THE CHARLESTON ORPHAN HOUSE

MARKETS AND GOVERNMENTS IN ECONOMIC HISTORY

A Series Edited by Price Fishback

Also in the series:

The Institutional Revolution: Measurement and the Economic Emergence of the Modern World
by Douglas W. Allen

THE CHARLESTON ORPHAN HOUSE

Children's Lives in the First Public Orphanage in America

JOHN E. MURRAY

THE UNIVERSITY OF CHICAGO PRESS

CHICAGO AND LONDON

JOHN E. MURRAY is the J. R. Hyde III Professor of Political Economy at Rhodes College and the author of *Origins of American Health Insurance.*

The University of Chicago Press, Chicago 60637
The University of Chicago Press, Ltd., London
© 2013 by The University of Chicago
All rights reserved. Published 2013.
Printed in the United States of America

22 21 20 19 18 17 16 15 14 13   1 2 3 4 5

ISBN-13: 978-0-226-92409-0 (cloth)
ISBN-13: 978-0-226-92410-6 (e-book)
ISBN-10: 0-226-92409-2 (cloth)
ISBN-10: 0-226-92410-6 (e-book)

Library of Congress Cataloging-in-Publication Data

Murray, John E., 1959–
  The Charleston Orphan House : children's lives in the first public orphanage in America / John E. Murray.
    pages. cm. — (Markets and governments in economic history)
  ISBN-13: 978-0-226-92409-0 (cloth : alk. paper)
  ISBN-10: 0-226-92409-2 (cloth : alk. paper)
  ISBN-13: 978-0-226-92410-6 (e-book)
  ISBN-10: 0-226-92410-6 (e-book) 1. Charleston Orphan House—History. 2. Orphanages—South Carolina—Charleston—History. I. Title. II. Series: Markets and governments in economic history.
  HV995.C32C459 2013
  362.73'2—dc23
                                                                    2012019387

Daughters of Carolina! . . .
you whose little prattlers are yet but tottering around your feet;
when you press them to your bosom . . .
thank God that they are not orphans,
cast upon the care and bounty of strangers,
bound to them by no stronger a tie than charity.
—Rev. George Buist, "An Oration, Delivered at the Orphan-House
in Charleston, on the sixth anniversary of the institution, 1795"

FOR SARAH AND ROSE

WITH LOVE

Οὐκ ἀφήσω ὑμᾶς ὀρφανούς, ἔρχομαι πρὸς ὑμᾶς.

Gospel of St. John

CONTENTS

ILLUSTRATIONS

Figures

Tables

THE CITY OF CHARLESTON, née Charles Town, has presented two different faces to the world from its founding in the late seventeenth century. It was the capital of the Carolina Low Country, a region from which valuable cargoes of tobacco, rice, and indigo, and later cotton, were transshipped to the greater Atlantic world. The planters who directed production of these valuable exports found it convenient to spend much of the year in the city, and so they built the famous Charleston single houses. In the exquisite balance and scale of these structures, many of which still stand and attract attention, the wealthiest of Americans announced their achievements in life.

At the same time, Charleston was home to about as many enslaved people as free people. Blacks had been present at the city's beginning, and a small population of free persons of color persisted in the city right up to the Civil War. Enslaved blacks provided the labor that built the wealth of Charleston, often while hired out from their owners. Many urban slaves learned a skilled craft, while others managed their owners' households. Thus, paradoxically, urban slaves sometimes found themselves in a position of some responsibility. That responsibility led to a bit of autonomy but no change in their legal position. In the eyes of the law their status ranked somewhere between that of a white person and a mule. They were bound to their masters, and their masters' heirs and assigns, for life, as were their children and their children's children. This was the lot of about half of all Charlestonians.

A third group of people in Charleston's early history lacked the numbers and ostentation that might have placed them in the written historical record. These were whites too poor to own slaves, and in many cases too poor even to maintain their own abode. By a variety of estimates they constituted between 15 and 20 percent of the white population, or perhaps 8 to 10 percent of the city as a whole. Many worked in the lower end of the skilled trades. They lived with a very slight margin for error. The sudden death of a husband or wife, a chronic illness, or the growing realization that available resources could not feed all household members might lead an adult to conclude that a child would have to leave the family. When that adult brought the child to the Charleston Orphan House, both people entered this book's story. In the Charleston Orphan House, the city—its elite, the white poor, and artisans and mechanics—created a world of children, one of several worlds through which these children passed as they grew up. The Orphan House was a unique venture, the first public orphanage in the United States, and an amalgam of public and private efforts to simultaneously care for the very poor and promote white unity. The wealthy organized the institution, the artisan classes found prospective workers there, and it gave poor families an early form of social insurance. It offers a case study of localized social welfare provision in the specific context of the urban antebellum South.

This book follows these children and their families from the events and decisions that led them to the Orphan House, through the time that the children spent in the institution, onward either to restoration of the children to their natal families or to their apprenticeship to learn a trade, and, in a few cases, to their later adult lives. The distinctive aspect of this history of the poor is that much of it can be told either in or through their own words. Letters and petitions of the poor whites of Charleston show them to have been plucky and determined, even as they sought the aid of the institution. Parents relinquished their children with regret, maintained contact during their time in the Orphan House, brought them back into the family if possible, and followed them through their apprenticeship if not. Children themselves appear as generally sober and occasionally rambunctious, aware after they leave the Orphan House of their disadvantaged status, but—and this is in the nature of the documents—willing to press masters, parents, and commissioners of the Orphan House to obtain their due.

My intention in this book is to let the children and their parents tell their own stories as much as possible. Rare are the historical documents in which law-abiding poor people appear, much less speak in their own words. These are not court cases, in which the poor appear as criminals. They appear here as ordinary, if unlucky, people, with little in the way of resources. They describe their own struggles to keep their families together after catastrophic loss, and to maintain loving bonds with children no longer under their roofs. Children and masters address questions of work and life of young adults. My hope is to present these people, as closely as possible, as they presented themselves, so that we might understand their lives and recognize their presence in one small part of the United States, from the era of Washington to the firing of Fort Sumter.

A NOTE ON EDITING PRACTICES

The Charleston Orphan House collection at the South Carolina Room, Charleston County Public Library, is an immense and priceless cache of records from the 1790s onward. The start of the Civil War marks a convenient end point of this study partly because the Orphan House personnel experienced much of the war from Orangeburg, partly because the records, particularly those relating to apprenticeship, declined in quality after the war, and partly because the early republic (1790–c. 1820) and antebellum (c. 1820–61) eras yield a cohesive periodization.

Many of the documents in the collection were written by poor and barely literate people, and many others were written for them. To maintain the spirit of the original documents and the personality of their authors I have tried to minimize my own editorial corrections. I have not changed spelling, capitalization, or grammar in the original documents, with one exception: where writers used a dash as a substitute for a period, I have replaced the dash with a period. I reserved the use of *sic* for a few situations in which the reader might be misled without it.

ACKNOWLEDGMENTS

I BEGAN WORK ON THIS BOOK not long before my own daughters arrived in 1998. What attracted me to the Orphan House documents initially was the chance to study a large number of children from the past, primarily in terms of causes and consequences of their acquisition of literacy. As it turned out, the records yielded quantifiable data that led to some statistically interesting stories, and this research has appeared in scholarly journals.[1]

That would have been the end of it, except that historian colleagues encouraged me to read deeper into the manuscript records to see what else might be there. So I returned to the microfilm of the commissioners' meeting minutes. Commissioners, it happened, spent a great deal of time on such prosaic matters as contracts for repairs, complaints by employees, orders from City Council to spend less—the sort of sleep-inducing issues familiar to all white-collar workers.

But those historian friends were correct: there was much more than institutional minutiae. In between the mundane bits were outlines of testimonies by recently widowed parents, impoverished neighbors, and inquiring tradesmen. I was unable to place these voices, which expressed all manner of pathos by people who did not seem to appear elsewhere in the historical record, at least not in such detail. It was as if a whole active world among the white lower classes of Charleston had thrived just out of sight of the written histories. I burned the last of my grant money on visits to the Charleston County Public Library, where I read and transcribed the as-yet unmicrofilmed letters. These offered rich, firsthand stories about the lives of these long-dead white poor—some tumultuous, others in steady decline, and still others who grew into a grateful adulthood. One particular young person's story compelled me to write this book, so that a history of the white urban poor in the antebellum South might enter the written record. The reader may find that person or others of particular interest, but I hope he or she will recognize the subjects of this history as once living people who, historiographically, deserve to be remembered by more than the epithet "poor white trash." I hope this book tells their story with due respect both to the lives of the subjects and to the rich historical literatures on Charleston and on the poor in early and antebellum America. Although I am not a member of the historians' guild, I tried to write the book as if I were. For collegial guidance toward that high standard, I express special thanks to historians Ruth Herndon, Billy Smith, Tim Lockley, and Chris Daniels.

Part of my good luck was coming to Charleston just after the 2002 transfer of records from the City of Charleston Archives to the Charleston County Public Library. At a stroke, the history of the Orphan House became accessible, and now the records are safe and well organized. During my visits to Charleston, librarians and archivists were extraordinarily knowledgeable and welcoming. At the City Archives, the College of Charleston Special Collections, and most especially the South Carolina Room at the Charleston County Public Library, I thank Marianne Cawley, Harlan Greene, Marie Hollings, Elizabeth Newcombe, and Nancy Phelps for all their assistance. Since then, Nic Butler has organized the Orphan House records and created an invaluable finding aid for them.

From the beginning of this project fellow scholars have been generous with their time and constructive criticism. I apologize for omitting any names, but I would like to thank the following for helpful comments, criticism, and encouragement, while exculpating them from errors due to my failure to follow their suggestions: John Alexander, Nancy Beadie, David Beito, Howard Bodenhorn, Chuck Bolton, Monique Bourque, Peter Coclanis, Chris Daniels, John Demos, Stan Engerman, Harvey Graff, Farley Grubb, Sally Hadden, Gillian Hamilton, Gloria Main, Anne McCants, Richard McKenzie, Darrell Meadows, Dave Mitch, Bill Pencak, Jon Pritchett, Dan Richter, Winnie Rothenberg, Billy Smith, Rick Steckel, Kim Tolley, James Watkinson, and Gavin Wright. Participants in seminars at Northwestern University, the University of Pennsylvania, Indiana University, the Ohio State University, and the University of Michigan, as well as at sessions at meetings of the Social Science History Association, Economic History Association, Society for Historians of the Early American Republic, and Southern Historical Association, and the 73rd Anglo-American Conference of Historians provided useful comments on drafts of particular chapters.

I want to thank a few people in particular. Ruth Herndon and I have discussed early American history for a good decade and a half now. Her comments on every part of this book, but especially chapter 9, have made it substantially stronger, and her scholarship, especially in *Unwelcome Americans*, has been a model for me. Many years ago at Yale, Ed Pauly stimulated my interest in children, schools, and policy. Michael McGandy advised me on manuscript organization and preparation. Gregory J. Kocken, reference archivist, American Heritage Center, University of Wyoming, helped with details of the life of Louisa Gardner Swain. Bill Fischer kindly sent along details of the later lives of the Erhard siblings. I thank Kate Lloyd and Sandee Jackson at the Orphan House's successor organization, the Carolina Youth Development Center, for providing the cover image.

My former colleagues at the University of Toledo encouraged my work, especially Mike Dowd, our department chair. My new colleagues at Rhodes College have been equally helpful, and I want to thank in particular our department chair, Marshall Gramm; and the chair of the program in political economy, Teresa Beckham Gramm. Department assistants Jeannie Stambaugh at Toledo and Linda Gibson at Rhodes helped get things done quickly and smoothly. Resources of the J. R. Hyde III Chair in Political Economy assisted in publication. It has also been a nice coincidence that I could discuss the Charleston Orphan House and its records with my history department colleague Gail Murray, whose fine essays on the Orphan House helped introduce me to the subject. Early in my time at Rhodes, history department chair Tim Huebner invited me to present this work to the Rhodes history faculty, which yielded many helpful suggestions.

Everyone at the University of Chicago Press has been a delight to work with. Price Fishback enthusiastically saw that this book would fit right into the Markets and Governments in Economic History series. David Pervin was especially insightful in getting me to see the big picture. Shenyun Wu was a big help and even came to a seminar I gave at the University of Chicago in fall 2011. The two anonymous readers provided helpful and critical comments that guided my revisions. This book is much improved thanks to Kailee Kremer's copyediting. It's a bit late for this, but I appreciated Holly Greenfield's excellent proofreading.

I am grateful for financial support from the Spencer Foundation and from the National Institute of Child Health and Development, National Institutes of Health, which sponsored initial research on pauper apprenticeship as an educational institution and literacy acquisition among institutionalized children, respectively.

Finally, my family. I cannot thank them enough. My wife, Lynn, read the entire manuscript and gave it the benefit of her well-informed and critical eye. Without her patience and encouragement, this book would never have made it out of my stalagmites of microfilm, photocopies, notes, and transcriptions. Lynn kept our daughters busy while I was mentally or physically visiting Charleston, and always found ways to let me write undisturbed. Then when I needed to be disturbed, Sarah and Rose had great ideas for hiking, biking, music, and all things canine. Throughout this project they were never far from my thoughts.

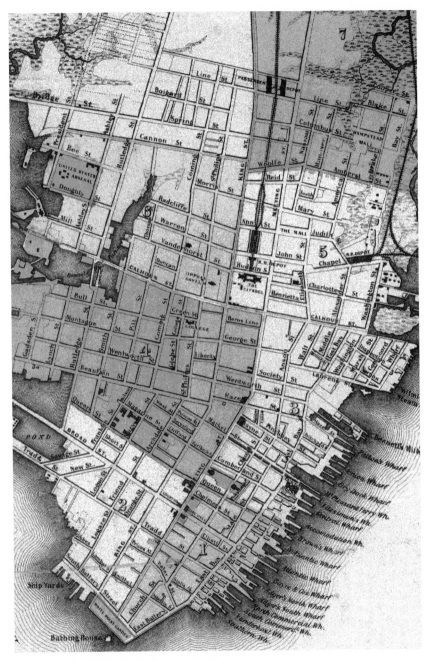

Fig. P.1. City of Charleston, South Carolina (1855). Courtesy of the Birmingham Public Library, Birmingham, Alabama. The Orphan House can be seen in the middle, near Calhoun Street at St. Philips Street, labeled "Orphan Asylum."

CHAPTER ONE

Introduction

O N JUNE 11, 1835, Caroline Hendricks sat down to write a letter. Two years before when her husband Frederick was still alive, business at their grocery in the Charleston Neck, the northern part of the peninsula on which Charleston sits, had slowed to a halt. Desperate to feed their children, she had hoped to send three of them to the Charleston Orphan House. Covering nearly an entire city block, the Orphan House faced Boundary Street, which ran across the peninsula between the Ashley and Cooper Rivers, thus separating the Neck from the city. The Orphan House did not ordinarily consider applications from Neck residents because they lived outside the city proper, and it rarely took in children whose parents were still alive, married, and living under the same roof. But in Caroline's case the institution accepted three: her stepson Richard, then aged nine; son Henry, then aged six; and daughter Louisa, whose age cannot be determined and who probably died not long afterward. Now, two years later, Caroline approached the Orphan House again, this time as a widow with few resources. She proposed to leave her youngest, five-year-old Lawrence, at the Orphan House. Caroline may have hoped for decent food and clothing for Lawrence, or perhaps she was drawn by the reputation of the Orphan House school among the poor. She must have thought that the Orphan House offered Lawrence more than she could, but no one looked forward to relinquishing a child to an institution.

One benefit for Lawrence was rejoining his brother and half brother. Lawrence, Henry, and Richard Hendricks lived in the Orphan House together for three years. Richard, the oldest, impressed the Orphan House staff with his diligence, for in 1838 they directed two prospective employers to discuss job possibilities with him. Later that year Richard left to become an apprentice apothecary, entering a trade generally reserved for boys who had excelled at the Orphan House school. In 1841 it was Henry's turn, and he left for the US Naval Apprentice School in Gosport (now Norfolk), Virginia. Meanwhile Lawrence steadily improved in his school work and earned special recognition when examined by the commissioners, or trustees, of the Orphan House. He scored well in arithmetic, and in October 1843 he addressed the crowd at the annual founding-day anniversary. A few months later, in February 1844, Lawrence's time at the Orphan House ended when he was bound apprentice to J. A. Stevenson, a shopkeeper in far-off Union District, 175 miles to the northwest.[1]

Before Lawrence Hendricks left for the Upcountry, he, his mother, and Stevenson all signed an indenture. In this contract, Lawrence promised to spend six years learning to operate a store, and Stevenson promised to teach him the skills necessary to keep a shop. Both parties fulfilled their commitments. After a year in the small settlement of Mount Tabor (it no longer exists), Lawrence wrote his mother to assure her that all was well. He described his happiness at attending church meetings and passed along his love to her and his two brothers. Because of a three-month-long drought, the harvest of fruit, including apples, peaches, cherries, and quinces, was thin, but the Upcountry was enjoying plenty of hickory nuts, chestnuts, blackberries, and persimmons. In part thanks to this healthy diet, Lawrence boasted, he had grown from 75 pounds to 125 pounds in just a year away from Charleston. As a result of his growth, he warned his mother, "you would not no me."

Stevenson, for his part, moved with Lawrence to Columbia in the autumn of 1845, when he opened his new store just in time for the drought that Lawrence described. When business proved slow he resolved to sell everything and move west. Lawrence Hendricks was not about to move away from his mother, and so Stevenson found another master for him, William J. Little. Stevenson informed the Orphan House about the transfer, writing that Little and his family were Methodists, "which would please his mother to hear that." With the change in employers, Lawrence took the opportunity to travel to Charleston by rail to see his mother. Little paid for his train ticket and told Lawrence to pass along good wishes from several other Orphan House apprentices in Columbia.

Lawrence left for Columbia before his indenture, or apprenticeship contract, could be revised, so the Orphan House promised to mail it as soon as possible. Back in Columbia, Lawrence became anxious about his status and wrote to Henry A. DeSaussure, the longest serving of all commissioners, to speed things up. Just to be sure, Lawrence apologized if he had misspoken while in town, but "it is my general way of speaking," the fifteen-year-old boy wrote. In good American fashion, he added, "I speak to everybody in like manner." A few days later, the indentures arrived, and Lawrence continued in his apprenticeship with Little.[2]

WHY DID CHARLESTON FOUND ITS ORPHAN HOUSE, and whom did the Orphan House serve? Most directly, the Charleston Orphan House protected the poor white population of Charleston by acting as an early social safety net *cum* life insurance policy. The Orphan House guaranteed the white poor that their children would be cared for should the family disperse due to death, disability, or abandonment. The place of the Orphan House in the city of Charleston and the mechanics of its operations are described in the first two chapters of this book, but the experiences of the families that relied on the Orphan House, and not least the children who lived there, are the main subject of this book. Their history is a part of Charleston's peculiar mixture of civic pride and racial anxiety. The ordinance that established the Charleston Orphan House in 1790 brought the city's abandoned and distressed children under the roof of the first public orphanage in the United States. The city was proud of its accomplishment. Local dignitaries escorted presidents from Washington to Madison to Taft up to Boundary Street (Calhoun Street after 1849) to see the bounty of the white upper class in action. In assuring poor whites of elite concern for their children, the Orphan House served a political function as important as its social welfare function. It did more than merely process vulnerable children.

The Orphan House was a focal point of white Charleston. It attracted the poor who needed it to care for their children, and the artisanal and mercantile classes who wanted those children to work as apprentices, and the wealthy elite who oversaw those efforts to care for young people, and then brought them all—poor families as well as merchant and artisan employers—together. As a result, it was woven into the city's fabric more deeply than any other institution. It brought all levels of white society together. But the Orphan House corporately embraced the poor.

To convince officials of their worthiness, adults who nominated their children for Orphan House admission wrote down their history of impoverishment, or, rarely, orally presented these stories to the Board of Commissioners. Skeptical commissioners then sent a board member to investigate. This initial process generated hundreds of letters in which poor families described their situations, all the while knowing that if they exaggerated, the visiting commissioners would likely find out and reject their children's applications. The result is a broad sample of reliable testimonies from the white urban poor during the early republic and antebellum eras, a time which has yielded scarce evidence indeed on this overlooked population. Later when an artisan or merchant contacted the Orphan House to obtain those same children as laborers, the process virtually repeated itself. Tradesmen, merchants, and a few planters described the work and life they expected the child to enjoy or endure, and the commissioners investigated and read reference letters to ensure that the children of the poor would encounter trustworthy guides into adulthood. Ever conscientious about monitoring the well-being of their former charges, the commissioners circulated letters to these masters, asking after their progress. The responses yielded eyewitness reports on the ordinary lives of poor children from early childhood to early adulthood. In many cases rather than being apprenticed to a master not personally known to the youth, the child returned to a mother or father who was newly remarried and capable of resuming family life. Even here, commissioners carefully vetted the new spouse to ensure that the child was reentering a proper family situation.

The sum total of all these inquiries and responses may be the single greatest collection of first-person reports on work and family lives of the poor anywhere in the United States that covers the entire period between the Revolution and the Civil War. The records illuminate the lives of the poor without losing any of the essential Southernness of their subjects. Managing the health of children and their families' fear of febrile diseases always took "the sickly season" into account, the families of the children (usually) showed deference to the commissioners of the Orphan House, and the Orphan House itself bought, sold, and rented slaves. As in the case of Lawrence Hendricks, fragments of many lives can be reconstructed to an extent that allows an unprecedented view into the lives of ordinary people, including the very poor. Their role in Southern history can now enter the published record.[3]

The Orphan House developed in parallel with the city of Charleston, the fortunes of which peaked early in the nineteenth century. Despite its dependence on agricultural staples such as rice and heavily subsidized indigo, before the Revolution the Low Country economy grew in terms of both wealth and breadth. Even including the black population, wealth per person exceeded that in most Northern cities. Along with that wealth came expanding networks of communication and finance.[4] But, as this book will show, wealth and sophistication were only necessary conditions for the establishment of the Orphan House.

Once founded, the Orphan House fulfilled a fairly simple charge. For local children it provided a bare-bones education of basic literacy skills, and then arranged for older children to enter apprenticeships in the various skilled trades that were flourishing along with the city's economy in the late eighteenth century. Over the course of the rest of the antebellum period, all those descriptors would change. The Low Country lost its position as chief export center of the South as cotton cultivation moved west. The value of traded goods stagnated along with transport industries such as shipbuilding. Population grew, but slowly, so that Charleston fell from its place among the leading cities of the nation. In the 1850s white population growth came from immigration, creating another headache for city fathers. Markets for the city's products grew torpid, thin, and disarticulated.[5] As the city's economy became more enervated, the skilled trades that had earlier employed Orphan House apprentices vanished. The Orphan House bound ever more young people to become farmers or domestics, and others were sent from the Orphan House so hurriedly that indentures reported their future trades as "unknown."

The Orphan House itself grew and changed over this time. Most obviously it moved from several buildings into the great structure on Boundary Street in 1794, which expanded in the 1850s. Internal changes followed trends in contemporary attitudes toward children. School subjects broadened to include geometry and history, and girls were examined regularly along with the boys. Corporal punishment, freely meted out in the early years, was virtually abandoned by late in the antebellum era. A few boys left the Orphan House for university study, and a few girls trained to be teachers. Perhaps most remarkably, in 1854 the all-male Board of Commissioners, which for six decades had governed the Orphan House collectively and more or less jointly with the informally organized Ladies Commissioners, ceded nearly all of day-to-day management to one woman, Agnes K. Irving, a twenty-three-year-old New Yorker. It was she who led the Orphan House through years of war and Reconstruction, and into the twentieth century.

Equally great shifts occurred among the children's families. At the beginning of the nineteenth century, the great majority of Orphan House children were bound out as apprentices, while a relatively small number of them were returned to their families. By midcentury, custody of an older Orphan House child was slightly more likely to be transferred back to a family member (usually a widowed mother who had remarried) than to a master who would direct an apprenticeship. This change—possibly a change of heart in some cases—was driven as much by families as by the Orphan House. It reflected increases in income that enabled families to raise the children they had previously relinquished to the Orphan House. Even here, the material explanation cannot suffice; over the early to mid-nineteenth century, Southern white families must have changed their minds about child raising. They wanted to have these children back under their roofs, in ways they had not in the late eighteenth century.

OUR KNOWLEDGE OF THE INTERIOR LIVES of families in the American past has been indirect, for the most part, and subject to few generalizations. Carl Degler inferred that the tendency of Puritan families, as demonstrated by Edmund Morgan, to send their children out to be raised in other families was a sign of parental detachment. And for later families, while acknowledging the paucity of sources on the working class, Degler endorsed the general view that the failure of eighteenth-century adults to discuss their children in letters indicated a more general lack of interest in them.[6] To break this absence of primary sources on children, Harvey Graff used some five hundred autobiographical accounts of childhood. But to generalize from an unrepresentative prosopography is dangerous indeed, and Graff concluded that "neither a simple summary nor a casual conclusion [was] possible."[7]

As a result, historians have tended to focus on a few examples with considerable intensity, beginning with Benjamin Franklin's spell as an apprentice printer. A later example is Lucy Larcom. Steven Mintz begins his chapter on working children with a vignette about this young woman, a rather ordinary mill worker about whom we now have a published autobiography (also examined in Graff's book); we also have an edited volume of her letters and diary, and two recent biographies.[8] Why this unexceptional woman should be the subject of such attention is explained by her authorship of *A New England Girlhood*. This book led to her posthumous fame less from its art than its representation of a rare type of writing: worker memoirs. The fundamental problem behind this concentration on so few individuals is the lack of primary material written by the poor and working class. This is hardly surprising, but at the same time we should not be too quick to dismiss the possibility of other documents on and by the poor that hitherto have been overlooked.

Domestic lives of the rich are far better documented. Recent efforts by historians of the South have generated insight into the families of the planter class and their slaves.[9] In one of the most systematic of such examinations, Bertram Wyatt-Brown considered Southern child-raising patterns in the context of honor. Mothers felt ambivalence toward their children, he proposed, but still permitted themselves to form emotional bonds with their offspring. The evidence for these assertions, though, was of questionable relevance to the question at hand, depending as it did on secondary literature on planter families plus assumptions that the poor acted pretty much the same as their betters.[10] Sally McMillen described the experiences of mothers in *Motherhood in the Old South*, focusing on pregnancy, child-birth, and infant care, but again, who else but the planter class would have had the time, ability, or desire to write about such things?[11]

Sideways views of ordinary families sometimes appear in legal set-tings. Peter Bardaglio described how Southern jurists failed to develop best-interests-of-the-child standards in adoption and public apprenticeship, in contrast to the North after the mid-nineteenth century. Bardaglio suggested that the Southern commitment to uphold blood ties as established in com-mon law, specifically to defend the father's prerogatives, directed such a strategy.[12] Suzanne Lebsock thoroughly examined most strata in one South-ern community, but few poor women and their families appear in it. Again, they left behind few of the legal records on which Lebsock relied, at least until the women were widowed.[13] Indirect views of working class women's capabilities appear in their use of public speech. Cynthia Kierner showed that in Charleston, working women took advantage of revolutionary-era discourse that emphasized equality. They then learned how effectively to petition men in politically superior positions.[14]

Such history of poor whites in the Old South as we know has been deter-mined by the nature of the primary sources, which are mostly court records. One result has been an overemphasis on the lawbreaking that led to creation and preservation of legal records. Charles Bolton and Bill Cecil-Fronsman each tracked poor whites through census, tax, and court records. They de-scribed people who, without much to live on, sought self-respect through belief in racial superiority.[15] Frank Owsley's long-influential *Plain Folk of the Old South* rehabilitated the rural yeoman class: those who may have owned a little land but few, if any, slaves.[16] His work influenced later his-torians such as Stephanie McCurry, who found in the South Carolina yeo-manry a strong element of patriarchy even at the lowest levels of material wealth.[17] More recently Timothy Lockley and Jeff Forret considered interac-tions among lower class whites and free and enslaved blacks in the antebel-lum period.[18] Reflecting the rural nature of the South, the subjects of these studies were nearly all country people; the working and lower classes in Southern cities appear in very few records before the Civil War.[19]

In the lowest of classes, ideology took a backseat to more urgent mat-ters. The poorest families spent their energies finding their next meal or, af-ter they were shown the door at a relative's already-crowded home, the next roof over their head. To follow the urban poor in eighteenth- and nineteenth-century America requires either a large database filled in with information on elusive people, or a particularly rich manuscript source in which the poor might appear in narrative. The best examples involve Northerners.

Billy Smith's "limited prosopography" held data on some fifty thousand Philadelphians of the "lower sort," which enabled him to view, with great insight and sympathy, their daily activities from a multitude of angles. Ruth Herndon concentrated on lives of a much smaller set of the poor, only forty or so New Englanders. When local poor officials interrogated them to determine the locality responsible for their relief, the humble applicants unwittingly provided what Herndon would need to piece together short yet compelling biographies, full of sympathy and far more humanizing than any other examination of the historical poor.[20]

To let the poor whites of Charleston tell their own stories, this book relies on letters and oral testimonies delivered by parents, their relatives and neighbors, their employers, and occasionally their children. By tracking one individual in as many different records as possible, it aims to follow particular lives over time. The poor families of Charleston are at the heart of this book, but the events that made up their lives, as documented here, illuminate from a completely new historical perspective the processes that moved Charleston as a whole.

And the white poor were a part of those historical processes, both as agents and as objects upon whom forces pressed. The poor whites of late eighteenth-century Charleston differed substantially in their identities, experiences, and hopes from the poor whites of the late antebellum period. In the earlier period most of the children who came to the Orphan House were Charleston natives, whereas in the later period substantial minorities of children had been born in Ireland or Germany. In addition to those children born overseas who were accepted, there were even more who were denied admission, and by the 1850s the commissioners feared being overwhelmed by foreign-born children.

Educationally, the Orphan House thoroughly reformed its efforts over this time. More or less independent schoolmasters taught the Orphan House's earliest groups of children. Throughout the middle of the nineteenth century the Orphan House shifted its educational goals away from simple literacy acquisition to a more rigorous and standardized curriculum. It provided a broad, if basic, education that would enable its best students to attend university. The most dramatic developments were changes in family hopes for their young kin. Before 1810 the great majority of children left the Orphan House to begin an apprenticeship in a trade. By the end of the period, nearly as many youths returned to a new configuration of their natal families as were bound out as apprentices. Further, among those indentured into a new household, the types of trades shifted over time, away from skills and toward manual labor. The orphans of Charleston became better educated over time, but to what economic end is not clear. What is clear is that the native-born white poor of Charleston, especially widows who had remarried, became better able over time to recover their children after relying on the Orphan House's care for a period of years.

THE CHARLESTON POOR were a living paradox. In the midst of the richest city in late eighteenth-century America, some free families owned almost nothing in the way of material goods. Around the corner from fabulously wealthy traders and planters, abandoned wives sold all of their property: clothing, furniture, dishes, until they had nothing left to sell, and thus no means to pay for food to sustain their children, who then entered the Orphan House. Near the wharves from which much of the world's most valuable crop, cotton, was exported, those women who could work found that washing or sewing brought in too little income to feed themselves and their children, who then entered the Orphan House. Within a few blocks of the most magnificent city houses in America, the fortunate, if that is the right word, found benefactors who let them stay in a spare room, but not their children, who then entered the Orphan House.

Contrasts among classes in Charleston have been previously examined. Barbara Bellows illustrated how benevolence worked in the city from the seventeenth century to the Civil War. The theme of her book might be summarized in that one word, paradox. The primary contrast was between black slavery and white charity, but the differences within white society between rich and poor were not just stark, but the motivating factor behind much of the benevolent activity, in order to maintain racial solidarity. Bellows devoted a chapter of her book to the Orphan House. Though she did present a few episodes in the children's lives, most of her concern centered on those providing the benevolence rather than those receiving it. Her evidence stemmed overwhelmingly from the 1850s, probably because records from that decade were the only ones available when she conducted her research. Today, all of the antebellum records of the Orphan House are available for scholarly inspection at the South Carolina Room of the Charleston County Public Library, and the present book draws on the entire body of these records.

Most of the poor families who appear in this book were not degraded victims of an early capitalist economy, although they may have appeared so at the time. In many ways the adults wrote their own biographies. Many simply experienced bad luck. They fell victim to a yellow fever epidemic, went to sea and never returned, or developed a chronic and fatal illness. It was their children who lacked agency and accepted their fate, however unhappily. But that is in the nature of childhood, not of economic forces. And at an individual level, some of the poor acted heroically. Widows showed resilience in keeping their children for months and years after the death of their husbands, strangers took in children living rough, and distant relatives opened their doors, at least for a time, to widowed and orphaned kin. Other poor folk were utter failures in life who defaulted in their obligations toward themselves and others. Husbands drank and beat their wives and children; wives found lovers and left the city. In other words, the experiences of poor families in these documents follow closely what we might expect to have been the experiences of many Americans at the time, or before or since. A few proved steadfast in devotion, some were scoundrels, and many raised themselves up from bed each morning hoping that when they lay down again that night their lives would not have gone too far downhill. But rise they did, to press on with life.

One thing poor families were not was alone. Of course, in the end the insufficiency of others' help drove the single parents of half orphans to the Orphan House; that is how we know about their lives. But for weeks, months, even years before they encountered the Orphan House, their letters described many different communities to which they belonged, some to more than one at the same time, and generally for long periods. Women abandoned by faithless husbands called on their own extended families for help. Many depended on sisters, brothers, and parents to care for their children or to take the entire family into their homes, at least temporarily. Neighbors fed and sheltered children who had been left by parents to their own devices, and other friends kept their eyes on older children apprenticed to nearby masters. If the master abused the youth, neighbors informed Orphan House officials. Former employers of deceased parents found apprenticeships for older orphans and housed younger ones until they moved into the Orphan House. Complete strangers allowed children who had been living rough on the streets into their homes, and sometimes their mothers as well, and then these strangers banded together to gain Orphan House admission for the children. Even outsiders to the Southern city were not alone, because they could join with fellow outsiders and find collective assistance. Recent German immigrants with limited English skills, Jewish merchants and artisans, Irish clergy and domestic servants all looked out for their brethren and their children. Perhaps the most underappreciated source of aid for the poor in the historical record is the church. Lutheran, Episcopalian, and Catholic clergy spent many hours aiding the poor, some not even members of their own denomination. Benevolent groups sponsored by vari-

ous congregations watched for signs of distress and stepped in when necessary, to represent, along with those clergymen, the poor in their approaches
to the Orphan House.

Ultimately, makeshift efforts fell short, and the children came to the
Orphan House. But we might infer from cases left out of the record that
many efforts by friends, neighbors, clergy, and extended family sufficed.
Because those children did not come to the Orphan House, they did not
enter the historical record. The notion of communities of the poor and near-
poor is noteworthy because it is overlooked in so much of the scholarly and
popular literature on the poor. Precisely because they lived outside of most
formal labor markets, the poor had little to do with the rise of any kind of
capitalist economy in the early republic, and so can hardly be pictured as
the victims of a capitalist economy that came to rely on commoditized labor. They were truly always to be with the rest of society, alternately looking out for each other and receiving the benevolence of the elites when they
could find no alternative.[21]

The Orphan House, for its part, aimed to turn its charges into "useful" adults. The definition of "useful," in their eyes, changed over time
and varied by child. At first, those boys with aptitude for schoolwork were
bound as apprentice merchants or apothecaries, trades that required such
aptitude. Later the very few who thrived in reading and writing entered
the South Carolina College in Columbia. The more adventurous entered
the US Navy or served apprenticeships on merchantmen. The typical boy
became a tradesman, and some who achieved mastership returned to the
Orphan House to find apprentices for their own shops. Girls looked forward
to much more monochromatic careers. Whether trained as domestics or
seamstresses, their future work lives for the most part lacked mental stim-
ulation, adventure, and remuneration. This was not the Orphan House's
doing. Its goal was not to raise the children far above their natural station
in life; after six decades of trying, one commissioner ruefully observed that
the children and their families wanted to avoid such uplift anyway. The
institution's goal was to give its charges training that would enable them
to earn a living in their adult years. The best outcome for a young woman,
in this view, occurred when she contacted the Orphan House to request a
fifty-dollar dowry before her wedding.

The Orphan House was a conservative institution. It sought to conserve
a social order in which whites who hit hard times would not fall below a
certain level. As a bonus, artisans and merchants who wanted to hire unskilled laborers could find a steady supply of same, and those who believed
in noblesse oblige could care for younger children who truly had nowhere

else to go. The Orphan House was an integral part of the city's collection of institutions that maintained the prevailing social order, the foundation of which was white unity.[22] Here was the sufficient condition for the early founding of the Orphan House: the desire to bind white Charleston together in the midst of more numerous blacks. The Orphan House was the mirror image of the nearby Work House; the former admitted helpless children and raised them up, if not too far, while the latter admitted hapless slaves and beat them down, with virtually no bottom in sight in terms of permissible violence. The Orphan House was at once an integral part of the most repressive social order in America, and the most humane and progressive child-care institution in America, and it remained both for decades. Like the elite who collectively performed acts of charity and beat their slaves, and like the poor who collectively loved their children and beat their wives or cheated on their husbands, the Orphan House was an amalgam of generosity and fear, love and violence, learning and ignorance. The division between good and evil, as in the human heart, ran right through its middle.

CHAPTER TWO

Charleston

FOR AS LONG AS CHARLESTON attracted free families, dissolution of some families would leave children in need of care from adults who were not their parents. Whether one or both parents had died, a child with no immediate or extended family members became a community problem. The community's response in Charleston eventually led to the Orphan House. How the city of Charleston managed care of orphaned, abandoned, and poor children is the subject of this chapter.

Before the Orphan House was founded, Charleston supported its orphaned and destitute children through its two Anglican parishes, St. Philip's (founded 1683) and daughter congregation St. Michael's (first building dedicated 1761). As local agencies of the established church, they collected poor rates and distributed them as relief. Churchwardens of St. Philip's gave cash grants to mothers of illegitimate children until the fathers were identified and made to support their offspring. Men who abandoned their families could expect similar treatment: child and family support payments as ordered by the church.[1] The parish paid women who took in orphaned and abandoned children and wet nurses who suckled infants. It also maintained older children here and there: at the Work House, in a hospital, and at the Provincial Free School, established specifically for poor and orphaned children.[2] Foreshadowing the Orphan House's policies, churchwardens bound out adolescents as apprentices.[3]

As early as the 1750s churchwardens sought to reduce child-care expenses. They observed that older children bound out as apprentices accumulated few "expenses on the parish."[4] Incorporation of the city of Charleston in 1783 shifted responsibility for these children from the now-disestablished Anglican parishes to the city itself. Like the wardens before them, city fathers wanted to spend less on poor children. They found an example in Bethesda, the first orphanage in America, founded by George Whitefield in nearby Savannah.[5] Convinced that centralized care of orphans would reduce costs, City Council passed an ordinance in 1790 that established the Charleston Orphan House.[6] The measure began by noting the "heavy expense" that attended the previous system of "supporting and educating poor children." Officials expected the Orphan House to mitigate those expenses.[7]

The immediate effect was to create a conceptual Orphan House, since there was no purpose-built structure yet. Until the new structure was ready, Mrs. Elizabeth Pinckney provided a large building on Market Street for children too young to be bound out. Its proximity to the Sailors' Home must have limited its appeal to city fathers, who hoped that the future Orphan House would shield children from the city's fleshpots rather than expose them to the aftereffects. Boys over eight years of age who showed promise lived with their teacher, Philip Besselleu. At his house commissioners conducted examinations to ensure a proper education. Propriety called for religious training, which some boys resisted. When the schoolmaster, J. H. Harris, could not persuade Mr. Besselleu's youths to accompany him to St. Philip's on Sundays, commissioners stepped in and ordered the boys to attend services.[8]

Authority over the Orphan House was exercised by a Board of Commissioners, which first met on October 28, 1790. The board included Arnoldus Vanderhorst—who had recently become intendant (mayor) of Charleston and would later be governor of South Carolina—and other leading lights. Commissioners needed to establish rules for daily operations, gather the scattered children together, and arrange for laborers to perform necessary chores. These men were supremely confident in their ability to manage several dozen children. This confidence appears in the specificity of their rules. The assistant to the matron was to "teach the Children to sew and read, [and] to sitt at one end of the Table." The nurses were to "make, wash, and iron the children's clothes, comb their heads every morning [for lice], [and] sleep in the room with the children under their care." For all that the assistant earned twenty-five South Carolina pounds and the nurses fifteen pounds each per year, plus room and board.[9] The commissioners also ordered that children scattered among different households be moved into Mrs. Pinckney's house. And not least, to work in the kitchen commissioners resolved to obtain one male slave and one female slave (a "wench"). Colonel Vanderhorst immediately offered to provide the woman for two years, gratis, and the man for 12 pounds per annum, which the other commissioners happily accepted. Inevitably in a slave-based economy, African

Americans would have entered the Orphan House story, but it is noteworthy that they were part of the institution from the very beginning.[10]

The commissioners were all gentlemen.[11] Officially, the only woman
with any authority was the matron, who cared for the girls, although initially
a nurse aided the matron. Reliance on just two women proved impractical
early on, and by 1800 a separate and unofficial board arose consisting of ladies of the city. This auxiliary board was so unofficial that it had no permanent title. In some records they were the Supervising Ladies, in others the
Ladies Superintending, in still others the Ladies Commissioners, and often
in the records they were noted simply as the Ladies, capital L. The work of
the ladies, and the respect with which the board treated them, made the Orphan House distinctive in another fashion. Throughout the South, even in
border cities such as Baltimore and St. Louis, benevolence was in the wom-
en's sphere, especially if it involved children, and few men participated.[12] In
Charleston the all-male Board of Commissioners, and above them the City
Council, had the final authority.

The ladies' work was invaluable for the Orphan House and its children.
They acted as the eyes and ears of the commissioners on those six days
of the week when a visiting commissioner did not inspect the institution.
Initially when prospective masters looked for apprentices the matron suggested eligible children, especially girls, but the ladies soon took over this
job. They were several in number, and their time spent around the Orphan
House made them well informed about individual children. The smallest
boys, under the age of seven or so, actually lived in the girls' section of the
House until they became of age to move to the boys' half of the building;
the ladies watched for signs of maturity that signaled time for these boys
to join their big brothers. The ladies organized girls into sewing teams to
produce bespoke goods, a service they advertised to attract "benevolent and
humane" customers. The ladies advised commissioners on the wisdom of
approving particular applications for admission and for binding out. And
it was the ladies who alerted commissioners to restock food, clothing, and
other necessary supplies. The commissioners never ignored the ladies' arguments and rarely refused their recommendations. Far from wealthy dilet-
tantes, the ladies provided as many worker-hours on behalf of the children
as the commissioners did, and perhaps more. Without the commissioners,
the Orphan House would have been leaderless, but without the ladies, the
Orphan House leaders would have been blind and overwhelmed.[13]

The great balancing act in which city fathers who operated the Orphan
House engaged was to take an institution with a poorly defined nature and
mold it into one with a sharply defined nature—not just in their own eyes,

but in those of its benefactors, its children, and all citizens of the old city. Before construction of the purpose-built Orphan House in 1794 it was hard to say where the institution was located, as it operated through several buildings and external homes, and it was about as hard to say what it did there. Despite the dispersion of personnel and resources, commissioners wanted the institution to watch over its inmates in every aspect of their lives, great and small. As a result they spent many hours on such details as enumerating appropriate menu items, so that children might be served decent breakfasts (hominy and molasses or mush and butter) and lunch (beef or pork with bread or rice). At the same time, many surviving parents did not want to cut their ties completely, and so commissioners had to manage them as well. Some surviving parents managed to get their children out of the Orphan House late in the afternoon and back home in time for bed, returning them the next morning. This the commissioners wanted to discourage.

Even before construction of the new building, the half-in, half-out status of Orphan House residents did not fit commissioners' ideal of the institution. Gradually commissioners developed the notion of the Orphan House as an all-or-nothing proposition and decreed an end to sleeping out. Indeed a few months after ordering resident children to stay overnight at the Orphan House they issued another order that nonresidents—brothers, sisters, and friends of the children—could not overnight inside any Orphan House building either.[14] Commissioners wanted to make the Orphan House an all-encompassing environment for its charges. With so many surviving parents and extended family members in town who were eager to see their little ones (and vice versa), the Orphan House became an institution that filled the interstices among other components of Charleston's civic society. The Orphan House was not the child's family, but the commissioners did stand in loco parentis; it was not a charity, but it did depend on gifts; it was not just another office of the city government, but it did benefit financially from special arrangements on escheated properties.[15] And to protect the children from the temptations of the city, as well as the citizens from the occasional wild child, a new building would be necessary. And where new buildings were concerned, Charlestonians did not act in halves.

The construction of the new Orphan House was a grand undertaking. The campus grew into most of a city block, within the confines of Boundary, King, Vanderhorst, and St. Philips Streets, on the edge of the Charleston Neck. The location served several purposes. Most of the north (far) side of Boundary Street was part of the Charleston Neck, but during the Revolution defensive works had been erected at King Street that remained within

Fig. 2.1. Detail of C. Drie's *Birdseye View of the City of Charleston, South Carolina, 1872*. The Orphan House (15) is center left, facing south toward Boundary Street. The street running from upper left to center right is St. Philips; the Orphan House Chapel, center right, faces northward toward Vanderhorst Street, which runs from lower center to the upper right corner. Building 9 is the Charleston Neck market. The church with the tall spire (41) is the postbellum St. Matthew's Lutheran, which faces King Street. Source: Library of Congress Geography and Map Division, http://hdl.loc.gov/loc.gmd/g3914c.pm008830.

the city limits afterward. Now with the plot available for peaceful purposes, the city's orphan institution stood near another educational institution, the newly established College of Charleston, which was built south of Boundary Street. Later these two schools were joined by the Military Academy of South Carolina (The Citadel), to the east of the Orphan House on Marion Square. As architectural historians Kenneth Severens and Maurie McInnis have noted, the choice of location for the Orphan House confirmed the community's view of its purpose, as educational and humanitarian. By contrast, several blocks to the south stood a complex of more ominous structures: the Poor House, the City Jail, and the Work House, for the poor and insane, the criminal, and recalcitrant slaves, respectively.[16]

Beginning in 1791 commissioners organized a variety of fund-raising ventures to pay for both the new building and operating expenses. In June Colonel Vanderhorst proposed that clergy throughout the city be invited

to preach charity sermons at their respective churches, after which there
would be a collection for the new Orphan House. The idea met with general approval, the one exception being the Quakers, whose meditative tradi-
tions, they reported, precluded preaching. And so a series of sermons at the
most prominent Protestant churches, as well as St. Mary's Catholic Church
and Beth Elohim Synagogue, both on Hasell Street, ensued. Each Sunday
morning in July, August, and September, the commissioners, staff, and children of the Orphan House processed through the city to a different church,
listened to a sermon with varying degrees of attentiveness, and returned to
the Orphan House while ushers collected gifts from audience members on
their way out. A total of £632 was raised this way, a substantial share of the
new building's projected cost.[17]

Charlestonians also approached commissioners informally with gifts.
A latecomer to the Beth Elohim sermon, who somehow missed the collection basket, sent twenty dollars, and one member of St. Philip's offered ten
pounds. A jury in the Court of Common Pleas contributed five pounds five
shillings. One raffish Charlestonian explained that his ten pounds were the
winnings from a bet with a friend. These sums added up as well. By September 1, 1793, religious congregations had contributed a total of £872, while
gifts from fraternal societies and other groups and individuals amounted
to £966. Commissioners had estimated to City Council that building materials, exclusive of labor, would cost altogether £2,200, thus indicating
that over three-fourths of the cost of bricks and mortar arose from private
donations.[18]

The people received for their generosity a solid and workable building.
With one major overhaul in the mid-nineteenth century, it would last for
a century and a half. The commission went to Thomas Bennett, a local
merchant-builder-architect. Sources of building materials show the degree
of specialization in the Charleston economy. Bricks were recycled from
pre-Revolutionary barracks; glass, paint, oil, nails, and locks were imported
from Rhode Island and England, and stone from Philadelphia. The wood
came from Bennett's own lumber company, Cannon and Bennett. The Orphan House opened to 115 children on October 18, 1794. The brick building
consisted of a center block, 40 by 40 feet, plus two wings each 65 by 30 feet.
Here its function more or less determined its form, with boys generally in
the East Wing and girls in the West. Standing four stories tall, the Orphan
House was the greatest structure in the City, larger than the Exchange or
the Court House. But its charitable purpose called for a lack of ostentatious
detail, with only a small cupola for decoration. The building answered its
purpose in the same form for six decades. Remodeling and expansion in the

mid-1850s resulted in an expanded structure described by a Scottish visitor as "[b]y far the most imposing edifice in Charleston," but the original was hardly less massive.[19]

A small but important building detail sheds light on the attitudes of commissioners toward their charges, the city, and interactions of the two. After the charity sermons of the summer of 1791, commissioner John Mitchell approached City Council for a dedicated budget line to pay for a "most substantial" wall around the Orphan House lot. Council agreed to pay a maximum of one hundred pounds. What makes this informative is the commissioners' interest in separating the children from the city a full year before the cornerstone of the new building was laid. Commissioners knew that behavior of the children outside the Orphan House reflected on the commissioners themselves, and so they wanted to make it difficult for residents to pass over the boundary between Orphan House and city. However, the plan did not go forward, and a year after the Orphan House had opened there was still no wall. As a result, observed Charles Lining, then chairman of the Board of Commissioners, "some of the children of the Orphan House frequently go about the streets & impose upon the citizens by informing them that they are in want of victuals" despite their actual "abundance at home." Worse in commissioners' eyes, neighbors accepted the children's claims at face value and fed them. No greater chagrin could fall upon the men of the board. In the absence of that brick wall, which at this point the commissioners were hoping to fund through a lottery, children escaped from the grounds for days at a time, injuring the reputation of the Orphan House and inconveniencing citizens. Therefore, the commissioners informed their neighbors in a *City Gazette* advertisement, children who were absent with permission must carry a signed ticket—much like slaves.[20] This point speaks to a motivation for Charleston to establish its Orphan House: Extensive experience with captive populations led its leaders to believe they knew how to operate such an institution. The wall, the absence of which left the boundaries between city and institution so open, was not built until after 1800.[21]

Commissioners, like white Charleston as a whole, took great pride in the fruits of their labor. Men of particular prominence were not only welcome, but expected, to enter the grounds when visiting the city. Thus came President Washington in 1791 and former President Madison in 1819 to observe the charity that white Charleston bestowed on its orphans.[22] The obverse of this pride appeared in response to criticism. Commissioners responded quickly and sharply to suggestions that the Orphan House failed in any way regarding child welfare. One rare example occurred in 1817 when

William H. Gibbes, a local judge, contacted the commissioners about restoring a boy to his newly remarried mother. Gibbes explained that if the boy could be removed from the Orphan House and "placed in a different situation from where [he] now is," he might "acquire more moral habits and improvement." The commissioners hotly denied the "illiberal insinuation" that the boy might be better off elsewhere than in the Orphan House. Gibbes must have seen some improvement in the Orphan House, because a few years later he contacted the commissioners to accept a child then in a situation "where his morals may be completely corrupted."[23]

THE STANDING OF THE ORPHAN HOUSE in Charleston's political economy is visible through its finances. Total donations for building purposes, including collections from charity sermons, were later estimated to be around $11,000.[24] Clearly much of the white community was invested in the success of the Orphan House. Some early accounts separated capital from current expenses and allow us to see how the Orphan House provided for its residents on a daily basis. For example, consider the fiscal year from September 1, 1793, to September 1, 1794. Commissioners paid some £421 as salaries for nurses and assistants, and for groceries, rice, corn, molasses, soap, candles, salt, and other necessities. City Council also bought supplies for the Orphan House, to the tune of £543 for bread, beef, wood, clothing, and other articles. In addition, the institution paid rent on the old Orphan House building, and salaries to the steward and matron that were accounted for separately. Construction costs for the new building during that year added up to £2,112, of which the City Council paid £1,274 and the commissioners paid £838. Concerning income, by this time donations for construction had dwindled to a mere £151. City Council contributed a subsidy that composed nearly all the Orphan House's revenue: £2,653. In addition, commissioners expected to get £341 from the estate of John Robertson, the commissioner who was the driving force behind the new building. His service as treasurer of the institution was less successful, and he died owing the Orphan House several hundred pounds, which commissioners recovered from his estate over several years.[25] Once the burst of early private fund-raising had passed, the Orphan House depended heavily on the city for its ongoing expenses. In February 1795 the commissioners were reduced to asking the intendant for an emergency sum to pay their wood and food suppliers, who had halted deliveries until the Orphan House paid its overdue bills.[26]

Gradually the city and state assumed responsibility of financing Orphan House operations. During fiscal year 1817–18, the city spent about ten per-

cent of its budget on the Orphan House, just over twenty thousand dollars.[27] In 1821, the city budget allocated some $16,489 for Orphan House
provisions, clothing, wood, and staff salaries—all of the Orphan House's
ongoing expenses. In addition, the Orphan House automatically received
the value of Charleston estates that had escheated to the state of South
Carolina. This source provided another $6,209. By definition the escheat
law collected funds from the estates of all Carolinians who died intestate
and without heirs, for example, George Champaign, a free man of color, in
1822: a man whose own surviving minors, if he had had any, could not have
entered the Orphan House.[28] Commissioners scrupulously followed the in-
tent of the escheat law. When family members of another free person of
color named William Butler petitioned city council to release property from
his escheated estate in 1852, the commissioners were quick to acquiesce in
the request and return the property.[29]

The Orphan House was a natural beneficiary of the financial charity of
the white working, middle, and upper classes. Throughout the nineteenth
century its charge was to enable the unfortunate poor white child to become "a useful, virtuous, and religious member of Society . . . not merely
to be kept from vice & want, but to be fitted for the higher walks of life."[30]
Soon Charlestonians returned to donating sums small and large. These collectively became the private funds on which the Orphan House could draw
for particular projects, to distinguish them from the public funds from the
state and city, which covered operating expenses. A typical bequest to the
private funds appears in the will of Charles Shetler, a rope maker who died
in 1802 without heirs. Shetler directed that a friend receive his sailboat,
that his two slaves be emancipated, and that one of them receive his rope-
making tools and the other ten pounds. Shetler then gave his house and lot
on King Street, worth $2,141, to the Orphan House, requesting in exchange
only that the children of the House join his funeral train through town.[31]
Later the Orphan House received by the bequest of Frederick Kohne some
sixty thousand dollars in cash and two houses, including the magnificent
Inglis Arch House at 91 East Bay.[32] By 1808 managing the considerable flow
of donations was so time consuming that City Council created a new set
of Trustees of the Orphan House Funds, consisting of the intendant, the
city treasurer, and the chairman of the commissioners. This ordinance also
directed the trustees to invest funds for the benefit of the Orphan House.
Thanks to generous donors such as Charles Shetler, by 1821 the institution's endowment had grown to $46,921, much of it held in bonds issued by
the Bank of the United States, the state of South Carolina, and the City of

Charleston, as well as in shares of various banks. The endowment returned a useful stream of revenue, although occasional capital calls from banks in which the Orphan House owned shares cost it several thousand dollars.[33]

As with any charity, income from the endowment enabled the commissioners to provide for the children in ways that would have been difficult otherwise. Under the 1790 ordinance that established the Orphan House, City Council hoped that "the benevolent [would] assist in the support of so charitable and laudable institution." Still, it kept control over the maintenance and education budget to itself, which left the commissioners unable to respond to financial emergencies or to defray expenses that alumni might bear once out of the House: college tuition, new tools for tradesmen, or dowries for brides. A later commissioner observed that under these rules, "good wishes were the cold substitutes at their disposal for well timed assistance." Endowment income paid for some of that well-timed assistance in the form of both durable structures and gifts for children and alumni. From 1837 to 1839 it covered a small land purchase in a corner of the Orphan House lot and renovations to turn a building on the lot into the school for boys, which cost $7,500. A new organ for the chapel required $954, and a new bathhouse for boys cost $400.[34]

The most long-lasting effect of the private funds was to enable the commissioners to get former residents off to a good start in life. Dowries, tuition charges for students at the College of Charleston and the South Carolina College in Columbia, a theological library for one newly ordained alumnus, fees for the bar exam of another, and expenses for a woman outside the Orphan House to whom they had sent a foundling all added up to several hundred more dollars. The popularity of the private fund among donors derived from its being a people's charity for diligent poor young folk who sought a good start in life. At one point City Council considered taking over the private fund. Communicating in the merged language of politics and benevolence, commissioners were quick to observe that if this account were to be combined with the general expense fund that Council managed, "such dissatisfaction will be treated among the citizens as in a great measure to extinguish the hope of future donations and bequests of the Institution." Council duly retreated.[35]

Donations continued to flow in, and from some unlikely sources. Shows of fireworks ("no person [to] be admitted without a ticket") mounted in the lot of the Orphan House were popular.[36] A Madam DeBonneville offered fifty-eight dollars, the net proceeds from "her farewell lecture on mesmerism."[37] From these and more traditional gifts and bequests, by 1855 the private fund held $64,460 in securities, which yielded a healthy 7 percent return. W. J. Bennett and George Buist, who formed the Orphan House Committee on Accounts at that time, observed that while this seemed large, additional expenses could be foreseen in the near future as the substantial renovations to the Orphan House building were nearly completed. Furnishing the interior, they estimated, would cost $8,600.

In the mid-1850s commissioners considered shifting one income to benefit apprentices more directly. Ever growing numbers of alumni who had been apprenticed were either running away or being returned by their masters, who complained of their bad behavior and were willing to pay the Orphan House the standard penalty (sixty dollars for boys) to be rid of them. Previously the Orphan House had established a penalty fund as one of the private funds, but at this time demands of dealing with broken indentures absorbed too much time and energy. The penalty imposed on the masters was insufficient, and led to no reward for the apprentice for staying to the end of the apprenticeship. The Orphan House needed a new approach to encourage young people to fulfill their indenture terms. Bennett and Buist proposed to create a financial mechanism for this purpose. In their proposal, the Orphan House would open an account for each newly bound-out child. At the end of each year, the master would inform the Orphan House of the apprentice's progress. If the youth had remained dutifully at his station, the commissioners would deposit ten or twenty dollars into the account, and if he ran away, he would forfeit the funds in the account. At the end of a successful apprenticeship, he would receive all the funds in the account. While this proposal was not adopted, it indicates the willingness of the commissioners to adapt their methods to deal with newly emerging problems.[38]

Commissioners may have spent as much time on relatively minor financial matters as on major strategic decisions. Approval or denial of payments for particular claims simply cropped up from time to time. The Orphan House replaced personal goods of apprentices who lost them in accidents or fire. It advertised the availability of former apprentices who were ready for adult work.[39] Retrieving runaways did not happen for free: a driver, cart, and two horses to bring back two boys cost fourteen dollars. When City Council ordered commissioners to hire a wet nurse for a foundling, they limited her fee to no more than ten dollars per month and expected the Orphan House to pay it. All these arrangements consumed the time of commissioners, whose oversight of the Orphan House was, to them, a civic duty.[40]

By default, the commissioners sometimes became trustees of small bits of wealth belonging to the children. The city intended that Orphan House residents be white children in dire poverty or who had lost one or both parents, and indeed that described most residents before their entrance. But occasionally a child appeared with a small amount of illiquid wealth, and no family member or guardian who could legally liquidate it. Thomas Knight entered the Orphan House at age ten, fully orphaned but with considerable wealth. He had inherited a seat in the city market, a female slave, and her three children. The executor of his father's estate offered to manage the wealth while he was in the Orphan House, an offer the commissioners accepted "to ensure his education and morals."[41] Other children inherited funds or a slave after they had entered. For example, Charles Payne entered the Orphan House in November 1815 at the age of five, along with his sister Harriet, aged twelve. Their father endorsed their indentures, which suggests that their mother had died. Seven months later, William Payne, explaining that he was then enjoying better prospects in his work as a stonecutter, retrieved Harriet from the Orphan House. Charles stayed behind, and eventually was bound out to Richard Steel, also a stonecutter, when he was fifteen years old. Three years after beginning his apprenticeship, Charles received a bequest from a Mrs. Elizabeth Frisch, which consisted of fifteen dollars in cash and three shares of stock in the Planters and Mechanics Bank. As Charles was still a minor, the commissioners held this stock in trust for him at the Bank of the State of South Carolina, diligently collecting dividends and adding them to his account. In 1833, when Charles was well into his majority, the commissioners gave him the shares plus some fifty dollars in accumulated dividends and interest.[42]

Ideally, a child bound out from the institution as an apprentice would spend several years living in his master's family and learning a trade, after which he would begin his life's work. But this did not always happen. Apprentices changed their minds about which trade they wanted to learn, or they did not get along with their masters, or surviving parents appeared to take the child back. Masters might not honor their obligations to an apprentice just out of his time. Such cases generated extra work for the commissioners, who had overseen the filling-in of the indenture, which had been printed to regulate the ideal case of binding a child to a master only one time. Commissioners recognized that some matches were not made in heaven, and allowed masters to void their obligations to the apprentice by returning the youth, the indenture, and, as mentioned earlier, a penalty fee to the Orphan House. At an early point these breach payments were 20 pounds for boys and 15 for girls, sums which were codified in a motion of the commissioners in June 1800. Beginning in March 1815 the penalty and forfeiture fund provided end payments to apprentices whose masters refused their contractual obligation to do so.[43]

MUCH OF COMMISSIONERS' TIME was taken up by the various people who made up the Orphan House. Commissioners managed conflict among Orphan House staff, and tried to monitor the progress of children once they had been bound out. Their diplomatic skills were tested most acutely in dealing with parents and guardians of their charges. These poorest of white Charleston residents, after all, had suffered catastrophic reverses in their lives that forced them to turn their children over to strangers. Some had gotten to that point by means of alcohol, and some were continuing past that point by means of alcohol as well. Some parents wanted their children admitted to the Orphan House, and other parents wanted them back. Some parents wanted to believe that the indenture had not ended their custody, like the mother who announced, "My children, Gentlemen, are my own," while others could not transfer custody soon enough, like the mother who informed them, "My children are yours."[44] All expected commissioners to look favorably on their demands, and usually that is what happened.

On one occasion the commissioners dealt with the consequences of an event that resounded throughout the Atlantic world: The slave rebellion at Saint-Domingue. In 1791 the slaves of Saint-Domingue, the French part of the island of Hispaniola, rose in violent rebellion and successfully threw off their masters. The shock to the American South was electric. The success of the freed slaves in defeating the French militarily and the bloodbath that followed alerted whites in all slaveholding areas that their safety was not certain. In Charleston, where blacks had formed a majority from time out of mind, fresh stories of atrocities that circulated with each new shipload of refugees only reinforced the acute fear of slave violence. Some refugees were children whose parents were killed in the rebellion, such as Marie Francoise Metayer, whose father "unhappily fell by the hand of the Brigands." The Charleston elite felt a particular bond with these children that crossed language barriers, and even superseded their relationship with the poor whites of Charleston. The poor of Charleston needed the Orphan House, but the rich of Saint-Domingue had suffered exactly the anarchy that establishment of such civic institutions had aimed to prevent. Thus, only weeks after waves of refugees began to appear in Charleston, commissioners agreed to suspend the mandated inspection of applicants and accept "any unfortunate sufferers" from Saint-Domingue on the spot.[45]

A LARGE SHARE of the Orphan House's daily chores and some skilled labor was performed by slaves. The first slaves who worked at the Orphan House belonged to Charlestonians who donated their services or who leased them to the Orphan House. A list of "Negroes" in 1796 carried the names of seven women and two men, none of whom belonged to the institution. Within a few years commissioners determined to liquidate some securities in order "to purchase ten Africans." In some cases the Orphan House took the long view of demand for slave labor. In 1837 they bound out Sam, a slave, as an apprentice plasterer, expecting that he would return to work in the Orphan House when the biennial whitewashing was necessary.[46] Commissioners hired slaves for skilled work, such as planting and tending the Orphan House garden over a period of several months, for which they paid ten dollars per month. Commissioners also rented out some of the Orphan House's slaves. In 1814 the commissioners resolved to bring Tom, a weaver who belonged to the institution, back into the Orphan House to process a large amount of yarn once his current engagement expired. Besides hiring, commissioners were also active in buying and selling slaves. The institution had expanded so much by 1813 that one commissioner estimated a need for thirteen slaves altogether: two male laborers, two cooks, and six washerwomen to be shared evenly by the boys' and girls' wings of the building, two men to work in the garden, and one weaver for the loom. To attain this level of staffing the report recommended that five Orphan House slaves be sold, four others purchased, and one retrained to cook. As the Orphan House child population grew and declined, so did its demand for slaves. An 1841 roster of slaves showed just three working in the East Wing, one of whom was hired, and four working in the West Wing, one of whom was hired.[47]

The charitable mission of the Orphan House may have led to somewhat more-humanitarian treatment of its bondsmen and women. Orphan House slaves appear to have received regular medical care. For as long as George Logan was House physician, he examined and treated "Negroes" almost weekly.[48] Commissioners attended to slave health in other ways also. In 1844 the Orphan House sold a "boy" named Sampson and used the proceeds to buy a woman named Hagar, who was set to work as a washerwoman. In 1852 Hagar's health failed, and she could no longer work. The commissioners agreed to send her for two weeks' rest at Mount Pleasant in the hopes of restoring her health.[49]

Commissioners did not hesitate to invoke coercion, however. The preferred method of dealing with troublesome slaves was simply to sell them. A woman named Mary escaped in 1825 and got as far as Bell County, Georgia, where she was captured. By order of the commissioners, she was sold, and the proceeds of $294.33 were turned over to City Council. Even if violence was not the first method they used to modify behavior, the threat always remained in the background. A recurring problem involved Tom, who knew how to obtain alcohol and was frequently drunk. Tom worked and drank quietly until during one bender he threatened to beat one of the nurses. While the commissioners contemplated their options, "a Negro man" named Jack approached them and offered to cure Tom of "the vice of drunkenness" for twenty dollars. The irresistible part of the offer was Jack's guarantee that he would refuse payment if the cure failed. In fact, Tom returned to drinking heavily and so commissioners sent him to the Work House to await his sale. The Work House was a grim destination. Slaves there spent their days grinding grain on a treadmill, breaking rocks to be used in street maintenance, and suffering the occasional whipping.[50]

AS AN INTEGRAL PART of white Charleston, the Orphan House interacted with other institutions that were on the periphery of civic Charleston. The Poor House, in particular, was less an institution that offered hope to the downtrodden than a holding pen for the deeply unfortunate, abandoned, and mentally ill. Commissioners of the Poor House acknowledged that the local poor saw it as "a place of punishment for the unworthy," and no doubt those poor who were content to receive outdoor rations from the Poor House were grateful to have a roof over their heads that was not the Poor House's.[51]

The Poor House, after the mid-nineteenth century known as the Alms House, and the Orphan House both had descended from the same parent institution: St. Philip's Church.[52] The colonial government established the Poor House by a 1732 statute that eventually led to the 1768 building near the Work House and the Jail. The location indicated the purpose of the Poor House: less to rehabilitate the Poor than to keep them near other undesirables and apart from the rest of the city. Its organizational structure, in which commissioners, led by a chairman, oversaw its operations, was similar to that of the Orphan House. There the similarities ended. While Orphan House inmates were winsome but unfortunate, Poor House inmates were hideous and unfortunate. They smelled terrible, some were close to death, and others suffered frightening mental illnesses. No ladies appeared to aid Poor House inmates, and few on the outside saw them as suitable objects of charity. Sporadically from the Poor House's opening, the city hoped that Poor House residents might reform themselves by their own labor, and in the process pay for at least some of their upkeep. One 1826 project to put residents to work aimed to force them to learn "habits of order, industry, and frugality," thereby "remov[ing] the causes of Indigence." Unfortunately for the commissioners' high hopes, demand for picked oakum and broken rocks (for macadamizing city streets) did not materialize, and

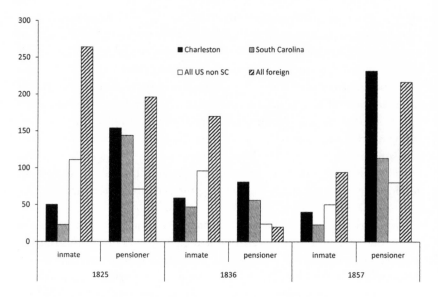

Fig. 2.2. Poor relief recipients by type of relief and nativity. Source: Klebaner,
"Public Poor Relief in Charleston, 1800–1860," 219.

the expenses of feeding (however minimally) residents were so great that
the project failed. Afterward, without any tradition of charitable donations
as the Orphan House had, the Poor House became even more dependent on
city subsidies.[53]

The conflicted relationship between the two institutions offers further
insight into the Orphan House's situation in Charleston. Poor House admission patterns describe the recipients of its grudging charity. Figure 2.2
shows the distribution of poor relief in Charleston by type of relief and
nativity of recipients in three sample years. For each year, the left-hand set
of bars ("inmates") indicates numbers of people resident in the Poor House
at any time that year, and the right-hand set the number receiving outdoor
relief ("pensioners"), typically in the form of "rations"—mostly bread. In all
three years numbers of out-of-towners, especially those from out of state, far
surpassed the number of local inmates. Of necessity, local residents formed
a plurality of out-relief recipients. Some of the foreign-born recipients were
sailors who had fallen ill while in port. These men provided the rationale
for building the Marine Hospital in the same block as the Poor House. The
Poor House did not inspire civic celebration or charitable donations in part
because of its diffuse clientele: it took all comers while the Orphan House
aimed to serve Charlestonians in particular. That particularity made the

Orphan House an instrument of white social unity in ways that the Poor House, with its many beneficiaries from out of town, could not be.

And so the two institutions engaged in constant conflict. The fundamental source of disagreement concerned the disposition of children. Each House had as many children as its commissioners felt it could handle, and so those commissioners wanted additional children to take up residence in—and add to the operating expenses of—the other House. When a child too young for the Orphan House entered the Poor House, commissioners of the latter reported to City Council that the child would be better off in the Orphan House. In May 1808, Benjamin Boyd, a Poor House commissioner, wrote to the Orphan House seeking the admission of three-year-old James Spencer. James's father had abandoned the family, and his mother, Margaret, had entered the Poor House with him and a sibling who was still nursing. Even the Poor House wanted to keep mother and nursling together, but James, Boyd felt, was ready for the Orphan House. The Orphan House "reluctantly resolved to receive the child."[54]

But then Orphan House commissioners were nearly always reluctant about receiving Poor House children. In August 1833 Poor House commissioner William Inglesby asked the Orphan House to accept four very young brothers at present living in the Poor House. Their mother was also in the Poor House, but was "subject to fits and in other respects a very unfit person to have charge of the children." The father of these boys was in "gaol on some criminal accusation" and not able to care for them.[55] The Orphan House accepted the two older children, but only after City Council forced the matter, and one of the younger two entered the Orphan House two years later.[56] In other cases City Council directed the Orphan House to take several children at a time from the Poor House: in one case four, in another case nine. The Poor House, for its part, also sought to discourage the City from forcing additional inmates through its doors. Regarding five potential residents who were putatively insane, Poor House commissioners described them as "unoffensive persons, with sufficient intelligence to perform the household duties which they were directed to do" and thus did not need to be institutionalized.[57]

Less clinically, Poor House officials used two arguments for moving children to the Orphan House. First, as they were quick to inform City Council, children were much better off anywhere other than in the terrible conditions of the Poor House. In August 1821 fourteen children were living in the Poor House, of whom ten were cared for by their mothers. The others were four girls aged seven and eight, without parents, for whom life in the Poor House (according to its own commissioners) "will deprive them of knowing and esteeming virtue and good morals, or of receiving education," whereas in the Orphan House "they may partake of the benefit of education and good morals." In response the Orphan House executed a dry calculus. One of the girls, Elizabeth Bourdenstine, had been born away in St. Paul's Parish, and her father died in St. Andrew's Parish. Although she "should have been considered as one of the poor" of St. Andrew's, the commissioners would accept her as long as City Council understood the burden Elizabeth placed on them. Susan Lamott was born in New York, but her mother had died in the Charleston Poor House. Emily Darnes had been born in Boston, but at the age of seven had already endured two years in the Poor House. Elizabeth Downie's mother was living on Anson Street in Charleston, but the child was a native of some other part of South Carolina. The Orphan House would accept them all, but notified City Council that the House held 188 children at the moment and was not eager for more.[58]

The other point Poor House commissioners repeatedly made was that a child moved to the Orphan House benefited both the city's budget and the child. The child entered an institution designed for children, and the Poor House had one less mouth to feed. In several cases the Poor House commissioners stressed that if transferring the child enabled the mother to leave the Poor House to work, the overall expense to the public would decrease. As a Poor House commissioner patiently explained to Orphan House commissioners, transferring a child out of the Poor House "would relieve this house of both trouble & expense, as we have at present both mother & child, whereas if the child was sent to the Orphan House the mother could be discharged & would be able to maintain herself which she is not capable of doing while her children are with her."[59] Civic duty called for the Orphan House to accept one five-year-old boy, argued a commissioner of the Poor House, because "as the city will probably be thereby relieved of its mother as a pauper, your honorable body will perceive that granting this application will not only be an act of benevolence to the parties but a benefit to the community."[60] An unhappy choice for the mother, but to move a woman from the Poor House into the ranks of the employed won over City Council members who adjudicated these disputes every time.

The commissioners of both Houses sometimes managed to work together so that different family members benefited from each House. A year after Rebecca Simmons had been bound out to Mary Johnson to learn "the art of sewing generally and particularly the art of making gentlemen's apparel," she began suffering from "fits," and so Mrs. Johnson asked to return her to the Orphan House. The commissioners usually denied such requests, but given Rebecca's decline in health, they decided that she could return to her mother, who would then receive two kinds of support. From the Orphan House, she would get five dollars a month for a year, and from the Poor House they both would receive rations.[61] More often the two sets of commissioners simply could not agree on how to act in particular cases. Martha Murrell, a quondam shopkeeper who lived near the Orphan House, asked the commissioners to let her son come home each morning after chapel, so he could run to the Poor House for her bread rations. The Orphan House commissioners rejected her request without explanation.[62] A high point of conflict occurred in August 1861 when each House took out dueling newspaper announcements to explain their decisions regarding a fatherless family of four children. The family at that time was in the Poor House, which shamed the Orphan House by noting that the father was a Confederate soldier serving in Florida, and the Orphan House replied by citing an ordinance that limited admission to those with a year's residence in the city.[63]

Some children in the Poor House were in custody of a parent who suffered from mental illness. These cases typically led to a transfer to the Orphan House. The Orphan House received from the Poor House five-year-old Peter Morgan in October 1822 at the request of his mother, who was still nursing an infant. Mr. Morgan was being held in the Poor House due to his insanity, so for a while the entire family was living there. Even in such cases, the Orphan House occasionally balked at taking a child. City Council forced the Orphan House to accept a girl named Mary Jane O'Brien, whose mother had just been confined in the lunatic cells at the Poor House. Mary Jane did not, however, fill in an indenture, because soon after her admission her mother had improved sufficiently to recover her child. The mother reported that her plan was to move with Mary Jane to Fort Moultrie, where they were "intitled to Rations & quarters," suggesting that Mr. O'Brien had been killed in military service.[64]

As with other Orphan House residents, parents who remained in the Poor House, even those suffering from mental illness, kept in contact with their children. This may be seen in the case of Peter Poulson. Peter first appeared in Orphan House records in July 1811, when he was fifteen months old. His (unnamed) father was a sailor, which meant that the family had little income. The owner of the vessel on which the father worked later reported that he had sent some of the father's pay directly to support Peter and his mother, Judith, at least until the father deserted.[65] Within a few months of Peter's birth, Judith had been committed to the maniac cells of the Poor House as insane.[66] A poor widow named Mrs. Mary Hammond then took Peter into her care when he was seven months old. After seven or eight more months, she sought help through an acquaintance named Benjamin

Johnson, who wrote to propose that the Orphan House pay for "a Negro girl for the purpose of assisting her in minding the infant." The commissioners at first refused, resolving to take Peter directly into the Orphan House. Unusually, Peter stayed right where he had been with Mrs. Whitney, née Hammond, uneventfully for the next seven years.[67] Mrs. Whitney described their life together in her petition to have Peter officially bound to her, an arrangement as close to legal adoption as was possible at the time:

> [Y]our petitioner has nursed & cherished the boy, till the present time, has supported him in sickness & in health and is still capable & willing to do so. She is ready to give any security to have the child educated & [illegible] in the most exemplary manner. A mutual attachment has grown up between herself & this object of her charity. She now feels for it a maternal tenderness and begs that the commissioners would transfer to her his indentures under any conditions their prudence may devise. She refers to the certificates enclosed to satisfy the commissioners of her capacity to discharge toward this child all the duties of a mother & of her continued care and attention to it, since she first took it under her protection. Your petitioner confidently relies on the sympathies of gentlemen who she feels assured will not unnecessarily rend those bonds of affection which unite your petitioner with her foster child.[68]

In one of the enclosed certificates, a neighbor described Peter as "a little boy adopted by her in infancy" and Mary as "fondly attached to the child, and bestowing upon him every care and attention which motherly tenderness & affection could suggest." Four women and three men testified that Mary was "better capable than any other person of educating & bringing him up" so that "it would be cruel" to disrupt the household.[69]

At this point, in October 1818, Judith Poulson was out of the Poor House. According to a physician she "continued to be afflicted [with mental illness] altho' less severely." Enjoying "moments of sanity now & then," she was lucid enough to file a writ of habeas corpus in an attempt to prevent Peter's binding to Mrs. Whitney.[70] A judge granted temporary custody to the Commissioners of the Orphan House, to whom Judith, who was illiterate, submitted a petition written by one A. Mazyck. The petition attacked Mary Whitney's ability to raise Peter properly: To make a living, Mary operated her late husband's grocery, which provided "examples of depravity and vice which were daily presented to his view by living in a grog-shop." Based on his circumstances Peter was "likely not only to grow up in profound ignorance but also in vice and depravity." As a result, "the affliction [Judith] suffers by his continuing in his present situation may greatly tend to make her mind relapse into that melancholy and unhappy situation from which the kindness and sympathy of her friends have lately relieved it." Judith reminded the commissioners "that tho' humble and dejected she is still a mother and feels for the fate of her infant."[71]

The commissioners, having considered the petition, "determined against the memorial, and [agreed] that they will do nothing further on the subject," and the Poulsons and Mary Whitney disappear from the record thereafter.[72] This case illustrates that even mentally disabled mothers maintained some kind of contact with the Orphan House, at least to the extent of learning the status of their children. It also illustrates the strength and viability of relationships between orphaned or abandoned children and unrelated adults. Finally, it suggests the existence of quasilegal adoption arrangements that predate those in standard histories. Most early statutes and court cases concerning adoption addressed the question of inheritance of property by the adopted child. But the institution of adoption may have been developing all along among Americans with no property to bequeath, who wanted legal recognition of their status as family members not related by blood.[73]

Financial pressure on the Orphan House intensified in the 1850s, when Charleston, like northern cities, received waves of immigrants. The commissioners' response to one particular application illustrates both the Orphan House's own straits and its view of the potential usefulness of the Poor House as a catch-all of the poor. A visiting commissioner reported on a family named Kelly whose children were prospective Orphan House residents. The parents were both alive, the husband a sober but unemployed baker. A pot of boiling water had seriously burned the wife across her torso and on her right arm, which kept her from attending to her three children, ages five, eight, and ten. Without either his unemployment or her injury, they could care for their family, but as things stood, wrote the visiting commissioner, "it [was] hard to procure food and raiment." Most unusually, another commissioner, Henry A. DeSaussure, in his twenty-eighth year of service, wrote a dissenting opinion on the application. DeSaussure acknowledged that the family was indeed destitute. However, as Liverpool Irish they were not exactly Charlestonians, and here DeSaussure reckoned that the price of white solidarity was larger than native Charlestonians wanted to pay. "If this application is granted," he forecast, "it will open a wide door for numerous similar applications from Irish and German laborers who would willingly throw their children upon the public for maintenance and education." Thinking of those ratepaying members of the public, he urged, "A stand must be made somewhere by the board for the protection of the citizens of Charleston from increased taxation & this is a proper case for such a stand." He recommended that in general the Kelly family should expect to "labor to support themselves & children," but that in the meantime "they can procure rations from the Poor House to supply their food." The Board of Commissioners did indeed reject the application, but the Kelly family does not appear in Poor House records. To judge by surnames, though, the Orphan House ended up taking in many dozens of Irish and Germans in the next few years; to judge by DeSaussure's fiscal advocacy, perhaps these numbers were smaller than they might have been.[74]

ALTHOUGH ETYMOLOGICALLY, RELIGION binds together (re-ligare), it did not unify the Orphan House children as much as commissioners might have liked, and in a few cases was positively divisive. All of Charleston's churches, plus its synagogue, contributed to the initial building fund. The next great building project was a chapel for the children. Around the turn of the century, the commissioners sought to build "an Edifice for the Service of the Supreme Being," which eventually became known as the Orphan House Chapel. Permission to begin the project was relatively easy to obtain from City Council, because the commissioners proposed to build it with no public money, only donations. Council accordingly approved a building "for public and religious purposes . . . provided the city is to be implicated in no contract therefore" and that the chapel would "be open to the Clergy of all denominations."[75] Since the Orphan House already had the funds in hand, construction began almost immediately. Only four months after City Council approval, commissioners staged a very Masonic ceremony to mark the laying of two cornerstones, one by John Drayton, South Carolina's governor and Right Worshipful Grand Master of Ancient York Masons; and the other by city intendant Thomas Roper. No specifically Christian terms appeared in either's speech, or in commissioners' description of the day. Instead the building was dedicated to the glory of the "Almighty Creator," and the "Great Architect of the Universe." The dates on the cornerstones were inscribed "anno mundi 5801" in the Masonic style, and "anno salutis 1801" in a more traditional style.[76]

The commission had been given to Gabriel Manigault, one of the more prominent gentleman-architects in Charleston. The classical revival building did not look particularly Christian. Later photographs show a façade of five vertical sections separated by four engaged columns (fig. 2.3). The façade was made of stucco over brick. No crosses appear, but the plaque above the center window unsubtly reads, "The poor shall have the Gospel preached unto them" (Matthew 11:5). Two sets of doors allowed interested

Fig. 2.3. The Orphan House Chapel, Gabriel Manigault, 1801. Destroyed 1953.
C. O. Greene, photographer. September 1940, northeast elevation.
Upper left: main Orphan House building. Library of Congress, Prints and
Photographs Division, Historic American Buildings Survey Reproduction
Number HABS SC, 10-CHAR, 137-1.

members of the public to enter and pray with the children. Inside was a
prominently displayed painting of Christ blessing children, copied by the local artist Thomas Coram from the original by Benjamin West.[77] The chapel
opened on September 19, 1802, only a year after the laying of the cornerstones. In a ceremony less Masonic and more traditionally Christian than
the groundbreaking, the widely respected Baptist minister Richard Furman
preached on a classic text for church dedications, Psalm 84, "How ami-
able are thy Tabernacles, O Lord of Hosts." The inevitable collection at the
doors gathered $144 "in aid of finishing the building."[78] Over the years it
became common for townspeople to attend church services in the chapel
along with the children, which led commissioners to hope in 1823 that
some might donate to replace an aging organ.[79]

The chapel brought church attendance home. Originally, adults led
groups of children to churches on Sunday mornings. Three churches were on
the circuit in August 1796. The steward John Wedderspoon and a nurse were
to accompany twelve boys and fourteen girls to the Presbyterian Church,

schoolmaster J. H. Harris and another nurse were to take twenty-six boys and thirteen girls to New Church, and the matron and a nurse would walk to St. Philip's with thirteen boys and five girls. In total, then, eighty-three children were to attend one or another church, and one "deformed" child who belonged to no church and three others who had just arrived and whose religion was as yet unknown were excused. Once the chapel was in place, the commissioners brought the clergy to the children rather than the other way round. They contacted representatives of the Episcopal, Independent (Congregational), Presbyterian, Baptist, German Lutheran, and Catholic churches to come to the chapel in rotating order and "perform divine service." On occasion they permitted Catholic children to leave the grounds to attend Mass with their surviving parent. This system seems to have worked adequately for some time.[80]

The population of Catholics in early nineteenth-century Charleston was probably quite small and adequately served by St. Mary's Church on Hasell Street. Similarly, it is reasonable to guess that there were few, if any, Catholic children in the Orphan House in its first decades, other than the Saint-Domingue refugees. By 1820, the number of Catholics in the city had grown substantially. When Rome determined to carve the two Carolinas and Georgia out of the Archdiocese of Baltimore, it made Charleston the seat of the new bishop, the newly consecrated John England.[81] Part of Bishop England's flock resided at the Orphan House. Given Catholic doctrine on the importance of weekly Mass attendance, and the desire of commissioners to limit each Sunday's preaching to one particular clergyman, conflict was unavoidable. The first disagreement surfaced in spring 1822. Dorothy Gallagher, a widow who had been sheltering her three children among the family of a Charles Prince, a tin plate worker, placed her two oldest in the Orphan House in September 1820, and the third child entered a few months later. In April 1822, at the request of Mrs. Gallagher, Bishop England approached the commissioners asking either to visit the Orphan House himself or to send another priest regularly to catechize the Gallagher children. The commissioners declined his request, stating that "other Clergymen of various sects" had made similar requests which they had turned down and that Bishop England was free to send a priest to the Orphan House in rotation with other clergy—meaning every six to eight weeks. While the commissioners continued what they saw as their balanced treatment of the different churches, Bishop England could do little other than stew.[82]

Three years later Bishop England again sought permission for his priests to come and teach Catholic children. The commissioners pointed to the previous decision not to allow Catholic clergy regular teaching visits and denied the request. Later during this particular commissioners' meeting, the prominent attorney Thomas Grimké proposed introducing Sunday school to the Orphan House—exactly the type of religious education that Bishop England had in mind when he wrote that Catholic children were being indoctrinated in "the catechism of a society which protests against the religion of their parents as erroneous." Indeed, a few years later Grimké suggested that the commissioners distribute to all children religious tracts from the American Tract Society, an organization described by one historian as "whole-heartedly opposed to Catholicism." To ensure that his views would not be overlooked, Bishop England published his letter to the commissioners in the *United States Catholic Miscellany*, the first Catholic newspaper in America, which he had established. The commissioners stood by their policy.[83]

The commissioners and the bishop clashed again over the children of an early acquaintance of Bishop England. Charles O'Sullivan, according to the bishop, had requested on his deathbed that the bishop obtain custody of his children and have them educated by the bishop's sister. In October 1827 the first of the O'Sullivan children, Christina, reached the age of binding out. In competition with the bishop, a Mrs. Fairchild applied for her. Apparently persuaded by the bishop's testimony regarding his friend's last words, the board granted the indenture to him rather than Mrs. Fairchild. But they maintained their suspicions about what the bishop really intended to do with the girl. When the bishop applied for the next O'Sullivan, Charles Junior, a commissioner wondered if the bishop really intended for the O'Sullivan children to become menial house servants. Bishop England shot back that he found it appalling that it was "necessary to have it enquired into whether I ask him for a 'menial' when I declare I <u>do not</u> & when upon enquiry it is easily ascertained that his sister is not educated for a 'menial.' " Charles was eventually bound out to a "printer of books" and Christina to a seamstress, typical trades for Orphan House apprentices.[84]

Commissioners were more relaxed regarding religious practices off than on the Orphan House grounds. In 1815 a widow named Jane Mordecai sought admission for her late husband's daughter Fanny, noting that she had three very young children to maintain and that Fanny was slowly going blind. Her appeal was endorsed by several members of Charleston's flourishing Jewish community, including Mordecai Cohen, a merchant and regular benefactor of the Orphan House. The commissioners allowed Fanny into the Orphan House temporarily until she was officially bound in the next spring. A few years later Fanny's uncle, Aaron Davis, asked permission to let Fanny stay with his family for two weeks including Passover, to which the commissioners agreed. A different result obtained some decades later, when a similar question arose concerning Jewish observance. In 1857, the rabbi at the Hasell Street Synagogue sought to withdraw two Jewish children for regular Sabbath worship and instruction. The commissioners rejected the request, basing their decision on the same grounds as in the case with Bishop England, that "the regulation of the House would be so materially interfered with" by such activity.[85]

However chary the commissioners may have been regarding Catholic and Jewish children, the Protestant Christianity that they promoted to their inmates was remarkably broad. In response to a Universalist minister's query, the commissioners noted that "there was no rule which would exclude any Protestant Clergyman from preaching in the Chapel of this House," and so the Universalist could be included in the rotation of visiting ministers.[86] Many children who came to the Orphan House without family were not baptized, or at least they did not know if they had been baptized. The ladies reminded the commissioners that it was their responsibility to ensure that Orphan House children received baptism. Most baptisms were conducted by Episcopal clergy, but in at least one case a Presbyterian minister christened a child. The children in most desperate need were foundlings. One night in January 1803, for example, the steward was locking the gates to the lot when he found an infant wrapped in flannel, with the name Clementina tagged to her blanket. Soon the pastor of St. Michael's Church visited the Orphan House to baptize the little girl, whose short life ended a few months later.[87] Other children near death were likewise given emergency baptism.[88] For a time, though, the Orphan House made it a practice to ask children or their parents about their baptismal status and make arrangements for baptism if they wanted it. Even so, few children accepted baptism in the months that followed, one example being the unfortunate William Tucker.[89]

As Bishop England deduced, the Orphan House operated as if Protestant Christianity were the standard religion and others a deviation from that standard. When the Religious Tract Society inquired in 1816 about distributing its evangelically oriented publications to the children, the commissioners responded immediately in the affirmative.[90] As Thomas Grimké had urged, the Orphan House did eventually accept some kind of Sunday school into its curriculum, although its effectiveness might be open to question. Each commissioner took his turn teaching on Sunday mornings some seventy students at a time.[91] Texts included Watts's *Psalms and Hymns* (1799) and the *Book of Common Prayer*.[92] A later project with tract distribution involved the American Tract Society. Thomas Grimké recognized the potential difficulty in finding "a supply of tracts so purely, simply, wholly Christian and so entirely free from any peculiarities of sect as to command the good opinion and approbation of the vast majority of all Christians, if not of all." However, he reported to the board, he was sure that those from the American Tract Society fit the bill. Grimké experimented with offering monetary prizes for children who learned their scripture and doctrine particularly well.[93]

What happened to children's religious practice after they were bound into their masters' households could not be foretold. The Rev. Benjamin F. Taylor embodied a nearly ideal case. In 1822 seven-year-old Taylor had entered the Orphan House, where he lived for three years before being bound out to J. N. Cardozo, publisher of the *Southern Patriot*, as an apprentice printer.[94] After completing the apprenticeship, he studied theology with Bishop Christopher Gadsden of the Episcopal Diocese of South Carolina and was ordained deacon and eventually priest. On Trinity Sunday, June 3, 1849, he preached a sermon at the Orphan House Chapel and afterward addressed the children. His theme, naturally enough, was gratitude for the care given by the Orphan House. "I know it is a sad thing to be an orphan," he mused, "but it is a great deal worse to be the children of rich and ungodly parents." Taylor well understood the generosity of the commissioners. Waiting for a suitable call to a church had left his family "in very indigent circumstances," commented a commissioner. The gift the Orphan House then provided to tide Taylor and his family over "struck [him] dumb," Taylor acknowledged. Particularly for Christian clergy, the commissioners did not stint in getting their alumni off to a good start.[95]

Certainly the general expectation of commissioners and masters alike was that children would continue in the practice of some type of Christianity; at least publicly no one proposed any other outcome as ideal. The institution encouraged its alumni to follow Christian precepts in various ways. Charities donated Bibles to be given to the Orphan House children when they left the House.[96] Commissioners looked for promises by masters to keep their apprentices on the straight and narrow; at least some prospective masters thought that promising visits to church would count in their favor. When Amelia Elmore applied for Mary Scherer, she offered not only to "treat her kind and endeavour to do a good part by her," but perhaps equally importantly she promised to "allow her all religious privileges such as church and Sabbath School which I understand was her greatest desire."[97] Alternatively, but rarely, the commissioners stipulated as part of an indenture that the master was obligated to take the child to church services on Sundays or at least allow the child to attend. After the dissolution of her first apprenticeship, as a domestic, commissioners approved the transfer of Jane Weathers to a second master named Joseph Moses, as long as "she be permitted to attend divine service on the Christian Sabbath in the Orphan House or some other Christian Church in this city." The reason for the stipulation is not given; perhaps Moses was Jewish. Later, the commissioners passed a resolution requiring all masters to promise, on the indentures, that they would send their apprentices to Sunday school.[98] While they could not determine what those children would learn or accept, the commissioners intended that their charges would receive a proper religious education that would point them in the right direction.

CHAPTER THREE

Orphan House

THE ORGANIZATIONAL SCHEME of the Orphan House, as ordained by City Council, called for commissioners at the top and ladies to the side, officers (as the managing staff were called) such as the steward and matron in the middle, nurses below them, and children at the bottom. It was misleading in its simplicity.[1] Commissioners and officers did not always have the same ends in mind, and any institution populated by dozens of children will see its share of chaos. This chapter describes daily life within the Orphan House. Between commissioners' desire to control the pace and content of daily activities and the ability of those who actually lived in the institution to do more or less as they pleased, most of the time, was a tension that remained unresolved.

Descriptions of the two main Orphan House structures, the Orphan House and the chapel, can be easily found in any number of architectural and local histories.[2] To learn about the condition of the enclosure as the children experienced it, its frequent state of disrepair, and the numerous outbuildings requires a look at the written rather than the visual record. The grand Orphan House structure officially opened on October 18, 1794, the institution's fourth anniversary. Thanks in part to private donations and the general tradition of stately architecture in Charleston, there could be no mistaking the grandness of the building's purpose: to protect helpless children of the white poor and working classes, and to lift them up through education and training.

The interior of the building did not quite live up to such glorious expectations. On June 13, 1796, a great fire broke out in Lodge Alley, on the east side of the peninsula. Winds blew it toward the center of the old city, where it burned "a vast Number of Houses and . . . left many Citizens without the Means of being otherwise accommodated," reported the commissioners.

They immediately opened their doors to dispossessed Charlestonians and offered them temporary living space in the Orphan House.[3] Two consequences followed. The first was the realization that opening the gates to all fire victims allowed in certain people contact with whom would not benefit the children, for example, one "woman of bad conduct." Thus the commissioners appealed to the intendant to allow them to move such "Persons of fame" to the more déclassé Poor House, which he granted.[4]

The second surprise for commissioners and refugees alike was the generally miserable state of the Orphan House on the inside. A quick head count in mid-August showed that the grounds held the following residents (153 in total): In the West (girls') Wing, the steward, the matron and her assistant, three nurses, and five hired slaves; and in the East (boys') Wing, the schoolmaster and a nurse (a married couple), and four hired slaves. Here and there in the compound were sixty-one boys and forty-one girls, as well as thirty-four people belonging to the eleven families driven from their homes by the fire. Once the guest families were in place, commissioners felt the need to investigate conditions within the Orphan House building, and what they saw appalled them. The children lived in an "extremely comfortless" state. "The children eat out of tin pans which there is great difficulty in keeping clean, and which in cleaning the servants frequently break, and make leaky," wrote a commissioner after inspecting the rooms. Children slept directly on the floor, since the House completely lacked any beds or bedsteads. For the 102 children there was a grand total of three sheets. A donation of bedtick had been cut and sewn into fifteen mattress shapes which were never filled, so a few children and nurses slept beneath the empty sacks. And that described the healthy residents. Sick children were reported to "lie scattered throughout the House in the apartments in which they are taken sick, or those they lodge in when in health." The rooms were swathed in darkness after sunset, because there were no candlesticks, and one broken, useless lamp. The commissioners sent to investigate urged that the House obtain "half a dozen rough bedsteads" and enough ticklenburgh, a rough cloth made of hemp or linen, to make as many bedclothes as necessary. They also noted that the Orphan House's garden was "very sterile," but could be fixed if it were "supplied with manure by the city scavengers."[5]

The other commissioners appear to have been shocked at these descriptions, but they should not have been. They could have consulted the steward and matron, who called the roll each evening at eight o'clock, and so had seen the appalling conditions, night after night.[6] They might have noted a report filed by a new teacher, who recommended that "beds & bedsteads may be procured at least for the sick orphans," suggesting that children had been sleeping directly on the floor as soon as the new building had opened.[7] But the commissioners were simply too busy with getting the Orphan House built and running to investigate.

Questions about the soundness of the building persisted through the early nineteenth century. In 1809 the Superintending Ladies reported intolerable conditions in the House. In the East Wing, sixty-eight boys were living in two leaky bedrooms, one of which was described as "very small" with "only two windows in it." In the West Wing girls shared four bedrooms, which leaked to the extent that they were "drenched with water when it rain[ed] so that they [slept] on wet beds." It was futile to try airing the linens out in the yard, since the loose chickens constantly soiled them; later the matron complained of horses and cattle as well as fowl walking on clothes and linens set out to dry. Further, a diet heavily dependent on offal must leave the children in ill health, the ladies asserted. Worse still, all these conditions were aggravating the current whooping cough epidemic.[8]

A commissioner who had inspected the House himself concurred with the ladies. Standing in just the right position in any of the third-floor bedrooms enabled one to see through holes in the roof all the way up to the bright blue Carolina sky. The commissioners resolved to fix these problems at their meeting of August 7, 1809, but as late as November a visiting commissioner complained that nothing had been done about leaks in the roof. By this time the bedticks had been filled, but the children were now suffering bedbug bites. Wall, window, and roof repairs began in January 1810, but problems with leaks persisted through the years—as did problems with a lack of airflow. When the kitchens filled with smoke, so did the children's rooms.[9]

The 1809 report also described the layout of the building, giving an illustration of how the Orphan House and its children interacted. The East and West Wings of the building were dedicated to children of one sex only, the boys in the East Wing and girls in the West. Thus, on the ground floor of the West Wing there was a special room for weaving that the East did not have. Each wing had a kitchen, a dining room, and a washroom, and the East in addition a store room. On the "first" (i.e., second) floor of both wings were classrooms. The girls' wing held the meeting room for the commissioners and a small chapel, while the boys' wing held an office for the schoolmaster. The "second" floor contained apartments for staff members. The matron lived in two rooms and the schoolmistress and sewing mistress in one room each in the West Wing. The steward lived with his family in three rooms and the schoolmaster in one on the East side. The third floor was for children's dormitory rooms. On the West Side were four rooms. Three nurses oversaw two large rooms that were each home to twenty-five girls and one small room with eighteen girls, which, just like one of the boys' rooms, had only two windows according to the ladies' reports. The spinning mistress managed sixteen children in a large room. On the boys' side there were also four rooms, but much more unevenly divided than among the girls. One nurse watched over a room with thirty-three boys in it, and the other nurse was responsible for a large room with thirty-five boys. Each nurse enjoyed her own room to live in. A visiting commissioner contrasted the "large and commodious and airy" nurses' rooms with the associated boys' rooms, which were "almost suffocating, and might in the end cause a contagious disease among the children."[10]

Water was a constant concern. The Orphan House initially used its considerable land, nearly an entire city block, to provide for both collection and dispersal, drilling wells for drinking water in one area and placing vaults beneath their privies in another. Later, rainwater collecting in a cistern was a source of potable water.[11] Clean water was especially valuable in the densely populated Orphan House. Bathhouses in the yard included furnaces to heat the water, a welcome treat for the children.[12] The eventual conflict between drawing clean water and disposing of wastewater came to a head in 1806, when wastewater from the vaults serving the West Wing was found in the wells, rendering the latter useless. Commissioners proposed to fill in both and redrill elsewhere on the lot, but farther apart.[13] A later project investigated the viability of "Scentless Privies." The need for them must have been overpowering within the Orphan House compound, for neighbors on the King Street (east) side of the block complained of the smell "in the strongest terms," in response to which commissioners ordered the steward to pour yet more lime into the vaults. More unnerving, perhaps, was the location of these privies: in the Orphan House garden.[14]

Until the renovations of the 1850s the Orphan House lacked indoor plumbing. In its absence, students simply answered nature's call in corners of the classrooms.[15] After the overhaul, the Committee on the Water Closets reported in 1857, bathrooms with toilets had been stacked one above the other on the various floors, with water for flushing recycled from the washrooms. Unfortunately, while up-to-date, the facilities were not numerous: the Committee estimated that about one hundred children shared each water closet made available to them. The infirmary had two water closets, which seemed not to work as well as the others. A lack of water and children stuffing "rags, shoes, hunks of bread and coal ashes" into them caused stoppages. The committee recommended replacing them with the more efficient pan-trap toilets and keeping them locked during the day, saving them for use only during the night and medical emergencies.[16]

Commissioners hoped off and on that the Orphan House might provide much of its own food through raising livestock, dairying, and gardening. Driven by budgetary concerns, commissioners failed to make a careful assessment of costs and benefits of urban agriculture. Horses running loose in the yard "improper[ly] restrain[ed]" children from doing the same, and it proved difficult to prevent cattle and poultry from "going at large" on the Boundary Street side of the lot.[17] Experiments with keeping a few dairy cattle in the hopes that they could feed on leftovers from the garden (fig. 3.1) came to naught.[18] Garden yields proved consistently, disappointingly thin. Although the garden produced only small quantities of vegetables and potatoes, commissioners remained eternally hopeful about its future bounty.[19] As measured by resources devoted to it, the garden was a high priority. Commissioners hired slaves trained as gardeners to manage it (at ten dollars a month), and later obtained skilled slaves for the institution as resident gardeners. They bought dozens of loads of manure to lavish on it. They tried to hire a white gardener who would train boys in the art and mystery of vegetable raising. The commissioners' hopes that the garden would produce enough fruits and vegetables to reduce food expenditures proved to be in vain.[20]

Food was one of the major expenses of the Orphan House, and as such it was a constant target for economizing. On Christmas Eve 1795 the children ate a special dinner that was "genteel, plentiful, & frugal."[21] In the fiscal year 1795–96, the Orphan House paid $2,661.80 in construction costs ("bricks, lumber, workmanship") to finish their new building, and another two-thirds of that amount ($1,679.10) for beef and bread. Other accounts from this time estimate that payments for "rice, grocery, corn, milk, butter, molasses, soap, candles, stationery" and other necessities totaled more than salaries paid to the steward, matron, schoolmaster, assistants, and nurses, plus rent on hired slaves, combined.[22] This pattern held over the next several decades. In the early 1830s provisions cost about half again as much as officers' salaries. Again, in 1846, separate bills for bread, beef, "corn, pease & hay, etc.," rice, and groceries added up to just less than the officers' salaries. In this year a non-itemized payment to the purveyor, who provided food other than meat and bread, involved a much larger sum.[23]

Exactly what the children got for this expense was probably quite monotonous. One visiting commissioner in 1809 described children as eating plenty of "corn beef with potatoes," after which, for the sake of some variety, Commissioners ordered the butcher to send over pork twice a week

Fig. 3.1. View from the Orphan House to the northeast, 1865. At this point, federal forces
were in control of the Orphan House and the rest of the city, while the children were in
Orangeburg. In the middle ground is the garden, better organized than under the Orphan
House staff and children. The Old Citadel, with crenellations, is in the background.
Photo attributed to George N. Barnard, Library of Congress, Prints and Photographs
Division, Civil War Photographs, LC-B8171-3419.

rather than beef.[24] Occasionally commissioners had to reproach their ven-
dors for selling spoiled or questionable meat or bread.[25] In 1846 the steward
presented a report of rations allowed to Orphan House residents (table 3.1).
It is possible that this list describes less food than the children actually ate,
since these estimates responded to threats by City Council to cut Orphan
House funding. In particular commissioners required that the steward reduce the beef allotment to seventy pounds per day, which this list happened
to achieve. The approximate daily totals per child included five ounces of

TABLE 3.1. Rations in the Orphan House

To whom	Weekly								Daily	
	Rice	Sugar	Coffee	Molasses	Soap	Butter	Candles	Milk	Bread	Beef
	qts	lb	lb	qts	lb	lb	lb	pts	lb	lb
Steward	7	2½	1½	1	1½	2	1	3½	2	2
Matron	7	2	1	1	1½	1½	1	3½	2	2
School mistress	7	2	1	1	½	1½	1	3½	1	2
Sewing mistress	7	2	1	1	½	1½	1	3½	1	2
4 nurses	14	4	2	4	2	4	3	3½	4	4
Miss E. Rivers	3½	1	½	1	½	1	¾	3½	1	1
Mary Gurfin	3½	1	½	1	¼	1	¾	3½	1	1
Ellen Carpentier	3½	1	½	1		1	¾	3½	1	1
Porter	3½	1	½	1	½	1	¾	3½	1	1
Cook	3½	1	½	1	½	1	¾	3½	1	1
P. M. Ryburn	3½	1½	½	1	½	1½	1	3½	2	1
J. M. Covert	3½	1½	½	1	½	1½	1	3½	2	1
Children	126	8		48	18	14	1	14	47	46
Servants	38½	Occasionally or when sick			1	—	—	—	—	5

Source: Minutes, 5 November 1846.
Note: Ryburn and Covert were to become students at the College of Charleston.

grits for breakfast and the same amount of rice at dinner, two fluid ounces of molasses, a third of an ounce of butter, a third of a fluid ounce of milk (meaning, a small glass once a week), and a half pound each of bread and beef. The children undoubtedly ate much less than half a pound of meat on a daily basis. Because adults in the Orphan House received one pound of beef daily, it seems likely that the measures of beef described what the steward was to expect from the institution's meat vendor. Thus, the butcher delivered to the Orphan House the equivalent of a half pound of beef per child per day, but much of those eight ounces consisted of bone, gristle, fat, and offal. Sick children were regularly granted extra sugar and milk, and Sundays saw pork substituted for beef for the entire House. A similar exercise from 1840 yielded much the same figures, with slightly more pork per person on Sundays. In both cases the commissioners reported back to City Council that scantier diets for Orphan House residents would not be possible.[26]

The Orphan House certainly attempted to economize in dietary provision. In early 1797 many children, especially boys, appeared ill, with "sallow complexions and sickly appearances." Consulting physicians determined that the problem was a diet out of balance: the children were being fed "too great a quantity of animal food without a sufficient proportion of vegetables." With the consent of the matron and other officers, the commissioners resolved the imbalance by ordering a *reduction* in daily meat allowances of ten pounds in the East (boys') Wing and seven pounds in the West, a roughly equiproportional decline for each sex that may have represented a 25 percent drop in the amount of meat given each child. The difference was to be made up in potatoes and other vegetables "until the garden should be sufficiently productive," which, as noted above, would not occur before the Second Coming.[27] Little had changed by the time of the Civil War, when commissioners estimated that the Orphan House paid 5 1/2 cents per day to feed each child.[28] At the centennial celebration in 1890 a guest speaker could boast, "The cost of maintaining the Orphan House has been brought to the lowest practical point."[29] He spoke for generations of commissioners and stewards.

Clothing the children presented another potential source of economies in the eyes of adults. Shortages appeared early on; in midwinter of 1803, several boys "were in want of shoes."[30] Girls prepared for training as seamstresses and tailoresses by making inmates' uniforms. They made undergarments from white homespun.[31] Although the spinning mistress directed some spinning of thread, the Orphan House made little of its own cloth, purchasing it instead. In 1825 the steward displayed samples of blue twill homespun, which he had obtained from a local merchant. The merchant had on hand 400 yards at 29 cents per yard, or about half the necessary quantity. To ensure that the boys would actually wear the uniforms, the board required that "all the children who are receiving the bounty of this institution be clad in the apparel obtained for and worn by the children of this institution" (emphasis in original).[32] The Superintending Ladies who oversaw the West Wing hoped for a different economy when they advertised the services of Orphan House girls to take in all kinds of sewing work, income from which would go to "a fund for the benefit of the female children coming of age." But because the girls were so busy making and repairing uniforms, it was donations that later financed the dowry fund.[33]

TO DISCUSS EARLY AMERICAN CHILDREN as mere consumers of food and clothing is to describe Charleston as a city with some old buildings. Children have an energy, a willfulness, a spontaneity, a desire for adventure, and a lack of foresight that makes them so qualitatively different from adults. And so with the Orphan House residents. Some energetic children stirred up trouble, but they seem to have waited for just the right moment to do so. In 1819 an epidemic of "the itch" reduced the number of adults who supervised children at mealtimes, leaving only a few nurses to watch. "In consequence," one commissioner warned, "there is not the subordination kept up that ought to be, and is so very essential." Not only children acted up; a nurse reported that a male slave "had grossly insulted one of the nurses in the children's dining room and threatened to beat her." This slave was Tom, whose excessive drinking was described previously. He received "immediate reprehension," meaning the lash. Alarmed, commissioners instructed the steward and matron to supervise children at meals, in person, and not to pass the buck on to the nurses alone. A lack of subordination by residents of less than full legal standing, commissioners realized, was as severe a threat to the miniature Charleston that was the Orphan House as it was to the great city as a whole.[34]

The prospect of trouble was always in the minds of commissioners, not unlike the lurking fear of a slave rebellion in the city at large. The 1806 bylaws of the Orphan House required "the aid and assistance of all the Officers of the house . . . to prevent or repress any disorderly, tumultuous, or improper invasion" against the theoretically standard environment of peace and quiet.[35] And at least once, trouble came, but in the timeless manner of young boys rather than the deadly serious violence led by a Denmark Vesey. In 1810 the "ungovernable and unbecoming conduct" of some boys was treated lightly, with just "an admonition and reprimand."[36] The precedent did not prove discouraging. The next summer five boys faced reprimands when they were thought to be playing with fire in the courtyard, fire being nearly as great a source of concern in Charleston as a slave insurrection. It turned out that the boys were not in fact guilty of this very serious offence, but the raising of these charges indicated a certain anxiety. At the time dissension was rife among the officers, increasing tensions further. George Peters, the schoolmaster, and Eliab Kingman, the steward, were constantly at loggerheads, raising their voices in front of the children and threatening each other with violence. Fed up with misbehavior by Orphan House personnel of all ages, when commissioners found boys in the chapel and the West Wing, they determined to make examples of them by whipping each one six to twelve times.[37] The lash for unruly youngsters was hardly unusual at this time, but for city fathers to order a public whipping of boys just as they would order stripes to be placed on the backs of their slaves was too much to bear—at least, for the children.[38]

A few days later the boys rose up, creating a "tumultuous uproar in the yard and house" and damaging some outbuildings. Described by one commissioner as a "Riot," it could only have reminded the board of the consequences of a lack of proper subordination in the greater urban order. Upon leaving the dinner table, the boys "commenced a great noise . . . they ran about the yard hooping and hurrahing with a most tumultuous clamor," according to the steward's later report. One boy beat a kettle with a stick, and others raced past him shouting at the top of their lungs. Boys climbed over the pump near the Boundary Street gate and vigorously forced water into the yard. Others unsuccessfully attacked the nearby sentry box, trying to push it over with a wedge of loose boards underneath. Still others threw rocks at outbuildings. Running back through the House, they alarmed the matron and nurses, who were all too aware of how completely outnumbered they were. Neighbors entered the compound to query the steward about the source of the commotion. Kingman, for his part, cowered in his apartment. Eventually the racket died down and adults restored order.

At a distance it is easy to imagine the whole episode as an epic adventure in troublemaking and dismiss it as boys being boys. But in Charleston, the prospect of large numbers of subordinate persons reacting violently to an exercise of the law would never have been interpreted so innocently. Afterward, Kingman, the steward, led the investigation. He claimed to have "learned the names of some of the boys who were chiefly concerned in the insurrection," and concluded after talking with them that the spark that ignited the tinderbox was the disrespect shown him by the schoolmaster. Kingman extracted confessions from some of the ringleaders, whom he named. The commissioners determined that the schoolmaster was to "inflict six lashes" on each but one of them, and that boy was to get eight lashes. In addition, the ringleaders were forced to stay within the Orphan House lot for two weeks, and commissioners ordered each personally to apologize to Kingman. A half dozen lashes seems a mild punishment compared to what slaves endured for less, but flogging eleven-year-old boys before an audience of other boys followed the model of slave discipline.[39]

Conflict among adult managers of the Orphan House illustrates another aspect of its operations that were, to a great degree, beyond the control of the commissioners. Part of Kingman's anger at Peters stemmed from Peters's use of Orphan House boys to assist in his off-grounds business and family activities. Kingman claimed in a detailed letter that Peters habitually removed boys from chapel to attend to his various concerns: helping Mrs. Peters and their children, carrying leftover food to Peters's dogs rather than the institution's cows, and taking grain from the Orphan House to Peters's farm to feed his horse.[40] Peters claimed ignorance of the events within the Orphan House walls but admitted to using the boys occasionally to perform farm-related chores. Still, he noted, even the half bushel of corn that boys carried hardly constituted a heavy load (modern estimates run to about thirty pounds). Exasperated commissioners demanded civilized behavior among the officers.[41] The officers did not end their conflict right away, according to a visiting commissioner's report a year later. He found "perfect harmony subsisting among the officers (except only that the Steward and Schoolmaster who as usual continue at variance)." Divided leadership may have encouraged the several Orphan House boys who were caught throwing brickbats at neighbor boys. To the commissioners, certainly, without cohesive leadership, a slave-based society was at risk of violence from below.[42]

Corporal punishment in the Orphan House was consistent with contemporary standards of child discipline, but in some cases reached extremes. Complaints of excessive punishment were common in the 1790s. One mother prodded the commissioners to investigate whether her eleven-year-old year old daughter had been "cruelly beaten." A report concluded "that she had only been twice whipped, during the time of her being at the Orphan House," and that the "moderate correction" received by the girl had matched her misbehavior. Commissioners invited the mother to remove her daughter or leave her as she saw fit.The girl remained and was bound out three years later.[43] Part of the problem, in the eyes of some parents, was that those doing the whipping were themselves unsupervised. James Barry claimed that the schoolmaster had inflicted "unmerciful floggings and whippings" on his thirteen-year-old son, which exacerbated his "fits." Henry Barry remained in the Orphan House for just another four days, after which he moved to the Poor House, which was thought to be a better place for a "lunatick."[44]

Not every infraction resulted in whipping. The mother of John Thomas Swords complained that he had been kept under lock and key (in the "penitentiary room") for four weeks after an unspecified infraction. Then after he was bound out his mother complained again about treatment by his master. John solved the immediate problem by absconding from his master and returning to live with his mother and stepfather, who "refused to give him up." The threat of legal action led the couple to return him to the Orphan House, where the commissioners decided to reprimand but not "correct" (i.e., whip) him, and to discontinue parental visits, "as it appeared he was encouraged by them to absent himself."[45]

Girls rarely received lashes. Once a visiting commissioner encountered "insubordination & negligence" while visiting the girls' quarters. They "behaved very disrespectfully to their officers & had been neglectful of their studies," he reported, and thus he felt "obliged to punish them." The penalty was likely whipping, because immediately, according to the matron and nurses, "the punishment had a salutary effect on them."[46] More typically they were reprimanded orally.

As the 1811 riot exemplified, boys were far more accomplished troublemakers than were girls. The gendered differential in troublemaking was evident even before children came to the Orphan House, as discussed in the next chapter. Once in residence, boys who were inclined toward aggression, destruction, vandalism, and other such pursuits enjoyed ample opportunities to indulge themselves. Eventually City Council put its foot down and called the commissioners to account in April 1835, demanding that they produce a list of changes in day-to-day governance that would lead to better "policing" of the Orphan House. The commissioners responded with a laundry list of ideas that they hoped Council would pay for. They requested additional funds to raise the walls around the Orphan House, especially near the trees that enabled boys to climb their way to freedom. They asked for a spare member of the City Guard to replace a boy acting as the porter who manned the entrance to the compound. Using a boy as porter, they acknowledged, kept boys on the grounds about as effectively as leaving the gate wide open and the porter's station unoccupied. Using a city guardsman should, they expected, send a different and more serious message to the boys. In the years since the Denmark Vesey events, the City Guard had been transformed from a ragtag band of watchmen to a force dedicated to keeping the city's black population "completely subordinate," according to one historian of Charleston, Walter Fraser. Still, commissioners pleaded, with a hundred or so boys under their roof, "it must be obvious to all who are in any manner accustomed to the management of boys that it is difficult to keep such a number in that order which is essentially necessary for their good, and the well being of the institution under any even the most favourable circumstances." Add to that the temptations of the big city, and it was no wonder that the boys were so unmanageable. But there were no such complaints about the girls.[47]

Sometimes, children committed violence on other children. In spring 1812 James Jones joined a group of boys in successfully tipping over the sentry box, which earned them a week without dinner, during which time they had to watch the other boys eat their dinner. Around this time Jones wounded a boy with a knife, for which he was whipped.[48] The degree of punishment depended to some extent on the identity of the victim. In 1812 an unnamed boy "in a moment of passion struck one of the Africans with a stick, in which there were one or two nails and wounded him severely on the arm." Given the use of a weapon that had few other uses than assaulting another person, and that the unnamed victim probably belonged to one of the Orphan House's benefactors, it is noteworthy that the boy was not punished. The steward reported, "It does not appear to have been the boy's intention to do much injury," and apparently because of this he decided to spare the rod.[49] When Joseph Rivers, aged fourteen, "committed an indecent outrage" on one of the girls, commissioners could not immediately determine how to punish him. Although his offense deserved a "severe chastisement," it did not appear that his physical health would allow whipping, so they merely "reprov[ed] him publicly" and then expelled him from the Orphan House.[50]

Running away from the Orphan House was not uncommon, although it is impossible to create statistics to show just how frequent it was (see chapter 8). Orphan House officials were determined not to let running away pay off in freedom, and so were willing to pay almost any expense to retrieve their charges.[51] Punishments for those captured varied over time. After the knife attack, James Jones escaped with his friend Charles Smith just days before his grandmother received permission to withdraw him and send him to his mother. After they were caught twenty miles north of town and returned to the Orphan House, they were whipped before all the boys.[52] In an 1817 episode, commissioners recognized the potential trouble that three would-be runaways, William Wilson, Hezekiah Wright, and James Spencer, could create within the House, and so bound them out before they could escape. One was apprenticed to a painter who had nearly received another boy who turned out to be too young, and the other two were bound over the next few weeks.[53] A boy who expressed contrition and promised to behave better in the future might be accepted back after absconding, but even in such a case commissioners would never regain their trust in him. And so they would keep an eye out for a merchant ship to whose captain he might be bound. William Frank absconded and remained at large for eight months, during which time he may have sailed aboard the brig *Sukey*. Once back in custody of the commissioners, they declared him "irreclaimable" and ordered him bound to go to sea. And in still other cases the boy might build up his courage and escape again.[54]

FOR ALL THE DRAMATIC EVENTS recorded by the commissioners, it is important to remember that day-to-day life in the institution was driven by a much calmer routine. A typical negative report from a visiting commissioner to the full board was submitted on November 8, 1849: "The Visiting Commissioner of the past week, Dr. [Edward] North, reported that he had visited the House several times & had not found it in as nice condition as it should be." It was still more common for a visiting commissioner to inform the board "that he had visited the House as was customary and had found all things in their usual order, & had nothing material to communicate."[55] Boys and girls who sat together in the organ loft of the chapel, or who talked to each other during religious services, were just as likely to be telling childish jokes and stories, and comparing experiences in school, as planning a tryst, riot, or escape. Boys who, in the manner of St. Augustine, stole fruit from trees within the compound may simply have been looking for something special to eat, as much as seeking to challenge orders to keep away from the trees. Bringing the children together for morning prayers every day and evening prayers five times a week may suggest more about the daily routine than occasional reports of violence and noise.[56] Even common kinds of troublemaking were often resolved without violence, as when John Kimmons was caught with some unspecified stolen goods. He was to be "confined in the penitentiary room" for ten days and restricted to the Orphan House grounds for three months.[57]

The occasional references to interactions between children and African Americans suggest that relatively ordinary acts of discussion and trading were more common than incidents like the assault with the spiked board described above. As in the rest of Charleston, black-white interactions were legally restricted but in fact quite common.[58] An intriguing but inconclusive episode from 1807 suggests that Orphan House children spoke regularly with blacks both within and outside the Orphan House grounds. In this case the schoolmaster complained to commissioners that several boys had "improperly purchas[ed] a number of penknives from a little boy in King Street." Given previous examples of weapon-related violence, it is easy to see why adult supervisors would be concerned about this exchange. In addition, these boys had also purchased "twine from a Negro," apparently also outside the House, and had "traffic[ked] with Negroes in the house." Trading with slaves was generally illegal throughout the South, since the presumption was that slaves could only have obtained tradable goods by stealing them from their masters.[59] In this case the children may have traded the knives to the slaves, since the entire event was described in the singular as "this wicked transaction," which would no doubt have led to a harsh penalty. Commissioners directed the schoolmaster to "punish two of the most guilty of them in the presence of the whole school," which meant a date with the cowhide.[60]

Rare reports describe violence committed by the Orphan House slaves against children, but in such guarded detail that it is very difficult to know what happened. In one case, commissioner Langdon Cheves, a future Speaker of the US House of Representatives, reported, "It has been also represented that one of the Negroes about the Institution has committed some personal violence on one of the children." No further mention of this event appears in the Minutes of the commissioners' meetings, consistent with the general lack of publicity surrounding black-on-white violence in the antebellum South.[61] In a possibly similar case several years later, "a charge of great enormity [was] brought against Jack, one of the Negro men belonging to the Institution." An investigation revealed its findings to the commissioners, but in an oral presentation with no details recorded in writing. Probably Jack's actions occurred while he was drunk, as a week later the commissioners committed him to the tender mercies of the Work House "for a week or 'till he is well again."[62] Jack returned after a week, but struggled with alcohol for years afterwards. In August 1825 he was again sent to the treadmill after having "been drunk for several days."[63] Further complaints in 1830, this time involving his wife, Flora, led to their sale along with their child, for $405. The funds were dutifully turned over to the city treasurer.[64]

ONE GROUP OF DEPENDENT PEOPLE who were a special quandary were foundlings and other infants. The paths of these children to the Orphan House tended to be shrouded with mystery. Often they first appeared at a planter's door, the gate of the Orphan House, or simply in the street. One well-documented case began shortly after the birth of a boy who never received a first name. On August 10, 1840, a man named Vizzara approached the commissioners claiming to be the father of a baby boy a few days old. The mother had died in childbirth or shortly thereafter, and Vizzara himself, according to a commissioner, was continually drunk. Commissioners initially denied admission for the newborn because he was far too young. At that point, Mary Johnson of the Ladies Benevolent Society took an interest in the case, which was similar to several cases they had managed over the previous two years. When the commissioners next met a week later, Vizzara had rounded up three "respectable" references, including Mrs. Johnson, to persuade the commissioners to review the case. Mrs. Johnson proposed that if the Orphan House allocated six dollars per month for a wet nurse, the Society would find the nurse and then make all necessary arrangements. The commissioners agreed to a stipend of seven dollars for the nurse, to be paid monthly or quarterly as the Society saw fit, until the child was weaned and could later move into the Orphan House. All arrangements were made and young Vizzara lived with his nurse for about a year, until he died. In July 1841 the commissioners paid eight dollars from the private fund for his funeral expenses, recording his name only as "_____ Vizzara."[65]

Since the Orphan House intended to take in children old enough for school and keep them until they were old enough to work, the institution had not prepared to receive the very young. Two alternative places for the smallest unfortunates were the Poor House and homes of private wet nurses. An infant with mother was likely to be directed to the Poor House. For example, in one of the earliest cases of a very young child, in 1794, a Mrs. Kruger sought admission for her child, "between two & three years old." The commissioners noted that the House had "no nurses or provision made for children of so tender an age," and so recommended that both mother and child apply for aid from the Commissioners of the Poor. The child may have been the Charles Kruger who was later admitted to the Orphan House at age five.[66] Likewise, when a mother of three who was already in the Poor House applied to get all three into the Orphan House, commissioners agreed to take the ten-year-old and the three-year-old, but since the "infant . . . of course would require a nurse to attend on it, they could not receive it at present."[67] In rare cases, probably when the mother was completely disabled, the Orphan House accepted an infant from the Poor House. In 1839 they agreed to take Mary Ann Winship, the seven-month-old daughter of "a pauper, epileptic . . . inmate of that institution." Probably she was assigned a wet nurse whom the steward hired, as happened to an even younger child who came from the Poor House, five-month-old Henry Smith in 1852. The two babies met very different fates within just fifteen months: Mary Ann (as we shall see) was adopted, whereas Henry died.[68]

For very young children who had not yet been weaned, the Orphan House arranged for them to live with wet nurses. At first, commissioners simply refused to make arrangements for children so young that they would need a nurse.[69] Within a few years, though, commissioners began to contract with wet nurses. In one early case of 1805, Mrs. Sarjeant brought an eighteen-month-old girl in "peculiar and distressing circumstances," probably related to the Saint-Domingue revolution, to the Orphan House. The first commissioner to deal with the case ordered the child placed with a wet nurse at the expense of the House. Commissioners then contracted with the wet nurse obtained by Mrs. Sarjeant to pay the nurse eight dollars per month as long as she brought the child "frequently to the board" for examination.[70] By the 1820s payments to wet nurses were common entries in financial records. Much later, in the 1850s, the Orphan House assigned infants to the short-lived Akin Foundling Hospital, but before transferring them there, and after the Hospital had failed, the Orphan House continued to contract with wet nurses.[71]

On occasion commissioners pieced together the previous lives of these little ones. In summer 1797 twins appeared on steps of the new Orphan House building one evening. Immediately the commissioners enlisted a wet nurse for them and took "considerable pains . . . to find out the parents." Within a few days, their efforts had "not yet been effected to a certainty," but they soon began to bear fruit. Discussions with a Captain Morrison at the harbor indicated that the parents had in fact died on board his ship. A "woman of colour" who was traveling with her own infant nursed them as best she could after the parents had fallen ill late in the voyage. Before the parents of the twins died, they asked this woman to care for the children, and it was she who brought the two to the Orphan House. The voyage and trauma of their parents' deaths proved too great for the babies, however, and they both died within a year.[72]

A similar case involved another free woman of color who took in a white infant. David Barre, a grocer, became aware of a baby "in the custody of a mulatto woman." The unfortunate child "appeared to be perishing, which induced Mr. Barre to take the child home to his wife." How the child came to the mulatto woman is unknown, as is her reaction to Mr. Barre's seizure of the child. A group of commissioners investigated and found that Mrs. Barre was taking good care of the child, and ordered her "not to part with it to any person without the direction of the board." Some inquiries led to a William Dorum, who acknowledged paternity to the commissioners. The identity of the mother remained a mystery. Dorum agreed to make child support payments to the commissioners, which they would turn over to the Barre couple. After some negotiating, the commissioners and the Barres settled on five pounds per month.[73]

The best of networks did not always yield information on paternity to the commissioners. No one knew the family of a two-year-old girl left at the gate of the Orphan House one evening in November 1810, although the commissioners' scribe attributed her appearance to "some unfeeling woman." The commissioners resolved to assign the child to the matron and to advertise her presence in the newspapers in case she was simply lost. A few months later, a woman presenting herself as Mrs. Mary Findley asked for custody, claiming that the girl was her daughter Margaret. Margaret was released to her putative mother, but returned to the Orphan House a year later under the care of the city's poor wardens, this time to remain for seven years until being bound out to learn mantua making.[74]

Sometimes commissioners did not bother tracking down the infant's parents. In June 1817 a wealthy planter named William Matthews contacted the commissioners about "an infant left at his door." Rather than seek the child's parents, the commissioners, with the approval of City Council, paid Matthews ten dollars per month, which he turned over to Mrs. Nealy, the wet nurse with whom he had contracted for the child's care.[75] Eventually the commissioners offered cash rather than undertaking shoe-leather detective work. A child who appeared at the gate of the Orphan House in September 1840 was given to Betsey, a hired slave, who was provided with extra milk and fifty cents a week for her trouble. Taking advantage of the growing value of the private fund, commissioners offered a fifty-dollar reward to anyone who identified the adult who had left the child.[76] Two years later, in the case of a newborn, they offered a one-hundred-dollar reward.[77]

Despite such efforts by commissioners, death was a common fate for foundlings. The shock of abandonment and lack of care left foundlings extremely vulnerable to disease and death. Elsewhere high death rates for foundlings were not unusual; at the Grey Nuns' Foundling Hospital in Montreal, death rates approached 90 percent between 1825 and 1845.[78] Reports of several foundling deaths appear in the Orphan House records. The death of Clementina, who had been hastily baptized by the Rev. Nathaniel Bowen of St. Michael's, was followed by a bill from her wet nurse for $27.60, for two months and nine days of nursing.[79] Sarah Cunningham served as nurse within the Orphan House to a foundling, at ten dollars per month. When the child died in late April or early May 1821 she submitted a bill for five dollars and was promptly paid.[80]

PERHAPS THE BEST WAY TO VIEW the inner workings of the Orphan House is through the experience of a girl who grew up there and never left. Ann Brooks spent nearly her entire life in the Charleston Orphan House. Her father, Jacob, an immigrant from Prussia, died when she was a toddler. Her widowed mother, Mary, toiled as a lowly nurse at the Orphan House but found work plus two small children too much to manage. So on November 18, 1790, she resigned on amicable terms and immediately requested that the Orphan House receive Ann, who was then just three years old. Although commissioners often recommended that mother and such a very young child be kept together, preferably at the Poor House, here, they knew both and may have felt that accepting Ann was a charity to her mother, a loyal employee. And so Ann remained in the Orphan House after her mother's departure.[81]

Uncomfortable with leaving her daughter at her old workplace, Mary Brooks tried to retrieve Ann the next spring. This did not work out. She took Ann to a friend named Mary Killen, asked her to keep Ann for a short while, and did not return. Killen took Ann back to the Orphan House. Mary Brooks soon became incapable of caring for herself, much less Ann, and entered the grim precincts of the Poor House.[82]

At the Orphan House the years moved on but Ann did not. She should have been bound into a local family right around the turn of the century. But at some point, perhaps in her later teens, the commissioners and the Superintending Ladies must have realized that Ann would remain in their custody for some time to come. Ann Brooks must have seemed like a physical part of the institution, having lived in one Orphan House building or another since before the main structure opened in 1794. In 1811, a secretary recorded that Ann had entered the Orphan House eleven years previously, which was off by a decade. It only seemed as though Ann had been around forever.[83]

No mistress looked at Ann and thought she had found a suitable domestic servant. "Her small stature and homely appearance as well as the scantiness of her intellectual endowments were apparently the cause," explained this secretary. Her mother was in no position to take care of her, and the Poor House was no place for a mentally challenged young woman, at least not one who was loved by anyone. And so the Orphan House essentially created a position for her. Recognizing that Ann too possessed her gifts, in her case "some dexterity in doing menial or drudgery work," the commissioners let her stay in the Orphan House and work as a domestic. She swept rooms and staircases, made beds, and kept furniture clean. Sparing the Orphan House from hiring someone to clean was sure to appeal to the commissioners of an institution founded to lower the cost of welfare provision.[84]

Ann worked without pay, receiving only room, board, and clothing along with the older girls. But as she grew into maturity she began to notice and take pleasure in small things. She became "desirous of being indulged with a little tea, sugar, coffee, and butter," in exchange for which she promised "uninterrupted diligence and fidelity in the discharge of the duties appertaining to her employment," wrote her amanuensis. Ann would probably have toiled diligently and faithfully for the Orphan House no matter what the answer was. But recognizing how modest the request was in light of her "peaceable behaviour and . . . her willingness to do such work as is fit for her station" in life, the commissioners gladly assented.[85]

In 1815 they promoted Ann to the position of assistant nurse to the Orphan House. As determined by a city statute, this position came with a cash salary as well as room and board. Ann was to be paid at the same rate as all the other nurses. In 1840 that would have included a ten-dollar monthly wage payment, 3 1/2 quarts of rice and 3 1/2 pints of milk per week, one pound each of bread and beef daily, plus Ann's favorites—sugar, coffee, and butter (but no tea). When such jobs came open the Orphan House usually received far more applications than available positions, so Ann's promotion was no small achievement.[86]

In 1819 a small scandal erupted with potentially serious consequences for the children. Someone had been stealing from the children's grain allotment. The commissioners suspected one or more of the officers—the employees who managed the Orphan House's daily operations—and that included Ann. Nobody believed she was the culprit, and she duly proclaimed her innocence. One of the nurses admitted having taken the grain, but claimed ignorance of its intended use for the residents. The commissioners moved to "acquit" the other officers and ordered that in the future none take so much as an "atom" from the children's allowance.[87]

After many years of service to the Orphan House, at some point in the mid 1820s Ann became unable to work, perhaps due to a chronic and fatal disease. The commissioners ordered that she be accommodated as comfortably as possible. On October 17, 1828, Ann Brooks died and was buried in the Orphan House cemetery. In 1831 the commissioners gave a woman named Mrs. Mary Durand permission to place head and footstones at her gravesite, a final tribute to a woman whose dedication to the Orphan House was surpassed by no one in its long history.[88]

Families

T HE ORPHAN HOUSE PROVED AN ATTRACTIVE OPTION not just for full orphans, but also half orphans and other children whose parents lacked
the resources to raise them. In fact, so many children hoped to enter the
institution that it established an admissions protocol for prospective residents. The standard for admission was poverty. Nomination by a poor warden was prima facie evidence of extreme want, and children so nominated
were admitted as soon as their residency in Charleston could be established.
A widowed parent or guardian who hoped to leave a child at the Orphan
House was expected to explain the child's circumstances in a letter to the
commissioners. If the message described a real need, a commissioner visited and interviewed the responsible adult and sometimes neighbors and
employers as well. From these letters and reports we can piece together the
prior lives of children who came to the Orphan House.

Verification by visiting commissioners makes these testimonies particularly trustworthy. Adults who hoped to place a child in the Orphan House
might well have been tempted to stretch the truth of their destitution, if
their exaggeration might lead to a more hopeful future for the child. Indeed,
a minor genre of popular literature at this time was the personal narrative
of those down on their luck. Ann Fabian colorfully analyzes these writings
in which, in many cases, "clever dissemblers could pass as deserving sufferers." But in the case of published tales, statements of verification were relatively easy to concoct. In the Charleston records the visiting commissioners
had no reason to approve applications based on inaccurate narratives, and
strong ideological reasons to accept appeals from the deserving white poor.
That is, the visiting commissioners were likely to have assessed the need of
applicants accurately, and because this role of visiting commissioners was

common knowledge, applicants in turn were likely to present their cases accurately.[1]

In most cases it appears the responsible adult wrote the letter him- or herself, but even those letters written by others reflected the parent or guardian's own story. About half of mothers and female guardians of these children signed their names to Orphan House documents, so a large share of them could have written their own letters. Literacy among fathers and male guardians was nearly 90 percent by early in the nineteenth century. Thus, most parents were capable of writing a description of their family situation.

Those who could not easily write found literate friends, relatives, or clergy to do so on their behalf.[2] Many women, and a few men, endorsed their letters with a simple "X," near which witnesses attested to the identity of the marker by signing their own names. In other cases a woman's signature differed so clearly from the handwriting in the rest of the letter that it seemed safe to infer that someone else had composed most of the document and the signer had contributed the story and her signature.[3] Indeed, some handwritten letters provided blanks for the name of the child as well, so that it could be filled in as with boilerplate. Ann Duncan intended to nominate one of her two daughters for the Orphan House, but she could not make up her mind whether it should be Catherine or Mary. Because Ann herself was illiterate, a friend wrote most of her letter to the commissioners, explaining in the first person, "My husband died on the 18th October 1817 & from his long infirmity expended all his funds & has left me with two children without anything to support us." This scribe allowed Ann to delay her decision, possibly until after speaking with commissioners, by leaving blank spaces where a second writer (here underlined) then inserted name and age: "Necessity compels me to request that you will assist me by taking under your care my daughter <u>Catherine</u>. She is <u>11</u> years old." Thus poor mothers either wrote their own stories or dictated them to literate friends.[4]

And it was mothers who sponsored most Orphan House children.[5] Over the course of the entire period from 1790 to 1860, 56 percent of children were bound in by their mothers. Only 11 percent were bound in by their fathers, and just 3 percent entered at the behest of other family members, as identified on their indentures. The remaining 29 percent of children were bound in by public officials such as representatives of the Poor House. In some of these cases, the poor wardens signed the indenture, but it was actually neighbors or extended family members who brought the child to the Orphan House's attention. The relatively small share of full orphans was typical of later nineteenth-century orphanages; the Charleston evidence suggests that

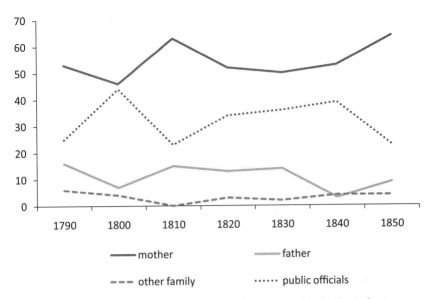

Fig. 4.1. Sponsors of Orphan House children by entrance decade. Vertical axis: percentage of children.

all along it may have been half orphans who dominated institutional populations.[6] Figure 4.1 shows trends in the share of entering children according to the identities of the adults who bound them in. Trend lines for mothers and public officials were, roughly, mirror images of each other, accounting for about 90 percent of all the children. Over the entire period considered here, few fathers and extended family participated in nominating children for Orphan House admission, and that did not change over time.[7]

In terms of sheer numbers, the population of the Orphan House followed an arc that both tracked the fortunes of Charleston's poor and showed their dependence on the "bounty of the institution," as it was often phrased. Figure 4.2 illustrates trends in admissions and total population of the Orphan House. Annual admissions remained around thirty, and the total number of children around 150, until the mid-1820s, when admissions began to decline to as few as nine in 1845. Given the general economic difficulties of the late 1830s into the 1840s, it seems likely that these numbers reflect the numbers of the poor present in Charleston rather than the degree of economic difficulties. That is, declining admissions at a time of economic stagnation in the city probably reflected the tendency of the poor to migrate westward in search of work rather than an era of prosperity for all white Charlestonians. From around 1850 the figures sharply increased, due

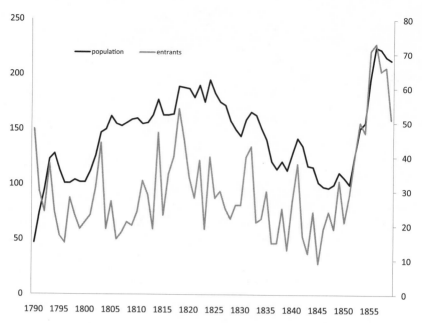

Fig. 4.2. Orphan House admissions and total population

to growing numbers of immigrants in the port city. Table 4.1 shows a similar arc, peaking in 1820 for girls and 1830 for boys, but it suggests a deeper
dependence of Charleston's poor whites on the Orphan House. In census
years, summary publications reported population numbers by age, race, and
sex. From these tables were drawn the first two columns, which show the
numbers of young white children in Charleston. In 1820 and earlier, the age
group shown was under ten years, and in 1830 and 1840 it was between five
and nine years. Estimates of the number of children in the Orphan House
at these same ages during these years appear in the second pair of columns.
The third pair of columns is simply the ratio of the previous columns. It
shows the share of the city's young white children who lived in the Orphan
House. At the peaks of Orphan House residency rates, about one in twenty-
five Charleston girls (in 1820) and one in twelve Charleston boys (in 1830)
lived in the Orphan House. This is a sizable minority of the population,
but as a share of the eligible population the Orphan House held an even
greater proportion of children. If previous estimates are only approximately
correct, that about one-fifth of the city's white population consisted of the
poor, then the share of poor white children in the Orphan House may have
been closer to one-fourth of girls and two-fifths of boys, which are very large

TABLE 4.1. Share of Charleston's young children in the Orphan House

Year	Charleston		Orphan House		Percentage in Orphan House	
	Boys	Girls	Boys	Girls	Boys	Girls
1800	1,323	1,321	50	38	3.78	2.88
1810	1,292	1,683	80	63	6.19	3.74
1820	1,408	1,359	111	55	7.88	4.05
1830	750	752	61	30	8.13	3.99
1840	648	620	49	22	7.56	3.55

Sources: Orphan House records; Dawson and DeSaussure, Census of the City of Charleston, South Carolina, for the Year 1848, 3–6; tables from federal Census reports.
Note: 1800–1820, children under ten years of age; 1830–40, children aged five to nine.

figures. A substantial share of the poor whites of Charleston depended on the Orphan House to care for their children in need. Even those who had not needed its charity previously expected it to be there should catastrophe strike.[8]

To discourage parents who might exaggerate their burden, the Orphan House required an official visit to their household. In many cases the interview included questioning of neighbors, landlord, employer, or clergy. Visiting commissioners investigated with varying degrees of diligence, depending on their caseload and on the space available in the institution. One typical report relayed that the applicant was a widow of three years and "in utter poverty," but that she had a plan to place her daughter at the Orphan House so that she could then go out to work as a domestic. The commissioner emphasized the reliability of this account by noting, "These facts I have ascertained by investigation and inquiry."[9] Other cases required multiple visits, which sometimes led to inconsistent information. Where one visiting commissioner saw a father who was "a worthless drunkard," another found a man "in the prime of life [who] could with proper diligence support his children."[10] Signs of living standards slightly above destitution sometimes led visiting commissioners to recommend rejection, in one case because the "mother appears to be a hearty woman & able to support" her children.[11] Aware of the potential scrutiny to which they might be subject, some applicants appealed to neighbors or town fathers to sign documents attesting to their industriousness and misfortune.[12] Commissioners treated testimony of women and men alike with little distinction between the two, accepting one petition signed by no fewer than sixteen women.[13] They also made no distinction between literate and illiterate witnesses, and many recommenders marked rather than signed petitions of support. The difficulty of misrepresenting one's situation must have been widely known, which implies that letters by and about Charleston's white poor are fundamentally trustworthy.

AMONG THE ADULTS WHO HAD BEEN CARING for children they brought to the Orphan House, one kind of person had no legal or kin relationship with the child. These people, mostly but not entirely women, might best be called foster parents, but as will become apparent, that is not to imply that they had a formal status by that or any other title. Thirty cases of unrelated women taking children into their homes appear in these letters of appeal to the Orphan House, plus a few others in which the patron was a man. As many foster mothers initiated contact with the Orphan House as did male intermediaries, themselves mostly clergy, who were acting on their behalf. Hopeful applications featured supporting petitions or letters from neighbors and friends on behalf of the foster mother. The numbers of people behind such petitions indicate that the poor belonged to a broader community that watched over their children. Between letters written by the foster mothers and those written for them emerge outlines of a previously little-noticed group of women. Most were widows, and a few stressed obligations to their own children. They emphasized their own penury by noting their occupations at the bottom of the scale: needlework or keeping a boardinghouse. One foster mother emphasized her poverty by noting that she was "receiving a pension herself from the Poor House." To assure the commissioners that the child she nominated came from a stable household she made sure that a former employer described her as "sober & industrious."[14]

Foster fathers lived more comfortable lives and were more articulate correspondents than foster mothers. John Farley, an Orphan House alumnus himself who had left the institution to join the class of 1815 at the South Carolina College, Columbia, was one foster father. Farley returned to Charleston to teach, and perhaps his occupation led the mother of four-year-old Edward Jones to leave the boy with him early in 1827. The father, whom Farley did not name but identified as another former Orphan House resident, died in Edgefield leaving his widow unable to support their five children. Farley kept Edward for "10 or 11 months" before turning to the Orphan House. Knowing its ways, he hesitated because he knew Edward's mother was living outside the city in the Charleston Neck, which ordinarily would have disqualified her children. In this case, the commissioners accepted Edward, perhaps because of his father and foster father's connections to the institution.[15] In a similar case, a free school teacher named Joseph Folker brought William Bradford to the Orphan House. The identity of William's father was unknown, possibly even to his mother, who was a prostitute. Still, someone enrolled him in a free school, where he met Folker, the schoolmaster. In 1819 when William was seven years old, his mother was unable to pay her rent and left Charleston without him. The procuress turned William out onto the street, and William turned to Folker for help. The commissioners immediately admitted William.[16]

Other foster fathers belonged to prominent Charleston families. William B. Pringle brought Thomas Lister to Charleston from Waccamaw. Thomas was ten years old and a full orphan, and Pringle hoped to get him educated and bound into a trade in Charleston. As a board member of the Bank of the State of South Carolina, Pringle was "much absent from town," and ultimately proved unable to make these arrangements himself. Instead, he turned to the Orphan House.[17] James Lowndes, a member of the South Carolina House of Representatives, took in two boys aged four and seven, whose parents had died while working for a neighbor of his. Lowndes also recognized that children from the neighborhood of his plantation were unlikely candidates for the Orphan House because they were not Charleston residents, so he offered to pay the House to support these two boys. The commissioners agreed to take the boys, and Lowndes agreed to pay the Orphan House eighty dollars annually for each.[18]

The impetus to many fostering relationships was an emergency to which foster mothers responded generously. In 1818, Margaret Denoon explained that John Campbell Sanders came to her as an infant after his mother died. She "took him into [her] family" for the next ten years, long after her last contact with his father. A boy named Thomas King lived with several different foster mothers. Two women cared for him after his mother died and his father abandoned him. Then an unnamed Irishwoman with a large family took Thomas in for a time. When this Irishwoman could no longer afford the extra mouth to feed, Mrs. Elizabeth McLaughlin took him into her home. Dying of cancer, Mrs. McLaughlin enlisted the aid of an Episcopal priest, A. Toomer Porter, in contacting the Orphan House. Two months after Thomas was admitted, Mrs. McLaughlin, his last foster mother, was dead.[19] Sometimes short-term caregiving by unrelated women led children into the Orphan House. Before Martha Bennett decamped to Columbia for what she claimed would be a brief visit, she left her three children "with a coloured woman named Youngblood" a few blocks from the Orphan House. In assessing the children's situation, the race of the foster mother was less

important than the reputation of the birth mother for poverty and misbehavior. "The mother of the children has no means and the sooner the children are out of the reach of her influence and control the better for them,"
urged the visiting commissioner.[20] The Orphan House admitted the Bennett
girls two days later.

Many a foster mother accepted a child into her home with the understanding that she might have the youngster on her hands for some time to
come. Clearly this was the case for foundlings. Finding a baby boy "but a
few hours old" on her porch was such a vivid event for Ann Creighton that
seven years later she could still recall that it happened "on the evening of
the 10th of October in the year 1845 between the hours of 9 and 10 Oclock."
She had him baptized at a nearby Episcopal church, where another priest
acted as godfather, with the name James Usher. Over the next few years, she
stressed to the commissioners, she "sustained him as a mother through his
tenderest years of infancy," and "entirely at her own expense."[21]

One path to the Orphan House involved calculation rather than chance.
Some foster mothers negotiated contracts for room and board of the child,
and when the parent or guardian breached the contract, the women turned
to the Orphan House for relief. Anna Wood explained to the commissioners
that while William Edmond Crowe had been "boarding with" her for some
two and a half years, she had only been paid ten dollars for her work. Her
inability to continue raising the child uncompensated, plus his new habit of
running away, led her to ask the Orphan House to take him. James Young's
wife died not long after giving birth to their daughter Jane. Young and Mary
Dunn agreed on a rate of eight dollars a month for Jane's care, a somewhat
higher-than-average wet nurse fee. Young paid for several months in ad-
vance, left for New York with his two older children, and was never heard
from again. Meanwhile, Mary Dunn struggled with caring for her now-
uncompensated charge, her own two children, her aged mother, and a husband in ill health. Her one possible source of relief was the Orphan House,
which took in Jane in July 1853.[22] William Player, whose father had been
killed in military service, was squeezed out of his mother's new household
by the arrival of his half sibling. William first went to board with a Mrs.
Armstrong, who became "a second parent" to him. On her death he entered
the household of a woman who boarded "several" children, but she determined that "his habits [were] bad and his disposition unmanageable," and
applied to the Orphan House for relief.[23]

These cases suggest that not all foster mothers accepted their burden as
an act of charity. Many of these foster mothers, in cases in which contracts
were honored by the child's parent or guardian, must have raised children

in exchange for money for some mutually agreed-upon length of time. Examples in Orphan House records suggest that a broad network of women participated in this market, which operated with standard contract duration (monthly) and remuneration. In Matilda Assalit's case, her mother gave her "almost stark naked to a strumpet, in order to beg alms through this city," as her angry uncle wrote. A member of the Ladies Benevolent Society who took Matilda from the unnamed prostitute then gave her to a Mrs. Hale on St. Philips Street, providing some clothes and a promise to pay her six dollars per month to care for Matilda. Because the girl was two years old at the time, this arrangement was probably for standard child care and not wet nursing.[24] Thus, as for Mrs. Hale, it seems likely that child raising was an occupation for some poor women. Most of those women performed their jobs in such a way that all parties were reasonably satisfied, and so the exchange never entered the written record. How extensive this network of foster mothers was is impossible to determine, but the fragmentary evidence from failed arrangements establishes that it did in fact exist.[25]

On the fringes of some cases were two interesting but most-shadowy groups of women who acted as accidental foster mothers: free women of color and prostitutes. They appear in the records usually because a neighbor or relative discovered a child in the woman's care and alerted authorities to this disorderly arrangement. The case of Martha Bennett's children above gives one example. One of the earliest items in the commissioners' minutes appeared in November 1790, when someone alerted them to the fact that a "Negro woman" was caring for a white orphan child. The woman, Jenny, produced the following letter: "Bearer Jenny has a poor Orphan under her care, my desire is that he remain there unmolested, at a proper time he will be sent to some school in the mean time any person interfering will do it at his peril Nov 6, 1790 [signed] Francis Kinloch."[26] Kinloch, a representative to the Continental Congress and Revolutionary War officer who had become a wealthy planter and politician, appears not to have been further trifled with. In a similar situation, when the grandmother of two-month-old Virginia Karnes could no longer care for her, she placed the infant "under the care & in the possession of a Negro nurse."[27] Authorities found children staying with prostitutes more alarming, not to say distasteful. When Mary Johnson of the Ladies Benevolent Society seized Matilda Assalit, she told the prostitute who had been caring for her "not to ever appear in her presence," and then almost as an afterthought "required to know the name of the child." Matilda seems to have stayed only a brief time with the woman before entering Mrs. Hale's home.[28] Two appeals to take children from their prostitute-mothers suggested that the children lived in a brothel, in a somewhat communal setting.[29] Unfortunately the lower reaches of the Charleston demimonde left little in the way of written records, so we cannot learn more about child-raising methods of these women.

Attitudes of foster mothers toward their children can be inferred from their letters. Abandoned as a foundling around 1815, Eunice Madison was twice lucky in her foster mothers. First she entered the household of a Mrs. Ferguson, who became unable to keep her but who found her a welcoming home in Georgetown, sixty miles up the coast. There, according to Mrs. Ferguson, she was "adopted and fondly cherished" by Mr. and Mrs. Ezra Benjamin, until Mrs. Benjamin's death. Once widowed, Mr. Benjamin relied on Mrs. Ferguson's recommendation in getting Eunice into the Orphan House. Other children were less fortunate in their foster mothers, among whom Eliza Smith was especially unlucky. Her first foster mother was a Mrs. Beswick, who after a while left Charleston. A storekeeper named Samuel Hayward took her into his home, aided by a wholesale merchant named Thomas Napier, who agreed to provide Eliza's clothing. An unidentified woman approached the Haywards to ask if the girl could move into her household, promising "to bring her up as her own child." Mrs. Hayward reluctantly agreed. But then both Haywards were horrified to find that the new foster mother "inhumanely whipt" Eliza and so they retrieved her, kept her at home for a few months, and then sought help from the Orphan House.[30] The reaction of the Haywards indicates that some foster parents continued to look after these children after surrendering custody, and at least in some cases could remove them from abusive adults.

Even if the typical fostering case involved a warm attachment in the adult's eyes, at some point the foster parent decided he or she could no longer raise the child. The most common reason for relinquishment was poverty. A barely literate neighbor described how one foster mother expected to care for John and William Calvert only a couple of days, but then "the Mother has now bin gon Eleven Weeks, & She has never herd of her Sence." Because the foster mother "is a poore woman her self," she needed the help of the Orphan House. Foster mothers needed cooperation from their husbands to keep above the poverty level, and when it was not forthcoming, the child headed to the Orphan House. Mary McCaffrey "adopted" a foundling in 1853, according to a neighboring physician, but "her husband does little or nothing for her support." After querying a neighbor for confirmation, the visiting commissioner recommended admission.[31] Especially with boys, foster mothers found that as children aged they required more attention and discipline, which the foster mothers were not able to provide. Some foster mothers reached this stage of resignation with children as young as three years, in the case of Charles Symonds, or six years, as in the case of Washington Stevenson, or with children as old as eleven, as with William Edmond Crowe.[32] In all these cases the foster mother hoped that the Orphan House would control the child more effectively than she could.

In most cases there is no way to know how attached a foster mother was to a child. For one woman the memory of a foster child stayed with her through the years until she felt compelled to learn of his fate. Around 1816 Jane Smith accepted a one-month-old boy from a desperate friend, a situation that she thought was manageable because her "circumstances at the time [were] very good." Some two years on, she wrote, "lately I have seen a great deal of distress." At the time of her writing she was supporting herself with needlework ("and that hardly suffices to clothe me") and living in a spare room of another family's house. If the commissioners accepted the boy, she wrote, she promised to come back for him as soon as her situation improved. The boy, named James Lawrence, immediately entered the Orphan House, and unusually for one so young, was almost immediately bound out as an apprentice. Seventeen years later, in 1834, Mrs. Jane Smith Page wrote from New Orleans to ask about James Lawrence, describing herself as "one who is deeply interested in his welfare." By that time, James had disappeared from the record, but not from Mrs. Page's memories.[33]

THE PROTECTORS AND ADVOCATES OF SOME CHILDREN fell into a liminal state between those with no legal or blood relation to the child and the child's parents. For convenience, adults in this group can be called stepparents, and some really were or had been married to the child's mother or father. Others were not stepmothers or stepfathers but held some kind of kin relationship to the child, such as that of a sibling, aunt or uncle, or grandparent. Among stepfathers, those who sent stepchildren to the Orphan House and those who aided their restoration to their mothers played very different roles. As discussed in chapter 7, many petitions for restoration came from widowed mothers who had just remarried to a man who agreed to help raise the child. While men who married widows with children may have known before the wedding that they wanted to reunite mother and child, few stepfathers whose wives had just died had the stomach for raising another man's child. These unlucky full orphans then entered the Orphan House. Among responsible adults, stepmothers outnumbered stepfathers. Partly this was a statistical artifact of higher mortality rates among men at older ages, which resulted in more widows than widowers. But unlike stepmothers, few stepfathers whose work required their absence from home even attempted to raise their stepchildren, although, as previously noted, they might have found a boardinghouse especially for children. Consider the example of John Tullock, who "work[ed] on the rivers in the boating business." His wife, the mother of his stepson, was "confined in the cells of the Poor House as a maniac," and so he hoped the Orphan House would raise the boy.[34]

Other stepfathers simply failed in their obligations. After being widowed in the War of 1812, William Player's mother remarried. William's stepfather must not have provided basic financial support to his new wife and her children, because the little family depended solely on "her daily labor as a spinner and washer-woman," according to Episcopal clergyman Christopher Gadsden. Gadsden referred to the remarriage of William's mother without reference to the stepfather's labor, which implied that he was alive but not contributing to the family's purse. Similarly, the widowed stepfather of Robert, Hugh, and Andrew Stenton did "not seem to be a person at all calculated to act a parents' part," as the Baptist minister Basil Manly delicately phrased it.[35]

Beyond neglect, other stepfathers abused their stepchildren. A mother's death could reveal how in life she had protected her children from their stepfather's wrath. After his mother and half sister died from fever, Joseph Ringland's intemperate and poor stepfather simply kicked him out of the house, forcing the boy to fend for himself.[36] Distant relations took in some of these children, but often not for long. "Connexions" (at least male ones) who were kin to the child only through marriage were rarely enthusiastic about cousins, nephews, or nieces entering the household. A visiting commissioner reported in one such case that "the aunt says she has done all in her power but that her husband objects to the keeping the children, as he cannot support them."[37]

Occasionally men emerged from children's extended family. Typically they passively accepted responsibility for their young kin rather than actively seeking to care for them. A good example occurred in the case of a full orphan named Conrad Rempp. Soon after his father's death, his stepmother proved unable or unwilling to support him, so Conrad was passed along to his maternal uncle, a cabinet maker named Ansell. After paying for his brother-in-law's funeral, Ansell reported that he himself could not support Conrad either, and so the boy entered the Orphan House.[38]

Most of the responsible adults in this situation were women, and among them, literal stepmothers were in a difficult position. Having married a man with offspring from a previous marriage, and in many cases having borne children by the recently deceased husband, the widowed stepmother was often faced with a most unpleasant choice: to institutionalize her own children or another woman's.[39] While the decision to keep her own children might seem natural, or even Darwinian, the chronology of events also often dictated that an older stepchild was better able to fend for himself in an institution than younger children of the second (or higher-order) wife. Thus, when Elizabeth Smith sought admission for her stepson, eight-year-old John Smith, she could note that both his parents were deceased and that she had five younger children of her own to care for.[40] In most cases, the stepmothers, like all other sponsors, stated that their poverty made it infeasible to raise the child in question, much less to provide any education.[41]

In many cases stepmothers themselves could tap into networks of extended family, friends, and patrons. Sarah Gibson Davis was the fourth wife of L. W. W. Davis, whose death left her with four children to care for, one from each of his first two marriages and two of her own. In frail health herself, she readily accepted an offer by Eliza Fludd to support financially the two oldest. Mrs. Fludd's description offers an example of the complex living and financial arrangements that the poor might find themselves in: "The step-mother Mrs Davis gave them up to me as soon as their father died and though they staid in the house with her, it was at my expense." Soon Mrs. Fludd and Mrs. Davis together agreed to place the stepchildren in the Orphan House.[42] Bridget Adams, a widow who was supporting her late husband's son, could not sign her name, but she not only found someone to write a letter to the commissioners but also obtained signatures of three people to endorse her appeal.[43] After Jane Mordecai secured admission for her late husband's daughter Fanny, the merchant Elias Abrahams and his wife offered to take Fanny under their care when she reached her majority.[44]

Commissioners conferred on stepmothers some of the legal rights ordinarily attributed to mothers of children. Caroline Hendricks, who appeared in the very beginning of this book, was the stepmother of Richard Hendricks, who entered the Orphan House in 1833 at age nine. When Richard was fourteen years old, an Upcountry man named Jesse Bates discussed the possibility of Richard serving as an apprentice to a merchant in Lexington Court House, near Columbia. Bates relayed to the commissioners that not only did Richard approve of the position, so did his stepmother. The commissioners voted to ask Caroline themselves, just to be sure. They thus extended to the stepmother the same right to approve an apprenticeship that they ordinarily granted to the mother.[45]

Women who were more distant relations to children found themselves in a spot in between complete strangers and stepmothers. Like stepmothers, they were privy to family information that one or both of the child's parents were ill, broke, alcoholic, or about to abscond. Even so, they often opened their doors on short notice. Like every other adult woman who brought a child to the Orphan House, they claimed that poverty kept them from providing for another child. The case of Michael Manihan is illustrative. Michael was born around 1846, and his mother, Rose, died in a cholera epidemic in 1853. His father, Richard, was a laborer who was "intemperate and poor," so his mother's mother, an Irishwoman named Mary Stanley, took him in. Eventually raising a young boy became too much for her and she brought Michael to the Orphan House. Given Richard Manihan's drinking and Mary Stanley's proximity, it seems likely that she was not completely surprised by the initial need to intervene on behalf of her grandson.[46]

Because extended family members were aware of developing problems, they were able to form part of a broad but unpredictably secure network before disaster fully struck. The pieces of this safety net consisted of aid from extended family, neighbors, and charities, and, in the last resort, the Orphan House. The experience of the Gilbert brothers early in the nineteenth century illustrates. Charleston in the very early nineteenth century was enjoying a boom like no other in its history, thanks to institutional growth that had led to new construction plans in the 1790s, the expansion of rice and cotton culture and marketing, and the reopening of the African slave trade in 1803.[47] A capable craftsman like Joseph Gilbert found regular work as a brick mason, and no doubt he and his wife greeted the successive births of three sons in 1801–6 with joy. Then when the boys were just toddlers, Mrs. Gilbert died in 1808, and Joseph soon unraveled. He became known as "a common vagabond about the streets," a "lazy indolent drunken man." To spare the children, Mrs. Gilbert's brother, William Ruberry, agreed to take all three boys into his home. This act pleased all parties since Ruberry was married but as yet childless. In spring 1814 Ruberry arranged for the oldest boy to begin an apprenticeship with the prominent Charleston brass founder Robert Wallace.[48] Unfortunately, William Ruberry died later in 1814, leaving his widow with two nephews of her late husband and deprived of her means of support. According to William's brother, John Ruberry, over the course of six years the ne'er-do-well father Joseph Gilbert "never [had] given one single fourpence to assist in providing for them." Instead, the widowed Mrs. Ruberry obtained support from the South Carolina Society, a private charity initially formed to benefit poor Huguenots, to send the nephews to school.[49] Eventually the burden of raising the two boys as a single mother became excessive and Mrs. Ruberry arranged for three men to contact the Orphan House on her behalf. Her brother-in-law John Ruberry wrote one letter, and the commissioners would have recognized the other letter writers immediately, as they were two future commissioners, Daniel

Stevens and James Jervey. Even with such aid in the admissions process, it was William Ruberry's wife and then widow, the aunt of these boys, who was no blood relation to them and whose first name appears nowhere in the records, who accepted responsibility for these boys when no one else would. The Gilbert brothers became full orphans when Joseph Gilbert died later in 1814. Joseph's brother Seth Gilbert, who as a wharfinger in a busy port must have been reasonably prosperous, then wrote to the commissioners for permission to take his nephews to their father's funeral. But Seth appears not to have aided his sister-in-law in any material way when she was widowed and distressed.[50]

As in the case of the Gilbert boys, when some women were overwhelmed with new responsibilities, they arranged for a man to deal with the male commissioners of the Orphan House. Other women addressed the commissioners directly in making their case. Elizabeth Morton just managed to sign a short note that was written for her, noting that her two grandsons William and John Morton had "sometime since lost their mother and a few days ago their father."[51] Christiana Jones hit all the right notes in appealing to the commissioners on behalf of her nephew James Allen. She had already cared for him over the eighteen months since his parents' deaths, she was grateful that the Orphan House had already received James's brother Charles, and she was currently raising a large family of young children of her own "with very slender means for their support."[52] Some of the female kin were sisters or sisters-in-law of the orphans. Mary Ann Hairgroves defied her alcoholic mother when she alerted the Orphan House to the danger in which her younger siblings found themselves after the marriage of their intemperate mother to a man noted for his "very hard" drinking. In this troubled family the mother kept her children from school and often sobered up in the confines of the Poor House.[53] Women with siblings in the Orphan House also demonstrated an ongoing attachment to them by seeking to take them out of the House and into their homes for holidays, such as Christmas.[54]

BY FAR MOST ADULTS WHO BROUGHT CHILDREN to the Orphan House were the parents of those children, and most of those parents were mothers. Again, the primary reason for the greater number of mothers was the higher mortality risk for their husbands than for themselves. Beyond statistical tendencies, mothers were not a homogeneous group. In marital terms alone, some had been widowed, others abandoned, and still others were living with their husbands in a more or less intact family.[55] Couples who approached the Orphan House often suffered from illness and destitution combined. As with other women who hoped to place children in the Orphan House, some mothers wrote their own letters and others marked beneath a message written for them. Many of these women had been born in Charleston, while others were immigrants. All communicated aspects of being poor and desperate in one of the wealthiest cities in America.

A decline in their own health drove many mothers to seek the charity of the Orphan House. Frances Bettison wrote that the sickness that had kept her bedridden "for many months" left her with "no hopes of ever getting out of [bed]." As a result she feared that her daughter Elizabeth would begin to keep bad company. Alas, at age thirteen the daughter was too old for the Orphan House, and within days Mrs. Bettison was dead.[56] Some mothers were simply described as ill or "suffering much under a disease which prevents her superintending her child."[57] In other cases it was obvious that the mother suffered from a particular disease. In January 1853 the mother of John Henry Jerrold, aged three, lay "in the Poor House, ill of consumption, and [could not] long survive."[58] Since Mrs. Catherine Gilbert had died on August 22, 1854, leaving behind an infant who was described on the 24th of August as one day old, it seems likely that she died in childbirth.[59]

A special type of ill health was mental illness.[60] Over much of the antebellum era, Charleston's facilities for the mentally ill were the basement cells in the Poor House. Persons confined to the cells were fed and protected from the elements, but received little else there. "[L]unatics" in the Poor House basement "filled the house with their unearthly whooping and hallooings."[61] Diagnostic practices changed over time so that whereas in the 1820s most inmates were considered incurable, by the 1850s many were discharged as cured, often after less than a year's stay.[62] Thus, the 1830 application of George Jacoby, "friend" to three-year-old Ann Iseman, noted that Ann's father was "a lunatic and now in the asylum for maniacs," probably a sign that his commitment was a long-term arrangement. In response, Ann's mother had abandoned both husband and child.[63] Similarly, Elizabeth King found someone to write a letter explaining that she was "the wife of a maniac" in the Poor House and so she needed to send her twelve-year-old boy to the Orphan House. Within a couple of years Elizabeth's husband, George King, had recovered to the point that he left the Poor House and retrieved the boy from the Orphan House.[64] The same destination awaited children of mentally ill mothers who were confined to the cells.[65]

It is hard to overstate how closely alcoholism was associated with destitution. Whether the already impoverished took to the bottle or otherwise capable adults drank their families into poverty, the frequency of drink as an explanation of poverty was striking. In some cases the applicant described the problem in straightforward fashion. Margaret Dooling hoped her five-year-old and three-year-old would qualify for entrance because her husband was in jail following a drinking binge. The air of resignation in her story suggests that she had told it many times already: "[W]e struggled long to support ourselves and children and might have succeeded had not my husband been unfortunately addicted to drinking. Gentlemen I shall not dwell on the melancholy effects of this passion on him and his helpless family."[66] In a densely populated city neighbors would have known with some precision where the loud and violent drunks lived, and so many reports came from neighbors. A Mrs. Moore approached the planter Lawrence Dawson to ask him to contact the Orphan House about receiving her twelve-year old son. Dawson readily wrote to describe how Mr. Moore was known in their neighborhood to be "from his intemperate habits . . . rather an incumbrance than a support to herself and family."[67] But even an oft-drunk father maintained legal rights to his children, so after two neighbors convinced the commissioners that John Rantin's "gross intemperance" had left his wife and six children in a state of destitution, it was still John Rantin's signature that endorsed the indentures that bound two of his sons into the Orphan House.[68]

Women as well as men drank to the point of endangering their families. In W. J. Rorabaugh's memorable history *The Alcoholic Republic*, women appeared about as often in the role of temperance activists as they did in the role of drinkers. Rorabaugh deplored the lack of information on women drinkers, especially those who regularly drank to excess, in the early nineteenth century.[69] Some such information appears in the Orphan House records, showing that a few female Charlestonians drank so much as to harm their family. Correspondents occasionally noted that a mother was, for example, "addicted to drink, & in very bad health, in consequence of the intemperate life she leads."[70] The most extreme cases again were well known to neighbors, who sought the help of nearby clergy or went directly to commissioners. James Caldwell, reporting as visiting commissioner on the case of Thomas Randles, aged four, passed along information from the Reverend William B. Yates "that the mother of the child is of bad moral character, of intemperate habits, and is a great measure regardless of the interest of the child."[71] A neighbor might note that a mother had been drunk so often she ended up in the Poor House, leaving her children to their own devices, or perhaps in the hands of "a servant of doubtful character."[72]

A recalcitrant and often intoxicated mother presented a real problem to the commissioners. In theory the mother had rights to custody of the children that only the father could trump, and by custom the Orphan House sought the assent of all parties to a change in the child's custody. But it might ignore the wishes of an alcoholic mother. The following episode illustrates a family in an extreme state of disarray, but one that may not have been untypical of the poor and desperate. On August 19, 1852, Rosanna Higgins, aged eleven, appeared before the commissioners. Her married sister, Mary Ann Hairgroves (previously mentioned), wrote to ask the board to take in Rosanna because their mother, Hannah, was "intemperate herself" and recently had remarried to "an intemperate and otherwise bad man" who was appropriately named Lawless. According to Mary Ann, their mother's drinking led to her being "oftener than once carried to the Poor House," nor would she allow the younger children to attend school. Although children nearly always communicated with the board through the steward or visiting commissioners, the Higgins family situation was so pressing that Rosanna herself came to the weekly board meeting that evening and requested her own admission for the reasons given by her sister. The commissioners moved quickly to receive Rosanna contingent upon the usual approval of her mother or, if she would not consent, the commissioners of the Poor House. Two days later the steward, Archibald Campbell, tracked down Rosanna's mother, who refused her consent and indignantly told Campbell that she "'never was Drunk' etc!" and that she was perfectly able to "maintain her children respectfully herself."[73]

At this point, the community of poor people to which the Higgins children belonged entered the picture. Rosanna's older brother visited her in the Orphan House to report that their mother and stepfather now lived somewhere on Market Street, but Rosanna failed to remember the exact address her brother had told her. Rosanna's godmother, a Mrs. Connolly, appeared at the Orphan House on August 25 to announce that "she was going to get a place for her in a respectable family." A few days later the visiting commissioner, having found the mother and stepfather's home on Market Street, interviewed their landlady about recent events. The landlady reported that on the night of August 25, Mrs. Lawless had suffered a "fit" that led all to believe she was in danger of death, and so someone had sent for the local priest. Father O'Neill came near midnight. After he gave the woman last rites, the landlady, tired of all the drama her tenants brought with them, announced that she "would not have her die there & sent her to Poor House." Lawless himself, described as a very hard drinker before his marriage, showed up and "cursed all of them." Ultimately it was officials of the Poor House and not her mother who signed Rosanna's indenture on September 2. Her mother's interactions with the Orphan House did not end here, however. In May 1854 both Mr. and Mrs. Lawless were tossed into the Poor House to sober up, him for the seventh time and her for the fifth. Because the Poor House was no place for her younger children, Daniel (aged eight) and Elizabeth (aged five), Poor House commissioners tried to send them to the Orphan House, and they partially succeeded. The Orphan House accepted Daniel, but young Eliza went to the Sisters of Mercy, who operated a boarding school on Queen Street. Over the next two years Hannah Lawless's life seems to have changed, possibly for the better. In 1856 she took Eliza from the Sisters and brought her to the Orphan House, signing the indenture as "Hannah Higgins." Perhaps by then she had been widowed a second time. Further, her direct involvement at the later date, without the aid of the Poor House, suggests that she had attained a degree of sobriety.[74]

EASILY THE GREATEST NUMBER OF MOTHERS with eligible children were widows. Their letters indicate that they lost their husbands in a variety of ways. Some, perhaps thinking in terms of a social contract and hoping to invoke reciprocity, carefully noted that their husbands were military veterans. Sarah Ann Grooms reported in 1804 that her late husband had suffered battle wounds while serving in the Continental Army.[75] A more direct connection appeared in letters for children of active-duty soldiers, such as the one written for Bridget McCluskey, whose "late husband was a member of the Irish Volunteers in the Seminole campaign in Florida," where he succumbed to a local fever.[76] Women hoped that military service by other family members would signal worthiness as well. Marie Allison had married a Philadelphian and worked as a midwife's assistant after his death. She could neither take her two young sons to work, nor could she afford to board them out. She noted that she needed help only with her younger children, as her eldest, like his grandfather, was currently serving in the Army.[77]

Service in the City Guard was of particular value to white Charleston. An early police force, the chief duty of the Guard was to keep slaves (and to a lesser extent, visiting sailors) in line. It formed the first line of defense against prospective slave rebellions, an ongoing concern of whites all too aware of their status in the numerical minority.[78] City Guard membership was a sure sign of a life spent contributing to stability of the social order. In addition, as Catherine Lowry noted in her letter, the Guard did not pay especially well, leaving her unable to support her five children on her husband's income as a guardsman.[79] When Elizabeth Stenton's husband, a city guardsman, drowned in pursuit of a runaway slave, Mayor Robert Y. Hayne ordered all three of their sons admitted to the Orphan House immediately.[80]

The most common situation among mothers was that they had been widowed and could no longer financially support the child or children whom they nominated for admission. Here is an entire, brief, and typical letter from one such woman, who probably wrote it herself in 1814:

Gentlemen

My husband (the late Lochlin Wright plasterer) died the latter end of September last leaving myself with four helpless children (three boys and a girl, the eldest in his tenth year and the youngest in arms) in the most indigent circumstances; such indeed were my distresses that had it not have been for some charitable aid, my children would have been without covering or nourishment. I was married to the late Mr Wright in 1801 and have been a resident of this city ever since. I humbly solicit your honorable board to take my situation into consideration and to receive two of my sons in the Orphan House viz Norman in his seventh year and Daniel in his fifth year.

Yr obt servt
S. L. Wright

The letter lays out the facts of the matter: A building tradesman had died, leaving his wife and four children destitute. While acknowledging the receipt of charity, the widow establishes her fundamental stability by noting her husband's trade and the length of their marriage, and by her willingness to raise two of the four children. She proposes to place the two middle boys in the Orphan House and to raise the ten-year-old and the infant herself. The message was accompanied by another letter signed by four men attesting to Mrs. Wright's probity. Two of the men, John and Henry Horlbeck, were building contractors who had probably employed the deceased man, and through their repair work on the Orphan House were well known to the commissioners. The commissioners immediately accepted the two boys.[81]

Only rarely could widows escape from poverty. Poor families lived under the constant threat of the wage-earning husband's death, a state dubbed by Jane Humphries "breadwinner frailty."[82] Death of a breadwinning husband caused his family to suffer beyond mourning. Poverty was common enough among widow-headed families that many women simply informed the Orphan House that they were too poor to raise a child, expecting their situations to be self-evident to visiting commissioners. In other cases mothers described their deprivation in some detail. Some widows struggled for years before surrendering their children to the Orphan House. Susan Adams lost her husband at sea, and tried raising their two young boys for two years before engaging a literate acquaintance to write a note to the Orphan House. She was unable to pay her rent, and caring for her sons kept her from working out in domestic service. In the end, she concluded, "Nothing but necessity could induce me to part with them, but for their support I have sold all that I had."[83] Eliza Connoly had left Charleston years previously with her husband to find work at a port in North Carolina, but his last voyage ended in New Orleans where he died of a "prevailing fever" six or so months before her writing. On her return to Charleston she found herself without friends or family who could help and so, she said, "I know not where to go, nor to whom to apply for relief." But she knew of the Orphan House, and assuring commissioners of her industriousness when in good health, she felt able to report that even now she "maintained a reputable standing in the community." Commissioners admitted all three Connoly children.[84]

Particular occupations served as sure indications of straitened circumstances. One such was washing. In 1856 a Mrs. Dooley reported that her income came from taking in washing, plus some rent paid by an older daughter who earned eight dollars a month as a domestic servant.[85] Washing was grueling work, and competition with slave washerwomen ensured that it would pay poorly. A hotel washerwoman in Charleston might earn six dollars per month at a time when a common laborer there made over a dollar a day.[86] In addition the transient poor found it difficult to build up a reputation as a reliable washer. Eddy Richardson, just arrived from Horry District, described her efforts to "take in Washing & sewing when I am able to get employ of which I have had little as yet." Luckily, a sympathetic neighbor enabled her to obtain bread for herself and her "poor boy."[87] Another low-paid job was domestic service. Perhaps surprisingly in a slave-based economy, it was common for poor white women to work in household service. They "scoured" and cooked in kitchens, mended the clothing and minded the children of the well-to-do. The frequency of mothers who reported working as domestics increased after the Denmark Vesey-related events of 1822, which may have reflected an increased demand for white domestic servants.[88]

But the occupation most widely associated with women's poverty was that of seamstress. Isabella Doyle described the scant returns to needlework: "I should not be able to support [five children] by sewing if even I could get a constant supply of work." As a result, she echoed Susan Adams in reporting, "We have indeed lived chiefly on the comforts of former days,

selling one article after another till little remains to be disposed of." The Orphan House agreed to take two of her boys, aged ten and eight. Mrs. Doyle
was then able to earn a bit as a wet nurse, but only after sending her own
infant out to a wet nurse who was cheaper still.[89] Similarly Martha Ann
Monroe described herself as depending solely on her needle for support, and
thus unable to provide any education for her son, William Calvert.[90] Dependence on the needle might be combined with outdoor relief, or bread distributed from the Poor House, to yield a somewhat less-desperate living, but
even then, observed a visiting commissioner of one unfortunate woman,
"her needle will not support her & her children & pay the rent, even with
the assistance of the rations."[91] The general understanding was summarized
by Barbara Quinnan's description of a woman whose son she had raised for
seven of his eight years on earth: "Her only dependence for self an another
child being the needle, which you all gentlemen must be convinced is not
sufficient ever to pay for room rent & the most common food."[92] In sum,
Sarah Connelly spoke for many poor women when she wrote in 1829 that
"needle work . . . yields but a poor subsistence for myself and children."[93]

A second category of mothers included those still married to the child's
father. Husbands in these cases were unable or unwilling to support the
family financially for a variety of causes. Sickness and alcohol were two
primary sources of such inability. In some cases of ill health a specific cause
can be identified. Elenor Bossell felt "obliged to beg relief from your truly
charitable institution" because her husband was suffering from "a tedious
lingering sickness." In the application their family physician described the
condition as "Painter's cholic"; that is, lead poisoning, a common occupa-
tional hazard in a day when lead was still an important component of paint.[94]
Unspecified chronic conditions plagued other men such as Ann Grainger's
husband, whom she and her neighbors described simply as a "cripple."[95]
Even more specific diagnoses did not always inspire commissioners to
move quickly. Thomas Hays suffered from a chronic "disease of the bow-
els & spine." In April 1856, a physician, probably the locally prominent
Dr. James Moultrie, described him as "permanently disabled" and recommended admission of his son, and there things stood for about two weeks.
Another visiting commissioner speculated in early May that Thomas could
"scarcely recover from his sickness" and again recommended admission
of the boy, William, who then entered the Orphan House on May 8, 1856.
Only two weeks later, Thomas died, aged 39. Now widowed, Mary Ann
Hays spent the summer of 1856 trying to keep her brood together. In October, she conceded and applied to send three of her four remaining children

to the Orphan House: two girls aged seven and five and a boy aged two. She kept her infant with her, and disappeared from the record thereafter.[96]

A peculiar type of family consisted of those women who were married in name only because their husbands had abandoned them. In some cases the departure was less shameful than it might sound: the man had left to go west and establish himself financially before sending for his family, or he might have gone to sea for an unexpectedly long time. The absence of a husband in these cases was more a mystery than a source of bitterness. Susannah Marriner was an Englishwoman who had lived in Charleston for some years. After her husband, William, failed to return home for an unknown reason, his prolonged absence cost his family dearly. In March 1824 Susannah sought to enter three of her children, explaining that she was

> utterly destitute of the necessaries of life for the support of herself & children and that she at present subsists on the bounty of her neighbours, that in January last the whole of her household furniture and most of their clothing was seized for rent by order of Mrs Prescott and taken to a magistrates' sale. Mr Joseph Young paid the debt, $89.26, and has given your petitioner the use of the same until she can repay him.

Later that year her infant daughter, Margaret, died, and her eight-year-old daughter, Susannah, followed her brothers into the Orphan House. In 1831 after Susannah and William, the eldest boy, had been bound out, the Orphan House attempted to contact the father in Chatham, England, about his remaining children. In 1833 the long-lost William Marriner, senior, appeared from New York to claim twelve-year-old Frederick and fourteen-year-old James. Commissioners, satisfied that he was indeed their father, simply granted his request.[97]

Sometimes the many solitary months endured by the wife of a sailor indicated a long voyage, and sometimes it indicated that her husband was lost at sea. Sophia Campbell anxiously begged the Orphan House to take her two sons because her husband had been at sea for six months and the family was destitute without his continued support.[98]

Cases where a wife and mother was intentionally abandoned by her husband for more nefarious reasons were numerous. Mary Hoare's husband, Thomas, had worked several years for the merchant William Clarkson. After being discharged by Clarkson he vanished from the city. After a good year of reliance on charitable donations to support her and two children, Mary approached Clarkson for help getting the children into the Orphan

House. Clarkson had recommended she do so some time ago, he told the commissioners, "but her maternal feelings could not bear the idea of parting with her children."[99] Usually the husband's departure was the end of contact between spouses, but in at least one case the disappearing husband tried to keep the wife from visiting her own children in the Orphan House.[100] It seems far more common for the husband to have fled far from Charleston: out of South Carolina or to Europe, for example. Finding a distant husband—such as that of Ann Wittencamp, who wrote, "[he] is gone I know not whither"—was not a priority for the Orphan House, but determining that he had, in fact, left the wife and children on their own was usually sufficient for the Orphan House to take the children in.[101]

A final group of married mothers consisted of widowed women who had remarried. These women tended to be either very fortunate or very unfortunate; those in the middle had no need for the Orphan House. The unfortunate women had remarried men who refused to take responsibility for their new stepchildren. Mary Anne McDermott sought admission for her two sons by her late husband because "the present step father Ed. McDermott will not allow them near the House or premises for sustenance."[102] Where exactly these children obtained their sustenance is not clear. A stepfather might explain his neglect. Ann Carter Wilson described her new husband's attitude toward her son and daughter: "Wilson . . . says he has not the means to support the children of Carter." In fact, the often absent Wilson provided little support for anyone in his desperately poor family. During her last pregnancy, Mrs. Wilson had worked with her needle and even went "out to scour houses when her health permit[ted] it." Despite her industry, the children were "obliged to go to the neighbors for bread."[103] Rarely, the remarried mother abandoned the child. In one case, the Poor House applied for admission for John Connolly, whose mother "deserted him" upon her remarriage.[104] These were the unfortunate women; the fortunate ones remarried men who supported their petitions to the Orphan House to have custody of their children restored to them.[105] The second husband was a powerful force for prosperity or destitution in poor widows' lives, as chapter 7 illustrates.

BECAUSE MOST HALF ORPHANS WERE IN THE CUSTODY of their mothers, and perhaps because surviving parents recognized that commissioners expected embellished tales of woe from women but not from men, the documentary record of the fathers' experience is not as rich as that for women. To be sure, fathers did care for some half orphans after their mothers had died, and uncles in particular took in orphaned nieces and nephews. But we know little more than that. In one example, Juliana Elliott sponsored Mary Clayton for entrance in 1811. She explained that after Mary was orphaned she moved in with an uncle, but the uncle had recently died. Now the uncle's large family was temporarily living with yet a different family member, who may or may not have been kin to Mary. In this situation, Mary was the odd one out and needed the shelter of the Orphan House.[106]

Most fathers were drawn from the lower ranks of laborers and artisans. They toiled as building tradesmen, shoemakers, and the occasional artisan. Usually these men could support their families, but they enjoyed little room for error. When epidemics, particularly of yellow fever, struck down mothers of young children, surviving fathers brought their children to the Orphan House.[107] Ill health could rob a father of the ability to support his family. When Sarah Anderson's father lost his sight, for example, her mother turned to the Orphan House to take in Sarah.[108] Nor could a disabled or imprisoned father support his family.[109]

As in all Atlantic port cities, families of men who worked on the sea barely scraped by.[110] In Charleston, they constituted a large share of those seeking the Orphan House's aid. A sailor on a longer-than-expected cruise might return to find that his wife remedied the family's financial distress by leaving a child or two at the Orphan House.[111] A widowed seaman named John Hanson had hoped to continue boarding his children with the neighbor lady who had taken them in upon his wife's death in 1825. "But," he explained, "the wages of a sailor are not adequate to do this." Indeed, this neighbor testified, Hanson had left for the sea without ever paying her, so it was she who applied to send the children to the Orphan House.[112]

The need for widowers to continue working prevented them from caring for their little ones during the day. Some took advantage of boardinghouses especially for children, but these were expensive. In an 1803 case, neighbors declared that a widowed father of four "has used every means to board these children out, but with all his exertions cannot pay for the same."[113] Bereaved fathers who drowned their sorrows in alcohol left their children to depend on the kindness of strangers. The Reverend John Bachman, a Lutheran pastor, reported that in the days after the death of Mrs. Cammer in May 1854, their father was "too far gone to hold up his head." Bachman despaired that the man would not sober up long enough to testify to the family's destitution before a city alderman, as the rules for admission then required.[114]

PERSPECTIVES ON HISTORICAL PARENT-CHILD RELATIONSHIPS have changed over the years, from emphasis on rather cold and violent Puritanical desires to break the child's will to the romanticized "sacralization" of child life.[115]

Parents who wrote letters considered here and those who were the subject of letters written by others were people of their own time. These letters reflect rhetorical conventions regarding parenthood that were abroad in their days. They also must reflect, to some degree, a deeper commitment to caring for their children, a strong desire to be reunited with them, and the empty pain of separation from them. This commitment, desire, and pain in turn reveal the love of the parent for the child at least as much as adherence to rhetorical convention. When we evaluate the letter by Ann Ferneau asking the commissioners not to bind out her son until she returned to Charleston, why should we not believe her when she writes, "my son is the only thing I have to make life desirable"?[116] Many letters describe the pain of separation.[117] As a final request, the dying Mary Hutchinson asked the Orphan House to return her four-year-old daughter because she was "extremely anxious to see the child in her hands before it pleases God to call her away."[118] Even fathers occasionally described their yearning to be near their children. A letter from the father of Joseph and Andrew Carson explained first that Andrew, who had run away from the Orphan House, was now living with him, and so the father was no longer "very sorry for us to be a part." And second, he liked having his one son nearby so much that he wanted the commissioners "to be so good as to give me back my little son Joseph." After all, concluded this father to the commissioners, "now gentlemen you no that they aint one of you that would like to part with your child."[119] James Carson was just making a commonsensical claim. Even among the poor, who would have felt most acutely the cost of an extra mouth to feed, no parents wanted to be apart from their children.

CHAPTER FIVE

Education

THE ORPHAN HOUSE DID FAR MORE THAN HOLD ITS CHARGES until they were old enough to be bound out. It offered them, their families, and by extension poor whites in Charleston generally, if the worst came to pass, the hope that impoverished children might receive enough education and training in a skill to make their adult life easier than that of their parents. Indeed, the first sentence of the 1790 city ordinance that established the Orphan House stated that the city's goal was to improve on the current methods of "supporting *and educating* poor children at different schools."[1] Chapter 8 will consider the assignment of children to particular trades as well as their experiences during their apprenticeships. The present chapter examines the expectations of parents and guardians for their children's education, as well as the learning experiences of the children themselves. Those experiences include what the children learned and when, and how the commissioners examined children to answer those questions. It concludes with a discussion of two documents written by Orphan House insiders on the evolution of the institution's school and the dampening of its expectations for educated children.

Children who came to the Orphan House began their lives in families that had little experience of formal education. One way to see this is the ability of the parent or guardian to sign his or her name on the indenture form. The ability to write one's name instead of marking a document with an X or some other symbol is one measure of basic literacy. To be sure, signature literacy is one particular kind of literacy, and in individual cases a signature may well indicate the ability to write one's name and no more. Alternatively, since reading instruction generally preceded writing instruction, the ability to sign may imply a basic ability to read. Thus has signature literacy come to imply a middling level of reading and writing ability, one

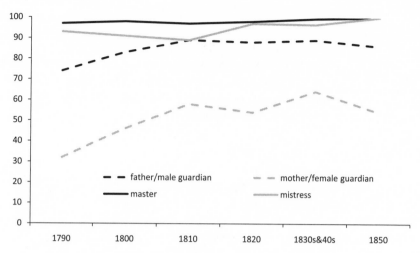

Fig. 5.1. Adult literacy rates in Charleston by sex and class. Vertical axis: percentage signing indenture.

that has been used by historians to make literacy comparisons across time and place. In addition, signature literacy measures the outcome of formal (school) or informal (home or church) education rather than the inputs into such a process, such as time spent in school. To understand the effect of education on a person, the outcome of an educational process is of greater interest. However, the temptation is to study the quantity of inputs into an educational process, which are typically easier to measure—if of dubious efficacy.[2]

Estimates of adult signature literacy rates in Charleston from 1790 to 1850 appear in figure 5.1. They are derived from the proportion of parents or guardians and masters or mistresses who endorsed indentures with their signatures.[3] Except for masters, who were nearly all literate, the curves show gradually increasing trends over time, suggesting that the overall level of literacy among white Charlestonians was rising during this period. In fact, the figures provided here roughly replicate data from the 1850 census, the first census to produce reliable literacy estimates, which suggests that the Orphan House records are a trustworthy source of literacy data.[4] Within each class, men's literacy rates exceeded those of women. For both sexes, those who took children into their homes were noticeably more literate, as a group, than the parents or guardians who entered them into the Orphan House. In absolute terms, only about half of women, who were far more likely than men to bring children to the Orphan House, were able to sign their names. The significance of this high rate of illiteracy was that those mothers and female guardians who could not sign their names were unlikely to teach their children basic literacy skills.

Despite their inability to read or write, or perhaps because of it, these parents and guardians wanted their children to be taught basic literacy skills. Parents and guardians emphasized in their application letters not only poverty but their desire to instill some education in their children. Many parents, especially mothers, reported in straightforward fashion that their inability to educate their children motivated them to come to the Orphan House. Sarah Estill explained that it was "impossible for [her] hands to support them or give them schooling." In the same spirit, Isabella Murphy felt it was "out of [her] powers to give them education or even maintain them."[5] The signatories might have believed that particular rhetorical formulas would appeal to the commissioners' sense of mission, and so it is possible that these phrases do not directly reflect parental desires. However, in many cases poor parents had in fact enabled their children to sign their names, or they reported that they had sent the children for a time to a free school. Thus, their actions, which the commissioners could verify by talking to the child or a schoolmaster, revealed their desire to gain the child some education. The most reasonable way to interpret, I think, assertions that parents wanted children to be educated, is to take them at face value. Unable to send their young ones to school for long, if at all, parents and guardians hoped that the Orphan House could provide that schooling.

Parental commentary sheds some light on the purpose of education as perceived by the poor. Schooling, as parents reported, benefited both child and community. Mary McGee found someone to write on her behalf that she was "totally unable to procure for [her son] that advantage of education which is to render him at a future period of benefit to himself and community."[6] Part of that benefit consisted of the inculcation of basic moral teachings, so that the child might learn how to play his role in the greater community. As Eliza Nelson assured commissioners, "I believe education which includes good discipline lays the foundation for good morals."[7] Education gave the child not just the ability to read, write, and cipher, but to live in the community.[8] As noted below, education for community life included instruction in proper race relations.

Many children came to the Orphan House with a year or so of school under their belt already. They may have attended an infant school, modeled on those in New England. These schools opened in the 1820s to teach basic arithmetic, spelling, and a little writing to children aged four to eight years.[9] Others, especially before the state school law of 1811, attended privately funded charity schools, which operated informally in manses, rectories, or other homes of educated tutors. Their quality was uneven. One boy who entered the Orphan House in 1818 had studied under the Rev. Israel Munds, who operated a private academy in his home. This seven-year-old boy, though, could not sign his indenture.[10] The South Carolina Society, founded in the eighteenth century as a benevolent association for Huguenots, operated one charity school. Because education was a popular charity among the descendants of Charleston's Huguenots, by the early nineteenth century the Society paid for orphans to attend various schools.[11] In the North, late eighteenth-century Sunday schools devoted much of their time to teaching basic reading and writing skills, but until rather late in this period, beginning in the 1840s, few children reported any previous attendance at Sunday schools in Charleston.[12]

For the poor, the chief alternative to the Orphan House school was a free school. After 1811 the state of South Carolina opened free schools for all white children. When the state, with good intentions, required that "a preference shall always be given to poor orphans and the children of indigent and necessitous parents," it indelibly associated the free schools with the poor. In turn only the poor who could afford no better sent their children to free schools.[13] A Charleston mother of two lamented that her utter destitution left her "not even able to clothe them decently to send them to a free school," implying that the typical free school pupil wore threadbare clothing indeed.[14] As this statement implied, the very poorest families (who could not clothe their children decently) might not turn to the free schools, but for the near-destitute one small step above, the free schools might be the only possible way to educate their children. A group of citizens who petitioned the Orphan House to admit two boys explained, "If the father was able to clothe and feed them he would get them at a free school but as he is not," the alternative for the boys was to "remain ignorant and unimproved."[15] The implication here is, again, that the very poorest could not afford to send their children to any kind of school, but poor whites who could at least dress their children in something better than rags sent them to a free school. That left the Orphan House to take in the very poorest of poor whites.

One result of greater availability of free schools thanks to the 1811 law was a decline in the educational level of entering Orphan House children. Comparing children's literacy rates at the Orphan House before and after 1811 reveals a sharp decrease following passage and implementation of the free school law.[16] Parents whose sole option was the free school did not enroll children there with enthusiasm, but these families did enjoy one great advantage over the poorest whites in Charleston: free school students could live at home, and, as noted in the previous chapter, poor parents valued the proximity of their children. Orphan House students, on the other hand, were required to live in the institution. And so after 1811, the near-poor kept their children in their homes at night and sent them to free schools in the day, but children of the very poorest families, who were the least prepared for formal education, were ever more likely to enter the Orphan House.

Why free schools might have appealed only to families with low educational expectations is not hard to see. Charleston's free schools were intended to be charitable, not universal, and to fulfill their mission they cut corners wherever possible, financially and pedagogically. The most famous and enduring half-measure of the day was Joseph Lancaster's, which reached America early in the nineteenth century. In the Lancastrian system, teachers worked relatively little while older students "monitored"—taught, really—younger children. Using older students as teachers, according to Lancaster, would solve the problem of teaching large numbers of poor children. Several of Charleston's free schools enthusiastically adopted the Lancastrian method. School commissioners proudly reported huge enrollment increases without additional expenditure.[17] From 1811 to 1846 state funding remained constant while free school enrollment doubled, which caused the student-teacher ratio to balloon from about 50 to 1 to over 100 to 1.[18] In Lancastrian theory such figures were manageable, but results in the classroom were grim.[19] An 1855 observer described the average Charleston free school as "a dirty hut" in which children were "tormented for six hours with books and birch" and were "injured physically, intellectually, and morally and learned only to hate school and books." According to this observer, prospective teachers qualified for the lowest level of free-school duty after a mere two years of their own attendance at a free school. No wonder many poor families who were motivated enough to enroll their children in the first place soon removed them and sent them to work instead, by one report as early as age eight.[20]

Thus, even if poor parents wanted to enroll a child in a free school, and they could afford the clothing costs, they remained unimpressed. In the nearby free school Agnes Kelly's children "scarce [had] advanced beyond the alphabet," and she hoped for better at the Orphan House.[21] Another mother complained that her son had "made no progress at all in learning" in a free school.[22] Advice circulated among Charleston's poor that reflected their opinion of Charleston's free schools. A boy named Louis Gesell came to the Orphan House in 1856 after getting "in bad humour" one too many times with his stepfather. In addition, his mother and the stepfather were disappointed in his progress at a free school and thought he could do better. The mother, Catherine Donecker, disclosed to the visiting commissioner that another reason for her application for Louis was that "she has been told that children is better attended to in the orphan house" school than at free schools.[23] Many parents desperate to educate their children felt the same way.

FROM THE START, SCHOOLING WAS an important part of Orphan House operations. Before the new building opened in 1794, Orphan House rules called for boys to attend school six days per week, for three hours each morning (four in summer) and three hours each afternoon except Saturdays. Girls' education received far less emphasis. Those who were "of ability" were tutored in writing and arithmetic for three hours each day. When boys turned eight years of age they were sent to an academy run by Philip Anthony Besselleu in his home.[24] The commissioners' expectations of Besselleu were simple: to conduct the school six days per week year round, with exactly two recognized holidays, the Fourth of July and October eighteenth (the Orphan House's own anniversary), and any ad hoc holidays the commissioners might determine. Exactly what was to happen during the six or seven hours school was in session was left to Besselleu to decide. Commissioners came to his house to examine the boys as to their readiness to be bound out to learn a trade.[25] The examinations also protected the good name of the Orphan House. Commissioners wanted apprenticed inmates to reflect well on the Orphan House. Boys who entered apprenticeships that were either technically demanding (for example, ship navigation) or with prominent local craftsmen had better be prepared to do well, and commissioners were not shy about failing students who might disappoint their masters and make the institution look bad.[26]

Before construction of the Orphan House on Boundary Street, boys lived in the teacher's residence, and so prospective masters contacted Besselleu directly about employing them as apprentices. If the boys passed their oral examination with the commissioners, they were bound out, and if not they continued under Besselleu's tutelage. In one exceptional case in May 1793, Benjamin F. Timothy, printer to the state and publisher of the *South Carolina State Gazette*, wrote to Besselleu requesting that Thomas Abercrombie, aged twelve, be bound to him as an apprentice printer. The examining commissioners "found he was not yet forward enough in his education to be bound out" and so refused. That much was fairly common, but the next step was far out of the ordinary: Abercrombie left Besselleu's house anyway and began working for Timothy. The commissioners first demanded his return, then waffled a few months later and agreed to examine him. When Abercrombie passed this later viva voce the commissioners officially bound him to Timothy, and so pleased all parties.[27]

Besselleu became ill late in the summer of 1794. With the help of a new assistant, he continued under contract to teach fifty boys ("more or less") from the Orphan House.[28] He died a few months later in 1795, but the records say little about his death other than its occurrence. His gravestone in the Huguenot Church cemetery says that he "was Tutor of the Orphants [sic] for many Years." No memorial to his work or memory appeared within the Orphan House, because his death occurred in the midst of one of the frequent financial crises. Commissioners lacked funds to pay their hired slaves and other employees, including Besselleu, who at his death was owed several dozen pounds. A new teacher was elected and soon the school moved into the new Orphan House compound.[29]

Besselleu's successor was a Lutheran clergyman named Frederick Daser, who began by reviewing the state of the school. Daser drew up a list of recommended texts, among them widely used books such as *Introduction to the English Reader* by Lindley Murray, Jedidiah Morse's *Geography Made Easy*, and J. F. Martinet's *Catechism of Nature*. Murray's grammars, which he had compiled from snippets of earlier grammars, were extremely popular around this time, running into some two hundred editions over the course of the nineteenth century. His *Introduction* consisted of poems and brief one- to three-page essays on moral improvement, with titles such as "Praise due to God for his wonderful works" and "The Brother and Sister; or mental excellence superior to personal beauty." American desires for an American-specific text led to the later popularity of McGuffey's readers, which came to succeed Murray's in the United States.[30] Morse, perhaps better known today as Samuel F. B. Morse's father, wrote *Geography Made Easy* just after graduating from Yale, and it became a surprise hit. He then expanded it into the even better-selling *American Geography*. Although Morse's work was criticized by Southern educators for its New England bias, Daser assured the commissioners that among geography texts Morse's was "the most commonly used in schools." In later editions the Orphan House itself appeared at the top of Morse's list of notable South Carolina charities.[31] Martinet urged young readers to recognize God in the splendor of his creation.[32] "[T]o further the education of . . . the cipherers" Daser suggested *The Schoolmaster's Assistant*, by Thomas Dilworth.[33] Dilworth marched

his readers through an impressive sequence of problems, beginning with basic arithmetic and building up to examples in the present value of assets.[34]

With the schoolmaster setting the curriculum but the commissioners
examining the children, conflict was perhaps inevitable. Frederick Daser
was a well-educated man by any standard. He held an advanced degree, had
served as a Lutheran pastor, favored the Loyalist side in the recent war, and,
as assisted by Philip Besselleu's son Mark-Anthony, was probably not one
to be instructed in his work's finer details.[35] Neither were the commissioners to be informed how to operate their Orphan House. Daser's submission
in March 1795 of no fewer than twenty-one recommendations to improve
all aspects of Orphan House operations and not just the school must have
seemed presumptuous and ill-timed to the commissioners. Many of Daser's
ideas concerned operations other than the school (e.g., "That wells & Bake
Ovens be built for the use of the House"), and he raised his points just when
commissioners were pleading with City Council for help to make their pay-
roll. In return perhaps, when three commissioners examined children at the
end of that summer, they found shortcomings in the students' preparation
and ordered Daser "to pay particular attention to" teaching proper punctua-
tion. To ensure that he got the point commissioners chose a new textbook
for him, Daniel Fenning's *Universal Spelling Book.* By autumn the children
were improving in commissioners' eyes, and the next year they found another schoolmaster for the Orphan House.[36]

By this time the free schools and the Orphan House school had come
to resemble each other in many ways. Each school allowed student-teacher
ratios to soar, as exemplified by the 107:1 ratio in the free schools of 1834.
In the 1820s when the free schools had 64 students for each teacher, there
were 120 or so Orphan House boys to challenge the schoolmaster, and about
60 girls for the school mistress. Likewise in the 1850s when the free school
ratio was around 60:1, the Orphan House was positively bursting at the
seams, with over 140 boys and about 75 girls per one teacher, respectively.
At some point even the Orphan House could see that there were too many
boys for an orderly class, and the Female School, which always had fewer
students, eventually took in several boys. Discipline operated much the
same way in the two schools, with little stinting on corporal punishment.
In September 1803 the angry father of thirteen-year-old Henry Barry lashed
out at Orphan House commissioners for allowing Henry to be beaten and
flogged by a young assistant teacher.[37] At one free school, a teacher who
administered punishments with "too great severity" was dismissed, leaving open the question of how harsh a beating had to be to qualify as too
severe.[38]

Classroom activities were similar in the two schools. After 1811 the length of the school day was the same in each.[39] While the free schools used the Lancastrian method, in 1818 the Orphan House introduced a competing scheme of Andrew Bell. Bell's technique was similar to Lancaster's but included specifically Anglican religious instruction in the curriculum. Bell's system was limited in its aims, which appealed to parsimonious commissioners. In Bell's own words, "It is not proposed that the children of the poor be educated in an expensive manner, or even taught to write or cypher."[40] He boasted that later improvements allowed his students to learn to write "in less than no time."[41] His intention to educate the poor with the strictest economy pleased commissioners and teachers alike. The Orphan House schoolmaster, John Kingman, thanked the board for sending him to learn Bell's system, "whereby my labors are much abridged."[42] But as those labors were abridged, so was the schoolmaster's authority. A problem of leaving the education of younger children in the hands of the older ones emerged in James Barry's bitter observation that it was the "boy schoolmaster" who had beaten his son.[43]

Whereas free schools appealed to the almost-but-not-quite-destitute because they could keep their children at home and send them, at least occasionally, to school, the all-inclusive nature of the Orphan House school offered a substantial pedagogical advantage: Orphan House residents had to go to school daily. As a residential institution, the Orphan House could and did require children to remain on the grounds, and it enforced school attendance even through the summer. Free schools could not enforce any attendance requirement, and board members usually reported derisively on the small proportion of registered pupils who actually came to school.[44] Given the importance of attendance in learning, mandatory Orphan House school attendance explains why its pupils learned so much. This is the most obvious difference between the Orphan House and the combination of free schools and home teaching available to children before coming to the Orphan House, since methods, books, student backgrounds, and length of the school day appear to have been similar.

To be sure, not everyone held the Orphan House school in high regard. Rarely, parents or masters of apprentices complained about the quality of the education the children received. George McDill of Chester District had taken in Eleanor Brown in spring 1810, and he kept in touch with David Moffitt, the master of Eleanor's twin sister Jane. Commissioners expressed alarm at a letter from Jane, apparently written by someone else, in which she proved unable to sign her name. McDill explained with some unhappiness that "The reason is they cannot do it [write] nor neaver could and wors than that could read very little when they left the Orphan-house." And indeed, neither Eleanor nor Jane could sign her indenture after eight years in the Orphan House.[45] But such complaints were few indeed.

AS THE NINETEENTH CENTURY PROGRESSED, the Orphan House school developed a much more sophisticated curriculum than it initially offered. Among these developments were age-specific standards and courses in different subjects. Commissioners also became aware of shortcomings in classroom equipment. Frederick Daser's request for candles suggested that classrooms had insufficient natural light. The need of a clock "so that regular hours may be attended to" indicated an informal attitude to the beginning and ending of the school day. Daser's request for textbooks may suggest that he was introducing something new into classrooms where children had been transcribing words and problems on their slates as teachers announced them. Closer oversight of language skills may indicate the beginning of a shift in their goals of education, away from preparation for apprenticeship and toward a more general type of learning.[46]

To see how these innovations were working out, commissioners began examining students in particular subjects before it was time for their binding out, rather than waiting for a master to request a particular child and then testing him or her, one-on-one. Regular examinations of boys and girls alike began not long after the move to the new Orphan House building on Boundary Street. The results were generally, but not always, satisfactory. Within a few years commissioners were comparing the results of their examinations to those in nearby schools, and not just free schools. They were pleased to announce "that the progress of the boys in general in writing, reading, and arithmetic was equal to any seminary in the city."[47] Relative to other schools in Charleston, the Orphan House educated its students to a level that made the commissioners proud.

Testing also revealed the relative educational achievements of the two sexes. Monthly examinations in late 1795 indicated steady improvement on the girls' part but uneven progress among the boys.[48] Later examinations led to praise for both boys and girls, complaints about the lack of progress of each, and sometimes commissioners praised one sex and complained about the other. When the commissioners felt that the girls were falling too far behind the boys, they specified to the schoolmaster that he had better pay more attention "in the future strictly to improving the girls in their branches of education."[49] But such orders meant improving girls relative to commissioners' expectations, not raising girls' capabilities up to the level of boys.

As broad as was overall development in methods and goals, education for girls evolved in lesser but parallel fashion compared to that for boys. Expectations for girls were simply lower. No one would have thought to send girls to college, for example. Girls' access to schooling did, however, expand along with improvements that boys experienced. Considering the thin educational offerings for Orphan House girls in the 1790s, relative improvements in the quality of girls' education must have been greater than that for boys. Early in the nineteenth century, the schoolmaster taught the boys from 8:00 a.m. to noon and then from 3:00 to 5:00 p.m., and the girls received his instruction in writing and arithmetic for an hour during the midday break.[50] When the schoolmistress proposed a few years later to lengthen the short school day for girls, the commissioners denied her appeal, declaring with emphasis that "the Rules relative to the School Hours [must] be adhered to."[51] To be sure, in the early Orphan House, masters who hoped to obtain a female apprentice from the Orphan House knew enough to specify that the girl should start "as soon as her education was finished." But education of girls simply was not the priority that boys' education was, not in the Orphan House, and nowhere else in America at the beginning of the nineteenth century.[52]

One reason for limited education of Orphan House girls was the institutional dependence on their labor. As early as 1801 the ladies had arranged for girls to produce "Sewing work of every kind," including "Tayloring [and] mantua making." The work would be "executed on moderate terms, with neatness and dispatch."[53] Later, separate rooms in the west (girls') wing were given over to training in spinning under the guidance of a spinning mistress. The yarn produced by girls then fed the looms in the weaving room, three floors up.[54] More critically for the Orphan House's day-to-day operations, girls worked alongside slaves who washed the clothes and linens. When epidemics struck, this chore proved especially time consuming, as sick children needed their bedding changed more frequently. While at times boys powered the primitive washing machines, it was always girls and hired slaves who labored steadily to keep uniforms and bedclothes clean. In 1843 the matron, who was charged with looking after the girls' well-being, complained that the girls' work assignments were interfering with their education. Since washing was so physically taxing, the largest girls were assigned to this task. These were just the girls whose last few months in the Orphan House represented their last chance to obtain some education. Washing might in fact have been very typical of the work that girls could look forward to in their apprenticeships, but eventually a matron did what she could to get the girls a few more months of school. The results were positive, but minimal.[55]

At the end of 1843 she reported that some of the older and bigger girls were still in the House because they had entered "in a state of great ignorance" and so needed extra time in the Orphan House school to catch up in their education. Unfortunately their washing chores interfered with schoolwork to such an extent that the matron found that these girls had learned even less than the schoolmistress had led her to believe. Thus, the matron recommended and the commissioners agreed, it would be better for these girls to be relieved of washing duties so they could study. The commissioners concurred, and ordered that a "washer"—undoubtedly a rented slave—be hired to replace them.[56]

Beyond the basics, the institution began preparing small numbers of students to study the liberal arts. This shift in educational goals began with an act of generosity. During the anniversary celebration of October 1807, ushers, as usual, took up a collection. In the basket appeared a donation of one hundred dollars attached to a note explaining that it was to be used for "the education of one of the Orphan Boys, selected for good Talents, and disposition for the Ministry of the Gospel, himself to chuse at a proper age the Church he is disposed to join." The anonymous woman who gave the sum promised to continue her gifts annually. To see the magnitude of this gift and promise, consider that the annual tuition charge around this time for the South Carolina College in Columbia was fifty-five dollars per student.[57]

Private and public funding for college led the Orphan House to embark on a new educational mission, at least for the boys chosen for further study. The anonymous donor continued her substantial gift over the next few years. Additionally, the state of South Carolina contributed a scholarship as part of the 1811 Free School Act, which specified that each year one Orphan House boy could attend the South Carolina College in Columbia free of charge. The resources spent on college preparation were all out of proportion to the small number of boys who would benefit. The president of the College of Charleston, George Buist, agreed personally to tutor the first two boys chosen in Greek and Latin. The Orphan House schoolmaster offered to teach them arithmetic in the evenings, along with some older apprentice-alumni whose indentures had called for evening school. The Orphan House itself paid for books, supplies, and clothes out of its private fund and the anonymous annual donation. Concern for these boys and management of their occasional peccadilloes took far more of the commissioners' time than did, for example, making arrangements for the boys who left Charleston to apprentice in the shipyards at the Gosport Naval Station in Virginia in the 1840s, although the numbers of boys in each category were about the

same. But the prospect of preparing boys for college, or at least for prepara-
tory study at the College of Charleston, and after 1839 the High School
of Charleston, led to curricula geared toward more academic pursuits and
away from strictly preparing children to learn trades.[58]

Another changing aspect of school life was the Orphan House school's
approach to discipline. Although never falling completely out of favor, corporal punishment declined in use over the antebellum era. In earlier times
Orphan House managers and staff occasionally sought permission of the
commissioners to whip children who had misbehaved, as in the case of
Thomas Holdup, who had been accused of theft by the schoolmaster in
1805. Thomas earned "correction" (i.e., from the whip), admonishment
(a public dressing-down), and even jail time—a week in the "penitentiary
room." As time went on commissioners became more likely to abstain from
corporal punishment if they thought a less-violent approach was justified.
More broadly, they aimed for the lightest sufficient punishment, as in the
case of Thomas Holdup's brother George, in which the schoolmaster released the boy from "confinement within the yard" two months early for
good behavior.[59] At times the Orphan House's public view on discipline
sounded positively progressive. An 1835 report acknowledged the power
of both pain and pleasure to form a young child's attitude toward learning.
"[W]e avoid the one, and seek the other," declared an Orphan House official.
Comparing learning by "birch and hard knocks" to one based on "kind and
tender instruction," the report claimed that the latter would be more likely
to lead the child to continue "his intellectual pursuits."[60] It seems likely,
then, that by the mid-1830s the Orphan House school was a less violent institution for study than the free schools of Charleston, which continued to
emphasize corporal punishment and produce learning at a very slow pace.

Attitudes toward liberal education in the Orphan House school as a
whole also began to change around this time. Whereas the 1835 report expressed doubt that making Orphan House students into "classical scholars"
would even be desirable, within a few years commissioners were giving
children pens and books as prizes at the annual anniversary fest.[61] In the
1840s commissioners examined boys' and girls' classes separately in each of
five subjects: dictionary and spelling, geography, grammar, arithmetic, and
history. They asked each child five questions and kept score of the number
answered correctly, by individual and by class grouping. These questions
may not have been particularly rigorous, and the execution of classroom
learning and grading of examinations was probably more lenient than strict.
A commissioner wrote one year that "the Examination was not conducted
with severity, & an impartial if not entirely indulgent feeling determined

the merit of each answer." In August 1840, each boy sat for three examinations, and the school committee recommended that prizes be given to
those scoring at least ten correct, as well as to fifteen-year-old James Will-
ingham, who had earned recognition for "his proficiency in arithmetic."
Another sign of the commissioners' growing indulgence in their charges
was the recommendation to award prizes even to underperforming children.
Commissioners acknowledged with regret their inability to test children
more precisely. As a result, "some injustice may be done to deserving boys,
since chance does in some degree interfere with the just assignment" of the
awards. The solution fell short of "all must have prizes," but commissioners drifted in that direction. Even after a relatively dismal performance, in
which one geography class answered ten of twenty-five questions correctly
and another scored three out of thirty, commissioners conceded that while
no classes had earned a prize, a few classes should be recognized in some
manner "as a mark of approbation for comparative diligence."[62] Expectations of commissioners had relaxed considerably since the 1790s, when
they rejected an application for a fifteen-year-old girl, probably to be a lowly
seamstress, because her education was not yet finished.[63]

Children who came to the Orphan House school varied tremendously
in levels of native intelligence, ambition, and preparation. As noted below,
large numbers of children, some as old as twelve, entered unable to sign their
names. Examination results suggested that a few children mastered enough
subjects to justify further study, but others learned very little indeed. Test
results from a century and a half ago are anything but self-explanatory, but
we can see that the examinations produced a considerable dispersion of
results. Classes were organized according to ability, which corresponded
loosely to age. Smaller "level" numbers indicated higher ability. In 1842
the girls' first-level geography class consisted of twelve- to fifteen-year-olds,
and the third-level geography class consisted of nine- to twelve-year-olds.
Table 5.1 provides the results of examinations of boys at the end of summer 1840. Each boy was asked five questions from the three subjects of
dictionary, geography, and grammar, for a total of fifteen questions. Out
of perhaps thirty boys only four could answer even twelve of those fifteen
correctly. Several classes answered fewer than half correctly, and two entire
classes could not answer even one-quarter of geography questions correctly.
A later report from 1842 indicates the distribution of scores within classes.
At least a few classes scored well. The second class of sixteen boys answered
five questions each on the five subjects of dictionary (spelling and vocabu-
lary), geography, history, grammar, and tables (i.e., arithmetic). Thus, out of
twenty-five questions, eight students answered nineteen to twenty-two cor-

TABLE 5.1. Test results, boys

Level	Subject	Number of students	Questions	Correct	Percentage
1	Dictionary	15	75	60	80
2	Dictionary	13	65	38	58
3	Dictionary	16	80	28	35
4	Dictionary	15	75	47	63
1	Geography	10	50	12	24
2	Geography	13	65	15	23
3	Geography	8	40	23	58
4	Geography	12	60	24	40
1	Grammar	14	70	38	54
2	Grammar	19	95	48	51

Source: Minutes, 18 August 1840.

rectly, four answered thirteen to seventeen correctly, and three answered between six and ten correctly. After checking the first class's answers and explanations in arithmetic, the school commissioner pronounced the subject as "well understood" by the boys.[64]

Some students enjoyed attending the Orphan House school. In the late antebellum period, the commissioners continued to refuse to bind out children with insufficient education. In one case, though, they did not need to exercise that prerogative. A girl whom a prospective master had approached about binding told the commissioners she did not want to leave the Orphan House just yet due to her "desire to complete her education in the Institution." The girl, Mary Burgrin, won recognition in her geography class, and later was bound apprentice to a milliner.[65]

THE GREAT MAJORITY OF CHILDREN who came to the Orphan House unlettered did in fact complete an education. It is possible to demonstrate the effectiveness of the Orphan House school among those children who entered with very little or no schooling; that is, among those children who were initially unable to sign their names to their indenture. If they were bound out as apprentices, then these children endorsed their indenture with either a signature or a mark when they left. Those who signed their names when they left must have learned to write their name, if nothing else, in the Orphan House, and those who marked remained illiterate despite the Orphan House school's efforts. Thus examination of signatures or marks at

TABLE 5.2. Descriptions of child literacy and ability to sign indenture

Year	Sex of child	Age	Comment in records	Sign (S) or mark (X)
1816	boys	9, 10	"without the smallest instruction"	X, X
1817	girl	12	"she has had no education"	X
1817	boy	7	"he can neither read nor write"	X
1819	girl	10	"can scarcely read"	X
1836	boy	10 to 13	"able only to read a little"	S
1855	boy	11	"mother can read & so can the two elder boys"*	S
1857	girl	11	"has no education except the knowledge of the alphabet"	S
1857	boy	11	"a regular attendant at St Michael's Sunday School & of some day school"	S

Sources: Applications and Indenture Books.
*Visiting commissioner also observed that the mother "cannot write," and she in fact marked her indenture; the other boy neither signed nor marked his indenture.

exit among those children who marked at entrance gives an indication of how effectively the Orphan House school taught basic literacy skills.[66]

Signature literacy was a good measure of basic education. Commentary on literacy skills matched up well with children's ability to sign. Table 5.2 provides short descriptions of a child's education or literacy according to Orphan House officials or letters that testified to the family's poverty. In general, children who were supposed to have been illiterate in fact marked the document, and those who were supposed to have been able to read or to have had a little schooling were able to write their names.

Enough signature data survive to estimate literacy rates of children when they entered the Orphan House, and then when they left. The comparison of the two rates by sex indicates that the Orphan House school was effective. In figure 5.2 the dashed lines show literacy rates at entrance, with boys in black and girls in gray.[67] Literacy was almost nil for both sexes before age seven, and then from age nine onward disparities grew between boys and girls. At each successive age among boys literacy rates increased at about 10 percent per year. The ability of many boys and a few girls aged eight to ten to acquire some basic level of literacy indicates that a few parents either taught the children to write or sent them to free schools to learn this skill. However, from age nine onward very few girls seem to have learned to write outside the Orphan House; if they had not learned to write by that age, they would never learn. It is highly unlikely that incoming children had benefited from private schooling or tutoring, the preferred modes of education for the well-to-do children of Charleston.

Compared to family and free schools, the Orphan House made a tremendous difference in the literacy acquisition of children entrusted to it. The curves made with solid lines in figure 5.2 indicate child literacy levels at exit. Children who were about to leave the Orphan House had resided there for some time and were about to be bound out apprentice to a master. At each age, children leaving the Orphan House were much more literate than those entering. For example, among twelve- and thirteen-year-olds, three-fourths of boys and one-fifth of girls were able to sign their names at entrance. But for girls and boys alike, about 90 percent of twelve-year-olds who were leaving the Orphan House signed. The large share of children who had come to sign rather than mark their names was due to the Orphan House school.

In particular the Orphan House school proved invaluable in teaching basic literacy to girls; there simply were no other schools, churches, or families in Charleston that passed along these basic skills to girls. Consider first the relatively flat trend in literacy acquisition pre–Orphan House among girls after age nine, and compare it to the sharp increase in literacy rates among girls at the same ages within the Orphan House. Clearly the Orphan House was instrumental in providing preteenaged girls with literacy skills; the implication of the graph is that a very large share of these girls would not have learned to write had they not entered the Orphan House. At the same time, compare the trends in literacy among boys over the same age groups. Outside the Orphan House, boys rapidly attained literacy over the preteen years. By age thirteen the gap in literacy acquisition between Orphan House and external sources had narrowed considerably, so that the implication is that most boys would have learned to write anyway. The Orphan House school, then, played an important and irreplaceable role in educating girls, with no parallel in the early republic–era South.

And their teaching took hold quickly. In many cases the Orphan House school taught children who entered as illiterate how to write not long after their admission. Literacy at entrance, for all 1,271 children who signed or marked, was 19 percent; but among those leaving the Orphan House within a year it was 61 percent (n=31), and after just one to two years it was 90 percent (n=61).

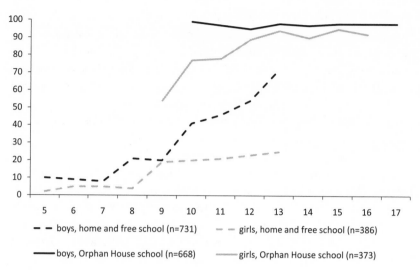

Fig. 5.2. Literacy rates by age, sex, and source of schooling. Vertical axis: percentage able to sign indenture; horizontal axis: age of child at signing or marking.

In a multivariate setting, these influences remain statistically signifi-cant.[68] Here some 782 children who were unable to sign their names at en-trance were followed to their departure from the Orphan House, when they signed or marked their indenture again. Among those children who had en-dorsed their indentures a second time, 96 percent of boys and 79 percent of girls were able to sign. Those children who had spent from one to two years in the Orphan House were 17 percent more likely to sign than a child who left the Orphan House after less than a year, controlling for age. The differ-ence between boys and girls in time spent in school influenced the girls' ability to acquire basic literacy skills. Boys became significantly more likely to learn to sign their names after just a year of residence, whereas for girls the effect did not take hold until they had lived at the Orphan House for at least five years, as over half of the girls in this sample did. It seems likely that the Orphan House was effectively providing basic training in literacy to its charges, but much more quickly for boys than for girls.

IN 1857 W. J. BENNETT SUBMITTED a report on the state of the school and its progress over the previous several years.[69] Bennett operated the largest local rice mill and belonged to the family that had directed construction of the Orphan House in the 1790s. Alongside his childhood friend Christopher Memminger, he worked to reform Charleston city schools, enlarging the district to include all white children and not just the poor.[70] Bennett committed himself to serve the Orphan House and to improve education in Charleston, and his knowledge of both came from years of close study. His report gives us an insider's picture of the Orphan House school at mid-century.

Bennett acknowledged that for all the good intentions behind the Orphan House's efforts, it could not replace a child's family. But once that responsibility had been given to the institution, the Orphan House needed "a school of the best plan and practices." The deficiencies of the Orphan House school in that regard needed to be seen in light of recent history. When Bennett paid his first visit to the school as a member of the school committee, in 1850, one master oversaw seventy boys. Students answered the master in their loudest voice so he could hear them, leading to a scene of "noise and confusion." The common belief was that "Geography and arithmetic were taught by guessing and spelling and reading by intuition." The physical resources were miserable. The furniture tortured the children, who, when nature called, relieved themselves in a corner of the schoolroom.

By the time of his next visit in 1854 things had improved very little. A year and a half of reforms had led nowhere. Evening prayer, which brought the girls and boys together, was particularly disorderly. Bennett recalled children who, when examined in arithmetic, answered by counting on their fingers. Readers had to spell out words, and the only geography question they could answer was the definition of an island. Weighing heavily on his mind was the high cost of this operation which produced "miserably low" results: twenty-four dollars per student annually.

Later in 1854 an event changed the fortunes of the Orphan House school for the next half century and beyond. This was the arrival of Agnes K. Irving in the new position of principal. Bennett had recruited her to come to Charleston from New York. Irving took the reins of the school at the advanced age of twenty-three. As a young woman and a Northerner she faced considerable opposition to her reforms, but soon enough her energy, imagination, and decisiveness won her supporters within and outside the Orphan House. The mayor of Charleston observed at her death in 1910 that Irving's strength of will enabled the Orphan House to reopen and thrive during Reconstruction, and that her reforms at the Orphan House had blazed a trail for reorganization of the city's public schools.[71]

Irving's impact on the Orphan House school was evident almost immediately. Within a week of her hiring, Bennett wrote, she "presented the school to the commissioners thoroughly classified and disciplined, and surprised them with its order & exercises." Chaos was a thing of the past. As principal, Irving kept a close watch on the teachers of the many classes, and the many new class sections that had to be added as the Orphan House went through one of its great growth periods. When Irving arrived in 1854 there were 150 children in the Orphan House school. By 1857 when Bennett wrote his review the population had grown to 253. Bennett gleefully noted that one advantage of Irving's system was a sharp decline of one-third in total schooling expenditures and an even sharper decline in the annual cost per pupil, from $24 to $9.60.[72]

The organization Irving imposed was similar to a present-day school. Primary classes comprised the first five grades. Students learned in first class to write letters and numbers and conduct basic arithmetic calculations, all on slates. In the second class they began spelling and reading lessons, still on slates, and were expected to articulate and enunciate their spoken answers clearly. Books entered in the third class, in the form of David B. Tower's *First Reader*, and emphasis on spelling and clear speaking continued. The new feature in the fourth class was the reading of maps, and students continued to write on slates. In the fifth class students began Tower's *Second Reader*, in which stories concluded with morals such as "we ourselves are the sources of our own content, and in many cases, of our own happiness."[73] The Grammar Department included sixth through eighth classes. Here students began to write in paper notebooks. Textbooks presented mixed messages. Students who read Samuel Griswold Goodrich's "Peter Parley" histories learned that the introduction of slavery was a "serious mistake." These books were soon replaced by the more region specific *Southern Reader and Speaker*.[74] Once in the eighth class students began twice-weekly singing lessons to form the choir for the Orphan House chapel.

To carry the teaching burden for this curriculum, Agnes Irving recovered a notion from earlier in the Orphan House school's history, of using older resident children as teachers. Irving arranged for the older girls who "evince[d] intellect," in Bennett's words, to become trained as teachers while their female classmates "of character and skill" who did not show such aptitude for schoolwork were "taught the use of the Scissors, the needle, and the Sewing machine," and thus learned "the arts of the Sewing Room."[75] As of June 1857 six girls had received pedagogical training and had begun teaching, two more were in the midst of their training, and two others were under consideration. Of the six who completed their training and actually had taught, two had left the Orphan House and gotten married, three continued to teach in the Orphan House school, and the sixth worked as a supervisor of the Orphan House infirmary. Bennett concluded that the use of "advanced girls" as assistant teachers not only "provide[d] most suitably for our better girls," but that it "work[ed] great economy and convenience to the Institution generally," thus combining the great goals of the Orphan House, to serve the children while not spending too much money doing so.

THE ULTIMATELY AMBIVALENT VIEW that commissioners held of the purpose of education emerged in an exchange of letters between the board and Robert W. Barnwell. A former congressman, Barnwell had returned to his home in Beaufort after concluding his service as president of the South Carolina College in Columbia. One day in 1840 he engaged a baker named James Vidal in a discussion about Vidal's apprentice, a former Orphan House boy named Thomas Stenton. Vidal believed, and convinced Barnwell, that Stenton had shown considerable promise, and was suited for "more important pursuits" than learning the baker's trade. Barnwell, a member of one of the state's wealthiest families, offered to send Stenton to school. Vidal may have been hoping merely to send Stenton to evening school while keeping him in the bakery during the day, because he gave his consent to Barnwell's plan to send Stenton away from Beaufort only reluctantly. To Barnwell, having just come from the university, sending the boy to Columbia seemed an obvious solution, and one that supported the public good. "The most useful men in our country," wrote Barnwell, "are those upon whose natural abilities poverty & necessity have superadded their powerful stimulants." Young Thomas Stenton, Barnwell believed, could be one of those useful men.[76]

The case for Stenton's further education was not as clear to the commissioners as it was to Barnwell. For one thing, Stenton himself seemed to have limited interest in Barnwell's generous offer. For another, the idea of interfering with a well-functioning apprenticeship did not sit well with the board, especially since Stenton was nearly out of his time anyway. Unanimously they voted to decline Barnwell's offer and tasked Henry A. DeSaussure with explaining why. Primarily, DeSaussure wrote Barnwell, the commissioners had limited legal abilities to come between master and apprentice. That was sufficient to explain their diffidence, but DeSaussure continued in a meditative vein. The boys sent by the Orphan House to college in Columbia, whom Barnwell probably had little chance to meet, proved to be disappointments to the commissioners. "With a few exceptions (distinguished), their anticipations have not been realized," DeSaussure confessed. The commissioners' efforts to "elevat[e] the children of the poor (taken as our little Inmates are, from the very lowest class of Society) beyond their Caste" had, in most cases, failed. Elevating the Orphan House children into the ranks of the highly educated had not worked because the children simply were not interested in moving upward. In DeSaussure's view they were best served by enabling them to rise above "the very lowest class" but not much above it:

> Their natural tendency & associations appear to be of the Mechanical or Operative Class; & unless a lad exhibit uncommon talents, we are disposed to believe, that his real happiness & interests are best promoted, by qualifying him for his natural rank in Society. If he have solid, useful talents, he will speedily emerge from his Class, to a higher & more fitting grade.

And so, the commissioners declined to disturb a boy's life by forcing him into an education that would only frustrate him. The value of a basic education as taught within the Orphan House was one thing, but the potential value of a liberal education obtained at the college in Columbia was sometimes just that: hypothetical. Stenton appeared no further in Orphan House records, and presumably continued on to his life's work as a baker. The commissioners continued their project of offering a liberal education, but with far less confidence in its results than when they began it several decades previously.[77]

CHAPTER SIX

Sickness

IN THEIR PHYSICAL AND MATERIAL LIVES, the children of the Orphan House were children of the Carolina Low Country. The diseases they suffered in the Orphan House were the same diseases that plagued the other young residents of Charleston, black and white, free and slave, native-born and immigrant. Once stricken, children received medical care derived from contemporary ideas on etiology and therapeutics. Medical practice in the late eighteenth century was on the cusp of breaking its Galenic fetters but was still in many ways bound by them. Balancing the four humors in standard therapeutics relied on heroic depletion, which wreaked violence on the patient in order to attack the disease. At the same time, new preventive approaches to ancient diseases appeared. Charleston was among the first locales in America to accept Jennerian vaccination against smallpox, and Orphan House residents were among the first Charlestonians to be vaccinated. The history of health and medicine in the Orphan House thus reflects and illuminates the state of both in the city at large and in the country as a whole.

The Orphan House stood on the northern edge of a city characterized by unhealthful conditions. When strong rains filled streets, holdings of wells and privies alike flooded and mixed together. One result was cholera. Cholera is an infectious disease, the primary symptoms of which include vomiting and diarrhea. Human excreta carry the causal agent, the cholera vibrio, so that an area with poor or nonexistent sewerage, like antebellum Charleston, may have had few uncontaminated water sources and thus widespread illness. The first worldwide cholera epidemic began in south Asia and carried westward over the next several years. Although North Americans hoped the vast Atlantic would keep the scourge away, the disease traveled on ships. It appeared first in Montreal in early June 1832, and later that month in New York.[1] That year Charleston enjoyed a fairly healthy summer, but October ended its respite. The brig *Amelia* sailed from New York for New Orleans with 108 persons aboard. Within a week passengers began falling ill with symptoms identified by shipboard physicians as cholera, and soon twenty were dead. Amid chaos on board, the ship ran aground at Folly Island, ten miles down the coast from Charleston. Survivors, scavengers, and residents of the island fell ill with the telltale symptoms, and so the intendant and Board of Health ordered the hulk and its cargo burned.[2] The desperate measures succeeded, and the city avoided the worst of the cholera. When the disease finally arrived in full force in 1835, the first of those cholera years in Charleston proved dangerous, as several hundred residents died.[3]

In the Orphan House, Dr. George Logan paid careful attention to the progress of the disease. He read the official report on the *Amelia*, which noted that cholera, surely from the ship and its cargo, had killed several scavengers. Two days after the report's release, Logan ordered that the children be kept within the Orphan House grounds as long as cholera was in the city.[4] These crude efforts at quarantine worked. Like the city, the Orphan House experienced relatively mild rates of cholera (seven to ten cases per year) up to 1835, when Dr. Logan reported 37 cases.[5] However in neither 1835 nor 1836 were there any cholera deaths in the Orphan House.[6] Part of the reason for the Orphan House's good luck might have been the relocation of the institution's privies in fall 1832.[7] When cholera eventually came to the city, it affected the Orphan House twice over. Within the Orphan House children fell ill, and outside in the city cholera killed parents of children who then came to the Orphan House.[8]

COMMISSIONERS OBSERVED THE HEALTH of prospective inmates and sometimes based decisions to admit or reject a child on those observations. In 1791 they accepted a boy on the condition that he first go to a hospital "until he is cured of a scrofulous humor." He was admitted unconditionally a few months later.[9] They accepted other physically disabled children without conditions. Margaret Zylk, admitted at age six in 1814, was blind.[10] Illness was precisely the reason for the nomination of some children. Commissioners admitted eleven-year-old Louisa Benton, who appeared to suffer from malnutrition, immediately upon hearing the visiting commissioner's report. "She was not in good health when brought into the Institution," he wrote, "being much swollen with stomach, & of a cadaverous appearance."[11] Visiting commissioners and clergy who supplied references occasionally described a child's health. Guardians realized this, as in one case in which an older woman informed the commissioners that the child she had been raising already "had measles and ha[d] been vaxinated."[12]

The health of entering children became another skirmish in the ongoing battles between the Orphan House and the Poor House. Before the opening of the Orphan House building, the two institutions agreed that on the order of a commissioner of either board or of the Poor House physician, a child could be moved from the Orphan House to the Poor House.[13] Orphan House commissioners could then relegate a child who was "represented to be diseased" to the Poor House, promising "when cured that then they [would] have no objections to receive her." In the case of Mary Turner in 1808, the Orphan House did in fact accept the girl six months after her initial application, when they had directed her to the Poor House until her health improved.[14]

Later, physical disabilities served as reasons for outright rejection. One such case occurred in 1857, when the Orphan House was unusually crowded. Henry W. DeSaussure investigated the case of twelve-year-old Alfred Sanders, who had only one arm. Alfred presented a mixture of promising and unattractive qualities to the commissioners. DeSaussure observed that Alfred was not a bad boy at all—he had "no vices" and was "not insubordinate," although he was uninterested in school. Unfortunately for Alfred, at age 12 he was older than the typical boy presented to the commissioners, which had allowed him to accumulate too much "knowledge of the world" for his own good or that of his prospective classmates. Even though commissioners expected Alfred to spend only a year or two in the Orphan House before being bound out, few trades were open to a one-armed boy. DeSaussure concluded, with emphasis, "Having lost an arm, there would be great difficulty in apprenticing him out, as he would be unfit for any mechanical employment, & what could the board do with him under these circumstances? The future embarrassment in the disposal of him admonishes the board of the inexpediency of admitting him."[15] And so the prospect of supporting an unemployable boy convinced the commissioners to deny Alfred admission. As a result, Alfred Sanders followed some other path to adulthood, one not in the historical record. Sometimes when presented with disabled children, the commissioners specifically sought to direct them elsewhere. Twice the commissioners considered the case of a child described as "an idiot," and twice they decided such a child was "not a proper object to be with the rest of the children." In both these cases they recommended admission to the Poor House.[16]

The health of a potentially admissible child entered into later negotiations between the Orphan House and the Poor House. In 1839 a boy of about twelve years named Malcolm McDonald came to the Poor House claiming to need medical attention. The Poor House commissioners allowed him to enter, but sought almost immediately to send him to the Orphan House. The Orphan House commissioners in turn replied that they regretted to exclude the boy, but he was "affected with a disorder which it would be dangerous to introduce amongst the inmates of the Orphan House." Should Malcolm be cured at the Poor House, though, the commissioners of the Orphan House would be happy to consider his application. Exactly what the boy's condition was cannot be determined now; at the time the Poor House's physicians claimed that he was harmless to other children. The Orphan House gave in and accepted the boy, and a year later bound him out to the US Naval School.[17]

Other children with recurring acute illness found it hard to enter the Orphan House. A prominent Carolinian named Harriott Horry took an interest in the mother of Frank and Isaac Smith, whom she had hired out of a local poor house in Santee. In 1816, Frank was ten and Isaac eight, and their mother had remarried to a man who abused the boys. Harriott made it her work to defend the boys from their stepfather and to protect their health. Despite her efforts to relocate the boys during the annual sickly season, she told the commissioners, "They are ill every year, often dangerously so, and I fear such continual repetitions of fever will prove fatal to them." This recurring fever may have been malaria. The Orphan House accepted both boys, but their mother prevented them from taking advantage of this offer. Some four years later Mrs. Horry hoped again to place them in the Orphan House, but by this time they were too old and the institution turned the application down.[18]

BY VIRTUE OF LIVING IN CHARLESTON, Orphan House children experienced some of the most up-to-date medical care available. Mid-eighteenth century interest in (and fear of) diseases carried by sailors resulted in construction of a marine hospital, then associated with St. Philip's Church. This occurred long before the federal effort to provide marine hospitals in port cities at the beginning of the nineteenth century.[19] By the late eighteenth century local physicians had formed the Medical Society of South Carolina, where they discussed new developments in medicine and the results of their own experiments.[20] And they had much to discuss, as by one account Charleston hosted more medical research before the Revolution than did Philadelphia, New York, or Boston.[21] From these conversations came a compendium of the state of the medical art, *A Review of the Improvements, Progress, and*

State of Medicine in the XVIIIth Century, by David Ramsay, the physician-historian. This culture of medical research and education produced the four physicians who cared for Orphan House residents for most of a century: George Logan Sr., John Noble, George Logan Jr., and William Harleston Huger. Logan père served until his death in 1793.[22] Of Noble little can be said beyond his membership in the Medical Society. In the very early nineteenth century he was serving as physician of the Poor House, and by 1809 he was submitting weekly Physician's Reports on his observations around the Orphan House.[23]

From this point onward, just two other physicians served the Orphan House into the twentieth century. In April 1810 George Logan Jr. succeeded Noble as Orphan House physician. Logan had earned his medical degree from the University of Pennsylvania in 1803. Soon after his return to Charleston he wrote a medical manual, and after some years in the Orphan House, he published *Practical Observations on Diseases of Children* in 1825. In 1810 Logan began his weekly annotations in the Physician's Record, in which he described health and disease among the Orphan House children. Logan continued to fulfill his duties until 1854.[24] That year the torch passed to William Harleston Huger, who carried the names of two of Charleston's most prominent families. Huger was a graduate of the Medical College of the State of South Carolina, class of 1849, and studied further in Paris and Dublin. One of the most prominent of Charleston's physicians in the late nineteenth century, Huger served the Orphan House until 1906.[25]

The Orphan House physician carried considerable authority over the diagnosis and treatment of up to two hundred or so children, resident staff, and slaves.[26] Bylaws forbade him to charge for his services and required him to submit regular reports on the health of the children and other residents.[27] Based on these reports, figure 6.1 illustrates trends in incidence rates for three broad classes of disease. Rates of fever cases were cyclical, spiking upward in 1838, 1844, and 1850. The first two of these peaks reflected high rates of scarlet fever, and the third an outbreak of measles and dengue or "break bone" fever, so named for its painful effects on joints. Another year of dengue fever was 1829, when it was supposed to have "prevailed." Rates of various diarrheal diseases, probably due to contaminated water, remained relatively steady, as did incidence of ophthalmia, a highly contagious inflammation of the eye, "the curse of children's asylums," according to a nineteenth-century physician.[28]

Another perspective is given by figure 6.2, which shows trends in death rates and infectious disease rates. The two rates were highly correlated with

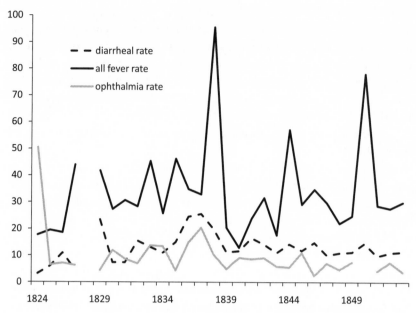

Fig. 6.1. Disease incidence rates and population levels. Vertical axis: Cases per 100 child-years. Source: Minutes of commissioners' meetings, annual physician's reports, each October.

each other (r=0.62), consistent with the notion that many child deaths were due to infectious disease. A difficult question is how high the death rate was relative to that for children outside the Orphan House. Statistics that would allow comparison of the Orphan House death rate with the mortality of other contemporary children are scarce, but the available data suggest that the Charleston orphans were not at a significantly higher risk than other children. About 2,000 children appear in the present data set, and each of them stayed an average of about 5.5 years at the Orphan House, yielding approximately 10,500 child-years at risk of death. Of all the children in the sample, 164 died in residence, making the Orphan House mortality rate 15.6 per 1,000 child-years at risk. For comparison, the death rate of inmates at the Philadelphia Children's Asylum in 1826 was 52.4 per 1,000 child-years.[29] Among the broader population, mortality data from the 1850 census, usually dismissed by historians because of uneven coverage, supply a comparison, even if one to be regarded warily. According to the census, the mortality of children and young adults aged one to twenty in the city of Charleston was 9.8 per 1,000. However, national estimates of child mortality were 28 per 1,000 among five- to nine-year-olds and 19 per 1,000 among ten- to fourteen-year-olds. Thus, relative to local death rates, the Orphan House residents appear to have been at higher mortality risk, but relative to national rates their risk of death was low.[30]

Isolation of sick children happened with varying degrees of urgency. Initially, children in poor health who needed special attention were sent to the Poor House, which had some space reserved for the sick poor. When the Orphan House building first opened, a room was set aside on the third floor of the West Wing as a "hospital or sick room" for the girls, and later a similar room was allotted to the boys on their side of the building.[31] As noted above (chapter 3), this space was inadequate or just unused, as an 1809 investigation found sick children left here and there in sleeping quarters. A near turning point came in 1817 and 1818 when a terrible epidemic of yellow fever swept through the city and then the Orphan House. That year 274 citizens of Charleston died of yellow fever, and within the Orphan House some fifty to sixty children contracted the disease. Isolating victims to prevent contagion was not a common practice at the time, although some physicians recommended it. More likely it was for the convenience of caregivers that the steward and matron and their assistants moved the stricken into the chapel. This was not the separate structure on the north side of the

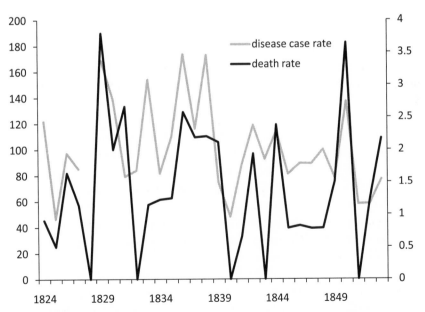

Fig. 6.2. Death rates and infectious disease incidence rates. Left axis: disease cases per 100 child-years; right axis: deaths per 100 child-years. Source: Minutes of commissioners' meetings, annual physician's reports, each October.

Orphan House lot, but a smaller prayer space on the first floor of the boys'
(East) wing of the building. Caregivers nonetheless found this arrangement
taxing, and the commissioners did not like using a worship space as an infirmary. With this episode clear in their memory, commissioners sought to
build a separate infirmary in 1823. Their committee noted that the Orphan
House had recently received a large bequest that could pay for this project.
However, it appears not to have gone forward. In 1855, renovations gave
over much of the new fifth floor to care of the sick. There could be found
a hospital, the convalescents' dining room, quarantine apartments, a laza-
retto for the long term ill, an apartment set aside for an apothecary, and
rooms for the hospital matron.[32]

A CLASSIC DISEASE OF CROWDING that illustrates the path of medical knowledge was smallpox. Smallpox is highly contagious, passing from person to
person via saliva emitted in spitting, coughing, or talking. It yields a high
case-fatality ratio but leaves survivors with lifetime immunity. As a result,
its attacks tended to be cyclical. It passed through previously unexposed
populations quickly, leaving some dead and others immune from further
attacks. Charleston's history with smallpox was part of the wider American
experience, and had unique elements due to its role as a major seaport. The
1760 epidemic sickened perhaps three-fourths of the city's residents, killing
700 of them.[33] At that time, the best available response was inoculation.
This term, literally meaning "in the eye," originally referred to grafting of
branches onto trees. In medicine, inoculation described the process of inducing a mild smallpox attack by inserting material from the pustules of a
victim into a cut in the skin. Inoculation often worked, but it was a crude
approach. In 1798 Edward Jenner publicized his newly discovered process of
vaccination, from the Latin word for cow. Vaccination involved a similar
process of insertion of material into a cut in the skin, but the vaccination
material derived from the much milder disease of cowpox. The practice of
vaccination spread quickly to America, and it came to South Carolina not
long after its arrival in Boston.[34]

Smallpox first appeared in Orphan House records in February 1791.
No children had fallen ill yet, but commissioners observed an epidemic
in Charleston not described in other published sources. "[M]any persons
in town have the small pox," commissioners wrote, making it "likely to
spread," and so the house physician asked whether he should inoculate
resident children who had not previously had the disease.[35] Four years later,
still in the pre-vaccination era, a child in the Orphan House died of the disease.[36] Then in 1801, the Charleston physician Benjamin Bonneau Simons

returned from medical studies in Edinburgh with a sample of the cowpox virus, and found David Ramsay enthusiastic about vaccination. Together with other local physicians they promoted vaccination as superior to inoculation.[37] Early the next year commissioners agreed and ordered not only that the physician should "inoculate the Children in the Institution with the vaccine matter," but as a standard test of its efficacy, the children should "afterwards be tested by the inoculation of the small pox." Noble soon reported that he was vaccinating the children. Speedy adoption of vaccination at the Orphan House may have followed the European precedent of using orphans and foundlings as experimental subjects in smallpox prevention.[38] Six years later, after considerable turnover among the residents, commissioners ordered Noble again to vaccinate the children who had not previously had "the small pox or the cow pox."[39] Further turnover in the child population required a further vaccination campaign in 1811, when Logan oversaw a process of "vaccine inoculation" in the Orphan House.[40] By the next smallpox epidemic in 1816–17, doctors in the city had completely abandoned inoculation, and Logan was ordered to begin vaccinating vulnerable residents.[41] Rather than wait for an epidemic, it became Orphan House policy to vaccinate children as soon as they came to the institution.[42]

Even after the beginning of general prophylactic vaccination, the question of smallpox remained an active concern for all associated with the Orphan House. In 1830 and 1831 a smallpox epidemic in Charleston sickened nearly 800 people and caused 46 deaths. The magnitude of the epidemic concerned medical officials who had expected previous vaccination efforts to limit the suffering caused by the disease. No cases of smallpox appeared within the Orphan House enclosure, however, despite occasional exposure to it during the previous year of its presence in Charleston. It was a tribute to Logan's insistence on prophylactic vaccination of the children. As a precautionary measure Logan decided to revaccinate all the children with "genuine cow pox." The notion that several varieties of cow pox existed, and that "spurious" cow pox would fail to confer immunity went all the way back to Jenner's original "Inquiry." One problem, Logan observed, was that spurious cow pox produced post-vaccination symptoms similar to genuine cow pox, so that it was difficult to tell which had constituted the vaccination material.[43] Later, the Orphan House desire to maintain a clear boundary between its grounds and the city was evident during the 1853 epidemic. Within the Orphan House 29 cases of "varioloid" or "modified" smallpox occurred. Even healthy children were affected by the outbreak. When Edward Cudworth's sister died of smallpox, he left the Orphan House without permission to attend her funeral. Once at home, his mother contacted the

steward to inform him of Edward's whereabouts. The careful response was
that Edward should stay with his mother until the epidemic had passed. At
the same time the Orphan House declined to pursue runaways as long as
smallpox prevailed in the city.[44]

A crowding disease that appeared but rarely in the Orphan House was
tuberculosis. The environment was probably ripe for its spread, but the patients were not. The disease, known as consumption or phthisis at that
time, is carried by bacteria that are excreted in coughing or spitting. At a
time when its etiology was unknown, diagnoses suggested that sick children
were likely to have been "the descendants of phthisical parents and those
of depraved habits."[45] Once the tubercle bacillus is in the body its most
common site of development is in the lungs, which leads to pulmonary
tuberculosis. The long and slow progress of the disease and its distinctive
wasting symptoms proved useful plot devices in *La Boheme* and *The Magic
Mountain*, which in turn hint at its low incidence in the Orphan House. Tuberculosis was largely a disease of young adults, not children. Thus, a routine census of the Orphan House infirmary in 1831 yielded 37 cases of five
different types of fever, but only one case of "tabes mesenterica," a form
of tuberculosis occurring in the abdomen, and three cases each of scrofula
(lymphatic tuberculosis) and "phthisis pulmonalis."[46]

A crowding disease of childhood was measles. Measles has much in common with smallpox, and on occasion in the past the two were mistaken for
each other. Measles is transmitted through nose and throat secretions passing through the air, only affects humans, and is highly contagious.[47] Thus,
measles also appeared in cycles. The earliest case of measles in the Orphan
House appeared in 1795 and resulted in a child's death.[48] A few years later,
in summer 1802, four children died of measles, which suggests an epidemic
involving more children.[49] An outbreak in September 1813 indicated the
speed at which the disease could spread through an enclosed group of children. George Logan reported the first cases, numbering six, as appearing in
the second week of September. The next week saw 13 more cases, the week
after 9, and the week after 13 more. By October 14, he wrote, in total at least
115 children had had measles in the past few weeks. Then, in the first week
of November 1813, reports of measles ceased and Logan could write, "The
children have been generally healthy during the last week."[50] The worst
measles epidemic occurred in 1829–30, which produced 180 cases in total
at a time when there were about that many children in the house. In October 1829, Logan reported that two weeks into the epidemic, seventy cases
among children and slaves had occurred. Altogether, in a seven-week period
during October and November 1829, 104 children contracted measles. In

later years there appeared 61 cases in 1836, 72 cases in 1842, and 56 cases in 1848.[51] Unlike smallpox, in reasonably healthy and well-fed populations, measles is rarely fatal. But among children who experience poor nutrition, measles is far more dangerous. Thus in the Orphan House persistent problems with measles mortality implied a low level of nutrition.[52]

No systematic data survive that would allow assessment of nutritional status among children in the Orphan House. Occasional references to tapeworms suggest that even those who ate sufficiently might not reap the benefits of that nutrition.[53] A suggestive entry in the annual Physician's Reports might explain why children occasionally died of measles and sequelae—that is, there was a small but persistent number of children whose cause of death was "marasmus." The term *marasmus* is today associated with a broader condition called protein-energy malnutrition, which manifests itself in the wasting associated with starvation. Six children died of this condition between 1838 and 1853.[54] These were very young children, all but one under six years of age. Their condition may have resulted as much from their Orphan House experience as from their earlier impoverished lives, because most had been in the Orphan House at least a year. Other children such as the four who died in the 1829–1830 measles epidemic may have been weakened by malnutrition before experiencing the convulsions, pneumonia, and dysentery that were recorded as having killed them.[55]

Besides chronic illness and infectious disease, children who lived communally in the Orphan House were also subject to parasites. Some children carried a considerable parasite burden, which would have exacerbated other health problems, especially those related to poor nutrition. Physicians diagnosed worm infections in children who also suffered from other conditions, but often only after their death. In 1844, nine-year-old William Fay died most clearly from dropsy, but he also suffered from an "obstruction, presumed by worms."[56] Many cases of fever were associated with worm infections.[57] Diagnosis was made when children voided worms. In at least one case George Logan Jr. conducted an autopsy that revealed "abdominal viscera . . . all in a highly morbid state, the omentum, mesentery, and valves of the intestines in particular were in several parts gangrenous." In this case, of the unfortunate eight-year-old John Sherer, the "post-mortem fully justified [Logan's] suspicion" that the "uncommonly large" worms played an important role in his death.[58]

Much less serious but still bothersome parasites appeared on children's heads. References to scald-head probably indicated lice, although it could have been ringworm. Therapeutic approaches to scald-head varied. One boy's stepfather applied to bring him home where he could be treated for the problem.[59] In another case, an infected boy who had already been bound out headed back to the Orphan House. A physician in Amelia Township, between Charleston and Columbia, complained that his new apprentice carried "scall or scurf on the head" and had "communicated the disorder to a servant in his family." A little investigation by the commissioners revealed that the "scald-head" on the boy had been noticed by the physician and schoolmaster when he was still in the Orphan House. Unusually in this case the board agreed to take the boy back, acknowledging their error in the binding of a sick child to an unsuspecting master.[60] While the Orphan House may have bred scalp problems by keeping children in close quarters, many children entered the Orphan House already infected. Without specifying the actions taken for a cure, Dr. Logan noted that two recently admitted children suffered from tinea capitis, or ringworm, and immediately subjected them to treatment.[61]

CHILDREN SUFFERED FROM TWO KINDS of vision ailments, acute and chronic. Most references to short-term diseases of the eye described the problem as "ophthalmia," which was probably conjunctivitis. Logan gave no specifics regarding the symptoms of this problem, but in one letter to the commissioners he did note potential causes of ophthalmia as well as its extent during a July 1833 epidemic. In the 1820s, nearly every child experienced ophthalmia soon after admission, and it was often painful. The disease spread through the Orphan House in epidemic form, as was typical "in all large institutions where young persons often assemble," according to Logan. He narrowed causal influences down to the "vehement and intense glare of light," probably in classrooms and outdoors rather than in sleeping quarters. In fact, bright light is known today to exacerbate the pain of conjunctivitis to the point of inducing photophobia, or fear of light. Logan offered no immediate solution but instead took the long view and recommended that commissioners plant more shade trees. He also noted an alarming tendency of laundresses to suffer diseases of the eyes, which he attributed to exposure to lye and the stress of carrying water. It was not Logan, though, but the commissioners who ordered children with ophthalmia to be isolated from healthier children during the 1833 outbreak, which may have limited the number afflicted that year to just 24 cases.[62] Cases of blindness and other chronic vision problems among Orphan House children may have been congenital or accidental, or they may have stemmed from high rates of smallpox, which often left victims blinded.

Treatment of children with chronic vision problems illustrates both sympathetic attitudes of adults toward these children and the general stigma of blindness. Commissioners proved sympathetic to children with chronic vision problems. When Fanny Mordecai first came to their attention in 1815, before they decided whether to admit her they called for her to be examined by a physician to see if her condition could be cured and (one suspects this mattered more) whether it was contagious. The doctor offered enough promise of the former and denial of the latter that they allowed Fanny into the Orphan House "in order that the physician might attend her and see if there [was] a possibility of curing her eyes."[63] It was not until the next spring that she marked her indentures, signifying her official and permanent entrance into the Orphan House and the commissioners' expectation that her condition was not contagious. Four years later her situation had not greatly changed. She could see little and sought permission to see a Dr. Gleize to attempt another cure. The commissioners resolved to let her do so as often as the doctor required.[64] In the contemporaneous case of Rachel Isaacs, though, commissioners refused to let her mother take her to a doctor to "promote the cure of her eyes."[65]

The concern of commissioners for children's vision was evident, but masters of bound-out children showed less concern. Since many of them had taken the child into their home and shop primarily to gain the apprentice's labor, near-blindness was a considerable obstacle to the youth's ability to work productively. Joseph Berry left the Orphan House in 1813, aged fifteen, to serve as an apprentice to Joseph McCullough, a prominent storekeeper and "man of large affairs" in upstate Greenville. A year and a half later, McCullough changed his mind about Berry, explained a Greenville physician named Thomas Williams to commissioners, because the boy's diminishing vision left him unable "to render Mr. Joseph McCullough any service for a number of years."[66] Presentation of other cases lacked that politesse and simply demanded that commissioners take the visually impaired child back as damaged goods. In the case of Elizabeth Sowers, her mistress asked to return her to the Orphan House after discovering that she was blind in one eye. The commissioners noted that because the mistress's husband had yet to sign the indenture, the commissioners could legally receive the child back into the Orphan House.[67]

Commissioners did not always accept masters' claims without verification. Harriet McNeil entered the Perrault household as an apprentice domestic in January 1806, when she was fifteen years old. A month later her mistress asked commissioners to take her back, because the "defect in her eyes . . . renders her incapable of doing sewing work." The steward and matron, at the request of the commissioners, examined Harriet's eyes and concluded that she was only nearsighted. Thus informed, the commissioners rejected the Perraults' request. Two months later, the commissioners gave in to Mrs. Perrault's repeated appeals and accepted Harriet back into the House, perhaps because they were tired of Mrs. Perrault's complaints. Within a year a woman named Ann Stewart took Harriet from the Orphan House to serve as an apprentice seamstress.[68] If all else failed, commissioners demanded that masters who returned apprentices, even for reasons of physical incapacity, pay a penalty fee. Thus the carpenter Thomas Hinson paid twenty dollars to return James McKie due to the "failure in the eye sight of his apprentice." As in the previous two cases, another master came along and found McKie perfectly fitting to serve as an apprentice tailor, and he even agreed to send James to night school for five years.[69]

THERAPEUTIC TREATMENT THAT ORPHAN HOUSE residents received was very much in keeping with standards of early republic–era medicine. In the late eighteenth century, when the Orphan House was founded, regular American medicine followed the lead of Benjamin Rush. He emphasized the power of the physician to disrupt the course of disease through vigorous application of powerful drugs. The obvious effects of cathartics (to induce defecation), emetics (to induce vomiting), and venesection (bloodletting) assured patient and family that something was indeed happening, and the physician's direction of all the violence assured patient and family that he was ultimately in control. This approach was difficult to implement in a communal setting. One consequence of heroic therapy was that sick children soiled their clothes and linens, so that, as in a commissioner's report on one epidemic, "sickness adds a great deal to the washing." This report recommended that the Orphan House rent "another negro" to deal with the increased burden of laundry. Heroic depletion also put the sick children in need of "small tubs" which "[could not] be dispensed with." A local cooper made them to order.[70] More ominously, Southern physicians, including some in Charleston, believed that fitting a course of therapy to local conditions required even more powerful drugs in the South than in the North, due to the naturally sluggish environment in the Low Country.[71]

The therapeutic approach to two diseases at the Orphan House illustrates the manner in which children were subject to techniques of heroic depletion. Pertussis, commonly called whooping cough ("hooping cough" in the records), was a common disease of childhood. Transmission is aerial via droplets emitted in coughing, the loud nature of which resulted in the common name for the disease. Immunity follows from survival of an attack.[72] The first appearance in Orphan House records was in 1809, when John Noble was house physician. By July 9 among forty to fifty sick children, he reported, six to ten were suffering from whooping cough. Later that month the number of afflicted children rose to fifteen to twenty, and cases persisted into the autumn.[73] The disease appeared in the Orphan House sporadically, with nearly fifty cases registered in 1824 and 1833; about two dozen cases in 1836, 1838, 1844, and 1850; and none at all between 1839 and 1843. In May and June 1831, reported George Logan, "the Hooping Cough prevailed as an epidemic from the 11th of May to the close of June," leading to nineteen cases total. Three of them were particularly serious, Logan observed, as the children presented "symptoms of violence and affections of the chest." As a result, Logan determined that these cases "required the Lancet, and Blisters, in general Emetics and Antispasmodicks."[74] With the lancet he was able to bleed the child, thereby breaking up the causal agent of the cough. Application of a chemical irritant to the skin for several hours produced the blisters that Logan had prescribed. The fluid that the blisters exuded was interpreted as evidence that the blistering compound worked as a counter-irritant, forcing the body to expel the problematic substance. References to use of the lancet suggest that venisection may have been more common in the Orphan House than elsewhere in the South, where the consequences of lost blood were thought to be more debilitating than in the North.[75]

Again in May and June 1833 an epidemic of whooping cough swept through the Orphan House. As often happened, it struck girls in particular, and among them especially those already ill with scrofula, or lymphatic tuberculosis of the neck. Again Logan resorted to venisection and blisters. From his materia medica Logan selected "antimonials, the squills, and occasionally the compound powder of Ipecacuanha, with the best effects." The antimonial may have been tartar emetic, a common emetic derived from antimony. Squills, a diuretic derived from the squill plant (a type of hyacinth), were more often used to treat dropsy (congestive heart failure) than an acute condition like whooping cough. Ipecacuanha was a powerful emetic. All together, the drugs used by Logan would have led to extensive purging of various bodily fluids, all in the hopes of disrupting the illness. In addition, during this wave of pertussis Logan arranged for cold baths for children, which "proved an excellent auxiliary antispasmodic[;] it suspended the Paroxysms and abridged the duration of the complaint." Probably this involved sending the children to the bathhouses in the Orphan House lot, where, in the ordinary course of things, children took baths and showers.[76]

Scarlet fever was another condition of childhood that plagued Orphan House residents. It too appeared irregularly, but it also tended to show up in years of great pertussis epidemics. For example, in 1831, 1838, and 1844 several dozen children suffered from each disease (and some undoubtedly from both).[77] Logan described particular characteristics of these waves. In 1844, the two diseases hit the Orphan House "in quick succession," and only those children who had suffered from scarlet fever went on to develop whooping cough. Logan described the disease in recognizable terms:

> The Symptoms were chill succeeded by a nausea head ache & fever, the Tongue, Tonsils, & Palate were painfully affected on the 2d day, the inflammation assumed a deep Scarlet Colour, on the 4th an Extensive Efflorescence appeared but in a few instances this was confined to the Arms or the Legs and Ankles, in one or two Cases the hands and fingers only exhibited a pink or red appearance. The Febrile Exacerbations recurred at Night with slight Delirium.[78]

Therapeutics for scarlet fever resembled that for whooping cough. Logan prescribed emetics and cathartics to cleanse the children's bodies. He specified calomel (a compound of mercury), rhubarb, and Epsom salts for this therapy, and later ordered a sulfate of quinine to control the fever. Gargling with cinchona bark derivatives also acted as a fever reducer.[79] This approach to scarlet fever was typical of the day, to judge from one contemporary medical textbook.[80]

Logan himself recognized the unique disease environment of the Orphan House. The 1838 episode was part of a more general scarlet fever epidemic throughout the city that had begun eighteen months previously. In the Orphan House, Logan proposed, the disease had become more virulent. In response to this development, sleeping quarters were disinfected with chloride of lime, vinegar, and niter, and the residents moved temporarily into the chapel. In the first day or so after a child was diagnosed, the very high fever began and was treated with the lancet. To deal with the fever, Logan ordered doses of calomel. For children who suffered from worm infections, he ordered castor oil or sulfate of magnesia as an antihelminthic. Some children received mustard plasters to raise blisters; others were given mustard internally, which, Logan noted, "produced a very favourable influence." One child who died had been given belladonna at the insistence of Logan's son, the third generation of the family to treat sick Orphan House children. Dr. Thomas M. Logan, recently returned from postgraduate study in London and Paris, assured the senior Dr. Logan that administering belladonna had been endorsed by the most eminent European physicians.[81]

Physicians could not resist the impulse to try new methods of medicine on Orphan House children. Their experimental design was too casual to yield much in the way of firm conclusions, however. During the next great epidemic of 1844, the younger Dr. Logan further explored the use of belladonna to treat scarlet fever. At his insistence, his father agreed to give belladonna as a prophylactic to children with no prior record of scarlet fever. At a concentration of five grains to each ounce of cinnamon tea, they gave several drops of this mixture daily to each child in the Orphan House, five drops to those aged three years or younger, and one additional drop per year of age for older children. They observed redness in their faces and throats but could not decide if the cause was the disease or the belladonna. After the epidemic had passed, they judged the therapy a success because only six or seven new cases emerged after dosing with belladonna began.[82]

DISEASE SUSCEPTIBILITY AND MEDICAL PRACTICE in an orphanage presented unique challenges to Orphan House medical and operational staff. Life in the Orphan House with several-score other children presented unusual risks to each individual resident as well. Physicians who worked in the Orphan House generally provided care in line with prevailing standards of the day, but as with the belladonna experiments, they were also not averse to trying unorthodox methods to break the momentum of epidemics. One thing they did not do was provide individualized care. There is no surviving evidence that they attempted to match courses of therapy to a child's particular age, sex, or ethnicity, which was a common approach in antebellum therapeutics.[83] That would have been costly, given the medical manpower requirements that would follow. But the standardized care children received did make for an interesting parallel with the other type of group medicine in the antebellum lower South: doctoring slaves. When physicians visited plantations to examine slaves as a group they recorded treatments and charges in a block, and not for individuals.[84] In John Noble's and George Logan's weekly reports, children almost never attained the distinction of individual reference by name, unless the recorded event was their death. Until then, sick children were either among the "several" who were ill, or perhaps one of the "two . . . boys [who] have been sick with Fever and Bowel complaints," or they might have been the "one case of Liver disorder."[85] Or, ideally, they were among the many "children [who] have been generally healthy during the last week."

Adults whom the physicians treated were almost always named, both in ill health and in recovery. Paradoxically, this included slaves. Thus we have these details from February 1811: "The Negro Dick has injured his foot which has confined him to the Kitchen during the week, he is getting better," and a week later, Logan reported, "Dick has recovered & is able to go to work." Over the two weeks afterward, Logan wrote, "The Wench Kate has been sick with a Catarrh, she is somewhat better," and the next week he recorded that "Kate has recovered."[86] Within the Orphan House the positions of black and white were reversed in terms of this one small detail, perhaps because it reflected how the doctors differentiated their patients by their ages. This approach was apparently acceptable to the commissioners who reviewed the reports simply because it was what the numbers dictated. The basic problem of providing medical attention to large numbers of children and of slaves determined physicians' approaches in both settings, but the children's medical needs necessarily rendered them in one more regard as a problem to be controlled. To achieve this control, the physician and commissioners relied on their considerable experience earned in management of bondsmen to organize the healing of the children who were temporarily bound to them.

DESPITE THE BEST EFFORTS of Orphan House physicians and nurses, some children died while in the institution's custody. As noted above, there is no reason to believe that children were at unusual risk of death in the Orphan House, relative to other institutions of the time. As melancholy as the death of a child is, the Orphan House aimed to observe with suitable ceremony the death of an orphan who left no (or few) kin to mourn his passing. In its earliest years, the Orphan House maintained its own burial ground on the institution's lot, but later in the period children were buried in a specially marked section of the Magnolia Cemetery in Charleston Neck. Commissioners arranged for clergymen to come and address the children on the somber topic. Sometimes they spoke with the coffin present, and at others the Orphan House physician convinced commissioners that for hygienic reasons they needed to bury the deceased child's body immediately. In one such case, Henry A. DeSaussure recommended contacting "the Methodist parsonage [to] procure a minister to perform the funeral service." This particular sermon went unrecorded, but no doubt the Orphan House children needed little reminding of the omnipresence of the threat of death, to themselves and to friends and family.[87]

CHAPTER SEVEN

Leaving

E VENTUALLY THE TIME CAME for each child to leave the Orphan House. This chapter examines the next steps of those children who did not enter an apprenticeship. A few children died in the Orphan House, their sad fates discussed in the previous chapter. In the late eighteenth and into the early nineteenth century, by far the most common outcome was for a child to be bound as an apprentice to learn a trade, and the situations young apprentices entered are the subject of the next chapter. This chapter describes fates of all the others: runaways, adoptees, and those who returned to the custody of a family member. Figure 7.1 shows how this pattern evolved over time. The trends suggest considerable change in the structure and goals of poor Southern white families in the years between the Revolution and the Civil War. In an initially small but growing number of cases, children returned to their natal families. By the end of the antebellum period, more children reentered their nuclear or extended families than were bound out as apprentices. Over the first half of the nineteenth century, the willingness, ability, or both, of families to recover their children grew dramatically.

CHILDREN WHO DECAMPED FROM THE ORPHAN HOUSE constituted a numerically uncommon but colorful lot. Boys far outnumbered girls among escapees.[1] While nineteenth-century runaways may conjure images of Huck Finn on the Mississippi, all rollicking adventures and learning about the nature of friendship, the reality of unskilled, young, and physically small people fending for themselves was considerably more sober. Whether young people ran away from the Orphan House to gain freedom, to relieve the stress of confinement, or to seek adventure, the world outside offered a harsh life as well as new opportunities. Those who found work that suited them, or who

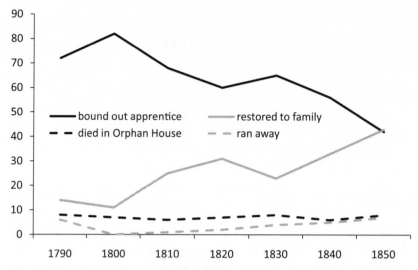

Fig. 7.1. Share of each entrance cohort by outcome. Vertical axis: percentage of children.

returned to a family that welcomed them back, saw no need to inform the Orphan House of their situation, so necessarily the written record primarily tells the stories of those who did not find the outside world quite so navigable. Thus when the grandmother of William Adams wrote from England to investigate his whereabouts, the steward could only reply that William had "left the House without permission two or three years ago" and since then no "precise intelligence which could be relied on [had] been had of him."[2]

Occasionally a runaway returned of his own accord, deciding that life on the inside was easier than being a lone child on the outside. However, commissioners viewed flight as a double betrayal: first, the child had failed to appreciate the charity given him up to that point, and second, the fugitive might provoke the same idea in others. Thus, in 1804 the runaway George Long returned and "promised he would behave himself in future so as to merit the confidence and approbation of the Commissioners." The commissioners accepted his apology to the extent of forgoing the lash, but wanting him out of the institution they "resolved that he be bound apprentice as soon as possible."[3] Another boy boasted to a poor warden that by his own cunning and will he had evaded the guard at the gate and then spent his nights within the Orphan House yard for a week before he was captured. He too was bound out ten days later.[4]

In many cases the self-liberating orphan returned to a parent. The earliest report of a runaway came from a woman who appeared before a regular Commission meeting to "declare that it never was her intention to take her son John Wm Rassdale from the Orphan House." Once he showed up at her door, though, "she was fearfull he might be much injured" by his punishment for absconding, so she did let her son in after all. The commissioners decided to pardon young Rassdale and told Philip Besselleu merely to "keep a strict eye on him in future," but at some point thereafter he ran away for good.[5] A letter written for Mary Buckingham explained that her son had absconded from the Orphan House because he wanted to accompany some friends who had been given permission to leave the grounds. Mrs. Buckingham or the friend who wrote her letter may have inadvertently discouraged commissioners from reclaiming the boy by writing, "He is very bad with the itch." They returned permanent custody to her three weeks later.[6] Occasionally a parent believed that the runaway child was better off at home. Catherine Biggs petitioned successfully for the return of her son Henry after he had "several times absented himself from the Orphan House." Each time, she wrote, his fear that she would return him kept him away from her as well, leaving him running loose in the streets, "and if he persists in that course [he] must inevitably go to ruin."[7] As in many cases of recaptured runaways, James Connelly's stepfather promised that if the Orphan House legally released James to his mother he would arrange a seagoing apprenticeship, in this case with a Captain Fox.[8]

In rare cases the children either were kidnapped or they colluded with the putative kidnappers. During the Napoleonic Wars, American neutrality attracted French privateers to the port of Charleston. Here they could repair and refit, dispose of prizes, and allow crew members time on shore. The years between federal closure of northern ports to French privateers and the onset of the Quasi-War with France, that is, 1794–96, saw the most intense activity.[9] During this time of unusual French activity in the Port of Charleston, commissioners feared that boys might be "decoyed on board a vessel" which would then sail off with them as unwilling crew members.[10] Decoys might have been unnecessary to enlist some boys as crew members. Several shifty-looking men "in the habit of french Sailors" were seen about the gate of the Orphan House in spring 1796. They managed to chat with William Walters, aged sixteen, and Pierre ("Peter") Cournand, a native of Martinique who was only eleven years old, and by one account gave each boy ten dollars. A few days later Walters and Cournand broke out and made their way to the vicinity of Fort Johnson, on James Island southeast of the city. There they boarded a French privateer and sailed off before their parents or the French consul could be notified.[11] French privateers were particularly attractive to boys who had been born in Saint-Domingue, and with their knowledge of the language, those boys looked like prime recruits to the ship captains as well. Both Louis Tardieu and Joseph LeTillier were among those boys, and when last seen in 1794 they had been "laid hold of by some of the French privateers." Two commissioners visited the captain of the suspect vessel, who assured them that no boy would be allowed on board without their permission. Two days later the Orphan House advertised for the boys in the *City Gazette* in a manner reminiscent of runaway slave advertisements, although the commissioners promised to pay, "cheerfully," expenses rather than a reward.[12]

As the advertisement suggested, catching fugitives who had limited legal standing was something the commissioners had some experience with. And their attempts to retrieve escapees often succeeded, according to the many reports of captured children from the early republic period. In the chaos following the 1796 fire Thomas Oliver and Peter Cooper managed to escape. Within a few months, a commissioner announced that "he had received information" on Oliver and Cooper's whereabouts, and so the board agreed to pay "any expense attending their removal" and return to the Orphan House. The two managed to remain at large for another year before returning.[13] In 1802 George Long, who had been "enticed by a waggoner" to abscond, made it all the way to Charlotte, North Carolina, before being captured. The board paid the man who brought him back twenty dollars.[14] After twelve-year-old Mary Ann Hampton left early in 1803, the commissioners ordered a newspaper advertisement to announce her absence; she was "restored to the House" within a week.[15] Within five days of absconding, James Jones and Charles Smith had been captured "near the Twenty three miles house," probably near Moncks Corner in Berkeley District, about thirty miles north of the city.[16]

While early on the standard "correction" for escaping involved the lash, later captured fugitives were incarcerated. Mark Thomason ran away in November 1842 at the age of eleven. After having "gone into the country" for nearly three years, Orphan House agents tracked him down, returned him to the city, and locked him in the Guard House, the police fortress at the symbolic heart of the city, Meeting and Broad Streets. His punishment was simply a loss of privilege to participate in the anniversary ceremony and of permission to leave the Orphan House yard.[17] Perhaps as a consequence of such leniency the number of runaways soared in the 1850s. The steward noted the names of seven recent escapees in 1853, one of whom had left for the third or fourth time, and plaintively asked the commissioners for directions on what to do about them.[18]

SOME CHILDREN LEFT THE ORPHAN HOUSE to enter a family, but not their natal family and not as an apprentice. These children were adopted. The process of adoption at the Orphan House, and even the use of the term *adoption*, sheds substantially new light on the history of this institution. The history of legal adoption in the United States usually begins by acknowledging its absence in the common law tradition passed down from England to America.[19] Legal histories then skip forward to the 1851 Massachusetts "Act to Provide for the Adoption of Children." This law did not create something new that had not existed previously. Instead it codified the legal structure of adoption, which by that time was a widespread practice of long standing.[20]

All Orphan House children who left to enter an adoptive family proceeded according to customary, not legal, practice. Adults who applied to adopt an Orphan House resident in the pre-legal era included among their motivations the desire to raise a child, a hope of future companionship, and the intention of doing a good deed. As early as 1802, Frances Pearson, the wife of a mariner, explained to the commissioners:

> With a view to contribute my mite towards the assistance of my fellow creatures and to furnish myself with a suitable companion during the frequent absence of my husband, I am desirous of taking a girl out of Orphan House. I have obtained the consent of Ann Ford [the girl] and accordingly by the direction and favourable report of the Ladies who superintend the female economy of that institution, solicit your approbation.[21]

Perhaps unsure how to categorize this case, which was neither a mother hoping for custody restoration nor self-evidently a woman who wanted household help, commissioners approved the application but inscribed "Domestic" as Ann's future trade. Probably Mrs. Pearson started to train Ann in the domestic arts, especially infant care, but the remarkable part of this application is the invocation of companionship (just after charity) as the motivation for Mrs. Pearson's application.[22]

By the early republic era, the language of adoption had spread beyond the immediate confines of the Orphan House and its residents. In one case, a woman who would probably have been described earlier in this book as a foster mother asked the commissioners to receive "a child which she had adopted" long before nominating him for residency. In this case the mother was still alive and in the Poor House, but the boy's surname in some Orphan House records, Chartrand, was the same as that of the adoptive mother.[23]

As time went on the permanence of the adoptive relationship came to the fore. Applicants began to describe the place within the family that the Orphan House child could expect to hold. The first use of the term "adoption" occurred in 1816 when Mrs. M. L. Horlbeck wrote that she was "desirous of adopting as her own a little girl" named Eleanor Kennedy. As in the case with Frances Pearson and Ann Ford, Mrs. Horlbeck had visited with Eleanor to ask about her interest in such an arrangement. As soon as the commissioners received Mrs. Horlbeck's letter they bound Eleanor to her immediately.[24] In later years the commissioners made sure to inform the child's surviving mother, if they could locate her, of the impending adoption and obtain her consent.[25]

At first, the distinction between living in a master's family as an apprentice and becoming a family member through adoption was unclear. Indeed, after observing his apprentice's demeanor for a year, one master applied "to adopt him as his own."[26] Later, a woman who sought a young girl wrote that she "wish[ed] to adopt one of the children," but also noted that "her occupation will be principally to attend in my confectionary store."[27] Only over time did adoption come to omit reference to the children's work when incorporating children not born to a couple into their legal family. For example, in November 1814 Mrs. Amelia Mimms of Orangeburg District wrote the commissioners to ask about obtaining two particular children, Louisa Gardner, age 12, and Mary Turner, age 11. Mrs. Mimms proposed to teach the girls needlework, spinning, and weaving, as well as to provide "at least three months schooling in a year for two years." In addition to bringing the girls into her own house, she promised, "Mrs. Mimms engages to bring them up as her own children." Thus, not only would the girls learn a trade, but, assured by two reference letters from Mrs. Mimms's neighbors, commissioners could be reasonably sure of decent living conditions as well, at least no worse than the other children in the family. The commissioners bound the girls to Mrs. Mimms immediately, and for over three years their relationship must have worked well. In 1818, however, Mrs. Mimms returned both Louisa and Mary to the Orphan House, which bound them out again, this time separately, to new mistresses in the needle trades.[28] Soon after this time, commissioners began writing "adopted" in the space usually given over to the trade; a total of thirteen indentures are so inscribed. The grocer Thomas Christburg, whom the Court of Equity had appointed to be the guardian of the four orphaned Erhard children, offered "to adopt as his own" the last one remaining in the Orphan House, ten-year-old Eliza.

Christburg "pledge[d] to do for the said Eliza the same as if she were his own offspring," and so her indenture described her as "adopted by" Christburg but did not report any trade she was to learn.[29]

By the 1840s indentures for adoptees left blank the space in which a child's future trade would have been written, rendering them difficult to distinguish from cases of restoration of custody. One indenture with a missing trade illustrates yet another motive for adopting children. Andrew Milne, planter and cotton merchant, adopted a toddler named Mary Ann Winship in 1842. At this point, Milne was fifty-nine years old, and his wife, Elizabeth, was forty-six, and they were childless, so they may have adopted because they were unable to conceive their own. It seems to have been a successful relationship, because three years later Milne again approached the Orphan House. He and his wife were "so much pleased with" Mary Ann, who was "so much in want of a playmate," that they were "determined to give her a sister." Mrs. Milne had her heart set on four-year-old Virginia Karnes, despite the fact that she was "rather delicate." Milne went on to describe expectations that resembled present-day adoption cases. The Milnes did not want just any child. They had determined that Virginia was "the only one in the institution suiting [them] in appearance, age, &c," which may have referred to Virginia's status as one of very few toddlers in the Orphan House. Another part of her suitability was that "the chance of her being claimed" was "so unlikely" that the Milnes were "willing to run the risk" of her parents demanding her back. Virginia had come to the Orphan House's attention when, at two months of age, her parents left her in the hands of her grandmother and left Charleston. The long odds of their return appealed to Milne, who described himself as "one who shall not be wanting in his endeavors to promote her health and happiness." The commissioners bound Virginia to the Milnes the day after receiving his letter, leaving blank the space for her future trade.[30]

Other prospective adoptees included foundlings and older children who were related to inquiring adults by blood. Extended family members invoked adoption language with little self-consciousness. One aunt was "desirous of adopting Angelina Hutchins who is her relation," and another aunt whose situation had improved was able "to support the child . . . the same as for her own."[31] Yet another aunt had assured her niece's dying parents that she and her husband would "adopt her as [their] own and do a parents part by her."[32] Adoptive parents of foundlings expected that birth parents would not return for their child, and did not hesitate to say they saw that as an advantage. Nina Mazyck's name practically shouted her foundling status. She had no known connection to the prominent family of that name, but was

discovered on Mazyck Street not far from the Orphan House. One prospective father wrote that his wife was "anxious to bring her up and adopt her as
her own child" because they had "no children of [their] own." He confided
to the commissioners that he was "more induced to adopt her on account
of being a foundling, where no claim can ever be made for her by any person
claiming to be her parent."[33] This particular application failed; the successful adoptive father proposed "to adopt [Nina] as [his] own, pledging [him]self
to do a father's part towards her" and did not mention the unlikely return
of her birth parents.[34]

The lives of such adopted children may not have differed much from
those of any other children at the time. No documentation exists of their
experiences, but several prospective parents offered promises of how they
expected the children's lives to proceed. Foremost was the child's integration into the adoptive family, and that chiefly consisted of not assigning
drudge work to the young person. As Ann Campbell noted in her application
for Mary Riley, "Mary's services are of no consideration to us. I only wish
her (from the regard I have for Mary) to live with us as one of our children."
A further sign of a serious parent was a promise to educate the child along
with some understanding of the purpose of such education. Mrs. Manson on
Sullivan's Island proposed to give her young niece Angelina Hutchins "an
education, to set her for maintaining herself by teaching." To the Goodrich
family Mary Shirer appeared to be both adoptive child and apprentice. From
conversations with her the Goodriches knew that she had no living relatives, and so Mr. Goodrich expected her to "look up to [him] & Mrs G as her
only protectors." They also expected that Mrs. Goodrich would teach her
sewing, and that Mr. Goodrich, a former teacher, would give her all the book
learning and practical instruction she would need later in life. Indeed, they
hoped that life in their home would induce Mary to "remain with [them]
even longer than the time specified by the indentures." But the relationship
lasted barely a year, and Mary then entered another household.[35]

Two of the most distinguished alumni of the Orphan House were
universally described as adoptees, although their paths into new families
were not quite so straightforward. They were Christopher Gustavus Memminger, future Treasury Secretary of the Confederate States, and Thomas
Holdup Stevens, a distinguished naval officer. Memminger was born in
1803 in Württemberg to Christopher Godfrey Memminger, a quartermaster,
and Eberhardina Kohler. His father died not long after his birth, and so his
grandfather, mother, and young Christopher emigrated to America around
1806, arriving in Charleston where Christopher's grandmother, Magdalena
Kohler, had already been living. Soon after arrival Eberhardina died, making

Christopher a full orphan. Magdalena then nominated Christopher for admission to the Orphan House. Although her initial appeal carried endorsements from three men, including the Lutheran minister John Faber, the commissioners waited six weeks to approve it, perhaps due to the family's status as recent immigrants. Once admitted, however, within a few years young Gustavus showed "a great native genius, particularly in mathematics," sufficient for him to be sent to Isaac Bennett for additional tutoring. In October 1813 he was given the great honor of addressing the crowd at the annual celebration of the Orphan House's anniversary. He delivered his speech with "ease and gracefulness of manner," and the crowd replied with "enraptured applause."

Once Memminger's promise was recognized, a leader of Charleston's white elite stepped forward to take the boy in and prepare him for better things. Thomas Bennett Jr., son of the Orphan House designer and builder, and himself future governor of South Carolina, informally adopted Memminger. Memminger then spent two years in the Bennett household, forming a lifelong friendship with Bennett's son W. J. Bennett. Both would eventually serve as Orphan House commissioners. In 1815 Memminger left the Bennett home and Charleston for the South Carolina College, where he distinguished himself in the study of the law. Thomas Bennett sponsored his first two years in Columbia, and then the state of South Carolina provided for Memminger as the Orphan House's annual scholarship boy at the college. He returned to join the law office of Joseph Bennett, the governor's brother, and began his ascent through local and regional politics that led to his cabinet post in the Confederate government.[36]

Thomas Holdup was the oldest of three brothers who entered the Orphan House very early in the nineteenth century. Like Memminger, Holdup made a quick impression on Orphan House officials, but in this case negatively so: after being accused of theft he was whipped. The punishment resulted in a considerable change of attitude. In 1808 the board authorized two commissioners to seek a warrant for Holdup's appointment as a midshipman in the US Navy. With the assistance of another commissioner, Revolutionary War veteran Daniel Stevens, they succeeded. Stevens's role in obtaining this warrant is not clear, but official naval histories describe his action as having "adopted" the boy in the process. After a few years in the Navy, Holdup felt himself a changed young man and attributed his maturation to his adoption by Stevens. To demonstrate his new identity in 1815 at the age of 20 he arranged for the South Carolina legislature to formally change his surname so that he would thenceforth be Thomas Holdup Stevens.[37]

Armed with a new quadrant from the Orphan House, Holdup sailed off
as an apprentice naval officer in 1809. Within weeks, from the sloop of war
Hornet he wrote the commissioners to acknowledge "the kindness done
him when a member of this House," which pleased the commissioners
immensely. In the War of 1812 Holdup volunteered for Great Lakes duty,
where he participated in amphibious commando attacks early in the war. At
age eighteen, he commanded the sloop *Trippe* in the Battle of Lake Erie, in
which he pierced the British line and then turned and attacked from the rear.
He attained command of larger ships during and after the war, until in 1836
he became a captain, then the highest naval rank. At the time of his death
he was commander of the Washington Navy Yard. The Navy later named
a destroyer (no. 86) *Stevens* to honor him, and a later destroyer *Stevens*
(DD-479) to honor him and his son, another distinguished naval officer.[38]

AS TIME WENT ON, AN EVER GREATER SHARE of children returned to some reconfiguration of their natal family. After the disruption in that family that
brought the child to the Orphan House in the first place, the makeup of the
family to which a child returned could vary considerably. In rare cases two
married parents sought the return of their child, typically after the mother
alone had brought them to the Orphan House and then later the father had
found steady work or recovered his health.[39] Alternatively, extended family
members retained an interest in the child and sought his return and integration into their families. In many cases they used the language of adoption
and presumably intended to treat the young relative as family. Thus, Francis Knieff asked for custody of Sarah Adams, his sister-in-law, because his
wife was "greatly attached" to her sister.[40]

Often enough, however, the request for custody followed some development in the receiving branch of the family, not always for the better.
Elizabeth Kennedy wanted to bring her niece Susannah Thompson into her
home after the death of her husband, expecting that "she will be a companion to me & I will be a friend to her."[41] Some efforts by extended kin to retrieve a child suggested underlying conflict within the family that the new
event had revealed. Lilias Denoon and her son Henry and daughter Margaret
lived with her brother or brother-in-law, Campbell Douglas. Lilias was fast
wearing out her welcome by drinking too much. "[O]f late her habits are
so bad that I cannot have her in the house any longer," Douglas wrote, and
further, he believed her "totally unfit to bring up children." In January 1837
Douglas petitioned the Orphan House to admit the boy and girl, and Denoon endorsed this move by signing their indentures. Within two months a

family named Keenan had adopted Margaret with the approval of Douglas. Around this time when Lilias was "not in a situation to transack business," according to Douglas, he obtained guardianship of Henry. That summer, Lilias may have achieved a degree of sobriety, and certainly had a change of mind regarding her son. Without permission from the Orphan House, she brought Henry back home. Her efforts to hide him from the commissioners brought a threat of legal action, after which she surrendered Henry to the Orphan House. Within weeks of her death in October 1838, Douglas abruptly informed the commissioners, "There is no longer any necessity for [Henry] to remain in the institution." And so he exercised his right as next of kin to "take the boy into [his] family."[42] In another case, Mary Barnes hoped to receive her niece, Catherine Bull, after some five years in the Orphan House. Catherine's mother had moved to New York after remarrying a man named Cantwell, and Mrs. Barnes suggested to the commissioners, "I believe it is well known to you that she and her present husband are not proper persons to have the care of her." She concluded, "I feel towards her as if she were my own child, and my husband and myself have the means of taking care of her."[43]

Other distant kin offered to take children in, but in an indirect fashion, thereby illustrating twists and turns in the children's lives as well as the breadth of their family connections. A woman wrote from New York to gain custody of Henry Pregnall. She claimed to be his aunt and for a time to have been his chief caregiver after Henry's mother abandoned him "when he was just twenty months old." Her father, Henry's grandfather, then moved to Charleston with Henry in tow. Upon the grandfather's death, she wrote, "it makes me feel very uneasy that the child is left there without any friends to take care of him." The commissioners apparently lost this letter and Henry remained in the Orphan House.[44] A local attorney, George W. Cross, initially asked the Orphan House to admit his three nephews with the hopeful contingency that the boys' grandfather in Rhode Island would "probably send for them" and so "these children may not be longer in the House than a few months." Indeed, a year later a local merchant named James Fife arranged passage to Rhode Island for the boys, which the Orphan House gladly paid.[45] In a third case, Mary Ann Myatt acknowledged that her brothers Edward and Lewis were "so discontented . . . thay where so verry discontented" at the Orphan House that they repeatedly ran away. Because her mother was unable to care for them, she offered to take them herself, promising to bind the older one to a trade and to send the younger one to school.[46]

THE SHAPE OF THE FAMILY to which children most commonly returned was much like the one from which they had appeared: a family headed by one parent (usually the mother) or by their mother's new husband. Among those children whose custody the Orphan House transferred to family members, the share who returned to parents rather than extended kin fell steadily from the 1790s (86 percent) to the 1840s (75 percent), but then in the 1850s it rebounded to 92 percent. The last decade before the war saw an influx of immigrants, mainly Irish and German, to Charleston, many of whose children ended up in the Orphan House for a time. The increased share of children returning to parents in the 1850s may reflect a conscious strategy on the part of those parents to use the Orphan House for temporary child care until the newly arrived family could stand on firmer financial footing.[47]

As time went on, it became more common for a child to return to his or her mother after she had married again. Mothers began to inform commissioners that it was now in their power to support, maintain, and even educate their children, hence the petition to restore custody. Indentures usually describe the person receiving the child as "mother" or "father" rather than by name, but it appears to have become increasingly common for the mother to sign with a different surname when she petitioned for restoration of custody. Of the 266 children bound into the Orphan House in the 1790s, eighteen (7 percent) were eventually returned to mothers. Four of these women had new surnames, and no doubt some of the unnamed others had remarried as well. Two children were returned to still-married parents, but in no cases did a father alone come back to reclaim his offspring. The share of mothers who had remarried increased over time. Of the 518 children bound in during the 1850s, 130 (25 percent) were returned to mothers and 12 to fathers. Here all fourteen mothers who were listed by name had remarried.

Petitions for restoration of custody give a fuller picture of the roles of stepfathers in a high-mortality regime. Widows were numerous, and their legal and financial quandaries common. When they remarried, the fates of their children were heavily influenced by the attitudes of their husbands. In the early republic, it was common for the new husband to deny his wife's children access to family resources and force them to the Orphan House. Then later in the antebellum era, a new husband enabled many a widow to regain custody of her children by allowing them access to the new family's resources. The transformation of step-patriarchy in this way indicates subtle shifts in the structure of white Southern families of the lower classes.[48]

Throughout this period, improved family finances were a powerful factor in enabling parents to recover their children from the Orphan House.

Widowed mothers who had remarried were potentially in a sounder economic position to resume custody. As early as 1796, Sarah Syms, formerly Sarah McKenzie, sought the return of her daughter Margaret, because, she informed the Orphan House, she was "now in circumstances to support her." Since Mrs. Syms had nominated Margaret by herself five years previously, her change of surname indicated a recent remarriage which accounted for her improved circumstances. Perhaps due to legal disabilities imposed on married women, Mrs. Syms did not appeal directly to the commissioners; instead a sympathetic man contacted the Orphan House on her behalf. Ultimately, her daughter, by this time aged nine, was delivered to her on the day the commissioners heard her case.[49]

Remarried women frequently reported that they were faring better materially than they had as widows. When Susan Adams Ridley first approached the Orphan House to take in her two sons, she had no trouble finding three men deemed trustworthy by the commissioners who would confirm her claim of poverty. Then at some point during the boys' time in the Orphan House, she wrote, "I have changed my situation by marriage and through my industry and that of my husband we have acquired some little property and are now capable of providing for these children." She assured the commissioners that Ridley, her new husband, had promised to do everything in his power to raise and educate the boys.[50] Indeed, an even more powerful witness was testimony from the stepfather himself. After John Burns had married the former Maryann Cook, a reversal caused her to send her son from a previous marriage to the Poor House. In May 1845, the Poor House ordered James Cook, just two years old at the time, sent to the Orphan House. A few months later, Burns, while unable to write in the articulate style of some parents or friendly scribes, made a detailed request for custody of his stepson:

> These few lines is to request you to let me have my son, as I am abel to support it my-self. I am truly thankful for the care whitch was taken of him during my misfortune, and am know abel and willing to take him and support him my-self, and he shal never be trouble any more. my business is a seaman, and riger whitch I am working at, and earns my $2.00 a day. my house is in Bufain Street No 40, and my childs name is James Coock. my-self and my wife live comfortably togeth. the child is my step-son. your most obt applicant John and Maryann Burns[51]

The material wealth of the stepfather was a necessary condition to reunite his new wife with her offspring. The sufficient condition was his desire to recover his stepchildren, and, in general, the degree of this desire increased over time. It became increasingly common for the new husband to permit his wealth to be spent on his new bride's offspring. Alexander Ballard informed the board "that he had married Mrs. Margaret Jackman the mother of Elizabeth Jackman, whom he now requests from the Orphan House as he is able to maintain and educate her."[52] While Mrs. Jackman was unable to support Elizabeth, not only was the new Mrs. Ballard able to care for her daughter, she and her new husband chose to do so, and there are many, many such cases in the records. Despite the legal doctrine of coverture, in which the wife's legal status was hidden behind that of the husband, some remarried mothers directly addressed the Orphan House rather than applying for their child through their new husband: "I respectfully beg that he may be restored to me," wrote one.[53] Martha Deliesseline anxiously wrote the commissioners: "I have taken to myself a husband, I now feel capable of taking care of my sons, John & Isaac, I would wish to take them from the Orphant Asylum if this meets your approbation. Please send me an answer as soon as possible."[54] All such cases of restoration illustrate how bonds between mother and child persisted after the child's institutionalization.

Some remarried widows recognized the importance of their new husbands' cooperation. Elizabeth Headwright Lodus Rhodes was illiterate, but she never lacked the ability to have letters written for her to the commissioners. As Elizabeth Headwright she was widowed around 1811, when her son William Headwright was born, or possibly in 1812, when she brought her daughters Evelina, aged five, and Mary, aged seven, to the Orphan House. At that time, she kept the infant William, a common strategy among mothers with several children, and a plan that also reflected Orphan House preferences for older children. In 1815 the burden of caring for a toddler as a single mother became too great, and a floridly literate friend wrote a letter for her in the third person, reporting, "[She] flatters herself that she shall again experience the liberality of the commissioners," and including her wishes for William's further education. She did not realize it, but she had hit bottom and things would start looking up soon. By 1817 she had remarried to a Mr. Lodus (or possibly Louis; neither appears in the city directories), whose job as a butcher provided a steady income. Her amanuensis wrote, this time in the first person, that the income provided by Lodus, "enables me to assist my children." At this point she was able to recover her daughter Mary immediately, but her other daughter, Evelina, had already been bound out as a domestic. Elizabeth had to wait until 1821, when Evelina's mistress, now in New York, wanted to send her back to Charleston. Elizabeth was very happy to have all her children back together, thanks to the "industrious good man" Lodus.[55] In the nearly two centuries since, no husband has received a higher compliment.

Commissioners had to decide whether to return a child to a remarried mother, and did not always approve of the potential reunion. Sometimes "due consideration of the character" of the mother motivated the denial. In other cases, the mother's situation looked fine but the commissioners determined that the child suffered from an "incompleteness" that could be remedied by more time in the Orphan House. But the commissioners might also get worn down by a mother's persistence, as in the case of Sarah Jane Gilbert. She had entered the Orphan House at the end of 1841 with four siblings, all of whom still lived there when their mother and stepfather began their campaign for the return of Sarah, the oldest. Over the course of 1843 her mother and stepfather petitioned the commissioners several times for her return. Each time visiting commissioners returned with reports that it was "inexpedient" for Sarah to join the new family. But inexpedient for whom? In November the commissioners finally concluded that "the anxiety of both mother & daughter was so great that it would be useless to refuse" another request, and so Sarah, now aged fourteen, and her mother reunited. But it turned out that Sarah's extra months in the Orphan House had benefited the institution as well. A week after she left, the matron complained that Sarah's exit left "no girl large enough to take her place" in washing the laundry, and so she asked for a servant to assume Sarah's duties. In this case the needs of the Orphan House may have postponed the official disposition of a request by a mother and her new husband.[56]

In addition to the fundamental desire of mothers and children to be near each other, particular factors moved women to recover their children. Because so many women continued to visit their children, they were aware when their children became ill and sought to aid their recovery by bringing them home for a brief time. Robert Clements appeared to be a fragile boy. Within a couple of years of his admission, an Orphan House nurse recommended to his mother that she bring him home for a visit, saying, "[H]e frets very much." His mother did so, but only temporarily, and not long after his return to the Orphan House, another nurse made the same recommendation, now noting that Robert was "dwindling almost to nothing." His mother had remarried to a man who was "very willing" to bring Robert home because "if he remain[ed] in the Orphan House," she wrote, "he no doubt would be in a short time consigned to the grave." Her efforts restored Robert to health, and some years later he was bound as an apprentice currier and tanner to an Alabamian.[57] Mothers understood the importance of their care. Ann Holway argued that the "peculiar disease" that afflicted her daughter required "a mother's unceasing & devoted attention."[58] Elizabeth Wolley's employer endorsed her appeal for her son by informing the commissioners that releasing her son Charles to her care "would be instrumental in saving a child evidently in bad health."[59]

WHILE SOME CHILDREN RETURNED to a mother who had remarried, others returned to a mother who had not. Typically, these women had recovered some semblance of economic security without the aid of a new husband, which alone makes their situations worth further scrutiny. In these cases the record reads that a mother with the same surname as a particular child wanted him or her back, and the board agreed with the motion.[60] Sometimes the mother reported that she was able to raise the child, but without explaining what had changed since poverty brought them to the Orphan House originally. In a very few cases the mother managed to improve her situation by her own persistence. When Elizabeth Wolley applied for her son's admission in February 1819, her claim of poverty was considerably strengthened by the endorsement it carried from no less than Charles Cotesworth Pinckney, one of the very best-known Charlestonians of the day. Within a few months, her son's health had deteriorated to the point that she wished to retrieve him. "[F]aithful & industrious" according to her employer, Mrs. Wolley had somehow set aside fifty dollars "in ready money" and was earning seven dollars a month. If the commissioners returned the boy to her, she planned to board him out at three dollars a month and would send him to a free school until his health recovered sufficiently for him to be bound apprentice.[61] Similarly, Elizabeth Welch asked for the return of her daughters because she had received "[a]n offer . . . to go into the country" where she could "obtain enough to support" them.[62] But these sorts of jobs were not very remunerative, nor were they very common.

In many situations a woman did receive help from a man she knew, typically a family member. Brothers came through with offers to support their sisters, or as tradesmen themselves they offered to take on a nephew as an apprentice. Isabella Doyle had particular luck in this regard, as she had hired into the household of Dr. Samuel Henry Dickson, a prominent local physician. When Dickson traveled to New York in summer 1835 to investigate a teaching position in a medical college there, Mrs. Doyle accompanied the family and visited her brothers. Not only were the men "very solicitous to have my children," she wrote, but Dickson, himself a future commissioner of the Orphan House, had the opportunity to meet the uncles and confirm to the board that they were in fact "willing and able to support" the two Doyle boys, aged ten and eight.[63] Other brothers who aided their sisters and nephews lived as far away as Alabama and were tradesmen and merchants, but in all cases it was the mother, acting as an intermediary, who officially received the child from the Orphan House.[64] Some women also received assistance from sympathetic clergy. The Catholic bishop John England continued to look out for the Gallagher children after they had entered the Orphan House. His offer to provide for John Gallagher's education led Dorothy Gallagher to petition the Orphan House for his release, and they transferred John's indentures to her, again as an intermediary, right away.[65]

THE CITY ORDINANCE that established the Orphan House explicitly charged it with "supporting and educating poor orphan children, and those of the poor, distressed and disabled parents," but implicitly the city wanted the Orphan House to care for white children.[66] Later, free persons of color formed their own charitable societies that cared for widows and orphans of members, such as the Brown Fellowship Society, founded 1790, and specifically for orphans, the Minors' Moralist Society, founded 1803. But the free black community, riven with its own class distinctions, had too little in the way of resources to care for all the children of poor, distressed, disabled, and deceased persons of color.[67] In two cases at least, the solution was to try to pass fair-skinned children as white to get them into the Orphan House. The partial success of these attempts only became clear when the mothers of the children came to retrieve them.

The early years of Caroline Lafar were murkier than those of most Orphan House children. At four years of age, she was nominated for admission by Mrs. Rebecca Ashford. Caroline had "been abandoned by her inhuman mother and left in the charge of a negro woman in a most deplorable state," in Mrs. Ashford's telling. Caroline entered the Orphan House that day. Five years later, in August 1812, "a mulatto woman" named Mary Flinch appeared at the Orphan House and, claiming to be Caroline Lafar's mother, asked for her daughter back. We cannot know how Mary Flinch convinced the commissioners of her story, only that her claim was "proven to the satisfaction of the Board," and that Caroline returned to her. The commissioners were likely surprised but happy to send out a free child of color, but the story raises further questions. Why did Mary Flinch abandon her child, and why did she return for her? Was Mary Flinch the "negro woman" who was caring for Caroline when Rebecca Ashford found the girl, and if so, was the "inhuman mother" a fictional white person whom Flinch created to make her daughter seem white? Was Caroline's father a prominent white man who approved of her return to her mother but did not want his paternity acknowledged in the written record? Except to note that at midcentury

Caroline was still in Charleston and unmarried at the age of fifty, the historical record is silent on the later lives of Mary Flinch and Caroline Lafar.[68]

Commissioners recognized and disposed of a similar case much more quickly a few years later. It began in 1819 with the death of the husband, as so many cases did. Seven months later the widow, Rachael Burbridge, found it impossible to manage all five of her children, and she hoped to place three of them into the Orphan House. Because Rachael was illiterate, several citizens wrote the commissioners on her behalf. A bit of research on the board's part revealed that one of the three Burbridge children was too old, but no comments appeared in writing about the other two, eleven-year-old Alfred and nine-year-old Harriott. The siblings entered the Orphan House two days after the board heard their case. Within two weeks, however, the board received the disturbing news that Alfred and Harriott "are now supposed to be coloured children" and ordered Rachael to appear for a discussion of the matter. Rather than submit to the board's interrogation, however, she arranged to send a letter that snapped with indignation: "Gentlemen, If you do not think that my children are white enough you will be pleased to send them home to me & I shall endeavor to maintain them." And that is exactly what happened: Alfred and Harriott returned to their mother the day that letter was written.[69] The record does not disclose how the commissioners learned of the Burbridge children's surprising ancestry.

A final family grouping accounted for a steady number of cases each year, that of fathers returning to obtain their children. It is more difficult to speak of general patterns in this group, in part because the nature of the records would keep any remarriage of a widowed father hidden (because his name did not change), and in part because fewer fathers than mothers returned for children (both because fewer children were sponsored at entrance by fathers than by mothers, and because after admission fathers continued to suffer higher mortality risk than did mothers). As with mothers, many men simply stated that their circumstances had changed and they were now able to provide for their children and to educate them.[70] A few provided clues as to the source of the improvement in their lives. Some had returned to Charleston from years away in which they had pursued business opportunities or served in the military.[71] Others regained health or sobriety.[72] Several made sure to note that their wives approved of their efforts.[73] Easily the most interesting, if unrepresentative, case was that of Thomas Gayner Jr., who came to the Orphan House in 1809. His sponsor was the state coroner in the absence of his father, who was about to be tried for the murder of his wife. Immediately upon his acquittal six months later, he applied to the Orphan House for restoration of custody. Because Thomas Jr. had never

completed an indenture that bound him to the Orphan House, the commissioners concluded, they had no reason not to return him to his father.[74]

JUST AS CHILDREN WHO RETURNED to some reconfiguration of their natal
families met a variety of new family structures, those who remained in the
Orphan House encountered a range of experiences. For those children who
survived and chose not to run away, but whose parents or other family members did not return for them, their experiences were in the labor market. As
their indentures called for, they were bound out as apprentices to masters
and mistresses, and their stories are the subject of the next chapter.

CHAPTER EIGHT

Apprenticeship

E ASILY THE MOST COMMON OUTCOME at the end of a child's time in the
Orphan House was to be bound out apprentice to learn a trade. Almost
three-fifths of the 2,000-plus children who came through the Orphan House
before the Civil War left to enter a master's house. This proportion is a rough
estimate; the previous chapter noted that children whose future involved
integration into a new family as an adoptee were often assigned a trade in
their indenture, as were some children who returned to a reconfiguration of
their natal family. If we accept the three-fifths figure as a rough average over
the entire period, it is important to note that in each decade the average
trended downward. The share of children who were bound as apprentices
declined over time, and the share returning to family increased, so that by
the time of the Civil War a child was about as likely to go back to family as
out to a master. Still, if as a rough approximation we can treat information
in indentures as literally true concerning the child's future, then from 1790
to 1860 about twice as many Orphan House alumni became apprentices
as returned to family. Thus, apprenticeship was in fact the most common
outcome for Orphan House children.[1]

The demand for Orphan House children as apprentices, especially where
boys were concerned, derived in large part from the pace and type of Charleston's economic activities. From the beginning of the nineteenth century
the trend in Charleston's economy was, relative to the South and cities
elsewhere in the country, mostly downward. When Charleston established
the Orphan House in 1790, it was the richest city in the nation. Studies of
probate records indicate that per-capita wealth of Charleston was twice that
of New England and the middle colonies, even including the substantial
slave population. Unbeknownst at the time, the city was near the peak of
its prosperity, and economic decline began early in the nineteenth century.

Development of the cotton gin initiated greater upland short-staple cotton production, but this occurred far from Charleston, in the western states of Alabama, Mississippi, and Louisiana. In 1810 South Carolina produced half the cotton grown in the South; by 1821 that share had fallen to 28 percent, and by 1834 it had fallen further to 15 percent. Gradually the center of the Southern economy was shifting westward, ever farther away from Charleston.[2]

In part as a hedge against the relative decline in cotton exports, some Charleston entrepreneurs tried to establish manufacturing businesses. One of the most prominent entrepreneurs was the eccentric apothecary-naturalist John L. E. W. "Doc" Shecut. His South Carolina Homespun Company did not survive the War of 1812, but it foreshadowed similar, later efforts. The devastating Panic of 1819, combined with a worldwide decline in cotton prices, led to increased interest in industrial and mercantile activities. By the time of Robert Mills's 1826 survey, the city held "two or three" iron foundries, "seven or eight" establishments powered by steam, including two each for rice and corn processing, and four sawmills.[3]

Charleston continued to industrialize slowly and very incompletely, which was typical of Southern cities. Through the next several decades, the number of mechanics and artisans in Charleston, many of them slaves or free persons of color, has been estimated at 1,200 to 1,500. Many tradesmen hired apprentices to help run their shops, and so provided work and homes for young people, including Orphan House alumni. Relative to northern cities, industry in Charleston had developed in only limited fashion, but by late in the antebellum period, Charleston was the third most prominent manufacturing center in the South, behind Richmond and New Orleans. Its industries included iron foundries, rice mills, gristmills, shipyards, carriage and wagon shops, saddleries, and brickyards.[4]

Within the old city, planters who saw Charleston as a pleasant residence contended with merchants who wanted to revive the city's economy. Symbolic of planter victory, the rail line from the cotton growing upcountry ended not far from the Orphan House at the city's boundary. The tracks were kept away from the old residential district, and, as a result, well short of the wharves from whence that cotton was shipped to textile manufacturers across the Atlantic world. But the planters could not hold this line forever. In the 1850s the city finally allowed the Charleston and Savannah and the Northeastern Railroads to extend their tracks to the dock area. The extension came too late. If railroads had arrived in the Holy City, broader economic development had passed it by, and as a result Charleston's wealth had already declined dramatically relative to that of the great northern cities. By Southern if not national standards, on the eve of the war, Charleston remained prosperous, but its days of economic prominence and dynamic growth were gone forever.[5]

That absence of large-scale industry aided the young folk of the Orphan House, because local manufactures tended to be made in small shops that hired apprentices. In eighteenth-century Charleston those shops and their apprentices were numerous. The market for apprentices was active and fluid. In the middle of the century advertisements for apprentice carpenters of either race promised graduated wages as the young man learned more of his trade. For the master, an apprentice typically brought with him a premium of twenty pounds, but as with unbonded orphan apprentices, many craft apprentices ran away or otherwise did not pan out. For those who completed their term as apprentices, a productive stint as journeyman brought admission to local societies of barbers, carpenters, coopers, mechanics, or tailors. Other craftsmen at the high end of the Charleston economy, such as silversmiths and cabinet makers, also employed apprentices. Into the early part of the nineteenth century furniture shops hired both black and white apprentices, and movement of apprentices between shops was easy and frequent.[6]

The later antebellum period saw the rise of racial conflict within skilled and unskilled labor markets. Opportunities for white craft apprentices were declining in the face of competition not only from journeymen, but from enslaved and free black craftsmen. In Charleston white artisans recognized the effects of competition from slave artisans who were hired out; the drumbeat of their complaints throughout the antebellum period indicates ongoing tension between the two groups. White artisans in Charleston petitioned the state in the 1820s: "The Black Mechanics enjoy as complete a Monopoly as if it were secured to them by Law." These monopolies were based on moral-economic networks of slave domestics to whom owners had delegated the authority to choose craftsmen to work in the house, and these women chose men whom they knew. White artisans hoped that these arrangements, monopolistic in their eyes, could be destroyed under common law. And so began legal efforts to drive out black craftsmen from Charleston. The city threatened to enslave free blacks who could not produce proof of their status. The state considered a bill to restrict free blacks to work only as day laborers and domestic servants. Hundreds of black craftsmen left the city and the state. But in the end Pyrrhic victories of the state over black tradesmen could not yield additional openings for Orphan House apprentices.[7]

Efforts to use apprentices in the occasional large-scale industrial start-up had mixed results. Especially when seeking capital from investors or financial assistance from the state, projectors liked to emphasize how they would employ the poor, as if they were launching a charity. Doc Shecut's South Carolina Homespun Company sought young folk who were to be styled apprentices, at the same time as Shecut solicited investment to finance its efforts to employ the indigent. Young workers from the Orphan House could perform double duty as both apprentices and indigent, and this ambiguity may have led to the commissioners' rejection of Shecut's applications for child workers. Not long after Shecut's proposals came another request from a prospective master whom the commissioners hesitated to rebuff, to the disappointment of all parties. David R. Williams, mill owner, obtained several apprentices from the Orphan House but was unimpressed with them. Williams also happened to be governor of South Carolina, which put him in a unique position to improve the preparation of young folk for work. His solution was compulsory school attendance, but compulsory only for the poor, and without regard to parental consent.[8] Orphan House children, then, made capable craft apprentices but inadequate industrial apprentices, a reflection of the Charleston economy as a whole.

THE PRINTED DOCUMENT CALLED THE INDENTURE codified all the terms of the contract that bound the parent, child, commissioner, and master. The form of the document confirms that binding a child out to a master was the expected result of a child's time in the Orphan House. Figure 8.1 below is an image of the rather typical indenture of John Fordham. According to the indenture, on February 20, 1817, Eliza Fordham bound her son John into the Orphan House, with his brother Benjamin, whose own indenture appears next to John's in the "Indenture Book." At that time John was eight years old and had already learned to write his name. From other records we know that Eliza retrieved John and Benjamin for a period of unknown length beginning in 1819, but at some point thereafter they came back to the Orphan House. On March 18, 1824, John signed the second half of his indenture, which bound him to John Leck, a farmer and blacksmith in Laurens District, about 175 miles northwest of Charleston. In other public apprenticeship systems, contracts were written out longhand, so that particular terms could be negotiated by town fathers and masters.[9] By this time in Charleston, much of the indenture was printed in standard boilerplate, in which most terms of the contract were fixed and not open to negotiation. Some blanks were intended to be filled in with the possessive

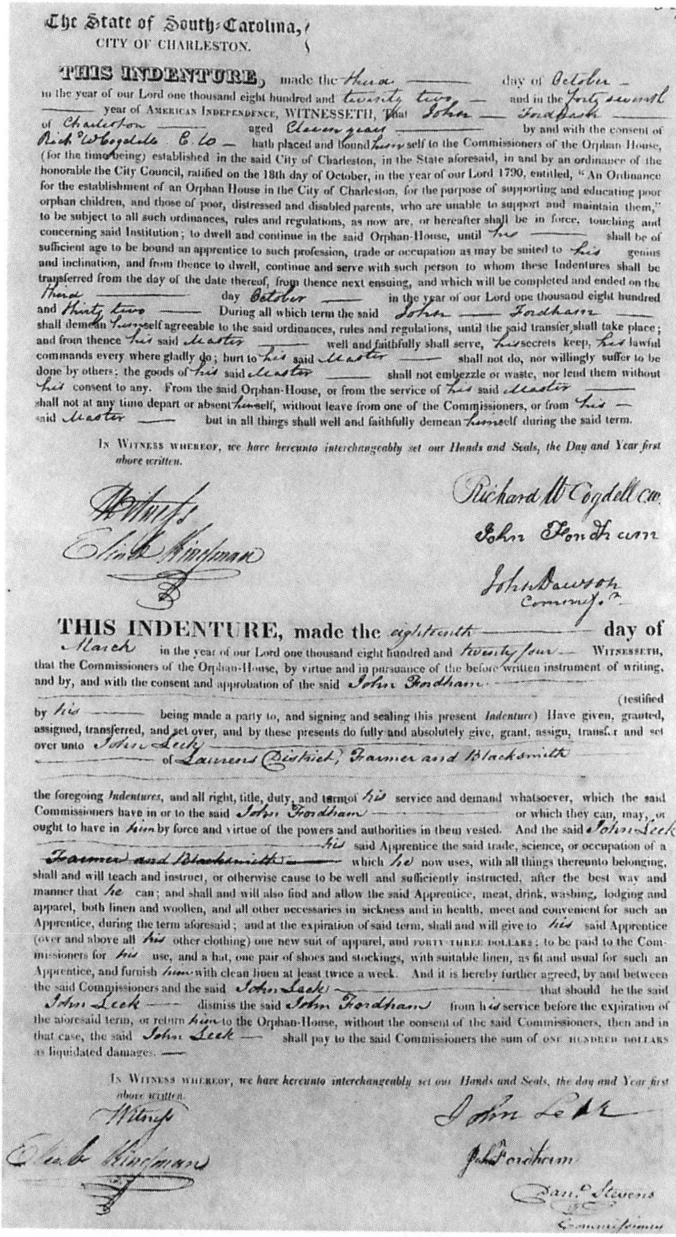

The State of South-Carolina,
CITY OF CHARLESTON.

THIS INDENTURE, made the *third* day of *October* in the year of our Lord one thousand eight hundred and *twenty two*, and in the *forty seventh* year of AMERICAN INDEPENDENCE, WITNESSETH, That *John Fordham* of *Charleston* aged *Eleven years* by and with the consent of *Rich. W. Cogdell E. Co.* hath placed and bound *himself* to the Commissioners of the Orphan-House, (for the time being) established in the said City of Charleston, in the State aforesaid, in and by an ordinance of the honorable the City Council, ratified on the 18th day of October, in the year of our Lord 1790, entitled, "An Ordinance for the establishment of an Orphan House in the City of Charleston, for the purpose of supporting and educating poor orphan children, and those of poor, distressed and disabled parents, who are unable to support and maintain them," to be subject to all such ordinances, rules and regulations, as now are, or hereafter shall be in force, touching and concerning said Institution; to dwell and continue in the said Orphan-House, until *his* shall be of sufficient age to be bound an apprentice to such profession, trade or occupation as may be suited to *his* genius and inclination, and from thence to dwell, continue and serve with such person to whom these Indentures shall be transferred from the day of the date thereof, from thence next ensuing, and which will be completed and ended on the *third* day *October* in the year of our Lord one thousand eight hundred and *thirty two*. During all which term the said *John Fordham* shall demean *himself* agreeable to the said ordinances, rules and regulations, until the said transfer shall take place; and from thence *his* said *Master* well and faithfully shall serve, *his* secrets keep, *his* lawful commands every where gladly do; hurt to *his* said *Master* shall not do, nor willingly suffer to be done by others; the goods of *his* said *Master* shall not embezzle or waste, nor lend them without *his* consent to any. From the said Orphan-House, or from the service of *his* said *Master* shall not at any time depart or absent *himself*, without leave from one of the Commissioners, or from *his* said *Master* but in all things shall well and faithfully demean *himself* during the said term.

IN WITNESS WHEREOF, *we have hereunto interchangeably set our Hands and Seals, the Day and Year first above written.*

Richard W. Cogdell E. Co.
John Fordham
John Dawson Comm.

THIS INDENTURE, made the *eighteenth* day of *March* in the year of our Lord one thousand eight hundred and *twenty four*, WITNESSETH, that the Commissioners of the Orphan-House, by virtue and in pursuance of the before written instrument of writing, and by, and with the consent and approbation of the said *John Fordham* by *his* being made a party to, and signing and sealing this present *Indenture*) Have given, granted, assigned, transferred, and set over, and by these presents do fully and absolutely give, grant, assign, transfer and set over unto *John Leek* of *Laurens District, Farmer and Blacksmith* the foregoing Indentures, and all right, title, duty, and term of *his* service and demand whatsoever, which the said Commissioners have in or to the said *John Fordham* or which they can, may, or ought to have in *him* by force and virtue of the powers and authorities in them vested. And the said *John Leek* *his* said Apprentice to the said trade, science, or occupation of a *Farmer and Blacksmith* which *he* now uses, with all things thereunto belonging, shall and will teach and instruct, or otherwise cause to be well and sufficiently instructed, after the best way and manner that *he* can; and shall and will also find and allow the said Apprentice, meat, drink, washing, lodging and apparel, both linen and woollen, and all other necessaries in sickness and in health, meet and convenient for such an Apprentice, during the term aforesaid; and at the expiration of said term, shall and will give to *his* said Apprentice (over and above all *his* other clothing) one new suit of apparel, and FORTY-THREE DOLLARS; to be paid to the Commissioners for *his* use, and a hat, one pair of shoes and stockings, with suitable linen, as fit and usual for such an Apprentice, and furnish *him* with clean linen at least twice a week. And it is hereby further agreed, by and between the said Commissioners and the said *John Leek* that should he the said *John Leek* dismiss the said *John Fordham* from his service before the expiration of the aforesaid term, or return *him* to the Orphan-House, without the consent of the said Commissioners, then and in that case, the said *John Leek* shall pay to the said Commissioners the sum of ONE HUNDRED DOLLARS as liquidated damages.

IN WITNESS WHEREOF, *we have hereunto interchangeably set our Hands and Seals, the day and Year first above written.*

John Leek
John Fordham
Dan. Stevens Commissioner

Fig. 8.1. Indenture of John Fordham.
Original image by Terry Richardson. Courtesy Charleston County Public Library.
Source: Bellows, *Benevolence among Slaveholders*, following p. 55.

of the proper gender ("until <u>he</u> shall be of sufficient age"), and in a few others concerning the apprentice's educational opportunities and endpayments
the recording commissioner inscribed more particular details. In this indenture Leck promised to teach Fordham his dual trades, to provide him with
"meat, drink, washing, lodging, and apparel, both linen and woollen" and
with clean linen twice a week during his time. When Fordham was out of
his time Leck was to give him a new set of clothes, including a hat, and one
pair each of shoes and stockings, and forty-three dollars. For Fordham's part,
he committed himself to "dwell, continue, and serve with" a master when
he first signed the top half of the indenture. In addition, Fordham agreed
to the following standard terms: "<u>his</u> said <u>Master</u> well and faithfully shall
serve, <u>his</u> secrets keep, <u>his</u> lawful commands every where gladly do; hurt to
<u>his</u> said <u>Master</u> shall not do, nor willingly suffer to be done by others; the
goods of <u>his</u> said <u>Master</u> shall not embezzle or waste, nor lend them without
<u>his</u> consent to any." Fordham also promised not to run away, "but in all
things shall well and faithfully demean <u>him</u>self during the said term." No
typeset provisions for returning to one's own family or being adopted into
another, or for a child's death, appear in the document. The Orphan House
expected, and children who came to the institution agreed, to the extent
that they were capable of such consent, that their future lay in learning a
trade in a master's household.

The first step in making a match between children and masters was to
get them to find each other. Because the Orphan House was a charity that
depended on public goodwill, it was open to visits during the day by interested Charlestonians "as often as they please." Thus, a master who lived in
Charleston and wanted an apprentice simply visited the House, talked with
a child or two, and tried to find one who was interested in his craft. By the
rule book, but only loosely enforced in practice, girls were to be bound out
at age 13 and boys at age 14.[10] By those ages, it was widely believed, children
themselves were old enough to form an impression of how well they might
like a particular trade, working with a particular master or mistress, living
in their house, and doing so for a number of years. The interview, then,
required each party to assess both his own interests and the ability of the
other side to fulfill the promises in the indenture, and then to act on that
judgment.

A successful binding resulted from a series of conversations. One necessary conversation was with the child. In 1793 commissioners approved the
application of Mrs. Henry for Maria Cox only after "they had made inquiry,
respecting the character & capacity of Mrs Henry." The future mistress

having passed this test, the commissioners then obtained the "consent and approbation of the girl." Another conversation was with the child's parent or guardian. The prospective mistress Mary Long made sure that her application for Charlotte Suder in 1802 had met "with her mothers approbation" before contacting the commissioners. Evidence of these discussions abounds throughout this period. In 1860 the saddle and harness makers Jennings, Tomlinson and Co. reported their interview with "the lad George Andrews." They emphasized to the commissioners that George was "anxious with the consent of his mother to come" and apprentice with them.[11]

These examples indicate that approval of the surviving parent, if he or she was in a position to grant or withhold it, was necessary for the apprenticeship to start. Tradesmen who had already gained parental approval made sure the commissioners knew about it. J. B. Duval, a tinsmith, wrote in his application, "I have consulted his mother on the subject and she consents that he should come to me." Printer and publisher, the Rev. Benjamin Gildersleeve, nearly forgot the critical piece of information in his letter for Oran Bassett: "P.S. I should have observed that I have had a conversation with his mother and her consent is obtained." Sometimes the mother herself expressed her written desires. "I the mother of R Taylor consent to his going with Mr Boling [sic] to the country. [signed] Ann Taylor" was scrawled at the bottom of Thaddeus Bolling's application letter. In other cases a parent initiated the apprenticeship conversation. Margaret Moles, who operated a dry goods store, noted that she was applying for a particular girl whose mother had approached her about a position.[12]

When commissioners informed responsible adults of the child's potential move from the Orphan House, they offered the parent or guardian a chance to reject the apprenticeship. Adult approval was not always forthcoming, and when the parent or guardian withheld it, the child stayed in the Orphan House. John Fairbrother's request for Charles Reyes to be bound to him was thwarted by Reyes's mother, who found painting "an unworthy trade" for her son. Reyes was bound to a house carpenter four months later.[13] Mothers exercised veto power over mistresses interested in their daughters. Sarah Airs offered to take in Louisa Carter "to live and reside with me as a domestic and be with me about the house to see and attend to my children and thereby relieve me from some of my domestic cares." This match was not to be, however; Louisa's mother, wrote a commissioner, "object[ed] particularly," so the commissioners "disagreed to" the proposal.[14]

Consistent with the goal of consent of all parties, commissioners even allowed children to reject applications from well-qualified and vetted prospective masters. After her brief time with Frances Pearson concluded, becoming an apprentice to William Hemmingway, a storekeeper, was "the choice of the girl," and Ann Ford was so bound. On the other hand, in the case of Eliza Walker, "[U]pon being enquired whether she was willing to be bound to Mrs. Mary Long, [she] replied that she was not—and therefore the binding committee declined to bind her."[15] Enough prospective apprenticeships ended this way to indicate that this was not just a hypothetical veto; children really had the ability to approve or reject their would-be masters and mistresses.

The greatest obstacle for prospective masters and mistresses was the Board of Commissioners itself. Two of the visiting commissioner's duties were to investigate prospective masters who lived in Charleston and to review letters regarding masters who lived out of town. If the master appeared not to offer a respectable setting for the child, commissioners rejected the application. A mistress who operated a boardinghouse was unlikely to receive a child.[16] They also rejected applications for children who were too young or who had not attained an educational level commensurate to the work to which the master proposed to put them. For the first decade and a half, commissioners consistently refused to bind apprentices to apothecaries, because the Orphan House's general schooling meant that "the children of this Institution received not an education competent for that business."[17] Commissioners looked especially skeptically on proposals for children to work in agriculture. In 1841 a sericulturist from Jacksonville, Florida, proposed to take six to eight children of both sexes and teach them to mind cocoons and make silk. The commissioners saw this labor as "not being a suitable situation for the children of the institution" and rejected the application.[18]

The complexity of fruitfully matching masters and children grew with the distance of the prospective master from Charleston. Those who lived in town and could walk to the Orphan House and chat with a child did so. Many letters to the commissioners in the early years referred to visiting the Orphan House yard. In the spring of 1818, Mary LeCompte, the wife of a local physician, described her experience:

> Desirous of obtaining one of the young females of the orphans under your guardianship, I visited them a few days ago and was recommended by the Matron to Miss Rachel Isaacs, who appeared to answer the expectations I had of her; and if our being mutually serviceable should be agreeable to you gentlemen to intrust her to my care, under the usual and established forms of the institution I shall pay every attention to her improvement in domestic oeconomy, needle work, &c, and she shall be treated with humanity and kindness.

Thus, Mrs. LeCompte already had some understanding of the Orphan House's workings. She knew that a girl in her household could lend a big hand to her daily work, and that she would be much less costly than a slave. But she did not know which girl would make a likely candidate. The matron presumably did. The matron suggested Rachel Isaacs, who at age sixteen must have been physically strong enough to manage chores such as washing, in addition to learning the skills of millinery as the indenture promised her. After conversing with Rachel, Mrs. LeCompte felt that she had found her girl.[19]

Those masters who lived out of town relied, when possible, on Charlestonians to act on their behalf. The order in which contact with the Orphan House might happen emerges in the 1803 case of inmate Charlotte Clark. A Mrs. Gillison of Coosawhatchie, about seventy miles west of Charleston, wrote the commissioners to ask for two girls as apprentices, one for her and one for her daughter's family. Probably Mrs. Gillison was part of a larger family that founded nearby Gillisonville, where they began a shoe manufactory. Mrs. Gillison and her husband arranged for one of the commissioners, Henry W. DeSaussure, to act on their behalf, and he consulted with the matron for suggestions. The matron recommended Charlotte Clark, "and upon enquiry of the girl, she declared her willingness to go," according to the commissioners. Something prevented the contract from being consummated, though, and Charlotte was bound a few weeks later to Joseph Byrnes, a merchant in Charleston. Similarly, in 1845 a Charleston cabinet maker named William Knauff, who had moved to far distant Pendleton District, sought two boys as apprentices. Knauff was busy enough making furniture for the likes of Floride Calhoun that he found "it inconvenient to come to Charleston," so he gave the Rev. John Bachman his power of attorney to execute indentures in Charleston. In some situations, the master happened to be in Charleston, perhaps on business, and so could discuss prospects with the child, as was the case with Christopher Orr, a merchant in Pendleton, who met up with his apprentice James Kean in April 1827. The commissioners bound Kean to Orr on the day they met.[20]

Masters' accounts of these discussions probably report actual events but in light of what they expected commissioners wanted to hear. One frequent message was the child's own wish to join the applicant's business or household. Cunningham and Neale, merchants, described the "earnest desire" of William Spence to become an apprentice with them. Joseph Milligan, a storekeeper, began his letter, "John Mitchell says he has a great desire to live with me and thinks he will like our business." The next-best thing to direct consent from the child was a conversation with his or her surviving parent. Occasionally masters and parents discussed the apprenticeship even before informing commissioners. A parent might come to the master, as in the case of the shopkeeper and mistress Margaret Moles noted previously. Josiah Finney, a harbor pilot, connected the two dots when he wrote of George Corker, "the boy has a wish to be with me and it is also the desire of his father." Although parents and guardians surrendered all legal authority over their children upon binding them into the Orphan House, the custom of obtaining parents' and guardians' consent, and honoring their refusal to grant it, insured that even after institutionalization parents and guardians would see the Orphan House as looking after their own interests as well as those of their children.[21]

The expectations of the commissioners became so well known that application letters began to reflect them. Masters planned their approach to the commissioners even before visiting the Orphan House. Letters described their home and work situations without knowing the particular children whom they wanted to fill those situations, so initial drafts of letters left a blank space for the child's name. Once at the Orphan House, someone with a different hand filled in the name. Different styles of handwriting or different colors of inks then reveal the two-stage composition of these letters. A typical example came from E. W. Whiting in 1832. The second hand is underlined.

> Being desirous of obtaining a boy from your institution by the name of <u>John Addams</u> he having signified his consent to be recd by me, my business is that of a turner should you favor my request I will cheerfully comply with all necessary regulations. [signed] E. W. Whiting[22]

Besides training in a skill, education, and occasionally treatment identical to their own children, masters specified characteristics they wanted in children. Unlike much later in history when the ideal of an unrelated child entering into a family meant an infant, masters expected their prospective apprentices to be old enough to work and educated enough to work well. In describing Eliza Vanorden as likely to be well prepared for an apprenticeship, an Orphan House nurse named Ann Bowles emphasized that Eliza had "a sweet temper" and was already "a good reader, marker, and sewer." An Upcountry merchant named G. D. Beckham described his interview with an Orphan House resident as follows:

> Being desirous of procuring a boy to assist in my store, as salesman & other matters pertaining to my store. I would be glad to get one from

your institution. The boy Wm R Bull, whom I have seen & conversed
with & whose writing, ciphering &c I have also seen, I am pleased with
him. I will do a faithful part by him. I should like to take him with me
to Lancaster on Saturday next.

This way masters could confirm that children whom the commissioners
had deemed as sufficiently educated to begin an apprenticeship had in fact
been educated to their own satisfaction.[23]

Masters indirectly described expectations of apprentices after youths
became too ill or disabled to work. Their main expectation was that the
young person should be able to work productively. Masters did not expect
the young person to produce enough to cover all the expenses of feeding,
clothing, and training, but they intended for the youth to close the gap
between costs and earnings as much as possible. In the first few years of
an apprenticeship, the child was a net liability who cost the master more
than the value of what he helped produce. If the apprentice never made it to
that later stage of helping to produce a good or service, the losses from the
earlier years fell on the master. A merchant, probably in Camden, reported
that he had successfully transferred a onetime apprentice to a prosperous
boot maker. Reflecting on his early experience, the master concluded, "[The
boy] has been an expense to me since the day I took charge of him to the
present." Similarly, another master believed that he "had not yet received
much advantage" from an apprentice who had run away.[24] Masters also understood that the net benefit of keeping an apprentice would rise as he aged
and grew into his skill, thereby becoming more productive. One mistress
calculated regarding an ultimately unsuccessful match, "The trouble and
expense of maintaining her in my service has already been likely to be more
than the proceeds of her future services can possibly repay." Her unspoken
implication was that in a successful match, the proceeds of the child's future services would indeed repay the trouble and expense of maintenance
early on.[25]

Masters expressed concern about disabled apprentices in similar cost-
benefit language. An apprentice who became chronically sick or permanently injured would find it difficult to work as productively as the master
had expected. Recall the case of the visually impaired girl Elizabeth Sowers.
One week after signing the indenture, her mistress, Mary Dupree, sought
successfully to return her to the Orphan House, complaining that Elizabeth
was blind in one eye. Mrs. Dupree explained to commissioners that Elizabeth's disability meant that she "would not answer her purpose, & therefore requested that she might be taken back." The commissioners allowed

her to bring the girl back to the Orphan House, and the next day bound Elizabeth out to a milliner. Eliza Egerton, a girl who was autistic or otherwise mentally disabled, cycled through a series of frustrated mistresses who reached the same economic conclusion about her time with them. The first found "her unable to earn even her food." The second complained that despite "all the pains" which she "had taken in teaching her" millinery, Eliza remained "perfectly ignorant." The third pronounced her "unfit to learn [the milliner's] or any other business" and so she was "incapable of earning her livelihood." Masters did not hire apprentices for their shops out of charity. They understood intuitively the precarious balance between costs and benefits, and they hoped to turn it in their favor. The apprentice's ability to work provided the goods or services that they sold, which in turn enabled them to provide for the youths. An unproductive apprentice was a costly error that masters wished to rectify quickly. As one master observed, because a nearly blind girl was "in no way able to earn her bread," he as a result was no longer "able to maintain her."[26]

For all the post hoc emphasis on the necessity of an apprentice's ability to work, in their applications masters wanted to stress that their goal was not simply to exact cheap labor. As publishers of the *City Gazette* and printers to the state of South Carolina, Peter Freneau and Seth Paine operated one of the largest printing shops in Charleston and were constantly looking out for capable apprentices. In 1796 they promised not only to treat two boys with "humanity and tenderness" and to send them to school in the wintertime, but said that "they shall not be employed to carry out newspapers." Printing was a skill that could lead a man to independence; work as a simple delivery boy was a dead end. Mistresses also anticipated that commissioners wanted to keep girls out of situations where their labor would not pay for some skill training, however lowly. Thus Margaret Smith's application for Ellen Carpenter promised that she would "subject her to no menial office."[27]

Avoiding menial labor mattered, because to antebellum Carolinians, menial, bound labor meant one thing: work by slaves. And so, many prospective masters explicitly stated to the commissioners that the children they hoped to obtain would not work as slaves or alongside slaves. Some masters expressed this in general terms. One assured commissioners, "I wish not to make slaves of my own race." Other masters made more particular denials. "I do not want her in the capacity altogether of a servant," wrote James Knight, whose ownership of several slaves precluded the need for more. In this regard, the odds of a yeoman farmer obtaining a child were probably long. The farmstead of a rejected applicant from Barnwell

District was described by a neighbor as having "no Negroes," so that with "a small family [of] only four children" the farmer worked the land himself. The commissioners may have thought that the farmer's children were being worked as slaves would have been, and to prevent this fate for Orphan House residents rejected this application out of hand.[28]

Commissioners' attitudes toward industrial labor, and perhaps even the issue of children working with slaves and free persons of color, changed over time. In the early nineteenth century, commissioners frowned upon factory work. When "Doc" Shecut founded the South Carolina Homespun Company, he applied for six boys by name. The commissioners noted that most of the boys requested by Shecut were not yet of age and as for the others, "it would not conduce to their benefit to place them to learn that business," and so they declined to bind any of them out.[29] Although the commissioners leaned toward getting their boys into a trade, they were willing to entertain prospects of factory work, at least for the right kind of factory owner. Governor David R. Williams's Cheraw Union Factory in Darlington District was to mill flour and manufacture cotton textiles and paper. Commissioners reported that Williams and his partners sought to "take boys from the Institution whom they will bring up as mechanicks and instruct in the various branches of the arts and manufactures which they will carry on." Commissioners approved, and four boys were bound to him. In this case commissioners may have felt pressure from the governor that the unconventional Shecut could never dream of bringing to bear. Not only were the four boys sent off to Darlington for factory work, but they were to labor alongside slave operatives as well.[30] Conceding boys to industry may have been part of a long-run trend. Much later, in 1847, four boys were bound to the newly reorganized Nesbitt Manufacturing Company, an iron furnace and foundry in Spartanburg, as lowly iron workers. Nesbitt Manufacturing's well-known reliance upon slave labor did not prevent commissioners from accepting this proposal. Other masters expected that the race of children's coworkers did matter, when they carefully noted that, for example, their apprentice "will not be allowed to associate with Negroes," a categorical statement that ruled out working alongside blacks, enslaved or free.[31]

Masters insured a positive impression on the commissioners if they could report success with previous Orphan House apprentices. The Orphan House kept track of interactions with masters, and this record influenced later decisions. For example, in 1796 they rejected an application from a Mrs. Henry because she had improperly discharged two apprentices some time before.[32] To avoid such an outcome, masters who could do so reminded commissioners of the successful apprenticeships they had overseen. A straightforward example was given by Charles Canning, printer of the Methodist newspaper *Southern Christian Advocate*, in 1852. In addition to benefits of a printing apprenticeship in his shop, including a promise not to assign night work that would keep the boys from studying, Canning noted that "the apprentices who have hitherto served their time in this establishment have been continued in its employment at full wages after the expiration of their indentures, as long as they desired to remain." He named one Orphan House boy, Charles Bremer, as a reference.[33] Other prospective masters made sure to tell the commissioners that their previous boys and girls had behaved so well and worked so hard they were coming back for more such diligent workers, thus communicating both their own success at supervising an apprenticeship and their appreciation of the commissioners' work.[34]

THE ORPHAN HOUSE SENT some 1,100 young people out into the antebellum Charleston labor market as apprentices. Table 8.1 indicates the variety of trades in which they were employed. For boys, the list roughly reflects both the nature of Charleston's economy and the types of trades for which apprentices were suited. In the first category, apprentice planters simply would not be found in most antebellum cities, and apprenticeships with goldsmiths and makers of elegant carriages and furniture reflected the fabulous levels of wealth among Charleston's white elite. Contrariwise, seafaring apprentices would have been fairly common in most Southern ports. Over the entire period, the demand for apprentice printers remained steady, and in construction trades apprentices continued to be useful to their masters and in demand once out of their time.[35] The options for girls were much narrower. A master bookbinder informed the commissioners that while boys had rarely benefited from learning his skill, "with females it is a lasting as well as a profitable trade."[36] But bookbinding was an exception. Beyond the needle trades and housewifery, few trades were open to women.

Because so many children entered apprenticeships, it is possible to determine with a statistical analysis which characteristics influenced their placement. For both boys and girls, the ability to sign one's name on the indenture at binding out raised the probability of being assigned to a skilled trade relative to being assigned to no trade at all. The effect of signature literacy was lasting, at least for boys. The ability to sign their names at entrance, years before being indentured, raised the probability of assignment to a skilled trade or to an apprenticeship as a planter or merchant. The initial ability to sign meant that the student could begin a step beyond the

TABLE 8.1. Types of apprenticeship by sex

Boys			Girls		
Occupation	Number	Percentage	Occupation	Number	Percentage
Skilled craft			Textiles		
Building trades	47	6.6	Needlework	102	25
Food processing	25	3.5	Other trade	10	2.5
Leather	40	5.6	Subtotal	**112**	**28**
Metal	71	9.9	Domestic		
Other	11	1.5	Domestic	**228**	**57**
Printing	85	11.7	No skill		
Seafaring/ shipping	56	7.8	No skill	**60**	**15**
Textiles	23	3.2			
Transportation	27	3.8			
Woodworking	71	9.8			
Subtotal	**456**	**64**			
Planter/merchant/professional					
Goldsmith/ jeweler	10	1.4			
Planter/merchant	124	17.3			
Professional	33	4.6			
Subtotal	**167**	**23**			
Farming/no skill					
Farming	61	8.5			
No skill	33	4.6			
Subtotal	**94**	**13**			
Total	**717**	**100**	Total	**400**	**100**

Source: Murray, "Family, Literacy, and Skill-Training in the Antebellum South."

basics, and then tackle more advanced studies before leaving the Orphan House school. Boys who had been bound in by their mothers also obtained better apprenticeships, compared to those who had been brought to the Orphan House by the poor wardens, clergy, or other unrelated adults. Fathers proved effective at getting sons into skilled trades.[37]

The process of binding out children from the Orphan House into appren-ticeships was influenced by both family preferences and the slow changes in the Charleston economy over time. The likelihood of being bound out dropped sharply in the 1840s and 1850s. Partly this trend reflected the greater desire of poor families, and stepfamilies in particular, to recover their children. Also important was the relative decline in Charleston's eco-nomic activity and the changes in its sectoral composition, as previously described. Craft goods that had previously been made in Charleston, in part by apprentices, were imported into the city, in exchange for bales of high-quality cotton. Thus the ability of the Orphan House to place its boys in prized craft apprenticeships diminished as the demand for skilled labor it-self declined late in the antebellum period. A good way to see this is simply to compare the trades entered by children at the beginning of the period to those entered by children at the end of the period. About the same numbers of children came to the Orphan House before 1810 as during the 1850s, 503 in the earlier period and 517 in the later. More returned to their fami-lies in the later period, but the proportion of those bound out who entered particular trades can be compared to see both the decline in apprenticeship and, simultaneously, the decline in Charleston's economy. For example, the earlier period was one of prosperity for all shipping-related crafts in port cities, thanks in part to American neutrality during the Napoleonic Wars.[38] Accordingly, eight boys in the earlier cohort were bound to become ship's carpenters or shipwrights. However, by the end of the antebellum period, shipbuilding in Charleston had virtually ceased. To the industrial-ist William Gregg the lack of any ship's carpenter apprentices in the city was powerful evidence of this collapse. And in fact the number of Orphan House boys entering in the 1850s who were bound as ship's carpenters or shipwrights fell to zero. Indeed, the same pattern can be found among pro-spective woodworkers overall. In the earlier period, of 224 boys who were apprenticed, four boys were bound to carpenters, two to turners, fourteen to house carpenters, and fourteen to cabinet makers. By the late antebellum era, the demand for future woodworkers had almost vanished. Among some 105 boys bound out, only four were to learn such a trade: one carpenter, two cabinet makers, and one turner-and-cabinet-maker. The sole apprentice carpenter was bound to George W. Egan, himself a future commissioner of the Orphan House.[39]

In good times and bad, Charleston boys found seafaring irresistible. As noted previously, some boys were so eager to go to sea they ran away from the Orphan House and effectively made their own arrangements to serve as apprentice seamen. Others stayed in the Orphan House and left to learn a seafaring trade with commissioners' approval. As early as 1794, Thomas McAvoy passed his examination with the schoolmaster Philip Besselleu and was then bound to a Captain Pratt "to be taught navigation and the art of a mariner." Similarly, mothers found captains to take their children, as in the case of Charles Vinro, whose mother arranged for him to be bound to his uncle after the uncle had returned from his current voyage to Cuba. But not just any sea labor would do; in 1818 commissioners permitted representatives of the Fishing Company to talk to boys in the Orphan House, but between the commissioners' veto of eight boys who were too young and the refusal of two older boys, the Fishing Company hauled up empty nets.[40] Again as with children bound to land-based tradesmen, when possible the commissioners waited for approval of the surviving parent of the boy. In May 1825 the commissioners approved the exodus of no fewer than eight named boys "or any other boys whom the binding committee" should "judge proper" to work on the sea. For Cornelius Clarke, his ship assignment would wait two months until the commissioners received his mother's consent. Two months after that, Joel Thorpe, captain of the ship of the line *Commodore Perry*, brought him aboard. Many other boys signed on as apprentices at the Naval Apprentices' School in the Naval Station, Gosport, Virginia.[41]

As attractive as the sea was to boys, it may have been even more useful to the commissioners as a way to unload troublemakers. One of them was Cornelius Clarke. As his mother explained once commissioners caught up to her, Cornelius held an "unfortunate antipathy" to the Orphan House which led to frequent escapes. Even though Cornelius had managed to avoid obtaining an education, his mother desperately wanted him to go to sea for two years in the absence of any alternative. The commissioners were happy to endorse Mrs. Clarke's notion.[42] When commissioners bound William Franks to learn a sea trade, they thought he was inclined to such work anyway, and they relieved the institution of a boy they had deemed "vicious & apparently irreclaimable." The commissioners were probably not very surprised when he soon returned after absconding from the brig *Sukey*.[43]

Experiences of boys aboard warships can be illustrated by the case of William Wish. Wish was eager to sail, and Lieutenant Lawrence Kearney brought him on board the US brig *Enterprise* in July 1814. Six months later Kearney attacked a British ship watering at North Edisto, Georgia, and during the battle *Enterprise* seized a British gunboat. After the engagement had rendered the ship unfit to cruise, it served as a guard ship in Charleston Harbor. Wish by this point had his fill of war, and his brother John convinced him to leave the Navy. As a former Orphan House inmate serving

as a midshipman on another ship, John Wish was in a similar position to
that of his brother. The elder brother thought the younger could do better in
a different line of work. Lieutenant Kearney relayed John's complaint that
"it was painful and mortifying to him to see his brother in the capacity of a
boy on board my vessel." Still, Kearney acknowledged that with the end of
the war it would take some time for William to rise in the ranks, and agreed
with the commissioners that William Wish could serve out his apprenticeship in the merchant fleet, which his brother arranged.[44]

ONE WAY TO RAISE THE CHANCES of a good match was to let the apprentice
try the work for a time, and many masters were willing to take children
provisionally. Economic historian Gillian Hamilton showed that probation
clauses were common in Montreal indentures around this time. She interpreted this as an effort to improve the likelihood that master and apprentice
would prove compatible. Inclusion of "tryal" periods appeared in several
Charleston indentures, and seem, as in Montreal, to have reflected all parties' desire to come to terms amicably. James Haig, printer and publisher
of the *City Gazette*, wrote the commissioners regarding several boys for
whom he had applied, "Should it be your wish therefore to bind them out I
would suggest the propriety of allowing them to remain at my office for ten
days or a fortnight to give them an opportunity of testing their capacity &
inclination for its duties." Their capacity and inclination, as well as the
printer's assessment thereof, must have been positive, as Haig proposed a
month later to formalize the apprenticeships.[45]

The classic arrangement of the apprentice moving in with the master's
family was common in antebellum Charleston. Explicit references to residence with the master appeared in letters from planters, merchants, and
professional men. Dr. John Hume Simons, widely known for his *Planter's
Guide and Family Book of Medicines* (1848), sought William Cantley as an
apprentice apothecary. Describing William's prospective situation, Simons
wrote, "[He would] reside in my family & attend to the business in which I
am now engaged."[46] Girls who were bound as domestics were by definition
to live with the master and mistress. Of Jane Thornley, aged thirteen, James
Knight promised, "[She would] live as we do and sleep in the room with
my children (they are girls)" while earning her keep by learning "to sew,
to wash and do up the lighter and finer articles of female apparel, to assist
to take care of the smaller children &c." The value of room and board provided to the apprentice could be substantial. In 1815 a merchant asked for
a boy on the condition that he live with his mother during the apprenticeship, and in exchange he would "offer his mother one hundred seventy five

dollars a year as a compensation for his board, washing, making, & mending his clothes." Even if that was an overly generous assessment, it indicates why masters whose compensation consisted of the apprentice's work expected those apprentices to begin earning their keep as soon as possible.[47]

Especially later in the period, the Orphan House sought to follow apprentices after they were bound out. Replies from masters tell us about the ordinary experience of young people at that time. Few letters survive from Charleston masters, suggesting that the commissioners checked on apprentices simply by walking around to local shops and interviewing young folk and their masters and mistresses there. Apprentices who remained in the city could also communicate with the board through family members. For children who left town, commissioners contacted masters by post. Replies included detailed pictures of apprentices' everyday lives. These letters are especially valuable because their ordinariness serves as a counterbalance to legal documents that stem from conflicted relationships, which have survived in greater number. However, those letters reporting a normal life must have been more typical of an apprentice's experience than the more numerous letters that describe conflict.

Here is an example of how a typical apprenticeship appeared in medias res. In June 1834, Theodore Sompayrac was bound to James McIntosh, a merchant in Society Hill, about 150 miles north of Charleston. At first, thirteen-year-old Theodore's "extreme youth and limited acquirements" led McIntosh to doubt whether he would succeed in his apprenticeship. However, within a few weeks, Theodore's "good disposition & industry" improved McIntosh's outlook. As of his writing, six months after Theodore's arrival, McIntosh could report that Theodore had enjoyed continuous good health, and that he was conducting himself pleasantly in the shop and at home. After he was out of his time, Theodore Sompayrac stayed in Society Hill, and later opened his own store, a perfect example of the apprentice continuing in the trade of his master.[48]

Some masters operated sufficiently large concerns that they took several apprentices at once. The baker J. C. H. Claussen filed a report on his three boys, and in the process he described the operations of a large-scale bakery in the antebellum South. Claussen first explained that an apprentice baker needed to learn how to make three kinds of goods: bread, biscuits, and cakes. Bread production required physical strength in order to manage the baking of several heavy loaves at once, while cakes, the lightest, required the closest attention. Thus, Claussen could report that Charles Girck was especially suited to cakes because he was "not very strong and very delicately built." William Buckheister had completed his courses in all three and was working again at biscuits, and James Cooks was trying his hand at bread, having completed courses in cakes and biscuits. Claussen gave thumbnail sketches of each boy: Girck was "the most good natured, generous, and best behaved of the three, very willing and [took] the trade first rate." Buckheister had "wild and playfull" moments, but "with strict and definite orders easily managed," and was also "very kind and of a sociable and generous disposition." The third boy, Cooks, was "strong and muscular for his age." Claussen wrote of Cooks, "[His] disposition is not so kind as the other two, but [his] general behavior (with a remarkable improvement of late) is now very good." Claussen understood the predilections of teenaged boys, for he was willing to "mak[e] a reasonable allowance for occasional small boyish freaks." Overall, he was very happy with his boys and expected to make good bakers out of them.[49]

The worst that could be reported in a reasonably positive midterm report was that a boy was acting as one would expect teenaged boys to act. R. E. and C. C. Seyle, merchants in distant East Florida, had obtained William Dunlap as an apprentice in February 1859. Later that year, they reported that Dunlap's "conduct has been that of most boys of his age." Dunlap was fifteen years old then. "[B]y watching him and being strict," they forecast, "he will someday make a useful man." It seemed that Dunlap's interests and those of the Seyles might merge more closely in the near future. The Seyles expected to leave the mercantile business to take up farming, and of Dunlap they reported, "[He] does not like his books as we might wish," and so it seemed he might want to accompany them rather than continue in commerce. But two years later they parted ways, with Dunlap's uncle receiving him for the rest of his term.[50] J. R. Frey, who operated a tannery near Spartanburg, related that his two apprentices, Daniel Higgins (aged thirteen) and Robert Murray (aged fourteen), were both "intelligent, industrious, and obedient boys" who were learning to tan and curry hides reasonably well. When conflict arose, Frey "had but few occasions to inflict corporal punishments," because "persuasion and reproof" instead generally got the boys back on track.[51] As apprentices aged, persuasion and reproof became more useful than corporal punishment. O. H. Wells, a printer in Greenville, wrote that his apprentice, Charles W. Evans, was "turbulent and more difficult to manage, when out of my sight, than any [apprentice] I ever had in my office." What Wells needed, he thought, were "harsher means" to make Evans work. Now that Evans was eighteen years old, though, he was too old and too large for physical correction, so as an alternative Wells did not "allow him any freedoms, or relax [his] discipline in the least."[52]

Probably most apprenticeships ended with both parties reasonably content with the results. Without comprehensive records of the outcomes of apprenticeships, this claim is based on interpreting the lack of written documentation as a sign of success. Of course, the declining share of Charleston children bound into apprenticeships and the general decline of apprenticeship in the United States as a whole may have been due to increasing chances of disruption of the apprenticeship over time.[53] While few bindings out that ended in success produced documentation of their outcomes, in two cases we can infer that the boys involved did become respectable tradesmen in Charleston, because they returned to the Orphan House for apprentices. In the earlier case, William Estill entered the Orphan House in January 1806, on his second try, as the commissioners had rejected his mother's previous application. As often happened, after his mother, now Sarah Estill Curtis, had remarried, she returned to the Orphan House and obtained custody of young William. She then indentured him to a bookbinder. William worked in printing shops from a relatively young age. When he was about thirty years old and married, he visited the Orphan House to obtain an apprentice bookbinder. Estill explained that he hesitated to take on Orphan House apprentices, because he knew from experience how great the responsibility was of directing an orphan apprenticeship. He also hesitated because he thought that in most cases prospective masters wanted children "without any intention beyond that of selfish interest," but he hoped that would not be so in his own case. Long after his apprentice, Margaret Cutter, was out of her time, Estill continued to operate his printing shop in Charleston.[54]

A second case is more inferential because, unlike William Estill, Henry Pregnall never explicitly stated to commissioners that he had been raised in the Orphan House. However, available information is consistent with two sets of references to a Henry Pregnall in fact alluding to the same person. Pregnall, who appeared in the previous chapter, entered the House in 1819 "entirely destitute," and apparently a full orphan. He was bound for a brief time, less than a year, to a Charleston physician. Then in 1825, when he was fifteen years old, he became apprenticed to a carpenter named William Bull, and here he found his life's work.[55] Soon after he was out of his time, around 1831, he entered into a carpentry partnership with a more experienced tradesman named Aaron Barton, and in this capacity they took on Lawrence Ridgeway, an Orphan House boy, as an apprentice in 1832. Within a few years Barton and Pregnall had moved up to specialize in sashmaking, and in 1840 Pregnall formed a new partnership with John Alderson, this one to specialize in blindmaking for the more elegant Charleston homes. During this time he returned twice more for orphan apprentices from the Orphan House, apparently happy with the work of the young men in whose place he had once been.[56]

A CONSIDERABLE NUMBER OF APPRENTICESHIPS did not succeed. In some cases the master failed to teach the apprentice his skill, in others he failed to care for the young person properly, and in still others the master balked at providing the end payment to the apprentice. Because the great majority of apprentices had been taught to write in the Orphan House, by the time conflict arose many of them could write the commissioners to complain. In other cases neighbors or family members learned about the breach of contract and contacted commissioners. In extreme cases, disputes followed from threatened or actual violence by the master, or theft or defiance by the apprentice. And in some cases the apprentice resolved the conflict by running away.

Breach of contract cases were relatively easy to resolve, although some required patient investigation and considered judgment by the board. Typically, it was the apprentice's parent, another family member, or the apprentice himself who brought the problem to commissioners' attention. Occasional complaints of masters providing insufficient clothing could be fixed by reminding the master of his obligations. Insufficient food was a more pressing matter, but masters could usually be convinced that a growing child needed more nutrition than he had been receiving. Of course, in some cases the master actually had fulfilled the terms of indenture and provided training, food, or clothing in quantities more generous than the apprentice's advocate had been led to believe. And so the commissioners reviewed all such charges. They took these claims seriously, sometimes deciding in favor of the apprentice, sometimes in favor of the master, and sometimes splitting the difference as a compromise.[57]

In cases in which a master was not teaching the apprentice his trade, or most distressingly, setting the youth to work in the field or at "menial service," the board moved quickly to order the master to cease and desist, or to turn the apprentice over to another master. In a typical breach case, Thomas Bowles had been bound to a local brickmason named John McKee in 1803. With two and a half years remaining in the indenture, Bowles charged that McKee was neither clothing nor training him properly. The commissioners promptly convened a hearing in which both McKee and Bowles spoke their piece. Concluding that Bowles's "complaints were well founded" they ordered McKee to surrender both Bowles and his indentures. Two weeks later Bowles was bound to another brickmason named John Martin.[58] A similar case a few years later involved one of the Saint-Domingue refugees, who was allowed to leave a tin-plate worker who did not provide training to join another tin-plate worker who promised to do so.[59]

Even far from Charleston, Orphan House apprentices were part of communities, members of which looked out for them. Those friends then contacted the commissioners about masters who were not training their apprentices. In the cases of John and Robert Davis, the community consisted of each other, and their correspondence demonstrated how commissioners collected information on out-of-town apprentices. The two brothers had each been bound to become merchants in the Upcountry, Robert to James R. Ervin in Marion District, and John about fifty miles away at the Cheraw Union Factory. In the aftermath of the Panic of 1819, Ervin's business failed, but because Robert's indenture bound him to Ervin and not to the business, Robert remained in Ervin's household. Ervin soon set Robert to work, which led Robert in turn to complain to his older brother. John, who was still an apprentice at the factory, wrote directly to the commissioners, "[Ervin] has put my brother in the corn and cotton fields, without your consent." Commissioners duly informed Ervin of his obligation, and threatened him with legal action if he failed to fulfill it.[60]

The reasons behind the failure of some masters to provide as they had promised did not always add up to a simple refusal to honor an obligation. Thomas Steenson was a millwright in Charleston who brought John Henderson King into his household in the autumn of 1822. Within months Steenson was explaining to commissioners that contrary to John's father's assertion, he had in fact provided John with three pairs of shoes, which he needed on short notice because he had begun the apprenticeship with none. In response to Leonard King's charge that he was not employing John at his trade and was in fact setting him to work in "menial service," Steenson replied that he had had to spend an "extraordinary" amount of time on "the manner [he had] taken to reform" John. Even after this time-consuming preparation, this apprenticeship never quite got off the ground. After providing shoes and some training in deportment, two months later Steenson handed John's indentures back to his father. He explained, "In consequence of the decline of truck in my line of business I have been unable to employ John King in a satisfactory manner either to his father or myself." Leonard King then found a more suitable, and busier, millwright for John.[61]

Claims of physical abuse were about as common as those of breach of contract, and in the worst cases demanded immediate resolution. Given the diminishing acceptability of corporal punishment over time, it is hard to interpret reports of minimal or reasonable violence directed toward young people. Claims by the apprentice of assault were difficult to verify at the time as well, so the commissioners investigated each allegation with some care. The quasi-legal process of investigating charges and countercharges sheds some light on circumstances surrounding each case, so that the record at least hints at each party's probable actions.

The apprentice himself provided some testimony. Several apprentices complained about being beaten. Henry Dicks composed the following missive, which he signed. It seems calculated to pull all the strings that would make commissioners act quickly:

> I don't want to stay with John Crittenden. If I go to church on Sunday he will whip me with a cow skin and I wish you would take me away. If you don't they will kill me and I want to know if Miss Crittenden is aloud to whip me. I want you to get me a traid and send me a letter as quick as you can so as to let me know what you are going to do for me. I can show you the marks as big as my fist I was in pain when I rite this letter. Remember that I am a poor orphan and have no friends to protect me have mercy upon me and do let me know what you are a going to do for me as quick as you can.[62]

Besides written testimony, a child's body might witness to his or her claims of abuse. Anna McNeal, who left the Orphan House as illiterate as she had entered, was bound to Mary Kreitsburg as a domestic on 1 June 1809. Ten weeks later a neighbor reported that Mrs. Kreitsburg "had cruelly and inhumanely treated her the said apprentice by beating her in an unwarrantable manner." The commissioners summoned Anna and "examined the bruises received." Satisfied of the accuracy of the neighbor's report, they kept the girl at the Orphan House. Four months later they bound her again, this time to a man whose wife promised to teach Anna the work of a seamstress.[63] In contesting claims by apprentices, masters summoned supportive testimony from their friends. When Susannah Lamott complained to commissioners that her mistress, Anna Small, had struck her, Mrs. Small's physician wrote to assure the commissioners that "Mrs. S. merely gave the girl a few cuts with a switch for excessive impudence and inattention."[64]

In a few cases the masters confessed, apparently quite readily, to having struck the apprentices, and thereby detailed the kind of violence they had employed. They also accounted for the violence by charging the youth with crimes ranging from impudence to theft to assaulting strangers. When a local carpenter named Michael Elland mistakenly supposed that his fourteen-year-old apprentice, Michael Brown, "had raised a report injurious to character," Elland's own letter reported that "in a heat of passion" he beat Brown with "the butt end of a horsewhip." Elland then conceded that he had "unjustly corrected" the boy. The commissioners removed Brown immediately and bound him to Elias Gregg, a storekeeper in far distant Darlington District the next week.[65] Because Margaret Charlton had been disobedient and impudent, Jane Johnston admitted that she "gave her 5 or 6 strokes across her shoulders with part of a small whip." In defense of his wife, Dr. Johnston wrote that such treatment was the same "as she is in the habit of whipping her own children with." Margaret, for her part, "increase[d] her impertinence" and soon ran away from the Johnstons.[66]

Commissioners adjudicated these charges carefully and dismissed some just as they accepted others. In several cases their research indicated that the child deserved the punishment that led to the complaint. In an early case of 1791 they found that one girl "was of a very evil disposition and deserved chastisement," but in this particular episode, the punishment "had been inflicted with rather too much severity."[67] In response to Henry Dicks's alarming charges against John Crittenden, a pillar of the Greenville community, commissioners asked a former Charlestonian named Thomas O. Lowndes to investigate. His report confirmed the story of the master, that Henry had in fact stolen goods from the Crittendens, stayed out overnight, and frequently lied about his activities. Thus, in Lowndes's view, however well Henry might be currently behaving, his past activities had justified his two whippings. Since Crittenden concluded that Henry could not be trusted to run a store, the training his indentures called for, Lowndes recommended, with Crittenden's endorsement, that Henry be re-bound to a tradesman.[68] The commissioners were aware of the consequences for a child of living with an abusive master. As the widow Elizabeth Hatter reminded them, she was searching carefully for a master for Thomas Torrens, because she wanted to prevent his meeting a similar fate as his brother, who "died under great hardships from being placed with so unkind a master."[69]

If the commissioners were sufficiently confident in their case and felt sufficiently frustrated by the master's lack of response to their demands, they resorted to the law. Here, the recalcitrant masters may have felt outgunned, as the Orphan House could rely on the pro bono work of such well known attorneys as James Petigru.[70] As a result, threats by the commissioners to take a master to court usually had the desired effect.

LIKE TEENAGERS BEFORE AND SINCE, apprentices misbehaved at times. Several masters complained about lies told by the apprentice, and a few charged their apprentices with intoxication. Beyond mundane white lies, masters needed to be able to trust a young person working in their shop or home, especially if he or she had access to the cash drawer. An untrustworthy apprentice was a burden on the master and a danger to his business. James A. Lyon, a merchant in Abbeville District, complained in 1859 of his apprentice, Langdon Cheves Riggs, "[He] deceived me more than any boy I ever met with." Since Lyon's intention was to make Riggs a clerk in his store, and as Riggs "proved himself not to be a good true & faithful boy," Lyon wanted to get rid of Riggs as soon as he could. The response from Charleston was to recommend that Lyon "call [Riggs] to a stricter acct for all the monies recd in the store," and failing that, to find another master. Lyon arranged for Riggs to move on to a baker's shop back in Charleston.[71] Ann Fash had obtained Mary Duncan as an apprentice tailor. For some time after her arrival she noticed that small amounts of money went missing, and one day she found four dollars on Mary's person, "which she [had] acknowledged that she took from [Ann's] drawer last week." Since Ann's husband was a grocer, and they all would have lived above or behind the store, the Fashes wanted the thieving girl to leave before she set her sights on larger amounts of cash in the store.[72]

Acts of theft might intersect with the hidden sides of a slave society. Just as residents of the Orphan House occasionally violated laws against trading with slaves, apprentices conducted such illegal transactions too. White fears that theft from masters lurked behind exchanges with slaves were justified, but in apprentice-slave exchanges the theft we know about had been committed by the apprentice. D. E. Sweeney, who seems to have been Henry Dicks's penultimate master, complained that the boy was "making bargains with Negroes and purloining my money to consummate them." Aaron Fairchild reported that Caroline Jewell had stolen from his family and then left the house after they had gone to bed, in order to "converse with a Negro fellow."[73]

The most ominous threat from an unruly apprentice was that of physical violence. While "impertinence" or talking back to the adults no doubt irritated masters and mistresses, the possibility of an apprentice assaulting a master, family member, or neighbor was unnerving. It was probably about as likely as an act of violence perpetrated by a slave, but the prospect of violence committed by a bound laborer who lived under the same roof frightened without regard to the race of the bondsman. Especially in the years following the Denmark Vesey events (1822), the mood created by an angry bound worker did not depend on the duration of the bond. In 1825, Francis

Poyas found that his apprentice had stolen not just from his own funds, and more than once, but from a nearby Sunday school. When Poyas "corrected him severally," the boy confessed. Afterwards, reported the master, "I feel myself in danger." Poyas was a gunsmith and may have feared the consequences of the boy's access to his shop.[74]

Apprentices did assault other people. The number of cases are few but well documented. George W. Cassidy, owner of a dry goods store in the Neck, complained to commissioners that his apprentice, James Carlton, had "beaten a Negro in our yard who came to purchase goods from us." After Cassidy gave him a "chastisement," Carlton ran away. One of the worst cases of apprentice misbehavior, which was then followed by the master behaving meretriciously and the Orphan House not much better, involved Henry E. Neil, who had been bound to G. W. F. Lankin, a merchant of Lawrenceville, Georgia. Early in 1840 Lankin reported to commissioners on Neil's first nine months as apprentice: "[His] conduct has bin good he is a fine boy his improvement in business is good as I could wish for he is a keen smart boy at any business I put him at." His progress ended that summer. In August 1840, a girl in Lawrenceville alleged that Neil had raped her. The evidence boiled down to each party's testimony, with no external corroboration for either. Lankin himself, claiming that "no person here . . . believes he commited the act but the girl swore it," then obstructed justice by hiding Neil "until the stage started and [Lankin] put him in it to go to Madison," about fifty miles away. "I thought it to be the best plan to send him off," Lankin explained, because otherwise "the laws of this state would have sent him to the penatentiary for five years." After Neil made his way to Charleston, the commissioners bound him into the Naval Apprentice School in Gosport the next year, thus enabling the boy to avoid facing justice.[75]

IT WAS COMMON FOR APPRENTICES to change masters in midstream. In these cases, commissioners ordinarily endorsed the transfer of indentures to a new master with a minimum of fuss, as long as the apprentice and his parent or guardian approved. Reasons for such transfers varied. The most common explanation from the child was that he had learned enough of a particular trade to conclude that he really wanted to practice a different one. Thus, when Zachariah DeHay tired of factory work in a yarn mill near Columbia, he moved into the apothecary shop of Dr. Edward Sill, also in Columbia.[76] In other cases the master met with misfortune in his business or personal life, and as his home or firm broke up, the apprentice had to be moved elsewhere. Thus Thomas Hagen moved from the failed grocery of F. G. H. Gunther to become an apprentice in chair making under John DeBow.[77] Rarely did the commissioners allow a concerned parent to break up a well-functioning apprenticeship, but it occasionally happened. At first, Benjamin Brown and his mother were happy for him to be bound to Daniel Mattison to be trained "in the mercantile business." However, within a couple of weeks, Matilda Brown had second thoughts about sending her son to far-off Anderson District. She arranged for a new apprenticeship with J. M. Eason and Brothers, a local metal foundry that soon would be forging gun barrels for artillery pieces, and then "urgently requested" the commissioners to break the indenture with Mattison and re-bind Benjamin to Eason and Brothers. The commissioners did as Mrs. Brown asked.[78]

Most apprenticeships ended with a minimum of drama. The indentures called for the master to pay the apprentice (or, indirectly, the commissioners) the appropriate amount of freedom dues: a cash payment and clothing. Into the nineteenth century, indentures required masters to pay boys ten pounds and girls five; then up to 1850 the payments became forty-three dollars to boys and twenty-two dollars to girls, and after 1850 it was set at twenty-two dollars for both boys and girls. Masters occasionally proved dilatory in providing the cash to the young person, who in turn pressed commissioners to get masters to fulfill their obligations.[79] Eighteen-year-old Anna Merrett produced a typical example of such a complaint when she wrote the commissioners the following letter from Columbia in 1815.

> I hope you will not be offended or surprised at my addressing you or troubling you with this letter for necesety obliges me to it it is now six years since i left the orphan house i was then put to live with mr Gladny and i have staid with him untel my time is up and he refuses to pay me the mony that my indentures requires my time has been up now befor [?] a year and i have been to him for it but he will not give it to me Gentlemen if you will make him pay either you or myself you will serve a distressed orphan for such i am i am in want of the mony or i would not trouble you it would relive me if you would send it up by the bearer [on reverse:] PS I will thank you if you get the mony to send it to Columbia to my sister Catharin Merrett. i can send my indentures if required A Merrett

In this case, commissioners received the fee payment from Joseph Gladney at the same time as Anna's letter, so they sent Anna a check for $21.50, the equivalent of the five pounds she was due and that Gladney had entrusted to a neighbor for delivery.[80] Fulfillment of these requirements generally, but not always, passed unnoticed, and so left no written record of how the indenture concluded in the most common cases.

Some masters might go beyond the written minimum of contractual obligations, at least in special circumstances. One apprentice, newly out of his time, "came to the board and complained that his Master did not find him regular employment in the way of his trade."[81] While the young man may not have obtained satisfaction from the commissioners, his expectation of help in the labor market suggests that at least on occasion masters supplied such aid to apprentices who had performed competently. Other masters provided extra material goods to their newly freed apprentices. William B. Neal had sufficiently frustrated his master that he agreed to let Neal go to sea. Having found a place for him on the *Caroline*, bound for Le Havre, the master sent him off with "an ample outfit of clothing and every thing necessary to the life he has chose," a trunk filled with a half dozen pairs of socks, seven shirts, and more.[82] Although this master was not pleased with the boy's work, he did want to do right by the boy and, not coincidentally, please the commissioners should he want another apprentice.

IN THE END, THE COMPLEX PROCESSES of matching children to masters, and balancing the early years of supporting the child with the later years of his greater productivity, enabled the Orphan House to provide a decent living for its children. Certainly it enabled the children, in most cases, to rise a step or two above the situations in which they lived before coming to the Orphan House. Ideally we could see what happened to the children as they entered their adult lives. In a very few cases is that possible, as the next chapter shows.

CHAPTER NINE

Transitions

IN THE GREAT MAJORITY OF APPRENTICESHIPS, young folk worked and learned their trades, and their masters fed, sheltered, and trained them uneventfully. At the end of the indenture the master gave the now-former apprentice all his or her current clothing, plus a new suit, hat, stockings, a pair of shoes, and some cash. Even among children who left the Orphan House to return to family, it was common for family members to sponsor them for apprenticeships, which undoubtedly proceeded much along the lines of those for children who were bound directly from the Orphan House. In a few cases, such as those of William Estill and Henry Pregnall, their later lives can be reconstructed from a variety of sources. This chapter reconstructs later lives of several other Orphan House children, to examine how they managed (or failed to manage) their transition into life away from natal family, Orphan House, and apprenticeship.

Our ability to follow these young people as they began their working careers, moved west or settled in Charleston, practiced a trade, married and raised their children, and held their grandchildren until they too entered the sleep of the just, is limited to the written record. Letters from former apprentices and their masters and occasional mentions in secondary sources yield bits of information that allow some lives to be reconstructed. In this chapter, lives of several Orphan House alumni exemplify particular aspects of apprenticeships and the transition into adulthood, marriage, family, and career.

The degree to which these lives are typical or not cannot be determined. Who has ever lived life typical of his or her age? How to determine the average life would be a massive problem, simply owing to the difficulty of following large numbers of ordinary people through time before the mid-nineteenth century. Even if we knew the average tendency in a population toward their age at marriage, number of children, occupation, location of residence, and so on, such an exercise really begs a question whether any one member of that cohort ever actually lived a life exactly like that in all its particulars.

The group of biographies offered here describes over a dozen lives of such ordinary people. While we cannot say that any one of them was "typical," we can say that each life included episodes that were common to many other Orphan House alumni, Charleston residents, and Americans of that time. The former inmates experienced success, failure, heroism, lawbreaking, family lives happy (which were not all the same) and unhappy, and relinquishment of their own children to the Orphan House. In short, this chapter encompasses many possible outcomes, reflecting the constraints imposed by the source material, but also the wide range of possibilities that were open to young white people in the antebellum South.

THE FIRST TWO CASES involve young people who did not complete their apprenticeships. Interruptions such as these occasionally happened, but probably in just a minority of cases. Here we know exactly why William Tucker and Mary Erhard were not able to finish their indentures. William Tucker was a troubled youth well before he attempted to sexually assault a young neighbor girl. His work history was checkered, but commissioners kept that fact from his eventual master while still requiring the master to submit customary character references. Although we do not know how his life turned out, at our last sighting his prospects looked dismal. Mary Erhard, on the other hand, was coldly dismissed by her master when her pregnancy became visible. Ignoring the fate of his own grandchild, the master sent her back to Charleston while claiming to the commissioners that she had chosen to end her apprenticeship. Mary approached her misfortunes with tenacity, equanimity, and dignity. When we leave Mary, her future hardly looks bright, but the strength of character she demonstrated as a very young woman suggests that she would cope admirably.

William Tucker's time in the Orphan House was quite similar to many dozens of other children. He was one of many Poor House residents who entered the Orphan House after lobbying by Poor House commissioners and arm-twisting by City Council. Like many of his fellow inmates, he learned to write his name at the Orphan House school. Besides penmanship, catechetical lessons must have appealed to him because after eight years in the institution, on Sunday, April 14, 1816, the Reverend Doctor Andrew Flinn of Second Presbyterian Church walked the two blocks to the Orphan House and baptized young William, with some commissioners as witnesses.

But there was something to William that kept masters from seeing him as a valuable apprentice. Twice he went out from the Orphan House on trial, once to a painter and once to a baker, and each time he returned. After just a few weeks, neither the baker nor the painter wanted any more to do with William. Perhaps it was his unattractive combination of aggression and self-pity that repelled the tradesmen.

The two failed trials indicated that placing William with a master would be more difficult than commissioners initially thought. Thus when Alexander Cabeau, a tanner and currier in Chester, far upstate near the North Carolina border, wrote the Orphan House asking for a male apprentice, they knew exactly which boy to suggest. They recommended William Tucker and kept silent on the two trial indentures. Cabeau responded with a formal application for William, which the commissioners were only too glad to approve on November 28, 1816. At age twelve, William was bound to Cabeau for nine years.

About three years later, William wrote to Charleston complaining of mistreatment at Cabeau's hands. The commissioners, in turn, queried Cabeau about what they believed was William's attempt to run away from this mistreatment. Cabeau's reply to the commissioners' query, written early in 1820, presents a very different picture. He denied that he had mistreated William, and claimed that to the contrary William was pure trouble. He "will not tell a truth when he can make a lie," charged Cabeau, plus he was "frequently drunk"—often after stealing the neighbors' spirits. Contrary to William's claim that he had been left "nearly naked," he had broken into a trunk, rummaged through a closet, and pried open the lock on a bureau to steal some of the nicest clothes the family owned. Between the commissioners having "recommended [William Tucker] to me for a very good boy and in every respect I have found him the reverse," and Tucker's retelling about his failure to catch on with the painter and the baker, Cabeau felt much put upon. Cabeau wondered how differently things might have turned out if only he had known of William's tendencies to misbehave.

As things stood, William had not run away. He was in jail on serious charges. Cabeau had needed to travel to Georgia, leaving William behind with his usual chores to do. In addition, Cabeau wanted William to go into town to change a five-dollar note. On William's return he met an eight- or nine-year-old girl named Millings, and offered her one of the dollars to "go off the road with him." She refused. He grabbed her, but she twisted away and ran to a neighbor's house. Tucker waited where he could keep an eye on the house. When she left, he would be there. He watched her exit, followed a bit, and in Cabeau's words, "attacked her again." This time too the girl escaped and ran back to the neighbor's house, where she convinced the man of the family to accompany her home.

She must have made it home, and presumably the neighbor man and possibly the sheriff caught up with William Tucker soon enough. After the assault he had intensified his drinking. With no man at home, to prevent Tucker "from strolling about" the Cabeau women somehow got all his clothes off him, perhaps after he had passed out, and at least temporarily hid them. Hence William's claim of being kept naked. He may have been drunk and dressed too lightly for an escape when the law caught up with him, and he may have resisted capture as well. Once in jail he wrote to the Orphan House asking for a visitor and describing himself as "both sore in mind & body." He would not tell the commissioners what had happened, only, "[I]f I am innocent I hope you will assist me." If? On the other hand, he wrote, "[If I am] culpable I can ask no aid & must resign myself to my fate." He wished, he wrote to his former home, he had followed the advice of long-time commissioner John Dawson in particular. Tucker did not specify what Dawson had told him, but if only he had obeyed, he would not "now be the inmate of a prisons walls." But such he was. William Tucker's story shows that not all Charleston orphan apprentices led upstanding lives.[1]

Mary Erhard illustrates both the courage a young person might summon in times of difficulty, and the extremes to which a master might go to rid himself of a problem apprentice (even one whose problem began with the master). It is noteworthy that Mary's master had hoped to return her to the Orphan House early in her time. Perhaps he had intuited the trouble that was to come. But in accordance with Orphan House practice, commissioners denied this request.

Mary Erhard came to the Orphan House with her brother, Daniel, and sisters, Eliza and Margaret, on October 16, 1817. She was eight years old. Her life might have proceeded on a very different path if the commissioners had bound her to Mrs. Adele Liman, when she applied for Mary as an apprentice in November 1819. During the weekly meeting they approved several such applications, and postponed consideration of one, but Mrs. Liman's they rejected without explanation. Two weeks later Thomas Hart of Lancaster, about seventy-five miles north of Columbia, wrote to ask specifically for Mary Erhard, and he enclosed recommendations from two men who described him as "worthy of your confidence." This time the commissioners approved, and Mary was bound to Hart to learn spinning and weaving.

The relationship between Mary and Hart must not have been exactly to Hart's liking, because in September 1821 he asked the commissioners to take Mary back. Perhaps Hart sensed trouble brewing between Mary and his family. Perhaps, according to an undated letter in Mary's file, the Hart family really did plan on moving west and Mary did not want to accompany them. In any case, the commissioners forbade him to return the girl but suggested that he could send her to a more suitable master and inform the commissioners afterwards. Neither option appealed to Hart, so when the Harts decided to remain in Lancaster, Mary stayed with them.

In the fall of 1825, when Mary was all of fifteen years old, Thomas Hart's son made an offer to Mary that generations of callow young men had made to their sweethearts. He promised to marry her if she would consent to sexual relations with him. Mary soon became pregnant, and the boy, as generations of callow young men had done, reneged on his promise. By early in 1826, Mary's situation must have become obvious to Hart. His cruel solution took advantage of his distance from the Orphan House and what he hoped would be his ability to force a now-sixteen-year-old girl to do pretty much as he pleased. He wrote the commissioners and claimed that Mary had suddenly developed a very strong desire to return to Charleston. Since she had not completed her time with him, Hart did not feel obligated to honor his end of the indenture, at least not immediately. He proposed to send her freedom dues of five pounds to Charleston in a year and a half, at the time when her indenture expired. He professed frustration and regret that Mary had such a volatile personality, which made it hard to fulfill his obligation to instruct her in spinning, weaving, and various country business skills. Off went Mary to Charleston.

Hart's explanatory letter to the commissioners took three weeks to travel from the Upcountry to Charleston, and commissioners still had not heard from Mary when it arrived. In fact, Mary's whereabouts at this time cannot be determined. She may have made contact with her siblings in Charleston. Her brother had just completed his apprenticeship with a local metalsmith. Her sister Margaret was still bound to Christopher Channer, a local clothier, as an apprentice tailor. Luckiest of the family was the youngest, Eliza, who as we have seen was adopted into the family of grocer Thomas Christburg. Perhaps Mary sought help from them or the families in which they lived. She seems not to have gone either to the Orphan House or to the Poor House for quite some time.

The commissioners, consumed with managing the institution in general and the comings and goings of several children at each board meeting in particular, treated the situation as a relatively common one of an apprentice and master who could not get along. Their first letter to Hart simply threatened to send Mary back to Lancaster when she did show up. Hart's reply was scripted in a wavering hand and with informal diction. Perhaps the prospect of setting his lies in writing and sending them to some of the most powerful men in the state gave him pause. So he decided to address the note not to the board but to the steward, Eliab Kingman. Hart complained to Kingman of Mary's constant misbehavior. In addition, Mary had threatened to run away. Still, in spite of all this trouble, Hart wrote, he had supplied Mary with what she would need for her trip and even "paid her freight" on a wagon that shuddered along roads in terrible condition. Hart begged Kingman to dissuade the commissioners from filing a suit against him until the fall of 1826, when he would make his regular trip to Charleston. Now Eliab Kingman was the last man from whom the commissioners would take legal advice, but he passed the letter along to them all the same. The board resolved to think about the situation—and then forgot about it. When last on their minds, Mary must have seemed to them like just another troubled apprentice. Without knowing her particular condition, the commissioners let the case of Mary Erhard lapse until the very end of 1826.

In the meantime, at some point in the summer of 1826, somewhere in Charleston, Mary gave birth to a little boy she named Thomas. (The name of Thomas's father does not appear in the records.) In the fall Mary and Thomas entered the Poor House together. At Christmas time they were still there, and at some point Mary realized that the eldest Thomas Hart owed her a potentially useful sum of money. To get it, she would have to go through the commissioners, who would have to be informed about her entire situation, including baby Thomas. So she wrote or dictated a letter that explained how she came to be living in the Poor House with Thomas, and that by her reckoning, more than seven years of work for the Hart family entitled her to the standard twenty-dollar payment due each girl apprentice on the completion of her time. After all, it was Hart who had prevented her from fulfilling the terms of the indenture, because he had shipped her back to Charleston ten long months ago. Mary concluded by describing herself as "an unfortunate, but not abandoned woman," perhaps referring to her son and companion Thomas. She offered the master and matron of the Poor House as character references.

The commissioners had previously dealt with a variety of unfortunate women and children—after all, that was the purpose of the Orphan House.

Bastardy was a much more manageable problem in Charleston than out of town, however. If commissioners could identify the father and he lived in town, they often had success at forcing him to pay child support. Dealing with an Upcountry lowlife like Hart was something else. Hart himself had acknowledged that Mary left before the end of her apprenticeship, and now thanks to Mary the commissioners knew that he was responsible for her doing so. From this perspective, it was obviously Hart and not Mary who had breached the apprenticeship contract, and in that case the sum due the commissioners was not twenty dollars (the five pounds Hart had mentioned) but the sixty dollars that was a standard penalty fee for girls. One typical, and here ironic, use for these funds was to provide dowries to alumnae of the Orphan House so that they could marry respectable yeoman farmers or mechanics. Mary Erhard was in no less need.

Armed with their new understanding, the commissioners stood up for Mary. They immediately threatened Hart with legal action to extract the sixty dollars from him. Hart whimpered that he might not be able to travel to Charleston until the fall. He reminded the commissioners, "I live a long way from the city & cannot without much inconvenience" come to Charleston in the spring. He begged the commissioners "not to push nor in force any thing." The commissioners were in no mood to hear about the difficulties of travel from Lancaster to Charleston. Hart finally conceded and paid the sixty dollars on April 27, 1827.

By this time Mary Erhard was out of the Poor House. She quickly learned that Hart had paid the penalty, and she knew that sixty dollars would go a long way toward giving her and Thomas more comfort than they had yet known. But when she wrote the commissioners about receiving the money, it was now their turn to balk at paying her. For no stated reason, the commissioners postponed consideration of Mary's pleas in May and then again in June 1827. It was another betrayal of Mary's good faith.

By early July, Mary was desperate and Thomas was ill. The two of them reentered the dismal precincts of the Poor House, and there Thomas died in the middle of the month. He was about a year old. Mary left the Poor House soon thereafter.

Seventeen years old, completely destitute, and in the eyes of most, utterly unmarriageable, there was really only one thing Mary could do, and that was work. She entered a family in Augusta for several weeks, probably as a wet nurse, and then arranged for further work in the family of a Charleston cotton broker. On her return to the city she sought once more to gain the sixty dollars from the commissioners. She explained that she knew Hart had paid the commissioners and that the funds would enable her to buy some clothes before her next job started. This time, the commissioners recognized their obligation to Mary and paid her, some six months after receiving the money from Thomas Hart. But their payment came with the caveat that it was a gift and not something she was entitled to. According to the commissioners, she had earned it through her "correct deportment" during all her trials. "There is every hope," the commissioners concluded, "that in the future her conduct will so continue."[2]

AT THE HEART OF AN INDENTURE was the contractual agreement by the apprentice to work and by the master to teach the youth how best to do so. James Nelson's story illustrates many aspects of the Orphan House experience, but none so clearly-as the life of a typical apprentice printer. Thanks to their facility with words as well as type, apprentice printers beginning with Benjamin Franklin have left us numerous accounts of their early lives and work.[3] James Nelson left a single letter that describes his experiences. Before coming to the Orphan House, James had been familiar with deprivation, and so the steady work of a career as a printer must have appealed to both him and his mother. But conflict with his master and homesickness for Charleston and his mother proved impossible to reconcile with his apprenticeship.

James Nelson was a second-generation orphan. His grandparents died when his mother, Susan, was very young, and then his father, John Nelson, died not long after James's birth. When Susan remarried, to Robert Kirk, James gained a stepfather. But in autumn 1845 Robert left South Carolina without a trace. Susan and James found themselves back in a desperate situation: no close relatives, no property, and Susan unable to work as long as seven-year-old James needed her care. Her predicament was well known to Orphan House officials. So that Susan could seek employment, they accepted James without the usual investigation. James must have already received some basic education, either from the local free schools or from Robert Kirk, because when he officially came to live at the Orphan House in 1846, he signed his indenture.

After seven years of basic education intended to prepare him for the working world, James Nelson came to the attention of E. A. Bronson, an upstate printer and publisher. James, at least at first glance, had gotten lucky. Although craft apprenticeship was in decline in the United States, printing remained the classic business in which an ambitious and literate young man could hope for some advancement after an apprenticeship. The previous year Bronson had founded *The Palmetto Sentinel* in Barnwell, one hundred miles northwest of Charleston. The publisher's ambition suggested that his was a star worth hitching one's wagon to. Early in 1853 at age fourteen, Nelson left the Orphan House for Barnwell Court House, to begin his training in the printing business under E. A. Bronson.

Bronson thought he saw some potential in the orphan. After a few months, he made Nelson an official "Carrier of the *Sentinel*" with his own route, which enabled James to net twelve dollars that he was allowed to keep. His duties sound typical of an antebellum apprentice printer. He worked long days, coming in before breakfast to sweep out the office. When the newspaper was ready to be distributed, James carried a bundle of them to the post office. James lived in Bronson's household and was treated as one of the family. Not only was he never whipped, reported Bronson, he got his share of any treats that the other children might enjoy. To celebrate their business success in spring 1854, Bronson acquiesced to James's request to travel to Charleston to see his mother. Susan lived just around the corner from the Orphan House, so no doubt James saw some old friends as well.

After returning to Bronson, James must have been meditating on the relative attractions of Barnwell and Charleston. On July 2, 1854, with his master's approval, Nelson left to spend the Fourth in Charleston. No doubt part of his desire was to see his mother. Bronson, however, suspected his real motivation was to visit with his old Orphan House friends, who had been encouraging his bad habits by writing him "obscene" (Bronson's word) letters. When James failed to return as promised, Bronson contacted the Orphan House and then went to Charleston himself to look for his apprentice. He went right to James's mother's home, where Mrs. Kirk produced the boy and took all the blame for her son's prolonged absence.

With James in tow, Bronson returned to Barnwell, fulfilling a promise to James's mother that he would receive James back into the shop. But even so, things were not well. Bronson did not whip James for his absence, but James did complain, "[H]e was very severe on me." Being apart from his mother and friends made James deeply unhappy. When he ran errands, local boys teased him with the epithet "runaway," and in the print shop itself he was at the beck and call of adults who were constantly demanding one more cup of water. Further, James felt that he was not learning how to print. In describing the progress of his apprenticeship to the commissioners, James wrote, "I am not swift in typesetting. and I am not satisfyed." It all became too much for the fifteen-year-old. One day he began to sob within earshot of Bronson. The master was quick to set him straight. "You damn little rascal," Bronson cried, "quit your snuffling!"

So James hatched a plan. One morning early in September 1854 he rose before sunrise, packed some clothing, and walked ten miles north to

Blackville, which lay on the rail line to Charleston. There he left behind a box with Bronson's name on it that held clothes he could not carry, hopped on a train, and rode the rails back to the city. Bronson was surprised the next morning by a black man at his door, returning the box of clothes. He bitterly complained to the commissioners that someone had to have paid Nelson's fare and other expenses—but who?

The next spring the commissioners of the Orphan House received Nelson's plea to get out of his apprenticeship with Bronson, and took the indentures back. What happened to Nelson after this is unknown. Bronson must not have been too discouraged by his experience with orphan apprentices, because he returned to the Orphan House for at least two more apprentices in the next several years.[4]

EXPIRATION OF AN APPRENTICE'S INDENTURES marked a transition from dependence on an adult who stood in loco parentis to a life of relative independence. In the many cases that created no written records, presumably the apprentice and master amicably agreed on the timing of the exchange and contents of the freedom dues, and the suit, hat, stockings, and shoes owed by the master to the now-former apprentice. In other cases, masters balked at providing what they owed, and the young people in that predicament called on the commissioners for help. In the two young people presented below, we see in Richard Leonard's case a good example of a successful apprenticeship successfully concluded. The reason it entered the record was that his master liked his work so much he offered Richard a bonus to stay on, and Richard later lost track of what he had been owed and what he had been paid. In Catherine Shefton Miot's case, early problems in her relationship with her master and mistress led them to try to annul the arrangement. Just as with Mary Erhard, the commissioners refused to take the young woman back, and so the girl remained. When Catherine was out of her time, though, her master refused to deliver her end payment, which was just the beginning of a bumpy transition into her adult life.

In September 1808, six-year-old Richard Leonard was found "going about the streets in a miserable situation" with no adult in sight. Later that day Thomas Somersall, a warden of St. Philip's Church, brought him to the Orphan House. Col. Daniel Stevens, chairman of the Board of Commissioners and that week's visiting commissioner, accepted Richard pending the formal decision of the full board, which came five days later at their usual Thursday meeting. Over his eight years in the Orphan House, Richard learned to sign his name and prepared for his working life.

On October 31, 1816, Richard entered the home and shop of William Timmons, an ironmonger and hardware merchant, as an apprentice. He came out of his time seven years later, on September 23, 1823. At that point, Timmons, having reckoned he had found a reliable worker worth hanging onto, began negotiating over a contract extension with Leonard. How Richard and Timmons approached this payment was later described by Peter DuBois, a journeyman carpenter also living in Timmons's household. On the last day of Richard's time, DuBois recalled, "Mr Timmons gave him his indentures, and askd him how much his cloathes would come to. he said about 50 dollars but he would be satisfied with 45 dollars. Mr Timmons then gave him a 100 dollar bill & said Richard here is 100 dollars for what I owe you, and now I want to employ you, as you know that I can not do well without you." DuBois concluded, "they then made an agreement which I did not hear."

Apparently that agreement satisfied Richard, because for seven months he continued to labor in Timmons's shop, only now as a waged journeyman. But eventually he changed his mind. As a reasonably skilled worker, he may have expected to earn more for his laboring time in a more prosperous city in another part of the country. In May 1824 he decided to strike out on his own, which must have meant leaving Charleston, since he appears in no city directory of the 1820s. On his last day of work, Timmons paid him the balance of his salary, twenty-eight dollars, and Richard signed a receipt that indicated Timmons had paid him all he owed.

That fall, Richard started wondering if he truly had received all to which he was entitled. His indenture, like others drawn up by the Orphan House before 1810 or so, required the master to pay ten pounds to the Orphan House "for his use." Although this sounded like a fee charged by the institution for the hire of its children, in nearly all cases it was turned around to the former apprentice as part of his or her freedom dues. Richard visited the Orphan House to inquire about the funds, and the Orphan House queried Timmons. Timmons's reply corroborated DuBois's statement. Timmons had divided his one-hundred-dollar payment to Leonard as follows. "The estimate (made by himself) of a suit of cloathing" came to $45. The "[f]ee to the Orphan House for his use £10" added $42.80. That left $12.20 "over & above what I was bound to pay, & which of course was a Gratuity." Richard Leonard had in fact received all he was due. With that, he headed out of the Holy City to strike his fortune elsewhere.[5]

Catherine Shefton was on her way home. She vowed to shake the dust of Winnsborough, South Carolina, from her feet, even if it was mid-December, and make her way back to Charleston. Between her and the city lay 150 miles of dusty, rutted roads and at least one good-sized river. At the other end of her journey were the commissioners of the Orphan House, who might be able to help her. Her indentures to Andrew and Jane Crawford had expired a month before, but despite her reminding and cajoling, Andrew Crawford refused to pay Catherine her freedom dues. Finally she gave up and arranged for a wagon to take her to Charleston. There the commissioners of the Orphan House, she expected, would know how to extract what the Crawfords owed her. With her trunk packed onto the wagon, Catherine and the driver set off on the long way south.

Eventually they came to what she described as a "creek" but what must have been a small river—perhaps the Broad or the Congaree, depending whether they crossed above or below Columbia. The driver estimated that here in the dry season of winter, they could ford the stream. Unfortunately, the river was deeper and the current swifter than it looked. Part way across the driver lost control of his wagon, which tipped over. Catherine's trunk slid into the river and cracked open, spilling out her clothes and personal effects. The river quickly swept them downstream and far out of reach. Catherine Shefton had just lost all her worldly goods.

This was only the latest of Catherine's frustrations. Three years previously Catherine and Jane Crawford had clashed, during the summer of 1807 when Catherine was about fifteen years old. Andrew wrote the commissioners then, asking them to take Catherine back due to her "improper conduct." The commissioners had set a firm rule against such transfers, believing that once the child had left their purview it was up to the master to maintain proper deportment in his home. They "recommend[ed] to him and his wife to exercise the duties required of them by the Indentures" and refused to receive Catherine. And so she stayed in Winnsborough.

Catherine had originally come to the Crawfords in 1805, when she was thirteen years old. After four years in the Orphan House, she was the subject of a letter from Andrew Crawford, who sought an apprentice for Jane. That Andrew or Jane had met Catherine before this solicitation is doubtful, given the distance to Winnsborough. And that Catherine was to be truly an apprentice worthy of the name is equally doubtful. The trade listed on her indenture is "domestic," which suggested that she would spend her teenage years cleaning, washing, and cooking. While this involved hard manual labor and, to be sure, a certain amount of judgment and foresight in running a kitchen, in Catherine's days the demand for white domestics would always be determined by the much easier availability of enslaved black domestics, and the unpredictable variations in the tendency of the middle class to prefer women of one or the other race to manage their homes. A white domestic could not expect much of a career. No doubt a key to Catherine's post-apprenticeship future as important as any training she might receive would be the clothes and cash she was to be handed at the expiration of her time. Andrew Crawford refused to hand over the cash, and the river had just taken her clothes. The rest of her ride to Charleston must have seemed endless.

Once she reached Charleston the commissioners did their best to make Catherine whole. In response to Catherine's report that all her clothes were lost in the accident, the commissioners voted an allotment of $71.42 to replace her wardrobe and make up her freedom payment. They would account for this sum by eventually recovering her end payment from Andrew Crawford. The commissioners then paid twenty-one dollars and sixty-two and a half cents for her clothing, and the rest became a cash payment to Catherine equivalent to that promised by her indentures.

Just as Catherine Shafton's bad luck began before the overturned wagon, her misfortune did not end with it either. After her return to Charleston in the spring of 1810, she was unable to find work as a domestic. She sought advice from the matron, who went to the board on her behalf. The commissioners decided to let her stay in the Orphan House while she looked for a job, which required her to perform some of the chores around the House. At least this arrangement provided room and board. Spring turned into summer, and the commissioners, eager to get Catherine off their hands, took to advertising her availability in the newspapers. Probably at some point in 1810 or perhaps 1811 she did in fact find a place to live and work as a domestic, although the records are silent on the question.

She did not, however, attain financial self-sufficiency. Six years later in April 1816, Catherine contacted the commissioners once more for their help. Now married, Catherine Miot found herself in Charleston, but her husband was in Savannah. The husband, she informed commissioners, was "in very ill health and in distress." They voted her twenty dollars for travel expenses so she could return to her husband. She received the money, and presumably returned home to her ailing husband.[6]

A THEME IN THE HISTORY OF POOR RELIEF is the potential for assistance to make dependence on that relief habitual.[7] There were in fact a few multigenerational Orphan House families, that is, consisting of one or both parents of Orphan House residents who themselves had lived part of their childhood in the Orphan House. We can only conjecture, but it is likely that the most common long-term situations of children from the Orphan House were that after a young man's apprenticeship he met with a degree of prosperity; among female apprentices, a young woman married a man who prospered; or in the case of either sex, the young person moved westward away from Charleston. Among those alumni who turned their children over to the Orphan House was Sarah Adams. After leaving the Orphan House she remained within her extended family and later married a young man who had also been raised in the Orphan House. After some reversals of fortune, she came back to the institution with her daughters, whose adult lives seem to have been more comfortable.

The story of Sarah Adams begins with her admission to the Orphan House on February 3, 1814. She was nine years old and could not sign her name. Since the poor wardens of Charleston bound her in, it is likely that both her parents were deceased. A few years later, in November 1818, a woman named Harriett Brown applied for Sarah to become an apprentice seamstress, but the commissioners determined that Sarah had too little education to leave the institution, and so she stayed on for another six weeks. On December 31, Francis Knieff, who claimed to be the husband of Sarah's sister, asked the commissioners to bind Sarah to him and his wife. "[M]y wife," he explained, "is greatly attached" to her sister. Skeptical commissioners demanded "satisfactory recommendations" from men known to them before binding Sarah to Knieff. When he produced them, early in 1819, Sarah entered her sister's household.

The story of Sarah Adams's life would end here with a concession of ignorance about her adulthood, if she had lived a life similar to those of her friends in the Orphan House. However, Sarah encountered more hardship than most other girls, or at least more hardship in Charleston than most. Around 1823, she married John Woolcock, who had also grown up in the Orphan House. John was twenty-six years old and Sarah eighteen at the time of the wedding. John had been bound to a bricklayer named Peter Gauth, and so probably worked in the building trades, a good source of steady work in architecture-conscious Charleston. John and Sarah had three daughters, Jane, born 1823, Elizabeth, born 1825, and Mary Ann, born 1831. Something happened not long after Mary Ann's birth that shattered the family. In September 1831 John brought Jane and Elizabeth to the Orphan House, where they were admitted with John alone signing the indenture. Mary Ann apparently stayed with her mother.

Sarah Adams Woolcock's life continued to deteriorate over the next two years. In December 1833 she wrote the commissioners a letter seeking to get Mary Ann into the Orphan House as well. She was, she wrote, "in the most distressed situation not having the means of supporting [her]self &

child." She explained that John had "rendered himself incapable of supporting his family," which usually meant that he drank too much to hold down a job. As a result, Sarah wrote, "[he] casts me upon the world for charity." Since both spouses had been brought up in the Orphan House, she hoped for a positive response to her plea. Her appeal was granted, and soon thereafter the commissioners admitted Mary Ann Woolcock. Again, John signed the indenture and Sarah did not, which suggested that he was still living in Charleston. Sarah wrote that she was "broken hearted" at leaving Mary Ann at the Orphan House. No doubt when she left the Orphan House for her sister's home fourteen years before, she could not imagine that her own children would need to move into the institution.

The lives of Sarah's daughters, as well as that of Sarah herself, improved from this point. Three years later in 1837, Sarah retrieved then-fourteen-year-old Jane from the Orphan House, which neither she nor the commissioners would have desired unless she had attained some degree of material comfort greater than at the time of the girls' admission. Then in December 1845 Mary Ann, at that point also fourteen years old, returned to her mother. This time, however, her mother signed the indenture as "Mrs. Sarah Page," indicating that John had died in the meantime and Sarah had remarried.

The middle girl, Elizabeth (known as Eliza), remained in the Orphan House an unusually long time. Like all the women in this story, she entered the House unable to sign her name, but she had ten years in the Orphan House school in which to learn to write, and like her mother and sisters she signed her own name when she was bound out. Finally in the spring of 1841 a man named B. E. Habersham obtained Eliza's services as an apprentice domestic. Soon he wished he had not. Eliza continued to visit with her friends from the Orphan House in her off-hours, which Habersham determined "to be very ruinous in its influence" and so ordered the girl to cease and desist. Eliza also continued to visit her mother, who, according to Habersham, told her to ignore him and keep up with her friends. The enraged Habersham protested at the "evil advice and example" given by Sarah to Eliza. In response Eliza fled, according to Habersham at her mother's suggestion, and also according to him, she had gone into the country far from Charleston. For his part, Habersham declared that he would find another master for Eliza, but no record survives whether he did so.

Eliza's whereabouts over the next few years cannot be determined, but she apparently stayed on the good side of the Orphan House commissioners. In the spring of 1846 word got back to the Orphan House that she was about to be married and, as the commissioners put it, "might require a little pecuniary aid." The commissioners ordered that fifty dollars "as a Marriage Portion" be drawn from the private fund for her, a standard gift for young women from the Orphan House. The money went to Eliza's aunt Mrs. Lambers, who spent it "very appropriately and judiciously" on the newly married couple, as she happily reported to the commissioners in some detail. Four years later Mary Ann also received a fifty-dollar dowry. By the time of that marriage, Sarah Adams Woolcock Page would have been forty-five years old, and perhaps a grandmother.[8]

THE EARLY ORPHAN HOUSE EXPECTED most of its charges, the boys in particular, to learn a skilled trade as apprentices and work at that trade as adults. Its notions of educating children gradually shifted from skill training to book learning, and a few of the boys even left to attend university. One of them was Albert Spalding. His story illustrates both the general opportunities that further education made available to Orphan House boys, and the more specific result of offering those opportunities to a young man who had trouble making up his mind.

From very unpromising beginnings Albert Spalding's intelligence and persistence made him one of the most educated of former Orphan House residents. He was born around 1807. At some point before 1813 his father died or left his mother, because by this time Jane Spalding had entered into a common-law relationship with James Thomas Watson. A child's relationship with his mother's boyfriend was as fraught in the nineteenth century as it is today, and after Jane bore two more boys in quick succession, the younger one in May 1814, Albert's days with her were numbered. Indeed, on September 15, 1814, Albert entered the Orphan House. Whether Watson forced Jane to send Albert to the Orphan House and then he abandoned her, or if she brought Albert to the Orphan House because Watson had already left her cannot be determined. In any case, Watson left Jane and their two young boys, but remained in Charleston.

With no means of support, Jane Spalding could not continue to care for her two youngest. In December 1814, just two months after relinquishing Albert, Jane asked the commissioners to take in the two Watson boys. Because James Thomas Watson Jr. was only two years old and seven-month-old John was still nursing, the commissioners declined to take them in. The next year, the two Watson boys "were found with their mother in St. Philips Street" at night. A nearby building tradesman named Dugan took in Jane for the time being, and a local Justice of the Peace, after throwing Watson in jail for failure to support his children, asked the Orphan House to take the boys in. The commissioners appear to have lost track of the request, writing "postponed" on the back of the J.P.'s letter and not addressing the issue during their weekly meetings. How long Jane Spalding and her boys remained in Dugan's house is not clear, but it may have been a matter of months. By March 1816 a physician who, like Dugan, lived on St. Philips Street, had taken Jane into his house. Both the doctor and Mrs. Spalding prodded the commissioners to receive the boys. To support the application another witness wrote that Jane had been "a quiet industrious person" as a neighbor, and that keeping the boys away from their father would benefit all parties. The commissioners relented, and finally the Watson boys joined their half brother, Albert Spalding, at the Orphan House later in March 1816. Watson himself remained in jail.

Meanwhile in the Orphan House the schoolmaster had begun to notice Albert Spalding's gifts for schoolwork. In November 1819 Albert's hard work and talent led the commissioners to nominate him to prepare for study at the South Carolina College in Columbia. That preparation required the commissioners to find a local schoolmaster who would take him on as a private student. They visited Abiel Bolles, a Brown University graduate who taught mathematics at the College of Charleston, and offered to bind Albert to him for two years as an apprentice, during which time Albert could work for his tuition. Abiel Bolles declined that arrangement, which would have placed Albert in the Bolles household, where Abiel conducted his own school. Instead, proposed Bolles, Albert could continue to live in the Orphan House and walk the block or two to Bolles's home. The commissioners accepted.

Albert entered a youthful limbo before his lessons could begin. Bolles insisted on the commissioners outfitting Albert in some decent clothes before appearing at the classroom in his home. As clothes were a standard part of the package given to scholarship boys sent off to Columbia, the commissioners were not about to buy them early and for a boy still living under their roof. Bolles stood firm on his sense of decorum, and Albert returned to the Orphan House school for the time being. Later, in the spring of 1821, two prospective masters applied for Albert by name, one a baker and the other an accountant. The commissioners turned them down.

Albert Spalding finally made it to Columbia two years later, where he studied at the South Carolina College. From 1823 to 1826 the state of South Carolina, through the Charleston Orphan House, paid his tuition and living expenses. He continued his studies after leaving Columbia, possibly matriculating at the Medical College of South Carolina, which had opened in 1824 in Charleston. He may also have studied medicine in Georgia, where he was admitted to the practice in 1828, when he was twenty-one years old.

By this time Spalding had grown into a thoughtful young man. In the course of medical training and practice, he wrote the commissioners in 1833, he had been looking back on his years in the Orphan House and how he had reached his current state in life. He was grateful to the Orphan House for all it had given him, and he was aware of the workings of Divine Providence in arranging for all his blessings. In fact, Spalding wrote, he was so aware of Divine Providence that he had forsaken the practice of medicine and had become an ordained minister in the Baptist church. He wrote that he was working "diligently" at his new calling, but still, he regretted his lack of "a finished education." That may have referred to a lack of divinity school training, since he both resigned his medical practice and received ordination in 1831. In January 1835 Spalding achieved a gratifying professional moment when he preached a service in the Orphan House chapel, where he himself had listened to many sermons as a boy. Afterward the commissioners learned—from whom else than Spalding himself?—that their protégé felt that a lack of books was limiting his ministerial work. So they resolved to send him one hundred dollars, specifically for religious books and other means of improving his ministry. His self-improvement campaign soon bore fruit, for the next year Spaulding was called to an important pulpit at the Greenville Baptist Church far upstate, where he served as pastor from 1836 to 1843, after which he and his family moved to Gainesville, Georgia, until 1851.

The life of the Rev. Albert Spalding never remained unexamined for long. In the midst of his pastorate in Greenville, he wrote the commissioners of the Orphan House once more to ask for financial assistance. His interest in medicine had rekindled, and he wrote to request financial support to attend lectures at the Medical College back in Charleston, some two hundred miles away, for three months. This time, however, the commissioners declined, and the Rev. Spalding continued in his newer calling.[9]

THE REMAINING LIVES INCLUDE one man and one woman who represent the most positive outcomes that the Orphan House commissioners might have hoped for. Neither remained in Charleston; the woman, Louisa Gardner Swain, went west, and the man, Thomas Gedney, to sea. He achieved professional success, and she did everything necessary to hold her family together. Actions of both appear in regional and topical histories, and illustrate lives of public and private heroism. What distinguishes them from Orphan House alumni who did not do as well was no doubt much the same mixture of personal character, circumstances, and luck as leads to success today. Unlike Sarah Adams's daughters, Louisa Swain did not receive a dowry from the

Orphan House, but she persisted through difficulties and raised her family all the same. Much as with Thomas Holdup Stevens in chapter 7, Thomas Gedney received assistance from the Orphan House in beginning his naval career. Gedney showed a truly remarkable talent for being present at historical events three times in his life. That must have been due largely to chance, but perhaps such luck really was the residue of design. Louisa Gardner Swain's life may have been marked most by her persistence in the face of disappointment. Such pluck and tenacity as exhibited by both Swain and Gedney may be the most enduring characteristic of all of Charleston's poor whites.

Louisa Gardner had been initially turned away from the Orphan House. Her father had been lost at sea, and so her mother returned to Charleston to be near her family. When Louisa's mother died she became a full orphan, but that could not change the fact of her birth in Virginia. Six weeks after rejecting her initial application, the board reversed itself, citing some undefined "peculiar circumstances of the case," and Louisa at age ten moved into the Orphan House. As described in chapter 7, Louisa Gardner and Mary Turner (who had entered at the same time as William Tucker, discussed above) stayed with their mistress nearly four years and then returned to the Orphan House in 1818. Louisa by that time was around seventeen years old.

Louisa was then bound into the Porter family for her final year of service. Even before she and Mary Turner had officially been received back into the Orphan House, W. L. Porter contacted the commissioners asking for Louisa by name. She was "to be brought up in his family under the direction of his wife." Porter and, no doubt primarily, his wife Anne promised to teach Louisa how to work as a seamstress. The relationship between Louisa and the Porters must have been a happy one, for in an 1823 letter, long after Louisa was out of her time, they reported to the commissioners, "[Louisa's] conduct has always merited our warmest approbation." They were so happy, in fact, that a few months after Louisa left their service they obtained another girl from the Orphan House, Mary Van Draper. Unfortunately, "circumstances of an extremely delicate nature" caused the Porters to send Mary Van Draper back to the Orphan House on short notice. They emphasized the sensitive nature of the situation by informing the steward of the events orally but not recording them on paper. To support their own probity, the Porters urged the commissioners to ask Louisa Gardner about life in their home.

Surprisingly, we know quite a bit about Louisa's adult life before, as the saying goes, she entered the history books. At some point while she was young, perhaps as early as 1821, the year after she left the Porter household, Louisa married a man named Stephen Swain. They spent some years in Baltimore where he operated a chair factory and she gave birth to four children. Then perhaps in the early 1830s, Swain sold the chair company and moved the family first to Zanesville, Ohio, and then to Indiana. Hard times came to the Swain family in Richmond, Indiana, and in 1845 Louisa, swallowing her pride, wrote to the commissioners to ask for money. By this time the Orphan House was regularly giving fifty-dollar wedding gifts as a dowry to young women who had lived there. But Louisa was not a young woman about to be married; she was middle aged and approaching her twenty-fifth wedding anniversary. The commissioners found no charge to care for alumnae old enough to have grandchildren in the institution and turned her request down.

Stephen and Louisa Swain kept moving west. In 1869 they moved to Wyoming, where they joined their son Alfred in Laramie. The Laramie *Daily Sentinel* described Louisa as "a lady . . . of the highest social standing in the community, universally beloved and respected." The occasion of this apotheosis was the 1870 election, in which Louisa cast her vote under Wyoming's new universal suffrage law. It happened that Louisa Gardner Swain was the first woman to vote that year in Wyoming, thus becoming the first woman in the United States to vote under an equal suffrage law. A statue to honor her stands today in Laramie, Wyoming.[10]

Thomas Gedney's first bout of notoriety came from breaking Orphan House rules, but those early misjudgments did not foreshadow his adult life of courage and action. One day in 1811 commissioners discovered that the Orphan House's chicken coop was holding ever fewer chickens that provided ever fewer eggs. The steward's stakeout revealed that Gedney was one of the thieves. Because the steward and commissioners concluded that the boys had "no evil intention" but "did it merely for fun," they were only "severely reprimanded" for their efforts. Besides his fearlessness, Thomas possessed considerable physical strength. When the steward and schoolmaster clashed over putting Orphan House inmates to work in and around their own homes, the schoolmaster confessed that he employed Thomas because he was the only boy "strong enough to render the requisite services." No doubt the commissioners hoped that Gedney would channel his strength and initiative toward something more constructive than stealing eggs and lifting heavy sacks.

That something turned out to be the US Navy. In July 1813 Captain E. P. Kennedy asked the Orphan House for permission to obtain two boys who would serve "as apprentices to the Sea." He chose Gedney and a boy named Samuel Mercer, and he chose well in both. Several decades later Mercer would remain loyal to the Union, and at age sixty-two he would command the unsuccessful relief convoy to Fort Sumter in spring 1861. While expressing their gratitude commissioners reminded Kennedy that part of his charge was to look out for Gedney's and Mercer's interests in the service. Because their own aim, they wrote, was "to place [the boys] in the service of the United States," they expected that "Captn Kennedy will favor their promotion and relinquish their indentures whenever it shall be for their interest." The commissioners must have been pleased with Kennedy's efforts as Gedney and Mercer rose through the ranks.

As an officer, Gedney participated in three activities of historical interest. In 1834 and 1835 while on survey duty, he discovered what became the Gedney Channel into New York Harbor. Not only was the channel, near Sandy Hook, New Jersey, named after him, but to honor this discovery some years later the US Coast and Geodetic Survey steamer *Thomas R. Gedney* was named after him as well. A second and better-known event involved the slave ship *Amistad* in 1839. The slaves on board had successfully risen against the captain and crew, and had anchored off Long Island, New York, intending to send out shore parties for water. Gedney, commanding the US Coast Survey brig *Washington*, encountered *Amistad* and seized it. He towed the ship to Connecticut and sued to be granted it as salvage. Eventually the US Supreme Court awarded the ship to Gedney and freed its slaves.

Gedney saved the life of Andrew Jackson in 1835. The president had attended a funeral in the hall of the House of Representatives. On Jackson's way out, a man approached within ten feet and shot twice. Each misfired. At the first shot, Jackson characteristically pushed forward to club the assailant with his walking stick. In between them leapt Lieutenant Gedney of the Navy. He knocked down the attacker, a mentally disturbed man, and saved Jackson from the threat of further violence. It is hard to be completely certain that this Lieutenant Gedney was Thomas R., but it is reasonably likely. The funeral at which the events occurred was for a South Carolina congressman, Warren R. Davis. Thomas Hart Benton, who was nearby but not an eyewitness, named the bodyguard as Lieutenant Gedney. Benton did not specify his first name, but Gedney at this time was in fact a lieutenant.

Gedney later rose to the rank of commander and served in the Far East. In 1849 the fleet surgeon of the East India Squadron notified his commanding officer of concern over Gedney's excessive drinking and gambling. Although this situation eventually resolved itself, Gedney died in 1857 at the relatively young age of fifty-eight.[11]

MORE THAN TWO THOUSAND CHILDREN LIVED in the Orphan House between 1790 and 1860. A mere dozen examples cannot represent all. But they do represent much that was common to many Orphan House children. William Tucker and Sarah Adams Woolcock and her daughters gained access to education and learned to write their names. Jane Spalding gave Albert up to the Orphan House and hoped to maintain her other two sons, until she was overwhelmed with poverty. James Nelson remained in contact with his mother even after he had been bound out apprentice. Thomas Gedney went to sea. Richard Leonard completed his apprenticeship and then worked in his chosen trade. Louisa Gardner Swain married, raised a family, and moved west. If we knew all there was to know about the paths of all Orphan House children through their lives, many of these themes would appear and reappear. We might guess that a life of steady laboring that Richard Leonard seemed poised to begin was much more common than William Tucker's lawbreaking, and that more children were born to former Orphan House girls within marriage, as in Louisa Swain's case, than outside of it, as in Mary Erhard's case. Still, even if we cannot know which lives were representative, the information we do have about these few of the Orphan House children is all the more valuable because it is real and well documented: it comes directly from testimonies of poor lives from some two centuries ago.

CHAPTER TEN

Epilogue

O N OCTOBER 18, 1810, THE ORPHAN HOUSE celebrated its anniversary, as it did on the eighteenth of every October. All but one of the commissioners were present that morning, as were "the Superintending Ladies of the female Oeconomy of the Institution."[1] At precisely eleven o'clock in the morning, the 150 or so children processed from the Orphan House to the chapel, and at noon they were followed by the city's poor wardens, various clergy, commissioners, city council members, and other dignitaries. The crowd marched down the front-entrance walkway from the Orphan House to Boundary Street, turning left for the half block to King Street, then left again at King. They walked the full block to Vanderhorst Street, where they made their final left turn to stroll the short distance to the chapel. Once all parties had entered and were seated, the children sang the Nineteenth Psalm ("The heavens are telling the glory of God") accompanied by organ. When they finished, one of the more capable boys approached the podium and began the first address of the day. This year it was thirteen-year-old John Wish, who was soon to begin service as a midshipman aboard the US frigate *John Adams*. Wish demonstrated "a manly deportment and dignity of delivery" in his speech, which "filled every bosom with sensations of rapture and admiration." After another hymn ("Hail Charity! Fair Daughter of the Skies") came the main event of the afternoon: a peroration delivered by the Rev. Christopher E. Gadsden, the prominent Episcopal clergyman. The children's chorus followed with its last effort of the day, and the Rev. Gadsden pronounced a benediction upon all present. Judge Henry W. De-Saussure, chairman of the commissioners, invited all the citizens to observe the children at their dinner to see for themselves how "happily and plentifully provided" the inmates were, at least at the anniversary dinner. The formalities concluded with an event important to the institution: a collection that gathered some $349, plus the usual hundred dollars from an anonymous benefactress. The commissioners were grateful for the support of the people.

The events of this anniversary celebration made for a typical October 18th at the Orphan House. From the late-eighteenth to the early-twentieth century, the anniversary was a holiday not just for the orphans within the institution; it enabled white Charleston as a whole to recognize the sacrifices of donors and taxpayers, the competence of the Orphan House's managers, and the resilient spirit of the children whose presence witnessed to great suffering. During the 1810 ceremony, the Rev. Gadsden described and analyzed the place of the Orphan House within the greater society of Charleston. First, the institution made the city a moral example to the nation as a whole. "Your country," he told Charlestonians, "calls on you to foster this Institution of national virtue."[2] By caring for the helpless the city was providing an excellent illustration of the Christian aim of loving one's neighbor. In addition, Gadsden observed, the Orphan House was a unifying influence among the "[f]ellow-citizens, of every class, and age, and denomination" that made up the city's population. In fact, in his opinion, the purpose of the Orphan House was only secondarily social welfare, or even Christian charity. "Ultimately," its reason for being was to promote "the virtue and happiness of the community." By producing "industrious, patriotic, virtuous, capable" young people, the Orphan House improved "the character of the community." Indeed, by "infus[ing] into the community virtuous principles," the Orphan House properly merged "the public good and the prosperity of this Institution."

Then Gadsden raised a rarely discussed possibility, the consequences of the absence of those virtuous principles. If his listeners proved unable to form a unified and cohesive community through the help of the Orphan House, he suggested, they might lose the society they had worked so hard to build up. To see the results of a factious and riven white community, he reminded them, "Ask the inhabitant of St. Domingo what vicissitudes have occurred in the short period of his life, and judge what may be expected in two or three generations." In Saint-Domingue the white elites (*grands blancs*) had not only mishandled the potential for slave resistance, but they ignored the increasingly violent and embittered white working class (*petits blancs*). In 1791 the slaves rose up and eventually, together with the free persons of color (*affranchis*), defeated their French rulers. The lesson was not lost on Gadsden or his listeners. A failure to promote unity and cohesion among the white inhabitants of Charleston, who were slightly outnumbered, but fully self-consciously so, by free and enslaved black Charlestonians, could carry dreadful consequences.[3]

In the years after the Saint-Domingue cataclysm, Charleston entered one of its periodic cycles of anxiety over the prospect of racial violence. From summer 1793 refugees had been landing in the port with eyewitness narratives of ghastly brutality. Among the city's responses was the Orphan House's decision to admit orphaned survivors immediately. In the midst of this elevated racial awareness, in 1803 the state of South Carolina re-opened the African slave trade. Before its constitutional end in 1808, some forty thousand unfortunate Africans passed through the city's slave markets. Uneasy about its growing black population, Charleston restricted legal activities of slaves and free blacks in 1806. Ordinances limited the number of blacks who could gather at one place, closely regulated or banned their commercial activities, and even forbade them from walking with a cane "or other stick" unless they had been certified as infirm or blind.[4]

Years before Christopher Gadsden's sermon, racial tensions had been part of Charleston's consciousness. Almost from its founding, and through to the Civil War and beyond, white Charleston concentrated, fixated even, on securing its position as a white island in a sea of blacks. In the colonial period leading up to the Stono Rebellion (1739), rising white fears resolved in early legal efforts to suppress black gatherings and other perceived threats.[5] Episodes such as the Denmark Vesey events triggered additional fears and legal repression in the 1820s. Eventually, restrictions on black movement and activities culminated in laws of the 1850s that aimed to enslave free persons of color who could not prove their free status. By this time where race relations were concerned Charleston had become, according to one historian, a "police state."[6]

Thus, Christopher Gadsden's 1810 commentary pointed to what was both a continuing source of concern in Charleston, and what had become, other than legal repression, the chief means of dealing with white fears of black violence: unity. Toward the end of the antebellum period, Southern writers emphasized how slavery led to a fundamental equality among whites, but Gadsden went further in his analysis. He sought to link white civic society with a broadly unified white population, forming a broad and united front that would discourage black resistance before it could get started.[7] Without that unity, the city was at risk of a Saint-Domingue-type conflagration. It is this link between civic society and racial unity that helps explain the puzzling question why the first (and for many years the only) large-scale public orphanage in America should have been built in Charleston.

The city's wealth was only a necessary factor; other important American cities produced and retained plenty of wealth also. What these cities lacked was the sufficient motivation of racial ideology.

This is not to deny all charitable motivations of commissioners and benefactors of the institution. They wanted to provide for helpless and vulnerable children, and many wanted so do so on the basis of specifically Christian teaching.[8] They proved their sincerity by the many hours and dollars they poured into the institution. And the effects of this labor were considerable. To the extent that its goal was to educate poor and distressed white children who would otherwise have gone uneducated, the Orphan House was successful. Many of the children who received a basic education would likely have learned very little otherwise, not enough even to write their names, to judge by signature patterns at entrance and exit, among same-aged children. And so each leader and donor, from Arnoldus Vanderhorst to Agnes Irving, from the clergy who preached charity sermons for the Orphan House to regular and generous donors such as Mordecai Cohen, to the anonymous benefactress who enabled Orphan House boys to attend college, all could look at their efforts and see that countless children would reach adulthood with more hopeful prospects than otherwise, thanks to their efforts. The city's pride in the institution was not misplaced, and its eagerness to display its charity understandable.

But to claim, as did the planter, merchant, and statesman Henry Laurens, that Charlestonians were more sensitive than other Americans to needs of the suffering poor begs the question, were Charlestonians so charitable? This book's answer is a qualified yes. Between 1790 and 1860 the Orphan House protected, educated, and otherwise cared for some two thousand children, nearly all of whom had lost at least one parent and whose alternative situations ranged from difficult to appalling. Recognition of this outstanding achievement must be qualified, as with so many aspects of Southern history, by reference to race. The qualification here must recognize that differential treatment of children by race went well beyond care for whites and simple exclusion of blacks. On the one hand, dependent whites were victims of bad luck (perhaps aided by alcohol), but on the other, white society as a whole acted positively to make life more difficult and painful for blacks. The astute social commentator Sarah Grimké excoriated the Charleston bourgeoisie who went out of their way to provide charity to the white poor and then showed no mercy to the poor under their own roofs: their slaves. In historian Barbara Bellows's view, neither Sarah nor Angelina Grimké could tolerate Charlestonians' acquiescence to "the complex mixture of good and evil in the human heart."⁹ Perhaps the problem was not acquiescence but active manipulation of good in the service of evil. That is, Charleston was unique in the early republic in creating the charitable Orphan House because in no other city did the elite need to make common cause with the white poor and working class against the potential common black enemy. The charity of the Orphan House thus unified white Charleston, so that it could preserve a culture based on slave labor.¹⁰

This social contract did not persist unbroken throughout the antebellum period. Not all whites appeared worthy to the commissioners. By the later 1840s, waves of Irish and German immigrants came to Charleston seeking little more than regular work. These newcomers fell into a far different category from the Saint-Domingue refugees, many of whom had owned slaves and nearly all of whom believed in the necessity of slavery. The later immigrants were numerous, permanent, and, worst of all, Charlestonians suspected they were "unprincipled . . . enemies to our peculiar institution," and so of questionable loyalty. Hardly less dangerous, perhaps, to the commissioners was the prospect of their impoverished offspring overwhelming the capabilities of the Orphan House, which, in Henry A. DeSaussure's words, would "greatly increase the burthen of the citizens by the increased expenses of the Institution." Thanks to fiscal limitations, white unity carried the whiff of Know-Nothingism by late in the antebellum era.¹¹

With that exception rather late in the period, making common racial cause helps explain the extraordinary degree of consensus among children, parents and guardians, masters and mistresses, and commissioners regarding the future of these children. The children themselves endorsed the contract that committed them to the care of the commissioners not once, but twice, agreeing to abide by Orphan House rules and then by the rule of their master or mistress. To enter the Orphan House a child had to want to live there. It would not be accurate to describe the parent's action as *relinquishment*, a term used in twentieth-century adoptions. While the parent did indeed agree to let the commissioners stand in loco parentis, rarely did the new legal parental figures deny the original parent a request to visit the child, to bind him or her to a particular master, or to remove a youth from an unsatisfactory apprenticeship. And indeed, for the transfer from Orphan House to the master's shop or home to occur, the master or mistress needed to obtain the agreement of the surviving parent or guardian. In many cases commissioners, who numbered among their ranks the most powerful and wealthiest men in a society characterized by fabulous (and fabulously unequally distributed) wealth, did exactly what half-literate and tattered women of utterly no social, political, or legal standing wanted them to do with their children. These actions were extraordinary demonstrations of racial solidarity across class lines.

The Orphan House itself did not come to an end in April 1861 but continued to care for abandoned, orphaned, and impoverished children into the twentieth century. The war, of course, shattered any sense of normality for the inmates of the Orphan House as it did for all other Americans. Anniversary celebrations were muted, and collections redirected to hospitals caring for wounded Confederate soldiers. In summer 1863 the children evacuated to Orangeburg, there to sit out the war in a disused seminary for young ladies. Discipline weakened considerably, and after the children and supervisors returned to the city, the commissioners knew just the person to solve this problem. Their appointment of Agnes K. Irving, already Principal of the school, to take over the duties of steward and matron made her the executive officer of the entire institution. Her service to the Orphan House extended into the twentieth century, and thus made her the single most important individual in the history of the Orphan House.[12] The fate of the Orphan House in the twentieth century was both typical of urban orphanages in America and an example of the Charleston we have lost. The form of the institution changed as the risk of parental death declined. In 1951 all children in residence moved to the new facility at Oak Grove in North Charleston, which continues to the present as the Carolina Youth Development Center. The Orphan House and its chapel, survivors of fire, hurricane, earthquake, and Union naval bombardment, were demolished soon thereafter. The loss of the Orphan House and its chapel helped inspire later historic preservation efforts in Charleston. The buildings were replaced by a Sears, Roebuck and Co. store, which itself closed in 1981.[13]

HOW TO ASSESS the first three-quarters of a century in the history of the Charleston Orphan House? No poor orphan had it easy in eighteenth- and nineteenth-century America, and many aspects of orphanage life must have been very difficult.[14] The steward Benjamin Cudsworth complained upon his resignation that while the girls were generally of "very good" character, the boys tended toward "malignant" behavior. Life in the Orphan House, he concluded, "was Hell."[15] However, we should note the experiences of other contemporary children before accepting these harsh judgments uncritically. In most of the North, binding poor orphans to local masters was a common practice with potentially grim consequences for the children. Barry Levy, among the more critical historians of extrafamilial child-raising institutions at this time, characterized the Massachusetts system of binding out abandoned or destitute children as "unsentimental, often abusive, [and] exploitative."[16] Town fathers in New England had the power to remove a child from the master's household upon proof of abuse, but how often that happened, and how effective it was in preventing abuse cannot be determined.[17] Certainly some orphans who were bound at a very young age were treated primarily as a cheap source of hard labor.[18]

The Charleston Orphan House must have been an improvement upon purely outdoor methods of orphan care in which the child's well-being was monitored only to the extent that neighbors or surviving parents complained about abuses.[19] Unlike the New England practice of using outdoor poor relief as orphan care, in Charleston "vicious" children stood some chance of being corrected in the Orphan House, adult supervisors were reasonably closely monitored, and educational efforts provided some minimal level of training. Children who passed through the Charleston Orphan House received an average of five years of care that included reasonably effective basic education. Had they remained with their impoverished family or been bound directly to their masters at age eight or so, their prospects for exploitation would have been greater and prospects for basic literacy training less promising.

But making a better life for luckless orphans and half orphans was only part of the Orphan House's charge. To the extent that the Orphan House aimed to assimilate the poor whites of Charleston into a unified white civic society, the Orphan House also succeeded. The ongoing role of widowed birth parents in children's lives after their legal separation at the Orphan House gate was part of a larger social process that enshrined consensus among white Charlestonians. This occurred across class lines and across religious lines as well. However upset Catholics and Jews may have been when local ministers preached lowest-common-denominator Protestantism to their children in the Orphan House, city fathers believed that it contributed greatly to white unity.[20] The emphasis on harmony of interests illustrated again the lengths to which Charleston's white elite went to accommodate the city's white poor.

Nearly all parties discussed in this book were white, but half of Charlestonians were black. A recurring theme in South Carolina historiography is the recognition by the white elite that racial unity was necessary to preserve the political and social order.[21] The Orphan House was a means to maintain that racial unity in Charleston. Through this institution the elite class could offer insurance to the city's poorest whites in case of disaster, and for many, hope of upward mobility. By contrast, public policy to provide for needy blacks tended toward incarceration. Immediately after the Denmark Vesey events, the pundit James Gregorie urged that the city invest in a "stepping mill" for the Work House, and then collar as many blacks as needed to grind grain for the city's institutionalized population.[22] It was important for the most powerful whites to address the situations of the white poor and black poor differently and publicly in antebellum Charleston.

The Orphan House was a benevolent institution, to be sure, but disinterested it was not. It was an institution with a charitable aim, to care for destitute, orphaned, and abandoned white children, and that charge it fulfilled with diligence. It was also a political institution that provided self-assurance to white leaders of their goodness, and it reminded the white poor of the paternal concern of the white elite. The Orphan House bound together all strata of white society, marking Charleston as the only city in America that would have thought to create such an institution at such an early date. Distressed parents and guardians sought its charity. Commissioners from the wealthy elite spent considerable hours enacting their magnanimity. Masters from the artisanal classes obtained the labor they needed while providing homes to luckless little ones. And the destitute children who hardly appear anywhere else in Charleston's rich history found some degree of compassion. Webs of white cooperation reached across class lines, as if the other half of Charleston's population weren't there at all.

NOTES

PREFACE

1. Herndon and Murray, *Children Bound to Labor*; Murray, "Literacy Acquisition in an Orphanage," "Fates of Orphans," and "Family, Literacy, and Skill-Training in the Antebellum South."

CHAPTER ONE

1. Until 1868, regional governments known as counties elsewhere were called districts in South Carolina.

2. Lawrence Hendricks, entered 11 June 1835; Henry and Richard Hendricks, entered 23 February 1833, Indenture Books. On Richard: Margaret Black to commissioners, 8 May 1838; Rejected Applications, file of Richard Hendricks; and Minutes, 29 March 1838, 16 May 1838. On Henry: Minutes, 27 May 1841, 24 June 1841. On Lawrence: Minutes, 7 April 1842, 14 July 1842, 19 October 1843, 22 February 1844, 5 March 1846, 12 March 1846, 1 April 1847, 22 April 1847; L[awrence] C. B. Hendricks to Mrs. Caroline B. Hendricks, 6 May 1845; J. A. Stevenson to commissioners, 23 February 1846; Stevenson to commissioners, 17 March 1846; Lawrence C. Hendricks to H. A. DeSaussure, 31 March 1846; W. J. Little to H. A. DeSaussure, 7 April 1846; H. A. D[eSaussure] to W. J. Little, 11 April 1846; Stevenson to DeSaussure, 20 April 1846; Hendricks to DeSaussure, 27 April 1846; Little to DeSaussure, 30 April 1846, all in Indentures, file of Lawrence Hendricks. Regarding the document categories Indenture Books, Minutes, Applications, Rejected Applications, Indentures, and Rejected Indentures, see the bibliography.

3. The finest collection of first-person narratives of the poor in the colonial and early republic period comes from warning-out interrogations in New England. Ruth Herndon analyzed these in compelling fashion in *Unwelcome Americans*.

4. Coclanis, *The Shadow of a Dream*, 48–110.

5. Ibid., 111–58.

6. Degler, *At Odds*, 69, 71.

7. Graff, *Conflicting Paths*, 184.

8. Mintz, *Huck's Raft*, 133, 403nn1–2.

9. Glover, *All Our Relations*; Censer, *North Carolina Planters and Their Children*; and Jabour, *Marriage in the Early Republic*.

10. Wyatt-Brown, *Southern Honor*, 126–37.

11. McMillen, *Motherhood in the Old South*.

12. Bardaglio, *Reconstructing the Household*, 97–111.

13. Lebsock, *The Free Women of Petersburg*, xvii.

14. Kierner, *Beyond the Household*, 124–128.

15. Bolton, *Poor Whites in the Antebellum South*; Cecil-Fronsman, *Common Whites*.

16. Owsley, *Plain Folk of the Old South*.

17. McCurry, *Masters of Small Worlds*.

18. Lockley, *Lines in the Sand*; Forret, *Race Relations at the Margins*.

19. Two exceptions that make imaginative use of limited data on bound white workers in early Charleston are Walsh, *Charleston's Sons of Liberty*, and Morris, "White Bondage in Ante-Bellum South Carolina." Topics in the latter essay also appear in Morris, *Government and Labor in Early America*.

20. Smith, *The "Lower Sort"*; Herndon, *Unwelcome Americans*.

21. On communities of the poor, see Rockman, *Scraping By*, and Snell, "Belonging and Community."

22. On racial politics of poor relief in rural South Carolina, see Lockley, "Public Poor Relief." On eighteenth-century concerns for racial unity, see Morgan, *Slave Counterpoint*, 307–11. Bellows (*Benevolence among Slaveholders*, 121) proposed that poor white support for the Orphan House "increased whenever Charleston society felt threatened," whether by racial violence or external political forces, such as federal responses to Nullification.

CHAPTER TWO

1. In Williams, *Vogues in Villiany*, court-ordered child support payments were meager, on the order of twenty-five dollars per year.

2. Pyburn, "The Public School System of Charleston Before 1860."

3. Fraser, "The City Elite, 'Disorder,' and the Poor Children of Pre-Revolutionary Charleston," 175.

4. Ibid., 178, quoting St. Philip's Vestry Book.

5. Cashin, *Beloved Bethesda*. Institutional histories from this time period continue to engage Rothman's landmark *Discovery of the Asylum*. The present book, while not a history of the Orphan House per se, is broadly sympathetic to Rothman's emphasis on social control of children and the poor. However, in the case of Charleston, for reasons that will become apparent, the socially controlled were not the children and the poor, but precisely those outside the purview of the institution: the slave population.

Histories of other American orphanages, most necessarily from a much later period than the present one, include Cmiel, *A Home of Another Kind*; Zmora, *Orphanages Reconsidered*; Polster, *Inside Looking Out*. See also Hacsi, *Second Home*; and Clement, "Children and Charity."

6. See *City Gazette* 8 (October 21, 1790): 4. The Charleston Orphan House was the first public orphanage in the country; the privately funded Bethesda was older by a half century.

7. "An Ordinance to Establish an Orphan-House in the City of Charleston," Edwards, *Ordinances of the City Council of Charleston*, 82–83.

8. Rev. Charles S. Vedder, D.D., "Centennial Oration," in *Charleston Orphan House: Centennial Celebration*, 19–40. See also King, *History and Records of the Charleston Orphan House 1790–1860*, 6; Fraser, *Charleston! Charleston!*, 296; Minutes, 28 October 1790, 4 November 1790, 27 January 1791.

9. The transition from colonial pounds to US dollars was gradual, and pounds continued to be used as the unit of account for some years under the Constitution. See Grubb, "Creating the U.S. Dollar."

10. Minutes, 28 October 1790; Fraser, *Charleston! Charleston!*, 174; Wallace, *South Carolina*, 347.

11. Pease and Pease, in *The Web of Progress*, note that relative to boards for other charities and civic institutions, the commissioners of the Orphan House were better educated and wealthier—really the elite of the elite (103, 293n41).

12. Lockley, *Welfare and Charity in the Antebellum South*, 60–114. On Charleston in particular see Bellows, *Benevolence among Slaveholders*.

13. Minutes, 5 September 1800, 19 September 1800, 22 February 1801, 19 March 1801, 9 May 1805, 12 June 1806, 7 August 1809, 3 August 1815, 1 July 1819, 10 February 1820, 18 January 1821, 28 June 1821, 19 June 1823, 10 March 1825, 21 January 1830, 22 April 1830, 5 May 1831, 14 June 1832, 14 December 1843. These represent a small fraction of the commissioners' meetings that involved consultation with the ladies or action on their recommendations. Compare Bellows (*Benevolence*, 122), who described their role as "marginal." More detail on the ladies appears in Gail S. Murray, "Charity within the Bounds of Race and Class."

14. Minutes, 4 November 1790, 14 July 1791.

15. The state law was enacted in 1799 and limited the value of escheated property that the Orphan House could claim to $50,000. See Meriwether, *History of Higher Education*, 82.

16. Fraser, *Charleston! Charleston!*, 142; Severens, *Charleston*, 182–85; Ravenel, *Architects of Charleston*, 81–82, 93; McInnis, *Politics of Taste in Antebellum Charleston*, 219–31. A fine study of community building through school building, set in the North, is Beadie, *Education and the Creation of Human Capital in the Early American Republic*.

17. Minutes, 10 July 1791 through 18 September 1791.

18. Minutes, 1 Sept 1791, 22 Sept 1791, 15 Sept 1793, 19 July 1792.

19. Severens, *Charleston*, 18; Ravenel, *Architects*, 81–82; Minutes, 7 August 1809. The number of children appeared on a cornerstone (*Charleston Orphan House: Centennial Celebration*, 62). The visitor was James Stirling (Clark, *South Carolina: The Grand Tour, 1780–1865*, 275).

20. Minutes, 17 November 1791, 23 August 1795. Similarly, one fear concerning literate slaves was that they would learn to forge passes. This was exactly how Mary Standford escaped from the Orphan House in 1794: by writing or otherwise obtaining a forged note that permitted her to leave the grounds (Minutes, 11 September 1794). On forged slave passes, see Franklin and Schweninger, *Runaway Slaves*.

21. Ravenel, *Architects*, 82.

22. Minutes, 7 May 1791, 25 February 1819.

23. Minutes, 24 April 1817; Indenture Books, Thomas Washington Giles, admitted 12 September 1811. Minutes, 1 December 1825. Gibbes's memoirs appear as Gibbes, "William Hasell Gibbes." As master in equity he oversaw trust arrangements for orphans with property.

24. Minutes, 1 September 1791, 16 July 1840. The commissioners recognized an exchange rate of about 4.3 dollars to the South Carolina pound; see chapter 9 on penalty fee equivalents. This is consistent with McCusker, *How Much Is That in Real Money?*, appendix C.

25. Minutes, 26 October 1794; Ravenel, *Architects*, 81; Keith-Lucas, *A Legacy of Caring*, 1.

26. Minutes, 26 February 1795.

27. "Domestic Occurrences," *American Monthly Magazine and Critical Review* 3 (October 1818): 469.

28. Minutes, 9 August 1821; *Revised Ordinances of the City of Charleston, South Carolina*, 391; Minutes, 11 July 1822 and 18 July 1822.

29. Minutes, 14 July 1852.

30. Minutes, 8 November 1855.

31. "Copies of Wills, 1804–1810," 9.

32. "Frederick Kohne." On the Inglis Arch House, see Poston, *Buildings of Charleston*, 103.

33. Minutes, 16 July 1840, 6 September 1821, 23 October 1834.

34. Minutes, 16 July 1840. Edwards, *Ordinances*, 83.

35. Committee on Private Funds report in Minutes, 16 July 1840.

36. Minutes, 2 December 1802. See also 3 March 1825 (fireworks to welcome Lafayette to Charleston), 9 February 1832 (fireworks for Washington's birthday).

37. Minutes, 13 August 1846. See also 20 January 1820, on a balloon exhibition.

38. Minutes, 13 September 1855, 5 April 1855, 19 April 1855.

39. Minutes 28 December 1809, 10 September 1807, 28 June 1810.

40. Minutes, 5 July 1816, 20 February 1817.

41. F. Lauer to commissioners, 14 February 1839, in Applications.

42. Minutes, 2 November 1815, 25 July 1816, 31 January 1828, 4 September 1828, 10 January 1833, 24 October 1833. Indentures, Charles Payne, entered 2 November 1815. Lesesne, *The Bank of the State of South Carolina*, 11.

43. Minutes, 6 June 1800, 23 March 1815, 24 September 1818.

44. Bellows, *Benevolence*, describes the two episodes on successive pages, 128–29, with no obvious sense of irony.

45. Fick, *Making of Haiti*. Minutes, 26 September 1793, 7 September 1794, 8 March 1804, 5 December 1805. On the mood in Charleston, see Rogers, *Charleston in the Age of the Pinckneys*, 131, 142, 153; Fraser, *Charleston! Charleston!*, 182–85. As late as 1805 the Orphan House accepted Saint-Domingue refugees under this rule (Minutes, 23 May 1805). Probably they were fleeing Dessalines's policy of ethnic cleansing (Hunt, *Haiti's Influence on Antebellum America*, 39–40).

46. Minutes, 29 June 1837.

47. Minutes, 18 August 1796, 18 September 1806, 1 August 1811, 16 April 1812, 16 July 1807, 8 December 1814, 1 July 1813, 27 May 1841. See also "Servants to the

Orphan House Institution," a list of enslaved workers. A study of institutionally owned slaves appears in Oast, "The Worst Kind of Slavery."

48. Physician's Reports.

49. Minutes, 12 August 1852.

50. Minutes, 17 June 1819, 15 July 1819; 5 May 1825, 23 June 1825, 20 May 1830; McInnis, *Politics of Taste*, 225–30.

51. The quotation is given in Fraser, *Charleston! Charleston!*, but no citation follows. Presumably it is from a contemporary document.

52. The next paragraphs are drawn from Klebaner, "Public Poor Relief in Charleston, 1800–1860," and McInnis, *Politics of Taste*, 93, 222.

53. Quotations in Klebaner, "Public Poor Relief in Charleston, 1800–1860," 211–12.

54. Minutes, 19 May 1808.

55. Wm. Inglesby to commissioners, 20 August 1833, Applications, file of Thomason boys.

56. Minutes, 29 August 1833, 5 September 1833, 2 July 1835.

57. Minutes, 11 August 1821, 13 January 1814; quote from McCandless, *Moonlight, Magnolias, and Madness*, 164.

58. Minutes, 9 August 1821.

59. Thomas Allen[?] to commissioners, 25 June 1835, Applications. Letter in file of "Mark Thomson" but the child in question here was Daniel McQuin.

60. B. Elliott to commissioners, 20 March 1826, Applications, file of John Utes.

61. Mary Johnson to commissioners, 10 June 1824, in Indentures, file of Rebecca Simmons; Minutes, 23 June 1825, 14 July 1825, 21 July 1825, 27 October 1825.

62. Martha Murrell to commissioners, 4 April 1816, in Applications, file of John Murrell; *Charleston Directory and Stranger's Guide, 1816*, in Hagy (ed.), *Charleston, South Carolina, City Directories*.

63. File of Moore siblings, opened 1 August 1861, in Applications; newspaper dated 18 August 1861.

64. Morgan: Daniel Hall to commissioners, [October?] 1822, Applications. O'Brien: Thomas Akin to commissioners, 28 March 1838, Applications; Minutes, 29 March 1838; Thomas Akin to commissioners, 17 April 1838, Indentures. A thorough study of mental illness and its treatment at this time in South Carolina is McCandless, *Moonlight, Magnolias, and Madness*.

65. J. Sanford Barker to commissioners, 11 October 1818, in Applications.

66. Minutes, 11 July 1811.

67. Minutes, 11 July 1811.

68. Mary Whitney to commissioners, 22 October 1818, in Applications, file of Peter Poulson.

69. Harleston Simons to commissioners, 8 October 1818, in Applications; no date, "We do certify . . . ," in Applications, file of Peter Poulson.

70. Geo. Logan, MD, to commissioners, 15 October 1818, in Applications; Ex Parte Peter Poulson, 18 October 1818, in Applications, file of Peter Poulson.

71. A. Mazyck to commissioners, 29 October 1818, in Applications, file of Peter Poulson.

72. Minutes, 29 October 1818.

73. Bardaglio, *Reconstructing the Household*, 106–12.

74. Form for Thomas and Agnes Kelly, 29 November 1855, Rejected Applications.

75. City Council to commissioners of Orphan House, in Minutes, 9 April 1801.

76. Minutes, 20 August 1801. Bullock, *Revolutionary Brotherhood*, dates the beginning of such Masonic cornerstone ceremonies at churches to around this time in the 1790s (150). After 1820 they became much more common throughout the country (178).

77. Mills, *Statistics of South Carolina*, 419.

78. Ravenel, *Architects*, 59–60; Minutes, 19 September 1802. See also Rogers, *Richard Furman*.

79. Minutes, 19 June 1823.

80. Minutes, 14 July 1796, 18 August 1796, 9 July 1801; Mary Anne Carroll to commissioners, 20 May 1819 and 25 November 1819, in Applications, file of Eliza and Maryanne Carroll.

81. John England was one of the most influential bishops in the history of American Catholicism. On England and the American Church more broadly, see Dolan, *In Search of an American* Catholicism, 35–43. On England's time in Charleston, and his foundation of a school for free blacks, see Saunders and Rogers, "Bishop John England."

82. Dorothy Gallagher to commissioners, 27 September 1820, in Applications, file of John Gallagher; Dorthy [sic] and John Gallaher [sic] in Indenture Books, entered 28 September 1820; and William Gallaher in Indenture Books, entered 21 May 1821; Minutes, 19 October 1820, 25 April 1822, 2 May 1822. John [England], Bishop of Charleston, to commissioners, 23 April 1822; John Dawson to John England, 2 May 1822; both letters transcribed in Minutes, 2 May 1822.

83. Minutes, 9 June 1825, 16 June 1825, 23 June 1825, and letters transcribed therein. These letters were also published in the *United States Catholic Miscellany*, vol. 4, 22 June 1825, p. 398; in other words, almost immediately after the exchange that left Bishop England so dissatisfied. On tracts, see Minutes, 6 August 1829; the assessment thereof is Billington, *The Protestant Crusade, 1800–1860*, 181. For more on Grimké and Sunday school, see Boylan, *Sunday School*, 54.

84. John [England], Bishop of Charleston, to commissioners, 29 May 1828, in Indentures (emphasis in original); Indenture Books, Charles and Christina O'Sullivan, entered 16 August 1827; Minutes, 20 September 1827, 4 October 1827.

85. Hagy, *This Happy Land*; Jane Mordecai to commissioners, 24 October 1815; Minutes, 26 October 1815 and 2 November 1815; Fanny Mordecai, Indenture Book, entered 25 April 1816; Aaron Davis to commissioners, 5 April 1819, in Applications, file of Frances Mordecai; Minutes, 8 April 1819. King, *History and Records*, 8.

86. Minutes, 18 August 1840.

87. Minutes, 23 January 1803, 27 January 1803, 2 June 1803.

88. Minutes, 20 December 1850.

89. Minutes, 3 August 1815. See chapter 9 on William Tucker.

90. Minutes, 21 December 1815 and 28 December 1815.

91. Minutes, 30 June 1830. On Sunday school more generally at this time, see Boylan, *Sunday School*.

92. Minutes, 7 April 1831, 9 July 1835.

93. Minutes, 6 August 1829, 14 August 1847.

94. King, *The Newspaper Press of Charleston, S.C.*, 78–83. Cardozo was a distant relative of Benjamin N. Cardozo (1870–1938), the associate Supreme Court Justice.

95. Rev. B. F. Taylor, "Address to the Children of the Orphan-House," *Charleston Gospel Messenger and Protestant Episcopal Register* (September 1849): 184. See added note on Benjamin Taylor's indenture in Indenture Books, admitted 11 May 1822. Grace Church, Charleston, Report of the Rev. B. F. Taylor, *Journal of the Proceedings of the Sixty-First Annual Convention of the Protestant Episcopal Church in South Carolina, 1850* (Charleston: Miller & Browne, 1850), 52–53. *History of Tioga County, Pennsylvania,* biographical appendix (New York: W. W. Munsell & Co., 1883) 23.

96. Minutes, 24 January 1811.

97. Amelia Elmore to commissioners, 20 August 1835[?], in Indentures, file of Mary Scherer.

98. Minutes, 12 July 1810, 17 March 1831. A Joseph Moses appears in several Jewish sources at this time (Hagy, *This Happy Land* 375).

CHAPTER THREE

1. Edwards, *Ordinances*, 83–84.

2. Fraser, *Charleston! Charleston!*, 179; Ravenel, *Architects*, 59–60, 81–82; McInnis, *Politics of Taste*, 61, 62, 126, 130.

3. Minutes, 14 June 1796; Rogers, *Charleston in the Age of the Pinckneys*, 142.

4. Minutes, 16 June 1796; John Edwards [intendant] to commissioners, 19 June 1796, transcribed in Minutes, 19 June 1796.

5. Minutes, 18 August 1796, 15 September 1796; Montgomery, *Textiles in America, 1650–1870,* 363. The chaos within the Orphan House stands in stark contrast to Rothman's emphasis on institutional regimentation and order (*Discovery of the Asylum,* 228).

6. Rule XX, *Rules for the Government of the Orphan-House at Charleston, South-Carolina* (Charleston: W. P. Young, 1806).

7. Minutes, 5 March 1795. By the mid-1820s boys were still sleeping on the floor in woolen coverlets, which were supposed to minimize exposure to bedbugs, according to Karl Bernhard, Duke of Saxe-Weimar-Eisenach, on his visit to Charleston. In his *Travels in North America*, Bernhard also noted "the exceeding cleanliness pervading the whole establishment." See Clark, *South Carolina*, 105.

8. Minutes, 7 August 1809; 24 August 1809.

9. Minutes, 7 August 1809, 24 August 1809, 2 November 1809, 11 August 1811, 30 November 1809, 28 June 1810; 19 June 1823, 14 December 1809, 11 April 1811.

10. Minutes, 7 August 1809; King, *History and Records*, 14.

11. Minutes, 21 June 1821.

12. Minutes, 29 July 1819.

13. Minutes, 20 March 1806.

14. Minutes, 19 June 1817, 29 March 1821; see also 27 September 1832.

15. Minutes, 25 June 1857.

16. Minutes, 30 July 1857.

17. Minutes, 13 June 1811, 30 November 1809.

18. Minutes, 1 July 1819.

19. Minutes, 26 January 1797, 7 August 1809, 1 August 1811.

20. Minutes, 1 August 1811, 1 July 1813, 1 July 1819, 4 January 1821, 7 July 1825, 18 November 1847, 23 August 1804. See also 1 July 1847.

21. Minutes, 24 December 1795.

22. Minutes, 4 August 1796. Both US dollars and South Carolina pounds were used as units of account at this time. See Grubb, "Creating the US Dollar."

23. Minutes, 17 May 1832, 16 August 1832, 26 February 1846.

24. Minutes, 28 September 1809, 9 November 1809.

25. Minutes, 24 May 1832, 29 October 1846.

26. Minutes, 5 November 1846; 18 August 1840.

27. Minutes, 26 January 1797.

28. Charleston City Council, *Circular of the City Council on Retrenchment, and Report of the Commissioners of the Orphan House*, 8.

29. Rev. Charles S. Vedder, D.D., "Centennial Oration," in *Charleston Orphan House: Centennial Celebration*, 35.

30. Minutes, 23 January 1803. See also Minutes, 18 January 1821 and 21 January 1830 for similar events, these triggered by the ladies.

31. Minutes, 21 January 1830.

32. Minutes, 24 March 1825, 23 June 1825. A separate issue arose in 1837 concerning whether girls could wear brighter calicoes instead of shabbier homespun. A Committee on Calico Dresses resolved the issue in favor of that fabric by noting that homespun was what slaves wore (Bellows, *Benevolence*, 137–39). Apparently in 1825 homespun was good enough for the boys. On children spinning cotton into thread, see Minutes, 3 January 1793.

33. Minutes, 19 March 1801.

34. Minutes, 17 June 1819. It seems likely that Tom's behavior was linked to his alcoholism, discussed in chapter 2. Tom had earlier earned stripes with the lash for keeping chickens in his room (Minutes, 18 April 1811).

35. *Rules for the Government of the Orphan-House at Charleston, South-Carolina* (Charleston: W. P. Young, 1806).

36. Minutes, 28 April 1810.

37. Minutes, 25 July 1811. Interaction between the sexes was an ongoing concern of commissioners. When a boy who had left the Orphan House and was working as an apprentice to a cabinet maker began bringing gifts to a particular girl, the commissioners, mindful of "the evil and pernicious consequences of such conduct," threatened to prosecute the youth, presumably for trespassing. Minutes, 8 March 1801, 12 March 1801.

38. Compare Wyatt-Brown, *Southern Honor*, 149–53.

39. Minutes, 1 August 1811, 18 January 1821.

40. Eliab Kingman to commissioners, 25 July 1811, transcribed in Minutes, 25 July 1811.

41. Minutes, 1 August 1811.

42. Minutes, 19 March 1812, 26 March 1812.

43. Minutes, 12 July 1792, Indenture Books, Catherine Marsh, entered 10 November 1791.

44. James Barry to commissioners, 5 September 1803, Applications, file of Henry Barry; Indenture Books, Henry Reynold Barry, entered 15 September 1797.

45. M. Swords to commissioners, 20 July 179[6?], Applications, file of John Thomas Swords; Minutes, 17 March 1798, 20 August 1798, and 27 August 1798. See Minutes, 7 March 1805, for "penitentiary room."

46. Minutes, 29 June 1843.

47. Minutes, 30 April 1835; Fraser, *Charleston! Charleston!*, 203–6.

48. Minutes, 9 April 1812.

49. Minutes, 23 July 1812.

50. Minutes, 21 July 1814.

51. Minutes, 20 October 1796.

52. Minutes, 11 November 1813.

53. Minutes, 26 June 1817; Indenture Books, William Wilson, entered 7 March 1811; Hezekiah Wright, entered 10 August 1816; and James Spencer, entered 13 May 1808.

54. Minutes, 8 December 1842, 23 May 1850, 14 December 1794; Indenture Book, William Frank, entered 29 October 1790. A note on the indenture reads, "absconded aboard the brig 'Sukey.'"

55. Minutes, 8 November 1849, 4 August 1842.

56. Minutes, 1 August 1811.

57. Minutes, 7 March 1805.

58. Fraser, *Charleston! Charleston!*, discusses the 1806 law that restricted black movement, assembly, and so on, and the appearance of the restrictions in the midst of the temporary revival of the international slave trade (190). These restrictions intensified after the 1822 Denmark Vesey events. Regarding everyday interactions between races in the Low Country, see Lockley, *Lines in the Sand*.

59. Stampp, *The Peculiar Institution*, 126.

60. Minutes, 11 June 1807.

61. Minutes, 30 November 1809. On lack of publicity, see Hinks, *To Awaken My Afflicted Brethren*, 120.

62. Minutes, 12 June 1823, 19 June 1823.

63. Minutes, 11 August 1825.

64. Minutes, 18 February 1830, 6 May 1830, 20 May 1830.

65. Minutes, 18 August 1840, 22 July 1841; Mrs. M. Johnson to commissioners, 11 August 1840, application form; H. A. D. [Henry A. DeSaussure] to Mrs. M. Johnson, 13 August 1840; Mrs. Mary Johnson to commissioners, 15 August 1840; all in Rejected Applications, file of "Vizzara." The 1840–41 Charleston Directory (reprinted in Hagy, ed., *Charleston, South Carolina, City Directories*) lists an H. Vizzara as a shoemaker at the corner of Green and St. Philips Streets, a block from the Orphan House.

66. Minutes, 8 May 1794; Indenture Books, Charles Kruger, entered 28 July 1796.

67. Minutes, 28 August 1800.

68. Indenture Books, Mary Ann Winship, entered 2 May 1839, and Henry Smith, entered 26 August 1852; Minutes, 1 August 1852; application form for Henry Smith, 1 August 1852, in Applications; and John Rogers, clerk [of City Council] to commissioners, 23 April 1839, in Applications, file of Mary Ann Winship.

69. Minutes, 18 December 1800.

70. Minutes, 13 June 1805, 20 June 1805, 11 July 1805.

71. Minutes, 28 October 1826, 3 March 1842, 2 March 1843, 14 February 1850. References to the Akin Foundling Hospital appear between 1849 and 1852 in the Minutes. This hospital was founded through the estate of Eliza Akin in 1844. Waring, *A History of Medicine in South Carolina, 1825–1900*, proposed that the hospital never actually opened (18), but it seems that it did in fact operate for a few years.

72. Minutes, 29 July 1797, 13 August 1798.

73. Minutes, 4 April 1800, 30 May 1800, 6 June 1800.

74. Minutes, 22 November 1810, 28 March 1810; Indenture Books, Margaret Findlay, entered 26 March 1812.

75. Minutes, 30 January 1817, 13 February 1817, 20 February 1817; *Charleston Directory and Stranger's Guide for the Year 1816*, in Hagy (ed.), *Charleston, South Carolina, City Directories*.

76. Minutes, 18 August 1840.

77. Minutes, 3 March 1842.

78. Hamilton, "The Stateless and the Orphaned among Montreal's Apprentices, 1791–1842," 170.

79. Minutes, 27 January 1803, 2 June 1803, 23 June 1803.

80. Minutes, 19 April 1821, 3 May 1821, 10 May 1821.

81. Minutes, 18 November 1790, 25 November 1790.

82. Minutes, 10 March 1791, 31 January 1811.

83. Minutes, 31 January 1811. Ann had entered the Orphan House in 1790 but was legally bound to the institution in 1801, at age 13. Unable to sign her name, she marked the document with an X.

84. Minutes, 31 January 1811.

85. Minutes, 31 January 1811.

86. Minutes, 23 March 1815, 16 July 1840.

87. Minutes, 1 April 1819.

88. Minutes, 7 July 1825, 28 July 1831; Indenture Books, Ann Brooks, entered 7 November 1801.

CHAPTER FOUR

1. Fabian, *Unvarnished Truth*.

2. Murray, "Family, Literacy, and Skill-Training." See chapter 5 for more on signature literacy. On literacy in the early republic more generally, see Gilmore, *Reading Becomes a Necessity of Life*, and Soltow and Stevens, *The Rise of Literacy and the Common School in the United States*. On literacy in the Colonial and Revolutionary Eras, see Grubb, "Growth of Literacy in Colonial America"; Lockridge, *Literacy in Colonial New England*; Herndon, "Literacy among New England's Transient Poor, 1750–1800"; and Main, "An Inquiry into When and Why Women Learned to Write in Colonial New England."

3. One example: Marie Allison to commissioners, 24 June 1825, in Applications, file of James and George Allison.

4. Ann C. Duncan to commissioners, 16 July 1818, Applications, file of Catherine Duncan. By contrast, perhaps 95 percent of mistresses who were accepting these appren-

tices into their homes could sign indentures. On illiteracy not hindering people either from acquiring information or committing to contract in nineteenth-century America, see Stevens, *Literacy, Law, and Social Order.*

5. On women in Charleston at this time more generally, see Pease and Pease, *Ladies, Women, and Wenches.* On working women in the South more generally, see essays in Delfino and Gillespie, *Neither Lady Nor Slave.*

6. Hacsi, *Second Home.*

7. Murray, "Fates of Orphans."

8. For similar estimates in the 1790s based on parental mortality rates, see Murray, "Bound by Charity," 215–17. On the one-fifth estimate, see chapter 5, note 4. By way of comparison, Barry Levy estimated that nearly half of children in eighteenth-century Massachusetts would lose one or both parents before reaching twenty-one years of age (*Town Born,* 245–46).

9. H. A. DeSaussure to commissioners, 28 March 1850, Applications, file of Amanda Luderwig.

10. Form for four Lonergan children dated 1 November 1855, Applications. The report appears in two different hands, the first unsigned and the second signed by M. Caldwell.

11. Application of Margaret Farrell, 9 December 1858, Rejected Applications, file of Farrell children.

12. One of many: R.W. Force et al to commissioners, 23 April 1857, Applications, file of Mary McCormick.

13. File of Rebecca Simons, 12 June 1816, Applications.

14. Women intermediaries: M. C. Wilson, Hannah Drayton, and Mary C. Gregorie to commissioners, 9 March 1815, Applications, file of Margaret Thompson. A widow with her own children: Margaret Church to commissioners, 19 May 1824, Applications, file of Thomas Devlin. Needlework: Jane Smith to commissioners, 9 January 1817, Applications, file of James Lawrence. Boardinghouse: Mary Byrd to commissioners, November 1829, Applications, file of Washington Stevenson. Quote from Letitia Glen to commissioners, 17 December 1803, Applications, file of Margaret Boyd.

15. John Farley to commissioners, 15 November 1827, Applications, file of Edward John Jones. Jones was eventually bound out to a cabinet maker. There were several possibilities as to Edward's father, as six boys named Jones passed through the Orphan House before Edward's birth.

16. Joseph Folker to commissioners, 20 May 1819, Applications, file of William Bradford. Bradford was eventually bound out to a ship's carpenter.

17. Wm. B. Pringle to commissioners, 4 June 1829, Applications, file of Thomas Lister. *Journal of the House of Representatives of the State of South-Carolina, Being the Annual Session of 1844,* (Columbia: A. H. Pemberton, 1844), 96, 173. Lister was eventually bound to an apothecary. On the bank, see Lesesne, *Bank of the State of South Carolina.*

18. James Lowndes to commissioners, 7 April 1803, Applications. This letter is filed under Lowndes's name. The identity of the boys cannot be determined; no pair of brothers in the Indenture Books fits Lowndes's description of them.

19. Margaret Denoon to commissioners, 10 May 1818, Applications. This letter is filed under Denoon, but from the minutes it is evident that the child is John Campbell

Sanders. A. Toomer Porter to commissioners, 21 March 1859, Applications, file of Thomas King. McLaughlin endorsed Porter's letter with her mark. Porter's autobiography is *Led on Step by Step* (New York: G. P. Putnam's Sons, 1898). The date and cause of McLaughlin's death are recorded in City of Charleston, Death Records.

20. M. Caldwell, reverse of application form, 27 November 1855, Applications, file of Lonergan children. The children stayed five years in the Orphan House until their mother, remarried and living in Georgetown, retrieved them. Catherine, Henrietta, and Laura Bennett, Indenture Books, all entered 29 November 1855. For another case of families of color raising a white child, see H. L. Gervais to commissioners, 21 July 1856, Applications, case of Thomas Richards.

21. Ann Creighton to commissioners, 22 September 1852, Applications, file of James Usher. Creighton gave no reason for the child's surname, and no one named Usher appeared in the 1841 and 1849 city directories. For a similar case see application form for James Calhoun, 18 March 1857, Applications, case of James Calhoun.

22. Anna Wood to commissioners, 14 May 1853, Applications, case of William Edmond Crowe; Archibald McLeish to Mr. Campbell, 20 July 1853; and E. Stoney to commissioners, 27 July 1853, both in Applications, case of Jane Young. Young was returned to an aunt in 1857 with the intention that she would continue on to her father (Indenture Books, Jane Young, bound in 28 July 1853).

23. Christopher Gadsden to commissioners, 7 January 1818, Applications, file of William Player. These Charleston examples date from much earlier than the child boardinghouses in Zelizer, *Pricing the Priceless Child*, 184.

24. J. Assalit to commissioners, 8 July 1830, Applications, file of "Assalie" children; Minutes, 30 April 1830.

25. Nancy Zey found similar networks of day care providers in Natchez, Mississippi, in "'Every Thing but a Parent's Love': Family Life in Orphan Asylums of the Lower Mississippi Valley" and "Children of the Public."

26. Minutes, 11 November 1790. *Appleton's Cyclopedia of American Biography*, vol. 3, Francis Kinloch, 550 (q.v.).

27. Visiting commissioner's report, 23 September 1841, Applications, file of Virginia Karnes.

28. J. Assalit to commissioners, 8 July 1830, Applications, file of "Assalie" children.

29. J. A. Johnson to commissioners, 14 October 1819, file of Julianna Barnes; and five women to commissioners, 21 February 1825, file of Salina Barto; both in Applications.

30. Ezra Benjamin to commissioners, 1 December 1819; Mrs. Ferguson to commissioners, 2 December 1819; and Mrs. Ferguson to commissioners, 14 December 1819; all in Applications, file of Eunice Madison. Saml. Hayward to commissioners, 8 November 1817, Applications, file of Eliza Smith. For other possible cases of abuse to be resolved by the child's admission to the Orphan House, see J. A. Johnson to commissioners, 14 October 1819, Applications, file of Julianna Barnes; and visiting commissioner's report on Louisa Benton, 1 August 1844, Applications, file of Louisa Benton. Note that there were no laws to govern adoption until the mid-nineteenth century, so that the terms "adopt" and "as her own" might be understood much as in their common usage in the present, but with no particular legal force behind them. Presser, "The Historical Background of the American Law of Adoption."

31. Application form for James Calhoun, 18 March 1857, Applications. The physician was W. M. Fitch. F. Keowin to commissioners, n.d., Applications, file of John and William Calvert.

32. Wm. Medlich to commissioners, 23 December 1802, Applications, file of Charles Symonds; Mary Byrd to commissioners, November 1829, Applications, file of Washington Stevenson; Anna Wood to commissioners, 14 May 1853, Applications, file of William Edmond Crowe.

33. Jane Smith to commissioners, 9 January 1817, Applications; and Jane Page to commissioners, 20 March 1834, Applications; both in file of James Lawrence. See also Indenture Books, James Lawrence, entered 9 January 1817, bound out 3 January 1818.

34. John A. Tullock to commissioners, 24 September 1829, Applications, file of Joseph Irvin.

35. Christopher E. Gadsden to commissioners, 7 January 1818, Applications, file of William Player. B. Manly to commissioners, 15 September 1836, Applications, file of Stenton brothers.

36. Joseph Johnson to commissioners, 11 July 1844, Rejected Applications, file of Joseph Ringland.

37. Report of George Coffin re Mary and Loretta Darby, 25 June 1857, Applications. For a few examples from many other cases involving extended family, see William Wish to commissioners, 14 May 1806, Applications, file of John and William Wish (uncle can no longer afford to keep nephew; note that both were named William Wish); and Rev. Cranmore Wallace to commissioners, file of James Willis, 18 July 1851, Applications (aunt cannot discipline nephew.)

38. Visiting commissioner's report by George W. Coffey, 5 July 1855, file of Conrad Rempp. Ansell appears in Baggett, *Directory of the City of Charleston for the Year 1852*, 3.

39. Stepfathers, by contrast, often held the key to reuniting mother and child. See chapter 7.

40. Elizabeth Smith to commissioners, 14 September 1818, Applications, file of John Smith.

41. Bridget Adams to commissioners, 28 February 1826, Applications, file of William C. Adams.

42. Eliza Fludd to commissioners, 9 November 1852 (formal application), and Eliza Fludd to Mr. DeSaussure, 9 November 1852 (cover letter), Applications, file of William and Ann Davis. Adding to the complexity of the Davis family, Laomi William Washington Davis may have been a free person of color. City of Charleston Death Records list a free black man named Wm. Davis who died of pneumonia around 1 October 1852, which was the time that L. W. W. Davis died, according to Eliza Fludd. Eliza Fludd's letter to the commissioners reported that Davis had worked as an overseer, and there were in fact a few black overseers. On overseers generally, see Stampp, *The Peculiar Institution*, 39; on reputations of and attitudes toward overseers, see Forret, *Race Relations at the Margins*, 115–22; on black overseers in South Carolina in particular, see Koger, *Black Slaveowners*, 10. The Orphan House records do not refer to the race of either Davis or his children, suggesting that if Davis was in fact a free person of color, the children were light skinned enough to pass for white.

43. Bridget Adams to commissioners, 28 February 1826, Applications, file of William C. Adams.

44. Jane Mordecai to commissioners, 24 October 1815, Applications; Aaron Davis to commissioners, 5 April 1819, Applications; E. Abraham to commissioners, 20 July 1820, Indentures, all in file of Frances Mordecai. On Charleston's flourishing Jewish community see Hagy, *This Happy Land*.

45. Richard Hendricks, Indenture Books, entered 23 February 1833; Minutes, 29 March 1838; Jesse Bates to commissioners, [late March] 1838, Rejected Applications, file of Richard Hendricks. Either Richard or Caroline ultimately rejected Jesse Bates's offer, because the board had approved it subject to their decision.

46. Visiting commissioner's report on Michael Manihan, 26 June 1856; City of Charleston Death Records, Rose Monahan, died 14 January 1953; Richard Monahan appears in Bagget, *Directory of the City of Charleston for the Year 1852*, 90.

47. Fraser, *Charleston! Charleston!*, 178–81, 187–88. On cotton in the southern economy as a whole, see Wright, *The Political Economy of the Cotton South*; and Woodman, *King Cotton and His Retainers*.

48. Rauschenberg, "A School of Charleston, South Carolina, Brass Andirons, 1780–1815."

49. Bellows, *Benevolence*, 16.

50. D. W. Stevens to commissioners, 4 May 1814; John Ruberry to commissioners, 16 June 1814; and Seth Gilbert to commissioners, 8 November 1814; all in Applications, file of Gilbert brothers. John Gilbert and William Gilbert, admitted 7 July 1814, Indenture Books. *Charleston Directory and Stranger's Guide for the Year 1816*, transcribed by James W. Hagy in *Charleston, South Carolina, City Directories*. Genealogical records suggest that the oldest boy's name was Joseph and the boys' mother's name Rebecca. See http://www.woodenshipsironmen.com/Humbert/gp130.html#head3, accessed 15 December 2011.

51. Elizabeth Morton to commissioners, 12 December 1818, Applications, file of Morton brothers.

52. Christiana Jones to commissioners, 17 March 1824, Applications, file of James Allen.

53. Mary Ann Hairgroves to commissioners, 19 August 1852, A[rchibald] C[ampbell], the steward] to commissioners, 26 August [1852], both in Applications, file of Rosanna Higgins.

54. Rebecca Kingdon to commissioners, 11 December 1817, Applications, file of Elizabeth Rhodes.

55. Less intact rather than more so: See Wm. Inglesby, commissioner of the Poor House, to commissioners of the Orphan House, 20 August 1833, file of Thomason siblings, Applications, in which the mother was in the Poor House and the father "in gaol on some criminal accusation."

56. Frances Bettison to commissioners, 4 September 1826, Rejected Applications, file of Bettison; see also postscript by Mary Parker and Mary Grimké.

57. Application form with note signed by John W. Mitchell, Eliza Thompson, and Mary Grimké, signed 28 June 1832, Applications, file of Elmira Lloyd.

58. Wm. Lawton, chairman of the commissioners of the Poor House, to Henry A. DeSaussure, 12 January 1853, Applications, file of John Jerrold.

59. Jas. R. Wood, MD, to commissioners, 24 August 1854, Applications, file of Henry Humbel.

60. A thorough study of the status and treatment of the mentally ill in antebellum South Carolina appears in McCandless, *Moonlight, Magnolias, and Madness.*

61. Quoted in Fraser, *Charleston! Charleston!,* 193–94.

62. McCandless, *Moonlight, Magnolias, and Madness,* 171.

63. George Jacoby to commissioners, 8 April 1830, Applications, file of Ann Iseman.

64. Elizabeth King to commissioners, 8 March 1838, Applications, file of George King II. See also George King's indenture in Indenture Books, entered 12 March 1838.

65. Thos. Akin, chairman, commissioners of the Poor House to commissioners of the Orphan House, 17 April 1838, Applications. This case of Mary Jane O'Brien was discussed above.

66. Margaret Dooling to commissioners, 1 July 1823, Rejected Applications, file of Dooling children. Mrs. Dooling noted that she was a New Yorker, her husband Irish, and that the family had arrived in Charleston just six months previously, which was probably the reason for the rejection.

67. Lawrence Dawson to commissioners, 20 October 1825, Applications, file of John W. Martin.

68. E. C. Holmes and M. E. Holmes to commissioners, 28 March 1831, Applications, file of John and William Rantin.

69. Rorabaugh, *The Alcoholic Republic,* 11–13.

70. Miss S. M. Drayton to John Dawson, 6 January 1814, Applications, file of Jane Elizabeth Page.

71. J. M. Caldwell to commissioners, 29 April 1852, Applications, file of Thomas Randles. Rev. Yates was well known for his ministering to sailors in the Port of Charleston.

72. W. A. Caldwell to commissioners, 6 September 1832, Applications, file of Bingley siblings.

73. Mary Ann Hairgroves, statement on application form for Rosanna Higgins, 19 August 1852, Applications; A. Campbell to Henry A. DeSaussure, 21 August 1852, Applications, in Rosanna Higgins file; Minutes, 19 August 1852.

74. A[rchibald] C[ampbell] to commissioners, 26 August 1852, Applications; Rosanna Higgins, entered 2 September 1852, Daniel Higgins, entered 25 May 1854, and Eliza Higgins, entered 20 March 1856, all in Indenture Books; S. J. Robinson, Poor House, to commissioners of the Orphan House, 25 May 1854, Applications, file of Bridget Crohan; Minutes of the Poor House commissioners, 10 May 1854 and 24 May 1854; *Metropolitan Catholic Almanac and Laity's Directory for the United States, 1859* (Baltimore: John Murphy & Co., 1858), 272.

75. [Sarah Ann Grooms] to commissioners, 8 February 1804, Applications, file of William Lansdel.

76. Bridget McCluskey to commissioners, 22 June 1837, Applications, file of McCluskey children. Bridget McCluskey marked all three indentures that bound her children. The "Seminole campaign" probably refers to the Second Seminole War, which began late in 1835. See Mahon, *The History of the Second Seminole War, 1835–1842.*

77. [Marie Allison] to commissioners, 24 June 1825, Applications, file of Allison

brothers. George and James Allison, entered 3 July 1825, Indenture Books. Marie Allison signed the indentures and the letter, but the body of the letter was written in a different hand. For another similar case see M. Magrath to commissioners, 28 July 1813, Applications, file of Edward Magrath.

78. McInnis, *The Politics of Taste*, 70–91; Fraser, *Charleston! Charleston!*, 171, 190, 203–4.

79. Catherine Lowry to commissioners, 15 September 1831, Applications, file of Robert Clements.

80. [Rev.] B. Manly to commissioners, 15 September 1836, Applications, file of Stenton children. Hayne was the first mayor of Charleston to carry the title "Mayor." He was also a fierce nullificationist and as a US senator attained national standing in his debates with Daniel Webster on the tariff.

81. S. L. Wright to commissioners, 8 December 1814, Applications, file of Daniel and Norman Wright; Minutes, 16 August 1827, 8 December 1814. It is possible that the infant mentioned in this letter was Margaret Wright, who was admitted at age 3 in 1817; if so, Mrs. Wright's first name was Susannah.

82. Humphries, *Childhood and Child Labour in the British Industrial Revolution*, 171, 367–68. As it also appears in Charleston, breadwinner frailty may have been more a characteristic of urban life than of industrialization, as in Humphries's analysis of the Industrial Revolution in Britain. Indeed, the Orphan House itself may be seen as a particular response to the problem of breadwinner frailty in a nonindustrial city.

83. Susan Adams to commissioners, 8 June 1824, Applications, file of Richard and John Adams.

84. Eliza Connoly to commissioners, 22 April 1813, Applications, file of Connoly children.

85. Visiting commissioner's report on Augustine Dooley, 14 February 1856, Applications.

86. Washerwoman: Unsigned report of visiting commissioner on Mrs. Pearce, August 24, 1858, Rejected Applications, file of Thomas Pearce; laborer: Margo, *Wages and Labor Markets*, 33. Presumably the washerwoman's pay included room and board, but the report is silent on this question.

87. Eddy Richardson to commissioners, 30 January 1823, Applications, re John Hardy Richardson.

88. Visiting commissioner's report on Catherine Blake, 31 January 1857, Applications; Archates, "Reflections," 18–19.

89. Isabella Doyle, April 1835, Applications, file of Doyle children. On the sure poverty of seamstresses in Baltimore at this time and other parallels in labor markets for unskilled women, see Rockman, *Scraping By*, especially 101–31.

90. Martha Ann Monroe to commissioners, 1 May 1827, Applications, file of William Calvert.

91. Visiting commissioner's report on Erasmus and Mary Ann Hodge, 26 December 1845, Applications.

92. B. Quinnan to commissioners, 8 August 1828, file of Joseph Alexander Clarke, Applications.

93. Sarah Connelly to commissioners, 8 June 1829, Applications, file of James Connelly.

94. Elenor Bossell to commissioners, 8 December 1803, and attached note by Jacob Williman, Applications, file of Elizabeth and William Bossell. Note that Williman wrote the name as Boswell.

95. Ann Grainger to commissioners, 16 July 1818, Applications, file of Mary and William Grainger.

96. Unidentifiable physician to commissioners, April 1856, and report of George Coffin, visiting commissioner, Applications, file of William Warren Hays; Minutes, 12 July 1855, 19 July 1855, 1 May 1856, 8 May 1856, 2 October 1856, and 9 October 1856; Indenture Books: William Warren Hays, entered 8 May 1856; Isabella Clara Hays, Margaret Anna Hays, and Thomas Heyward Hays, all entered 9 October 1856; City of Charleston Death Records, Thomas Hays, died 25 May 1856 of hydrothorax.

97. Susannah Marriner to commissioners, 11 March 1824, Applications, file of Marriner children; Joseph Young to commissioners, 7 September 1824, also in Applications file; Minutes, 14 February 1833. No information survives on Susannah's location at the time of William's return to Charleston, nor on the length of time or circumstances in which William had been in New York.

98. S. B. Gilliland to Mr. DeSaussure, February 4, 1858, Applications, file of Charles and John Campbell.

99. William Clarkson to commissioners, 13 February 1806, Applications, file of Thomas Hoare.

100. Bridget Kean to commissioners, 10 September 1818, Applications, file of Ferdinand and James Kean. See also Minutes, 19 February 1818, on Mrs. Kean's "improper conduct to one of the nurses," for which Bridget apologized in a letter of 16 February 1818, which also asked the commissioners to take in yet another Kean child. That application was rejected.

101. Susannah Marriner, 11 March 1824, Applications; visiting commissioner's report, unsigned, file of James Nelson, 12 February 1846, Applications. Ann Wittencamp to commisioners, 19 August 1823, Applications, file of Christopher Wittencamp.

102. Mary Anne McDermott to commissioners regarding Deignan children, 29 October 1831, Rejected Applications. Commissioners offered no reason for rejecting this application. See Minutes, 17 November 1831.

103. Unsigned visiting commissioner's report, file of Hester and Ruben Carter, 2 June 1842, Applications.

104. Thos. Akin, chairman commissioners of the Poor House to commissioners of the Orphan House, 20 May 1841, Applications, case of John Connolly.

105. Examples (among many): Edward Kent and Eliza Kent to commissioners, 9 January 1834, Indentures, file of Robert Bassett; Samuel Morris to Mr. DeSaussure, 7 March 1839, Indentures, file of Robert Brown.

106. Juliana Georgiana Elliott to commissioners, 7 February 1811, Applications, file of Mary Clayton. Elliott returned for Mary three years later, and received her into her own home as an apprentice.

107. Yellow fever was a notoriously urban disease, a kind of counterpart to malaria in the countryside. See Chaplin, *An Anxious Pursuit*, 94ff. See also Humphreys, *Yellow Fever and the South*.

108. Visiting commissioner's report on Z. Y. and Sarah Anderson, 7 May 1846, Applications.

109. Regarding a father imprisoned for debt: Richard Boak to commissioners, 19 March 1818, Applications, file of Richard Boak.

110. On straitened circumstances among seafaring families in New England, see Herndon, "The Domestic Cost of Seafaring."

111. Anna Zylks to commissioners, 4 August 1814, Applications, file of Margaret and Thomas Zylks.

112. John Hanson to commissioners, 13 October 1825; Mrs. L .M. Bennett to commissioners, 24 January 1826 and 24 August 1826, Applications, file of John and Samuel Hanson.

113. Seven gentlemen to commissioners, 25 November 1803, Applications, file of Charles and Harriott James. Most signatures not legible.

114. Bachman to H. W. DeSaussure, 1 June 1854, Applications, file of Cammer children. On heavy alcohol consumption in the early republic, see Rorabaugh, *The Alcoholic Republic*. Bachman was a well-known Lutheran pastor and temperance activist, and a friend of John James Audubon, who named Bachman's Warbler in his honor. See Stephens, *Science, Race, and Religion in the American South*.

115. Greven, *The Protestant Temperament*; Zelizer, *Pricing the Priceless Child*.

116. Ann Ferneau to commissioners, 17 January 1813, Applications, file of Francis Henry Ferneau.

117. Examples from among many: Mary Hazzard to commissioners, 12 August 1818, Applications, file of Richard and Oliver Hazzard; Catherine Lambers to commissioners, 7 September 1837, Applications, file of Bernard, Mary, and Rebecca Lambers; Catherine Shelbock, 8 May 1823, Rejected Applications, filed under Shelbock.

118. Mary Hutchinson to commissioners, 15 September 1820, Indentures. The daughter was also named Mary.

119. [James Carson] to commissioners, 28 January 1854, Indentures, file of Joseph Carson. This letter is unsigned but attributed on the back to Mr. Carson.

CHAPTER FIVE

1. Edwards, *Ordinances*, 82–85. The ordinance may also be found transcribed on page 1, volume 1 of Minutes. Emphasis added.

2. Graff, *The Legacies of Literacy*, 3–4. Other studies of signature literacy include Mitch, *Rise of Popular Literacy*; Grubb, "Growth of Literacy"; Herndon, "Literacy Among New England's Transient Poor"; Murray, "Generation(s) of Human Capital"; Murray, "Literacy Acquisition"; Murray, "Family, Literacy, and Skill-Training"; Lachance, "Literacy and Provisions"; Perlmann and Shirley, "When Did New England Women," and Main, "An Inquiry." Over two decades ago, Perlmann and Shirley could propose that women's literacy in the late eighteenth and early nineteenth centuries "deserves much more empirical study," while Grubb (477) could report that, in the historical literature, "studies of literacy among children and young teens are virtually non-existent." Variation in literacy rates by age, class, and sex implies that Perlman and Shirley's imperative

remains true today. Studies of literacy among children and teens can be found in the list reported above in this note.

3. Duplicate signatures or marks from parents who entered several children, or masters who obtained several apprentices, were omitted from each decade's figure.

4. This comparison assumes that the parents and guardians came from the roughly one-fifth of the population considered poor and that the masters and mistresses were representative of the other four-fifths. The one-fifth figure is a rough guess, but its pedigree extends back to Governor James Glen's 1751 estimate that the bottom quintile of Carolina society could only afford "a bare subsistence"; see Olwell, *Masters, Slaves, and Subjects*, 34. Later quantitative estimates corroborated this figure closely. Coclanis, *The Shadow of a Dream* (90), concurred with Glen's estimate, based on probate inventories. Richard Waterhouse found that a fifth of Charleston's white population just before the Revolution did not own any slaves, and a fifth owned less than £100 worth of goods at death, with plenty of overlap between the two groups (Olwell, *Masters, Slaves, and Subjects*, 45). Main estimated the figure to be between one-fifth and one-seventh, according to quit rent rolls (*The Social Structure of Revolutionary America*, 60–65).

5. Sarah Estill to commissioners, 30 April 1806, file of William Estill; Isabella Murphy to commissioners, 31 March 1825, file of Edward and Henry Murphy; both in Applications.

6. Mary McGee to commissioners, 11 May 1816, Applications, file of John Frederic Courtman. Although this letter bears a signature in McGee's name, her mark on Courtman's indenture indicated that she was illiterate. A similar case was that of William Calvert, admitted 10 May 1827; see his indenture in Indenture Books and Martha Ann Monroe to commissioners, 1 May 1827, Applications, in Calvert's file.

7. Eliza Nelson to commissioners, 31 October 1839, Applications, file of George, John, and Washington Nelson.

8. On moral education in the New York schools, see Kaestle, *The Evolution of an Urban School System*, 112–37. On the need for institutions to inculcate morality in orphans and other vulnerable children, see the classic by Rothman, *Discovery of the Asylum*, 210.

9. Pyburn, "Public School System," 89; Vinovskis, "Early Childhood Education."

10. Mrs. Whitney to Dr. Israel Munds, 15 July 1818, in file of Peter Poulson, Applications; Poston, *The Buildings of Charleston*, 134.

11. William Wish to commissioners, 14 May 1806, Applications, file of John and William Wish; J. W. Stevens to commissioners, 4 May 1814, Applications, file of John and William Gilbert. Bellows, *Benevolence*, 16–17. Note that three persons named William Wish appear in Orphan House records. The eldest was the uncle, who wrote the letter cited here; his nephew, the subject of this letter, was born c. 1800 and appears later in this book as a midshipman in the US Navy. The third William Wish was born c. 1822, came to the Orphan House after the death of his father in a hurricane, and served his apprenticeship to Dr. James P. Jervey, as an apothecary. His indenture appears in Indenture Books, entered 21 July 1825.

12. The earliest reference in Charleston is Jos. Johnson to commissioners, 11 July 1844, Rejected Applications, file of Joseph Ringland; in Darlington District a reference

appears in 1835: James McIntosh to James Jervey, 30 January 1835, file of Theodore Sompayrac, Indentures. On Sunday school pedagogy in the North, see Boylan, *Sunday School*, especially 8–10 and 22–59. Still, Boylan notes, literacy training was a less important part of American Sunday school curricula than in Great Britain.

13. "An Act to Establish Free Schools Throughout the State" (No. 1980), in Cooper and McCord, *The Statutes at Large of South Carolina, Edited, Under Authority of the Legislature*, vol. 5, p. 639. Jordan, "Education for Community," and Pyburn, "Public School System." See also Copeland, "A Note on South Carolina Teachers, 1811–1860."

14. Martha Lund to commissioners, 18 March 1830, file of Zachariah and Robert DuHay, Applications.

15. Elizabeth Ann Yates, Josiah Smith, Mary C. Gregorie, Samuel Wilson, Caroline Ann Spindle, and Sarah Hollinshead to commissioners, 30 January 1813, Applications, file of James and William Bozeman.

16. Murray, "Literacy Acquisition." Note the break in trend of parental literacy around the 1810s in figure 5.1. See also Minutes, 30 April 1835.

17. Kaestle, *Joseph Lancaster and the Monitorial School Movement*, and Pyburn, "Public School System," 88–89.

18. Jordan, "Education for Community," 108.

19. On Lancaster's method in Charleston's free schools, see Pyburn, "Public School System."

20. Jordan, "Education for Community," 105–6. A broader view of the market for teachers at this time, and including the South, appears in Tolley and Beadie, "Socioeconomic Incentives."

21. Visiting commissioner's report of H. A. DeSaussure, 29 November 1855, Rejected Applications, Kelly children. It is unclear whether the assessment came from Mrs. Kelly, DeSaussure, or another commissioner.

22. Catherine Bennett to commissioners, 22 September 1853, Applications, file of John Riens.

23. Visiting commissioner's report of Wm. H. Gilliland, 5 April 1856, Rejected Applications, file of Louis Gesell.

24. Minutes, 28 July 1791. Besselleu's name is spelled several different ways in various records, including Besselieu in some Orphan House records. In the city ordinance of 1790 that founded the Orphan House, he was Philip Anthony Besselieu (Edwards, *Ordinances*, 85). Besselleu is the spelling on his gravestone in the Huguenot church cemetery. Cf. Philip A. Bazeleau in 1790 Census: one white male head of household, thirty-six free white males under sixteen years, five free white females, no other free persons, and three slaves. US Department of Commerce and Labor, *Heads of Families at the First Census of the United States Taken in 1790: South Carolina.*, 44.

25. Minutes, 31 March 1791, 7 April 1791, and 3 January 1793.

26. Minutes, 2 October 1794 (failed examinations), 23 January 1794 (navigation and examination of John Groath); Indenture Books, John Groath, entered 29 November 1790, bound to Jacob Sass 29 November 1794. Sass "produced a prodigious amount of furniture" during his half century of work in Charleston. Burton, *Charleston Furniture, 1700–1825*, 118–19.

27. Fraser, *Charleston! Charleston!*, 171; Minutes, 2 May 1793, 6 June 1793, 17 October 1793, 24 October 1793. King, *Newspaper Press*, 50–53.

28. Minutes, 29 August 1794, 16 November 1794.

29. Minutes, 27 November 1794, 9 January 1795.

30. Fries, "The Rules of Common School Grammars." Murray, *Introduction to the English Reader.* Elson, *Guardians of Tradition,* 6.

31. Minutes, 5 March 1795. Brückner, "Lessons in Geography." Morse, *Geography Made Easy,* 207.

32. Reinier, "Rearing the Republican Child," 161.

33. Pyburn, "Public School System," 87; Minutes, 5 March 1795, 13 June 1811.

34. Dilworth, *The Schoolmaster's Assistant.*

35. A letter from Frederick Daser to the commissioners, inscribed in Minutes, 5 March 1795, was signed "Frederick Daser, A.M." On his pastorate at St. John's Lutheran in Charleston and in Orangeburg, see Bernheim, *History of the German Settlements and of the Lutheran Church in North and South Carolina,* and note on p. 212 the description of Daser as "a certain Master of Arts."

36. Minutes, 6 August 1795, 1 October 1795, 5 November 1795, 4 February 1796; King, *History and Records,* 14.

37. Minutes, 21 September 1843. James Barry to commissioners, 7 September 1803 and 10 September 1803, Applications, file of Henry Barry; Minutes, 1 September 1803.

38. Pyburn, "Public School System," 87–88. See also Copeland, "A Note."

39. *Rules and Regulations for the Government of the Orphan House in the City of Charleston,* rule 6, in Minutes, 28 July 1791; Pyburn, "Public School System," 87; Minutes, 6 June 1811.

40. In *Elements of Tuition* (1805), cited in Kaestle, *Joseph Lancaster,* 20. Further comparisons of Bell and Lancaster appear in Salmon, *The Practical Parts of Lancaster's Improvements and Bell's Experiment.*

41. Barnard, "Andrew Bell," 485.

42. Minutes, 16 July 1818.

43. James Barry to commissioners, 7 September 1803, Applications, file of Henry Barry.

44. Pyburn, "Public School System," 88.

45. George McDill to commissioners, 21 December 1816, Indentures, file of Eleanor and Jane Brown; Indenture Books, Eleanor and Jane Brown, admitted 21 July 1802. Their older sister (by two years), Elizabeth, left the Orphan House a year before the twins and had learned to sign her name by then. Even at the end of their apprenticeships Eleanor and Jane marked the receipts they gave their masters for their freedom dues. The receipts are in their Indentures file.

46. Minutes, 5 March 1795, 6 August 1795. It is worth noting in this context that boilerplate language in the printed indenture changed between 1822 and 1832. The earlier indentures bound the child "to the Commissioners of the Orphan House" (see John Fordham's indenture in chapter 8) whereas the later documents bound him "'as an apprentice for Education' to the Commissioners of the Orphan House" (see indenture of Archibald Kelso, Indentures).

47. Minutes, 1 October 1801.

48. Minutes, 1 October 1795, 5 November 1795.

49. Minutes, 1 October 1801.

50. Minutes, 13 June 1811.

51. Minutes, 4 January 1816, 11 January 1816, 12 December 1816, 9 January 1817.

52. Minutes, 6 March 1794, case of Bridget Carew. The commissioners approved the application.

53. Minutes, 18 March 1801.

54. Minutes, 7 August 1809, 14 September 1809.

55. Matron's report, Minutes, 14 December 1843.

56. Minutes, 14 September 1809, 17 February 1820, 14 June 1832, 14 December 1843.

57. Minutes, 12 November 1807, 16 May 1811. The donor may have been the woman identified by Bellows, *Benevolence* (40), without citation, as Mary Christiana Hopton Gregorie. Mrs. Mary C. Gregorie did bequeath some shares in the Union Bank of Charleston to support an Orphan House boy who wanted to prepare for the Christian ministry (Minutes, 16 July 1840).

58. Minutes, 4 June 1807, 17 October 1822, 16 May 1811; Meriwether, *History of Higher Education*, 143. Minutes, 24 June 1841; Gosport was across the Elizabeth River from Portsmouth and later became the Norfolk Naval Shipyard; its early history is summarized in *A Naval Encyclopedia*, 593–601. On numbers, compare comments on indentures in Indenture Books. On the College and High School of Charleston, see Fraser, *Charleston! Charleston!*, 179, 215, respectively. On the close association of apprenticeships, literacy, and schooling in Baltimore at this time, see Moss, *Schooling Citizens*, 74–78.

59. Minutes, 7 March 1805, 11 July 1805.

60. "Qualifications of a Guardian of Children," 544.

61. Minutes, 24 October 1844.

62. Minutes, 18 August 1840, 24 February 1842, 14 July 1842.

63. Minutes, 7 July 1791.

64. Minutes, 10 August 1840, 14 July 1842.

65. Indenture Books, Mary Burgrin, entered 18 August 1836. See also the similar case of Eliza Kimmey, Minutes, 14 November 1844.

66. The following analysis is condensed from Murray, "Literacy Acquisition."

67. Only those rates based on the signs and marks of ten or more children appear in this figure.

68. For details see Murray, "Literacy Acquisition."

69. All references below to this report appear in Minutes, 25 June 1857.

70. Meriwether, *History of Higher Education*, 116.

71. *Yearbook, 1910, City of Charleston, So. Ca.* (Charleston: Daggett Printing, 1910), 278–89.

72. Minutes, 25 June 1857.

73. Tower, *Tower's Second Reader*, 163

74. Roselle, *Samuel Griswold Goodrich, Creator of Peter Parley*; Ezell, "A Southern Education for Southrons," Peter Parley quoted on p. 315.

75. All quotations from Bennett's report, Minutes, 25 June 1857.

76. James Vidal to commissioners, 3 September 1840, and R. W. Barnwell to commissioners, 27 December 1842, both in Indentures, file of Thomas Stenton. Hollis, "Robert W. Barnwell."

77. Minutes, 5 January 1843, and transcription of Henry A. DeSaussure to R. W. Barnwell, 9 January 1843 in Minutes of 12 January 1843. DeSaussure spoke frankly of his experience at the Orphan House. A different view of turning poor boys into college students came from Thomas Jefferson, according to whose educational plan "twenty of the best geniuses will be raked *from the rubbish* annually." My emphasis. *Notes on the State of Virginia*, Query XIV. See Jefferson, *Writings* (New York: Library of America, 1984), 272.

CHAPTER SIX

1. Rosenberg, *The Cholera Years.*

2. "Review of Bernard M. Byrne, An Essay to Prove the Contagious Character of the Malignant Cholera," *Baltimore Medical and Surgical Journal and Review* 1 (1833): 429–34.

3. Waring, "Charleston Medicine, 1800–1860." Fraser, *Charleston! Charleston!*, 211; Physician report in Minutes, 15 October 1835.

4. "Review of Byrne," 432; Minutes, 9 November 1832.

5. Physician's Report, Minutes, 4 Oct 1832, 10 Oct 1833, 16 Oct 1834, 15 Oct 1835, 13 Oct 1836.

6. Minutes, 16 October 1835, 13 October 1836.

7. Minutes, 27 September 1832. Compare 20 March 1806 for report on mixing of well water and privy effusions.

8. Case of Andrew Stenton, 14 June 1838, Applications. Stenton's mother had died in 1836 of cholera.

9. Minutes, 25 August 1791. Indenture Books, John Burns, admitted 7 May 1792. This hospital seems to have been connected to the Poor House. See Minutes 28 August 1791.

10. Ann Zylks to commissioners, 23 December 1815, Applications, file of Margaret and Thomas Zylks; Jane Mordecai to commissioners, 24 October 1815, Applications, file of Frances Mordecai.

11. Visiting commissioner's report, 1 August 1844, Applications, file of Louisa Benton.

12. Edward McCrady Jr. and Edward B. White to commissioners, 27 November 1858, Applications, file of Elizabeth and William Henderson. Note the attached, unsigned visiting commissioner's report. A. Toomer Porter to commissioners, 18 June 1860, Rejected Applications, file of Ann Kain. Mary Byrd to commissioners, November 1829, Applications, file of Washington Stevenson.

13. Minutes, 10 October 1793 and 17 October 1793.

14. Minutes, 23 June 1808; Mary Turner, Indenture Books, entered 16 December 1808.

15. H. W. DeSaussure to commissioners, April 1857, Rejected Applications, file of Alfred Sanders. Emphasis in original.

16. Minutes, 1 February 1799, 10 September 1812.

17. Thos. Akin to commissioners of the Orphan House, 18 April 1839 and 27 May 1839, Applications, file of Malcolm McDonald. In a similar case, commissioners rejected

a child with whooping cough; see H. L. Pinckney to commissioners, 31 May 1838, Applications, file of Mrs. Susan Hopkins.

18. Harriott Horry to commissioners, 8 June 1816 and 31 May 1820, Rejected Applications, file of Frank and Isaac Smith. Harriott Horry was the sister of Charles Cotesworth Pinckney and the daughter of Eliza Lucas Pinckney, who developed a commercially viable process to transform indigo into blue dye. More on the family and the city at this time is in Rogers, *Charleston*.

19. Waring, *A History of Medicine in South Carolina, 1670–1825*, 110–11; Terris, "An Early System of Compulsory Health Insurance in the United States, 1798–1884."

20. Waring, *A History of Medicine in South Carolina, 1670–1825*, 118–29.

21. Richard H. Shryock, foreword to Waring, *A History of Medicine in South Carolina, 1670–1825*, viii.

22. *City Gazette and Daily Advertiser*, 26 August 1793, p. 4.

23. Waring, *A History of Medicine in South Carolina, 1670–1825*, 134; Report of Steward and Physician, 1809–1816. On Logan, see King, "Dr. George Logan."

24. King, "Dr. George Logan"; Waring, *A History of Medicine in South Carolina, 1670–1825*, 260–63.

25. Waring, *A History of Medicine in South Carolina, 1825–1900*, 248.

26. For more on the work of physicians in the antebellum South, see Stowe, *Doctoring the South*.

27. *By-Laws of the Orphan House of Charleston, South Carolina.*, 23–24.

28. Folks, *The Care of Destitute, Neglected, and Delinquent Children.*, 21.

29. Ibid., 20.

30. DeBow, *Statistical View of the United States*; Steckel, "A Dreadful Childhood." See also Murray, "Fates of Orphans," for further statistical analysis of Orphan House death rates.

31. Minutes, 23 October 1794, 15 September 1796.

32. Fraser, *Charleston! Charleston!*, 195; Waring, *A History of Medicine in South Carolina, 1670–1825*, 157; Minutes, 3 April 1823; Cooper and Kiple, "Yellow Fever"; Messrs. Jones and Lee, Architects, "Description of the Orphan House," in *Charleston Orphan House: Centennial Celebration*, 78–80. Forbes et al., *Cyclopaedia of Practical Medicine*, vol. 2, "Fever (Yellow)," 247–79 (q.v.).

33. Waring, *A History of Medicine in South Carolina, 1670–1825*, 74–77. The city's population at this time was ten to twelve thousand (Fraser, *Charleston! Charleston!*). The implied case fatality rate of about 10 percent was very close to the 14 percent in a well-documented 1721 epidemic in Boston (Crosby, "Smallpox").

34. Glynn and Glynn, *The Life and Death of Smallpox*, 4–5, 111–13; Rusnock, "Catching Cowpox," 28.

35. Minutes, 17 February 1791.

36. Minutes, 22 October 1795.

37. Waring, *A History of Medicine in South Carolina, 1670–1825*, 132–33, 301.

38. Glynn and Glynn, *The Life and Death of Smallpox*, 119–21.

39. Minutes, 18 March 1802, 4 April 1802, 26 May 1808.

40. Physician's Report, 21 March 1811.

41. Waring, *A History of Medicine in South Carolina, 1670–1825*, 155–57; Minutes, 20 February 1817.

42. Minutes, 14 July 1825.

43. Waring, *A History of Medicine in South Carolina, 1825–1900*, 40; George Logan to commissioners, transcribed in Minutes, 17 February 1831.

44. Waring, *A History of Medicine in South Carolina, 1825–1900*, 40; Minutes, 14 April 1853.

45. George Logan to commissioners, 11 July 1833, Physician's Reports.

46. Minutes, 13 October 1831. On crowding and tuberculosis mortality, see Murray, "The White Plague in Utopia."

47. Kim-Farley, "Measles."

48. Minutes, 22 October 1795.

49. Minutes, 14 July 1802, 19 August 1802.

50. Physician's Reports, various weeks, September–November 1813.

51. From annual Physician's Reports in Minutes for those years.

52. "The Relationship of Nutrition, Disease, and Social Conditions." Note Minutes, 14 July 1802, 19 August 1802, and especially 18 October 1830 on measles-related deaths.

53. E.g., Minutes, 20 June 1822.

54. Indenture Books: see William Nettles (entered 24 July 1834), George Haggemyer (entered 6 December 1838), Phoebe Vantine (entered 1 December 1842), Thomas Grogan (entered 7 November 1850), and Mary King (entered 29 January 1852). Apparently Mary Ann McGinnis, who died in 1850 at age twenty months, was too young to have appeared in the Indenture Books.

55. Physician's Reports, 29 October 1829, 14 October 1830.

56. Geo. Logan, MD, to commissioners, 30 June 1844, Applications, file of William Fay; and Minutes, 18 October 1844.

57. Minutes, 23–30 October 1800; Physician's Reports, 3 September 1809, 10 September 1809, and 4 June 1812.

58. Geo. Logan, MD, to commissioners, 5 October 1823, Applications, file of John Sherer. Sherer's younger brother Francis (entered 17 July 1823) died a year later of worms, according to his indenture; see Indenture Books.

59. Minutes, 16 November 1820.

60. Minutes, 25 July 1811 and 1 August 1811.

61. Physician's Report, 2 April 1812.

62. Logan to commissioners, 11 July 1833, transcribed in Minutes, 11 July 1833. Minutes, 25 July 1833. Karasch, "Ophthalmia: Conjunctivitis and Trachoma."

63. Minutes, 26 October 1815, 2 November 1815.

64. Indenture Books, Frances Mordecai, entered 25 April 1816; Fanny Mordecai to commissioners, 24 August 1819, Applications, file of Frances Mordecai; Minutes, 9 September 1819; E. Abrahams to commissioners, 20 July 1820, Indentures, file of Frances Mordecai. Little is known of Dr. Gleize, who had previously opened an "Infirmary for Sick Negroes" (Waring, *A History of Medicine in South Carolina, 1625–1800*, 143). On Elias Abrahams's promise to care for Fanny in her adulthood, see chapter 4.

65. Minutes, 18 September 1817 and 25 September 1817; see Minutes, 9 October 1817, for a suggestion that the commissioners believed her mother would take Rachel to the Bahamas.

66. Indenture Books, Andrew Berry, entered 27 September 1804; Yates Snowden, ed., *History of South Carolina* (Chicago: Lewis Publishing, 1920), vol. 4, pp. 9, 196; Dr. Thomas Williams to commissioners, 20 May 1815, Indentures. No records exist on what became of Berry.

67. Minutes, 19 September 1793; Indenture Books, Elizabeth Sowers, entered 20 November 1790.

68. Minutes, 27 February 1806, 6 March 1806; Indenture Books, Harriet McNeil, entered 26 August 1802.

69. Minutes, 5 January 1809; Indenture Books, James McKie, entered 1 December 1808.

70. Minutes, 14 September 1809.

71. The great history of nineteenth-century therapeutics is Warner, *The Therapeutic Perspective*. See p. 18 on Rush, and p. 71 on more powerful treatments in the South, Charleston in particular.

72. Hardy, "Whooping Cough."

73. Physician's Report, weekly, July–September 1809.

74. Logan to commissioners, transcribed in Minutes, 13 October 1831 (copy also in Physician's Report).

75. Forbes et al., *Cyclopaedia of Practical Medicine*, vol. 1, pp. 528–31. Warner, "The Idea of Southern Medical Distinctiveness," 182.

76. Logan to commissioners, transcribed in Minutes, 10 October 1833 (copy also in Physician's Report). See chapter 3 above for a brief description of water and bath availability at the Orphan House.

77. From the Physician's Reports, in 1831 there were 19 cases of hooping cough and 16 of scarlet fever; in 1838, 27 of hooping cough and 67 of scarlet fever; and in 1844, 25 of hooping cough and 44 of scarlet fever.

78. Physician's Report, 13 October 1831.

79. Physician's Report, transcribed into Minutes, 13 October 1831.

80. Forbes et al. *Cyclopaedia of Practical Medicine*, vol. 4, pp. 67–82.

81. Logan, "A Brief Account of the Scarlatina, as It Prevailed in the Orphan House, Charleston, South Carolina."

82. Logan, "Belladonna in Scarlatina."

83. Warner, *The Therapeutic Perspective*, 58ff.

84. Examples given in ibid., 305n3.

85. Physician's Report, 9 August 1810, 4 October 1810.

86. Physician's Report, 21 February 1811, 28 February 1811, 7 March 1811, 14 March 1811.

87. Minutes, 5 April 1791, 22 September 1796, 17 March 1803; 1861 *By-Laws* V.8 (p. 17); Henry A. DeSaussure to John Dewees, 16 March 1842, in file of Angelina Richter. DeSaussure also apologized for his inability to attend the child's funeral, as his presence was required as a pallbearer at the funeral of Charleston's mayor, Jacob Mintzing, to be held the same day.

CHAPTER SEVEN

1. Murray, "Fates of Orphans."

2. Elizabeth Adams to Orphan House, 25 July 1830, and J[oseph] J[ohnson] to Elizabeth Adams, 3 May 1831, Applications, file of William Adams.

3. Minutes, 8 March 1804.

4. William Roselle (?) to commissioners, 22 August 1824, Applications, file of John Van Hagen; Van Hagen, admitted 13 April 1820, Indenture Books.

5. Minutes, 28 November 1793; see also 17 March 1798 for the case of James Marsh, escaped to his brother-in-law's pilot boat.

6. Mary Buckingham to commissioners, 1 December 1819, Applications, file of Joseph Wilson; Wilson in Indenture Books, entered 10 April 1817.

7. Catherine E. Biggs to commissioners, 31 May 1832, Indentures; Indenture Books, Henry Biggs entered 22 May 1831.

8. Sarah Adams and Hugh Adams to commissioners, 23 April 1834, Indentures, file of James Connelly. Note that Sarah Adams, neé Connelly, had previously described her impoverished widowhood in a letter cited in chapter 4, note 93.

9. Jackson, *Privateers in Charleston, 1793–1796*.

10. Minutes, 7 August 1794.

11. Minutes, 28 April 1796. A similar case appears in Minutes, 11 September 1794.

12. Indenture Books, Louis Tardieu, entered 26 September 1793; and Joseph LeTillier, entered 10 March 1794; Ed. Penman to commissioners, 23 July 1794, transcribed in Minutes, 24 July 1794; Minutes, 7 August 1794, 14 August 1794; *City Gazette*, 9 August 1794.

13. Minutes, 20 October 1796; Thomas Oliver, Indenture Books, entered 11 December 1794.

14. Minutes, 12 November 1801, 3 March 1802.

15. Minutes, 13 January 1803, 20 January 1803.

16. Minutes, 11 November 1813.

17. Minutes, 17 July 1845, McInnis, *Politics of Taste*, 82, 86–87.

18. A. Campbell, Steward, to commissioners, transcribed in Minutes, 14 April 1853.

19. Bardaglio, *Reconstructing the Household*, 106–12; Grossberg, *Governing the Hearth*, 268–80; Kawashima, "Adoption in Early America"; Presser, "Historical Background." The gaps in the history of adoption might be illustrated by Presser's claim of an odd custom in the eighteenth-century South in which "those of great wealth" adopted orphans in very large numbers. He provides an example of a "Mr. Whitefields" in Georgia, whose household included no fewer than sixty-one orphans. The example clearly refers to George Whitefield's Bethesda, the Georgia Orphan House, the first orphanage in America, in Savannah.

20. An example of this kind of history of adoption appears in Melosh, *Strangers and Kin*: "Adoption gradually became established in the 1920s and 1930s," (3). For stories of adoption in Massachusetts that predated the 1851 law, not unlike the stories presented here, see Porter, "A Good Home," on the Boston Female Asylum.

21. Frances A. R. Pearson to commissioners, 21 October 1802, Indentures. Two Pearsons are listed in the 1802 directory, both of them mariners.

22. The emphasis in this story is on the word "companion." Mrs. Pearson would just

as likely have obtained a girl by asking for help with child raising, with the promise of teaching her eventually how to run a household. In this case it seems likely that Frances Pearson really needed a child minder, much as did many other young married women who came to the Orphan House seeking youthful help. Of the two men named Pearson in the 1802 directory, one of them, named Benjamin, was probably Frances Pearson's husband. In that case, one reason that Ann Ford's indenture was broken a year later and Ann then bound out to a shopkeeper in "Newburgh" (probably Newberry) might have been the son who Benjamin and Frances Pearson welcomed into their family, who was baptized in the Independent Congregational (Circular) Church in June 1802. Thus, while the sixteen-year-old Ann might have eagerly served as a companion to Mrs. Pearson, she undoubtedly also cared for the infant James Pearson as well, and perhaps with less enthusiasm. See Ann Ford, Indenture Books, entered 27 June 1793; James W. Hagy, *People and Professions of Charleston, South Carolina, 1782–1802*, 84; "Register," 312.

23. Minutes, 5 June 1817. There is no indication of a blood relation between the woman and the child. For a similar case see Minutes, 3 March 1825

24. M. L. Horlbeck to commissioners, 19 September 1816, Indentures. Eleanor's indenture reports that she was to learn the trade of a seamstress; Eleanor Kennedy, Indenture Books, entered 5 January 1809.

25. Minutes, 26 September 1850, re Louisa McCabe ("with the consent of its mother"); and 3 October 1850, re Amanda Ludwig ("with the full acquiescence of the mother of the child").

26. Minutes, 8 September 1825.

27. Eliza Mitchell to commissioners, 31 December 1855, Indentures, file of Martha Smith.

28. Indenture Books, Maryann Turner, entered 16 December 1808, and Louisa Gardner, entered 23 January 1812; Minutes, 10 November 1814, 28 May 1818, 9 July 1818 (Gardner), 16 July 1818 (Turner). For more on Louisa Gardner, see chapter 9.

29. Thos. Christburg to commissioners, 1 December 1825, Indentures, file of Erhard children; Indenture Books, Erhard siblings, entered 16 October 1817.

30. Milne obituary: *New York Times*, 16 December 1857; *Du Pont v. Du Bos et al.*, 52 S.C. 244, in *The Southeastern Reporter* 29 (15 March–31 May 1898): 666; Andr. Milne to commissioners, 29 October 1845, Indentures, file of Virginia Karnes; Minutes, 9 September 1841, 30 October 1845; unsigned visiting commissioner's report (probably by N. R. Middleton), 23 September 1841, Applications, file of Virginia Karnes.

31. Unsigned letter, possibly from Mrs. H. Horlbeck, to commissioners, 1 September 1830, Indentures, file of Angelina Hutchins. Mrs. Jane Corkran to commissioners, 4 October 1820, Indentures, case of Agnes O'Farrell.

32. Mrs. Ellen M. Nelson to commissioners, 30 March 1854, Indentures, file of Mary Whitemore.

33. Minutes, 19 February 1852, 23 October 1856, 30 October 1856; L. J. Runkin to commissioners, 20 October 1856, Indentures, file of Nina Mazyck.

34. J. Witz to commissioners, 6 September 1859, Indentures, file of Nina Mazyck. Compare a similar case in Minutes, 22 February 1844 and 3 March 1842, in which the successful application stopped with the offer to "provide for the boy as his own, as he had no son, & his wife was anxious to procure a little boy."

35. Ann Campbell to commissioners, 16 May 1855, Indentures, file of Mary Riley. Emphasis in original. Mrs. Campbell conceded that she "[had] no place to put her to sleep in, at this time," and a week later withdrew the application. See Minutes, 24 May 1855. Unsigned letter, possibly from Mrs. H. Horlbeck, to commissioners, 1 September 1830, Indentures, file of Angelina Hutchins. G. M. Goodrich to commissioners, 15 December 1833, Indentures, file of Mary Shirer; and Mary Shirer in Indenture Books, entered 4 August 1825.

36. Henry D. Capers, *The Life and Times of C. G. Memminger* (Richmond: Everett Waddey, 1893), 7–15, 21–28. Christopher Gustavus Memminger, Indenture Books, entered 28 January 1807; Minutes, 18 December 1806, 29 January 1807, 9 January 1812 ("great native genius"), 19 October 1813, 27 January 1814, 20 November 1817. Capers omits reference to Memminger's grandmother (except to quote the order to admit Memminger on 29 January 1807 in the Minutes), but it was Magdalena who signed the indenture. In addition, the indentures of Christopher Frederick Kohler and Maria Catherine Kohler, who both entered 5 December 1805, indicate that Magdalena's son Frederick (Christopher's uncle) was already living in Charleston, possibly with Magdalena under his roof, when the Kohler-Memminger party arrived, which would explain their destination of Charleston. The relationship between Isaac Bennett and Thomas Bennett is unclear (Poston, *The Buildings of Charleston*, 502). Thomas Bennett may have met Memminger through Isaac Bennett or at the Orphan House while he was a commissioner, 1811–14.

37. Minutes, 24 March 1808, 31 March 1808, 16 April 1808. *Dictionary of American Naval Fighting Ships* (http://www.history.navy.mil/danfs/s18/stevens-i.htm). Stevens's memoirs concentrate on his Revolutionary War service and do not mention Holdup, although he did discuss his service on the Orphan House Board ("Autobiography of Daniel Stevens, 1746–1835"). Stevens was sixty-two when Holdup left the Orphan House.

38. Minutes, 31 March 1808, 6 July 1809. *Appleton's Cyclopedia*, vol. 5, "Stevens, Thomas Holdup," 678 (q.v.).

39. W. Dukes (visiting commissioner) to commissioners, 3 April 1851, Indentures, file of William and Francis Shecut; Edward and Mary Farrell to commissioners, 10 July 1856, Indentures, file of Farrell children. The Farrells judged that Edward's current earnings of ten dollars per week—a handsome amount indeed—was sufficient to support the entire family.

40. Francis Knieff to commissioners, 30 December 1818, Indentures, file of Sarah Adams.

41. E. Kennedy to commissioners, 20 January 1803, Indentures, file of Susannah Thompson.

42. C. Douglas to commissioners, 30 October 1838; R. Keenan to commissioners, 23 March 1837; both in Indentures, file of Margaret and Henry Denoon. C. Douglas to commissioners, 5 January 1837, Applications, file of Margaret and Henry Denoon. Minutes, 31 August 1837.

43. Mary Barnes to commissioners, 31 October 1834, Indentures, file of Catherine Bull. Appended to the letter is the postscript, "I consent to and unite in the above application. [signed] Thomas Barnes." Mary Barnes alone, though, signed Catherine's indenture, Indenture Books, entered 22 October 1829. Minutes, 20 November 1834.

44. Mary and Wm. Pregnall to commissioners, 12 July 1819, Indentures, file of Henry Pregnall. Minutes, 12 August 1819: "The Chairman reported that . . . he had received no

application from Mrs. Pregnall." The exact relationships among the Pregnalls are any-thing but clear: the letter writer was married and signed the letter as Mary Pregnall, but referred to Henry's grandfather as "my father," as if she were a Pregnall before marriage. Possibly the older man was her father-in-law. Mary clearly identifies her relationship to Henry: "I was his aunt."

45. Minutes, 16 June 1825 and 28 October 1826; James Fife to commissioners, 10 May 1826, Indentures, file of Joseph and Nelson Lawton.

46. Mary Ann Myatt to commissioners, 8 May 1839, Indentures, file of Edward and Lewis Myatt.

47. Identifying the relation of the receiving adult from indentures was considerably enhanced by transcriptions by King in her *History and Records*. On strategies of the poor to use almshouses for child care, see Bourque, "Bound Out from the Almshouse."

48. For more on remarriage at this time, see Grigg, "Toward a Theory of Remarriage."

49. Minutes, 19 May 1796; Indenture Books, Margaret McKenzie, entered 14 April 1791.

50. Minutes, 10 June 1824; Susan Ridley to commissioners, 20 April 1826, Inden-tures, file of Richard and John Adams.

51. John and Maryann Burns to commissioners, 3 December 1845, Indentures, file of James Cook. On James Cook's previous whereabouts, see his indenture in Indenture Books (entered 8 May 1845) and the Minutes of the commissioners of the Poor House, 7 May 1845, in which he was described as "the child of Mrs Burns."

52. Minutes, 6 April 1815.

53. Mary Kirkpatrick to commissioners, 27 February 1834, Indentures, file of James Caulfield. On coverture in South Carolina, see Weir, *Colonial South Carolina*, 232–33.

54. Martha Deliesseline to commissioners, 22 February 1855, Indentures, file of John and Isaac Deliesseline.

55. Minutes, 13 August 1812, 22 June 1815, 20 February 1817, 10 February 1820, 15 November 1821; Elizabeth Headwright to commissioners, 22 June 1815, Applications, file of Evelina, Mary, and William Headwright; Elizabeth Lodus to commissioners, 20 Feb-ruary 1817, Indentures, file of Mary Headwright.

56. Due consideration of character: Minutes, 4 April 1800; seamstress: Catherine Ben-nett to commissioners, 3 March 1853, Rejected Indentures, file of Alice Riens; Minutes, 10 March 1853. On Sarah Jane Gilbert: Peter Mangan and Elizabeth Mangan to commis-sioners, 31 May 1843, and Elizabeth Mangin and Peter Mangin [sic] to commissioners, 22 November 1843, both in Indentures; Minutes, 1 June 1843, 8 June 1843, 23 November 1843, 30 November 1843, 14 December 1843. On the use of older girls in washing, see chapter 5 above. Similarly, Lockley found evidence of dependence on the labor of older (and "larger") girls in orphanages in Mobile, Beaufort, and Savannah (*Welfare and Charity*, 110–11).

57. Catherine Clements to commissioners, n.d., and Catherine Lowry to commis-sioners, 28 July 1829, Indentures, file of Clements children; Robert Clements, entered 13 July 1826, Indenture Books.

58. Ann Holway to commissioners, 11 May 1856, Indentures, file of Mary Holway; Mary E. Holway, entered 29 November 1855, Indenture Books. The phrase "peculiar disease" appears on her indenture.

59. Alex. Gillen to commissioners, 23 June 1819, Indentures, file of Charles Wolley.

60. An early example: Minutes, 21 February 1800; a late example: Minutes, 10 May 1855.

61. Minutes, 4 February 1819. The reference in the Minutes to "Genl" Pinckney indicates that this was Charles Cotesworth Pinckney the statesman. For more on Pinckney, see Rogers, *Charleston in the Age of the Pinckneys*, 121–136. The younger Charles Cotesworth Pinckney, a clergyman, also appears in Orphan House records. Alex. Gillen to commissioners, 23 June 1819, Indentures, file of Charles Wolley.

62. Elizabeth Welch to commissioners, 16 January 1834, Indentures, file of Harriett Welch.

63. Isabella Doyle to commissioners, 6 April 1836, Indentures, file of Doyle children, postscript by Henry Dickson. On Dickson, see Cardozo, *Reminiscences of Charleston*, 68–69.

64. L[ouisa] Ryan to Mr. DeSaussure, 22 March 1855, Indentures, file of Theodore Ryan, and Theodore Ryan, entered 22 July 1846, Indenture Books; E. Stiefvater to commissioners, 1 September 1853, Indentures, file of Juliana Stiefvater, and Juliana Stiefvater, entered 1 July 1852, Indenture Books.

65. Dorothy Gallagher to commissioners, 29 May 1826, Indentures, file of Gallagher children; John Gallagher, entered 28 September 1820, Indenture Books.

66. Edwards, *Ordinances*, 162. The term "disabled" referred to any inability to support a family, not just a loss of physical capabilities.

67. Wikramanayake, *A World in Shadow*, 81–86; Harris, "Charleston's Free Afro-American Elite." See also Myers, *Forging Freedom*, on free women of color in Charleston. Some Charleston charities did help both white and free black families (Lockley, *Welfare and Charity*, 113).

68. Minutes, 29 January 1807, 6 August 1812; Motes, *Free Blacks and Mulattos in South Carolina*, 125.

69. G. A. Schroebel, Wm. [illegible], and Mary Gregorie to commissioners, 25 January 1820, and Rachael Burbridge to commissioners, 17 February 1820, both letters in Applications, file of Burbridge children; Minutes, 17 February 1820. That is, on the afternoon of the day when Rachael Burbridge wrote to the commissioners, they determined to release her children to her. So swiftly did this happen, in fact, that Alfred and Harriott's indentures omit the date of their departure.

70. Minutes, 3 January 1811.

71. Roger Jones to commissioners, 8 January 1828, Indentures, file of Ormsby and William Jones; John Gordy to commissioners, 1 January 1819, Indentures, file of Peter and Nathan Gordy.

72. William Milligan to commissioners, 1 May 1828, Indentures, file of William Milligan; Wm. Dunlap to commissioners, 2 June 1831, Indentures, file of Samuel and Lucinda Dunlap.

73. A postscript to J. R. Cook to commissioners, 5 May 1859, Indentures, file of David, Samuel, and William Cook, reads, "I fully coincide with the requests of my husband. [signed] Martha H. Cook."

74. Minutes, 20 July 1809, 1 February 1820; steward's weekly report, 28 January 1810. Gayner's side of the story appears in Thomas Gayner, "[A] report in part of the trial of

Thomas Gayner for the alledged murder of his wife. . . ." (Charleston: W. P. Young, 1810);
Early American Imprints, Second Series, no. 21390.

1. Murray, "Fates of Orphans." On Southern children's labor, see Zipf, *Labor of Innocents*, and Sundue, *Industrious in Their Stations*. On rural children's labor, see Craig,
To Sow One Acre More. See also figure 7.1.

2. Coclanis, *The Shadow of a Dream*, 125–30. DeBow, *The Industrial Resources,
Statistics, &c. of the United States and More Particularly of the Southern and Western
States* vol. 1, p. 123·

3. Griffin, "An Origin of the New South." On the Panic of 1819, Rothbard, *The Panic
of 1819*. Mills, *Statistics*, 428·

4. Lander, "Charleston: Manufacturing Center of the Old South."

5. Lander, "Charleston: Manufacturing Center of the Old South"; Fraser, *Charleston!
Charleston!*, 178–243, railhead discussed at pp. 208, 233. See also Stavisky, "Industrialism
in Ante Bellum Charleston." The most vivid and poignant history of this gradual decline
is Peter Coclanis's *The Shadow of a Dream*.

6. Cooper and McCord, *Statutes at Large*, vol. 3, 544–46; Brevard, *An Alphabetical
Digest of the Public Statute Law of South Carolina in Three Volumes.*, 25–28; Walsh,
Charleston's Sons of Liberty, 22–23, 120, 143. See also Sundue, *Industrious in Their
Stations*. Burton, *Charleston Furniture, 1700–1825*, 109; Rauschenberg, "Evidence for
the Apprenticeship System in Charleston, South Carolina." On goldsmith apprentices in
early Boston, see Ward, "Boston Goldsmiths, 1690–1730."

7. Fraser, *Charleston! Charleston!*, 227, 242–43; Rorabaugh, *Craft Apprentice*, 182.

8. Griffin, "Origin of the New South." Minutes, 4 May 1815, 25 May 1815, 18 January 1816, 5 February 1818; Knight, *Public Education in the South*, 216.

9. Herndon and Murray, *Children Bound to Labor*.

10. From the Rules listed in Minutes, 28 July 1791.

11. Minutes, 25 July 1793; Mary Long to commissioners, 21 September 1802, Indentures, file of Charlotte Suder; Jennings Tomlinson & Co. to commissioners, 19 August
1860, Indentures, file of George Andrews.

12. J. B. Duval to commissioners, 18 June 1840, file of George King; Benjamin Gildersleeve to commissioners, 24 October 1832, file of Oran Bassett; see also King, *Newspaper
Press*, 172; Thaddeus C. Bolling to commissioners, 4 February 1838, file of Richard Taylor; M. Moles to commissioners, 7 January 1815, file of Sarah Fields; all in Indentures.

13. Minutes, 30 June 1808, and indenture of Charles Reyer, Indenture Book, entered
21 October 1805.

14. Sarah Airs to commissioners file of Louisa Carter, 3 April 1816, Rejected Applications.

15. Minutes, 7 November 1803, 4 April 1800.

16. Minutes, 9 November 1809, 21 May 1818.

17. Minutes, 28 November 1805. See also 27 September 1800.

18. Minutes, 30 December 1841.

19. M. LeCompte to commissioners, 26 March 1818, Indentures, file of Rachel Isaacs; Rachel Isaacs, entered 18 November 1813 in Indenture Books. Rachel had earlier been a subject of some concern to the commissioners, as chapter 6 recounts; she may have had vision problems, and commissioners were concerned that her mother would use medical treatment as an excuse to remove her from the Orphan House and spirit her away to the Bahamas. Rachel probably went on to marry John Calvo, a "Professor of Languages," in 1821 (*City Gazette*, Saturday, 19 May 1821).

20. Charlotte Clark, entered 27 June 1800, Indenture Books. Minutes, 2 June 1803, 8 December 1803, 15 December 1803. Rowland et al., *The History of Beaufort County, South Carolina*, vol. 1, p. 385. John Bachman to commissioners, 2 October 1845, Indentures, file of Rueben Terry. Christopher Orr to commissioners, 26 April 1827, Indentures, file of James Kean.

21. Cunningham & Neale to commissioners, 10 August 1802, Indentures, file of William Spence. Joseph Milligan to commissioners, Indentures; also on Milligan, Minutes, 28 September 1809. An example of a tradesman's discussion with parents is Jacob Henry to commissioners, 9 December 1813, Indentures, file of William Veronee. Josiah Finney to commissioners, 21 March 1826, Indentures, file of George Corker.

22. E. W. Whiting to commissioners, 26 July 1832, Indentures, file of John Addams. See also Henry A. Smysen to commissioners, 12 July 1836, Indentures, file of Mary A. Barrett; Jas. D. Knight to commissioners, 30 October 1832, Indentures, file of Jane Thornly.

23. Ann Bowles to commissioners, 5 January 1816, Indentures, file of Eliza Vanorden. G. D. Beckham to commissioners, 18 May 1852, Indentures, file of William R. Bull.

24. Mrs. L. Smith to commissioners, 2 September 1819, Indentures, file of Eliza Miller. Wm. E. Hughson to commissioners, 16 January 1843, Indentures, file of Wm. L. Meray. John McMillan to Col. Danl. Stevens, 27 March 1815, Indentures, file of James Holdup. Minutes, 19 September 1793.

25. Mrs. L. Smith to commissioners, 2 September 1819, file of Eliza Miller, Indentures.

26. Elizabeth Sowers, entered 20 November 1790, Indenture Books. Johan H. Wienges to commissioners, 15 June 1820, Indentures, file of Ann Gladden. In a similar case Robert Wallace lost his vision, leading his master, a blacksmith, to seek to return him. A. Roulan to commissioners, 11 January 1838, Indentures, file of Robert Wallace. On Eliza Egerton: [Mrs.] C. F. Wright to Mrs. J. Johnson, 26 November 1834; Eliza M. Bonner to commissioners, 26 November 1834; Catherine Johnson to commissioners, 27 November 1834, all in Indentures, file of Eliza Egerton. Some children whose intelligence did not permit the learning of a trade ended up in the Poor House (Minutes, 12 June 1856).

27. Peter Freneau was the brother of Philip Freneau, "Poet of the Revolution," but was much better known than Philip at this time (Davis and Seigler, "Peter Freneau, Carolina Republican"). Minutes, 6 October 1796. King, *Newspaper Press*, 37–38. Margaret Smith to commissioners, 30 October 1839, Indentures, file of Ellen Carpenter.

28. Unsigned fragment in Indentures file of Marion Hendricks, no date but possibly early in 1858; Jas. D. Knight to commissioners, 30 October 1832, Indentures, file of Matilda Kennedy; E. B. Benson to William McBurney, 23 December 1857, Rejected Indentures, anonymous file. No reference to this case appears in the Minutes.

29. Minutes, 17 August 1809; Griffin, "An Origin."

30. Minutes, 4 May 1815, 28 May 1815, 18 January 1816; Knight, *Public Education*, 216. Cook, *Life and Legacy of David Rogerson Williams*, 138–43.

31. Lander, "Iron Industry"; indentures of Robert Joel Buckheister (entered 1 October 1840), William Hafer (entered 1 July 1841), Joseph James Evans (entered 9 August 1838), and Hugh Stenton (entered 15 September 1836), Indenture Books; Mary Ann Judge to commissioners, 22 June 1837, Indentures, file of Jean Chennell.

32. Minutes, 4 February 1796.

33. C. Canning to commissioners, 26 February 1852, Indentures, file of Richard Lennox; King, *Newspaper Press*, 171.

34. Wm. Smith to commissioners, 24 July 1819, Indentures, file of Ann Downie; Anna Porter to commissioners, 11 May 1820, Indentures, file of Mary Van Draper.

35. Rorabaugh, *The Craft Apprentice from Franklin to the Machine Age in America.*

36. William Estill to commissioners, 21 July 1831, Indentures, file of Margaret Cutter.

37. Murray, "Family, Literacy, and Skill-Training."

38. Adams, "American Neutrality and Prosperity, 1793–1808."

39. Lander, "Charleston: Manufacturing Center," 341; Indenture Books; Garlington, *Men of the Time*, 130. Gregg's advocacy of manufacturing as a source of demand for labor of poor whites is described in Martin, "The Advent of William Gregg."

40. Minutes, 14 May 1818, 25 June 1818.

41. Minutes, 23 January 1794 (see also 22 November 1810), 2 March 1815, 19 May 1825, 18 August 1825; Cornelius Clarke, entered 19 February 1818, Indenture Books. On Gosport, see Minutes, 24 June 1841.

42. Elizabeth Clarke to commissioners, 18 August 1825, Indentures, file of Cornelius Clarke.

43. Minutes, 27 March 1794, 14 December 1794; William Franks, entered 29 October 1790, Indenture Books.

44. Roosevelt, *The Naval War of 1812*, 119–21, 227–28. Lawrence Kearney to commissioners, 2 July 1814; Lawrence Kearney to commissioners, 1 June 1815; Lawrence Kearney to commissioners, 3 June 1815; all in Indentures, file of William Wish.

45. Hamilton, "Enforcement in Apprenticeship Contracts," 568; Haig to commissioners, 19 January 1826, and Haig to commissioners, 16 February 1826, both in Indentures, file of John Downie. King, *Newspaper Press*, 62.

46. J. Hume Simons to commissioners, 23 July 1840, Indentures, file of William Cantley. Brief biography of Simons is in Waring, *A History of Medicine in South Carolina, 1670–1825*, 292–93.

47. Jas. D. Knight to commissioners, 30 October 1832, Indentures, file of Jane Thornley; Robert Stevens to commissioners, 30 November 1815, Indentures, file of Charles Church. Stevens's offer really was remarkable, as the sum of $175 was about what an unskilled agricultural laborer could expect to earn in a year; see Adams, "Prices and Wages," 633.

48. James McIntosh to James Jervey, 30 January 1835, Indentures, file of Theodore Sompayrac; National Register of Historic Places, Inventory-Nomination Form, Welsh Neck–Long Bluff–Society Hill Historic District, Darlington County, South Carolina,

16 December 1974 (http://www.nationalregister.sc.gov/darlington/S10817716003/
S10817716003.pdf).

49. J. C. H. Claussen to commissioners, 8 October 1859, Indentures, in file of William Buckheister. Cooks had been withdrawn from the Orphan House, as described above in chapter 7, and then brought back in 1848, probably after the death of his mother. See his indenture and the Charleston death records for Mary Ann Burns, d. c. 1 March 1848 of intemperance, on the timing of these events. Claussen later established bakeries in Columbia, Greenville, Augusta, and Savannah. See another National Register application: http://www.nationalregister.sc.gov/richland/S10817740095/S10817740095.pdf.

50. R. E. and C. C. Seyle to commissioners, 12 October 1859, Indentures, file of William Dunlap; William Dunlap, entered 13 December 1855, Indenture Books.

51. J. R. Frey to commissioners, 14 October 1859, Indentures, file of Daniel Higgins.

52. O. H. Wells to H. A. DeSaussure, 9 January 1843, Indentures, file of Charles Evans.

53. On apprenticeship more broadly at this time, see Rorabaugh, *Craft Apprentice*; Elbaum, "Why Apprenticeship Persisted in Britain but Not in the United States"; Jacoby, "The Transformation of Industrial Apprenticeship in the United States"; and Hamilton, "The Decline of Apprenticeship in North America."

54. "By-Laws and Rules of Order of Solomon's Lodge, No. 1 Free and Accepted Masons," Savannah, Ga., 1881; Sarah Estill to commissioners, 30 April 1806, Applications, file of William Estill; William Estill to commissioners, 21 July 1831, Indentures, file of Margaret Cutter; Minutes, 15 May 1806.

55. This William Bull should not be confused with the orphan William R. Bull, whose master examined his writing and calculating skills, and who lived several decades later.

56. Henry Pregnall, entered 25 February 1819. Pregnall's apprentices included Lawrence Ridgeway, entered 14 October 1830; Alexander Sivil, entered 14 August 1834; and Thomas Kilroy, entered 6 December 1849; all in Indenture Books. Minutes, 25 February 1819, 11 March 1824, 17 February 1825, 18 May 1837, 27 July 1837, 3 August 1837; Henry Pregnall to commissioners, 1 June 1855, Indentures, file of Thomas Kilroy.

57. Minutes, 28 January 1808, 4 February 1808, 17 May 1799.

58. Minutes, 28 April 1808; Thomas Bowles, entered 11 August 1797, Indenture Books.

59. Minutes, 15 May 1817; Felix Papillot, entered 6 October 1814, Indenture Books.

60. John M. Davis to commissioners, n.d., Indentures, file of Robert Davis; Minutes, 6 April 1820; John and Robert Davis, entered 9 January 1812, Indenture Books.

61. Leonard King to commissioners, 13 March 1823, Indentures, file of John King.

62. Henry Dicks to commissioners, 30 August 1830, Indentures, file of Henry Dicks.

63. Minutes, 10 August 1809; Anna McNeal, entered 26 August 1802, Indenture Books.

64. Thomas Y. Simons to commissioners, no date but after February 1825, Indentures, file of Susannah Lamott.

65. Minutes, 25 January 1821, 1 February 1821, 8 February 1821, 15 February 1821, and 22 February 1821.

66. J. A. Johnson to commissioners, 11 August 1825, file of Margaret Charlton, Indentures; Minutes, 11 August 1825, 22 September 1825.

67. Minutes, 10 March 1791.

68. Henry Dicks to commissioners, 30 August 1830; Thomas O. Lowndes to commissioners, 19 September 1830; John Crittenden to commissioners, 23 September 1830; all in Indentures, file of Henry Dicks. James Calvin Hemphill, *Men of Mark in South Carolina*, vol. 3 (Washington, DC: Men of Mark Publishing, 1908), 105.

69. Elizabeth B. Hatter to commissioners, 27 October 1814, Indentures, file of Thomas Torrens.

70. Minutes, 14 June 1821, 28 June 1821. It is probably no coincidence that a good share of South Carolina case law on apprentices concerns the Orphan House. *South Carolina Digest*, 109–10.

71. James A. Lyon to commissioners, 25 May 1859; Henry A. DeSaussure to James A. Lyon, 3 June 1859; both in Indentures, file of Langdon C. Riggs. 1860 Census manuscripts, James McIndoo.

72. A. R. Fash to commissioners, 3 January 1828, Indentures, file of Mary Duncan. Mary Duncan's indenture notes that she had been returned by her previous master, the Rev. Edmund Rutledge, also for stealing; Indenture Books, entered 26 November 1818.

73. D. E. Sweeney to commissioners, 9 February 1832, Indentures, file of Henry Dicks; Aaron Fairchild to commissioners, 17 June 1824, Indentures, file of Caroline Jewell. On the active black market in stolen goods exchanged between slaves and poor whites, see Forret, *Race Relations at the Margins*, 74–114.

74. Francis Poyas to commissioners, 15 August 1825, Indentures, file of Andrew Rou.

75. George W. Cassidy to commissioners, 18 December 1823, Indentures, file of James Carlton. Henry Neil: G. W. F. Lankin to commissioners, 11 January 1840, and G. W. F. Lankin to commissioners, 8 August 1840, both in Indentures; Henry E. Neil, entered 15 June 1837 (aged fourteen), Indenture Books.

76. Z. I. DeHay to commissioners, 13 July 1835; E. H. Fisher to commissioners, 13 July 1835, Indentures, file of Zachariah DeHay. Lander, "The South Carolina Textile Industry before 1845."

77. Thus Daniel Bainest to commissioners, 22 September 1831 (Gallagher), and F. G. H. Gunther and John DeBow to commissioners, 5 June 1828 (Hagen), both in Indentures.

78. Daniel Mattison to commissioners, 24 October 1857, Indentures, file of Benjamin Brown; Minutes, 12 November 1857. On Eason and Brothers, see Ripley, *Siege Train*, 23–24.

79. Daniel Stevens explained the process: "It has been usual for the Chairman to give the youth an order on his late master to pay the Fee to him, or to give an order to the Steward to receive it and pay it to the apprentice." Stevens to Judge Lee, 21 October 1824, Indentures, file of Richard Leonard.

80. Anna Merrett to commissioners, 24 June 1815, Indentures, file of Ann Merritt [*sic*]. Minutes, 6 July 1815.

81. Minutes, 25 July 1805.

82. Robert S. Oakeley to commissioners, 25 March 1853, Indentures, file of William Neal. The entire list reads, "3 pair worsted socks, 3 pair cotton socks, heavey monkey jacket, 1 pair drab felt pants, 1 pair blue pants, 3 red flannel shirts, 2 check 2 white shirts, 2 silk pocket handkerchief, 2 white pocket handkerchief, 2 double rose blankets, 1 mat-

tress & pillow, 1 pair boots & shoes, new; 1 belt with case & knife, 1 glaze cap, 1 souester cap, 1 cloth cap, 2 pair cloth pantaloons, 2 pair white drawers, 1 looking glass, 3 silk neck handkerchiefs, 2 towels, 1 trunk, $10 in gold."

CHAPTER NINE

1. William Tucker, entered 5 January 1809, Indenture Books. Minutes, 17 November 1808, 5 January 1809, 25 April 1816, 28 November 1816. Letters (all in William Tucker file, Indentures): Alexander Cabeau to commissioners, 20 November 1816; A. Cabeau to commissioners, 5 January 1820; William Tucker to commissioners, 4 January 1820. Cabeau appears as "Alexander Cabeen" in genealogical publications; see Catherine Reuther, "Descendants of Abraham Patterson & Margaret Caldwell and related Ellison & Terry Families" (Atlanta, self-published, 2008). Cabeau moved to Georgia before 1830 and participated in the Cherokee land lottery there.

2. Erhard children, entered 16 October 1817, Indenture Books. Minutes, 16 October 1817, 25 November 1819, 9 December 1819, 6 September 1821, 16 March 1826, 27 April 1826, 4 January 1827, 8 February 1827, 10 May 1827, 7 June 1827. Letters (all in Mary Erhard file, Indentures): C. S. Simonton and Robert Martin to commissioners, 8 December 1819; Thomas Hart to commissioners, 9 December 1819; Thomas Hart to commissioners, undated; Thomas Hart to Eliab Kingman, 25 February 1826; Thomas Hart to Eliab Kingman, 10 April 1826; Mary Erhard to commissioners, 28 December 1826; Thomas Hart to commissioners, 9 February 1827; Thomas Hart to commissioners, 20 February 1827; Mary Erhard to commissioners, 11 October 1827. Poor House Register of Transient Sick and City Poor, 25 September 1826; Minutes, Commissioners of the Poor House, 5 July 1827, 19 July 1827, 15 September 1827. I am grateful to Bill Fischer, whose genealogical research indicates that Thomas Christburg, Eliza Erhard's adoptive father, included Mary Erhard in his will. When Christburg died in 1828, he left $1,000 to be divided evenly among the three Erhard sisters.

3. See especially Rorabaugh, *Craft Apprentice.*

4. James Nelson, entered 12 February 1846, Indenture Books. Minutes, 12 February 1846, 20 January 1853, 27 January 1853, 5 April 1855, 10 May 1855. Letters: Unsigned visiting commissioner's report, 12 February 1846, in James Nelson file, Applications; E. A. Brunson to A. Campbell, 10 July 1854; James Nelson to Mr. Campbell, 21 July 1854; E. A. Brunson to A. Campbell, 25 September 1854; all in Indentures, file of James Nelson.

5. Richard Leonard, entered 29 September 1808, Indenture Books. Minutes, 29 September 1808. Letters (all in Richard Leonard file, Indentures.); Wm. Timmons to commissioners, 31 October 1816; Danl. Stevens to Judge Lee, 21 October 1824 (on reverse of this letter is Peter DuBois to commissioners, 11 November 1824); Wm. Timmons to commissioners with signed DuBois testimony on reverse, 11 November 1824.

6. Catherine Shafton, entered 10 November 1801, Indenture Books. Minutes, 21 March 1805, 10 September 1807, 28 December 1809, 31 May 1810, 28 June 1810 (loose pages tipped in), 25 April 1816.

7. The best-known argument comes from T. R. Malthus. See *An Essay on the Principle of Population,* xv–xvii.

8. Sarah Adams, entered 3 February 1804; John Woolcock, entered 10 May 1804; Elizabeth Woolcock, entered 8 September 1831; Jane Woolcock, entered 8 September 1831; Mary Ann Woolcock, entered 23 January 1834; all in Indenture Books. Minutes, 12 November 1818, 31 December 1818, 7 January 1819, 17 February 1842, 24 February 1842, 26 March 1846, 5 April 1846. Letters: Francis Knieff to commissioners, 30 December 1818, Indentures, file of Sarah Adams. Sarah Wilcox/Sarah Adams to commissioners, 20 December 1833; B. E. Habersham to commissioners, 17 February 1842, both in Indentures, file of Woolcock children.

9. Albert Spalding, entered 15 September 1814; John and James Watson, entered 28 March 1816; in Indenture Books. Letters on Watson boys in "Rejected Indentures" files: Jane Spalding to commissioners, 15 December 1814; Samuel A. Ruddock, J.P., to commissioners, 30 November 1815; Jane Spalding to commissioners, 27 March 1816; Edward Jones to commissioners, 27 March 1816. On Albert Spalding: Minutes, 15 September 1814, 4 November 1819, 4 January 1821, 11 January 1821, 18 January 1821, 1 March 1821, 15 March 1821, 29 March 1821, 17 October 1822, 1 August 1833, 27 June 1834, 29 January 1835, 19 November 1835, 16 December 1841. Samuel Boykin, *History of the Baptist Denomination in Georgia* (Atlanta: J. P. Harrison, 1881), 490.

10. Louisa Gardner, entered 23 January 1812, Indenture Books. Minutes, 28 November 1811, 23 January 1812, 10 November 1814, 28 May 1818, 18 June 1818, 9 July 1818, 16 July 1818, 4 September 1845. H. L. Porter to commissioners, 31 July 1823, Indentures, file of Mary Van Draper. Professor Phil Roberts, Department of History, University of Wyoming, "Wyoming Almanac of Politics," http://www.wyomingalmanac.com/. 110th Congress, 2nd session, H. Con. Res. 378, "Expressing support for designation of September 6, 2008, as Louisa Swain Day."

11. Thomas Robert Gedney entered the Orphan House 14 June 1810; his brothers entered 31 May 1810 (John) and 30 August 1810 (Joseph), Indenture Books. Minutes, 17 May 1810, 31 May 1810, 14 June 1810, 30 August 1810, 11 July 1811, 25 July 1811, 8 July 1813. On Gedney's channel, see documents transcribed in *Army and Navy Chronicle* 4–5 (1837), 357–58. On Gedney and the ship *Amistad*, see the National Archives web page "Teaching with Documents: The *Amistad* Case Libel of Lieutenant Thomas R. Gedney, on behalf of himself and the officers and crew of the U.S. Brig *Washington*, August 29, 1839" (http://www.archives.gov/education/lessons/amistad/gedney-statement.html). On the assassination attempt, a contemporary report is in Thomas Hart Benton, *Thirty Years' View: Or, a History of the Working of the American Government for Thirty Years*, vol. 1 (New York: D. Appleton, 1865), 521. End-of-career letters in Virginia Historical Society, Mason family papers.

CHAPTER TEN

1. All references to the events of the day, except for the Address, taken from Minutes, 18 October 1810.

2. Gadsden reprinted the speech in a publication he edited, the *Gospel Messenger and Southern Episcopal Register*, in the October 1831 issue, p. 289.

3. The Haitian Revolution began in 1791 on the French part of the island of Hispaniola, known at the time as Saint-Domingue and afterwards by its aboriginal name of

Haiti. About thirty thousand whites and twenty-five thousand free blacks lived alongside a half million slaves. While the *grands blancs* preached white unity, the *petits blancs* saw their economic position deteriorating relative to that of the *grands blancs* and the relatively prosperous *affranchis*, or free persons of color. See Fick, *Making of Haiti*, a classic bottom-up history of the revolution, but nevertheless one that concentrates on activities of the vastly more populous enslaved revolutionaries. Gadsden was referring primarily to this class division among whites in Saint-Domingue, and not political divisions such as those relating to the French Revolution. On Charlestonian attitudes toward the Haitian Revolution, see Hunt, *Haiti's Influence*.

4. Fraser, *Charleston! Charleston!*, 188–90.

5. Wood, *Black Majority*, 218–38, 271–84.

6. Fraser, *Charleston! Charleston!*, 200–206, 242–43. A good example of the translation of racial anxiety into political action was the connection, stressed by William Freehling in *Prelude to the Civil War*, between real and imagined slave insurrections of the 1820s and Nullification in the 1830s. See Freehling, *Prelude to the Civil War*, 49–86.

7. Fredrickson, *The Black Image in the White Mind*, 62.

8. Buist, "An Oration, Delivered at the Orphan-House in Charleston, on the sixth anniversary of the institution, 1795."

9. Bellows, *Benevolence*, 45–46.

10. In this sense, the purpose of the Orphan House was a form of social control, however indirect, much as Rothman discusses in *Discovery of the Asylum*. The Orphan House, which makes a few guest appearances in Rothman's book through contemporary publications about it, aimed to provide stability in response to a fear of disorder. Crucially, though, the mechanism through which the Orphan House exercised its social control was the *promise* of care to its inmates rather than any *threat* to institutionalize those on the outside.

11. Cited in Fraser, *Charleston! Charleston!*, 227; form for Thomas and Agnes Kelly, 29 November 1855, Rejected Applications.

12. Jones, "The Charleston Orphan House, 1860–1876."

13. Fraser, *Charleston! Charleston!*, 400–401; Poston, *Buildings of Charleston*, 29–30. Detail on the transition from a Sears store to the site's current use by the College of Charleston appears in Laura Nelson, "Orphanage, Sears Preceded Dorm on Site," *News and Courier* (Charleston), 18 August 1985.

14. Indeed, by way of comparison, Barry Levy emphasized that the fate of orphans in eighteenth- and nineteenth-century Massachusetts was invariably to serve as cheap labor, with almost no hope of education or acquisition of a trade (*Town Born*, 254–62).

15. Keith-Lucas, *A Legacy of Caring*, 9.

16. Levy, "Girls and Boys," 303. See also his *Town Born* on orphan labor in colonial Massachusetts.

17. Herndon, *Unwelcome Americans*.

18. Walsh, "Child Custody in the Early Colonial Chesapeake."

19. Still, some historians have judged that this system, too, was about as humane as could be expected, given the general lack of resources and attitudes toward children and their labor. See Towner, "The Indentures of Boston's Poor Apprentices, 1734–1805," 53.

20. Ramsay, *The History of South-Carolina from its First Settlement in 1670, to the Year 1808*, vol. 2, pp. 25–26.

21. Weir, "'The Harmony We Were Famous For.'" Regarding white racial unity in the South broadly, see Fredrickson, *The Black Image in the White Mind*, especially 58–64.

22. Steffen, "In Search of the Good Overseer"; McInnis, *Politics of Taste*, 82.

BIBLIOGRAPHY

I. CHARLESTON ORPHAN HOUSE RECORDS IN SOUTH CAROLINA ROOM,
CHARLESTON COUNTY PUBLIC LIBRARY

These documents have been organized into several categories, in each of which they are further ordered either (roughly) chronologically or alphabetically. The finding aid created by Nicholas Butler is extremely useful in navigating these documents.

The Indenture Books include two dozen volumes of printed, filled-in indentures. That is, these volumes contain the Orphan House's copies of the apprenticeship contracts. The child's copy of the indenture went with him or her, usually to be held by the master until the apprenticeship ended. Some Indenture Books are for one sex only, but most include all children bound in during a particular period, in the order in which they entered the Orphan House. They are available on microfilm from the South Carolina Department of Archives and History (SCDAH) and have been transcribed by Susan L. King in *History and Records of the Charleston Orphan House 1790–1860* (Easley, SC: Southern Historical Press, 1984).

The Minutes of the Board of Commissioners meetings are also available on microfilm from the SCDAH. A very few pages suffer from legibility problems, either due to the secretary's handwriting, the fading of his ink over the years, or poor-quality filming. The first twelve volumes informed this study. Volumes after 1830 or so usually were indexed not long after they were completed.

Letters and admission forms have been organized into four categories. In citations I used the name of the type of file that appeared in the file boxes, which make convenient abbreviations for the category names as in the collection's finding aid. Those cited as "Applications" can be found in Charleston County Public Library, Charleston Orphan House records, series II, section A, "Applications to Admit Orphans." These letters were generally written by parents, guardians, other relatives, or neighbors, and often included the visiting commissioner's report back to the board on the particular child's family. These materials are ordered alphabetically by surname of the child or sibling group. Citations to "Rejected Applications" refer to material in "Rejected Applications to Admit Orphans, 1802–1929," series II, section B. Letters cited as belonging to the "Indentures" files can be found in series II, section C, "Applications for Indentures." It is important to note that citations to the "Indentures" collections refer to file folders organized by child or sibling group, contents of which typically consisted of letters pertaining to that child or children. References to "Indenture Books" refer to a completely different set of records, the apprenticeship contracts that were called indentures and signed by all parties. The letters in the "Indentures" files were mostly from masters who applied for children to be their apprentices. Letters post-binding from masters, parents, children, and commissioners also appeared here. Citations as "Rejected Indentures" refer to series II, section D, "Rejected Applications for Indentures, 1802–1928." These letters came from disappointed masters. The materials in these boxes have been microfilmed.

Some other document groups have been microfilmed. They include "Copies of Wills, 1804–1810" (series IV), "Financial Records," and "Weekly Reports of the Physician and steward." The latter two both appear on reel 10 of the microfilmed records. "Servants to the Orphan House Institution," a list of slaves owned and rented by the Orphan House, appears as the second document in the unpaginated "Register" of 1791–1831, immediately following "Officers Belonging to the Orphan House Institution" on reel 6.

II. CHARLESTON ALMS HOUSE RECORDS AT THE SCDAH

Records of the Charleston Poor House, later the Alms House, are available on microfilm from the SCDAH. These records include minutes of the commissioners' meetings (which themselves typically describe flows of people in and out of the Poor House), registers of the sick and poor, indentures of apprentices bound out from the Poor House, and death records.

III. CONTEMPORARY WRITINGS AND PUBLICATIONS

Archates [Thomas Pinckney]. *Reflections Occasioned by the Late Disturbances in Charleston.* Charleston: A. E. Miller, 1822.

Baggett, J. H. *Directory of the City of Charleston for the Year 1852.* Charleston: Printed by Edward C. Councell, 1851.

Barnard, Henry. "Andrew Bell and the Madras System of Mutual Instruction." *American Journal of Education* 10 (1861): 467–90.

Bernheim, G. D. *History of the German Settlements and of the Lutheran Church in North and South Carolina.* Philadelphia: Lutheran Book Store, 1872.

Brevard, Joseph. *An Alphabetical Digest of the Public Statute Law of South Carolina in Three Volumes.* Charleston: John Hoff, 1814.

Buist, Rev. George. "An Oration, Delivered at the Orphan-House in Charleston, on the sixth anniversary of the institution, 1795." In *Sermons by the Reverend George Buist, D.D.,* vol. 1, 349–81. New York: D. and G. Bruce for E. Sargeant, 1809.

By-Laws of the Orphan House of Charleston, South Carolina. Charleston: Evans and Cogswell, 1861.

Cardozo, J. N. *Reminiscences of Charleston.* Charleston: Joseph Walker, 1866.

Charleston City Council. *Circular of the City Council on Retrenchment, and Report of the Commissioners of the Orphan House*. Charleston: Evans and Cogswell, 1861.

Charleston Orphan House: Centennial Celebration. Charleston: Walker, Evans and Cogswell, Printers, 1891.

City of Charleston. *Death Records*. South Carolina Room, Charleston County Public Library. Digital copy transcribed by Elizabeth Newcombe.

Clark, Thomas D., ed. *South Carolina: The Grand Tour, 1780–1865*. Columbia: University of South Carolina Press, 1973.

Cooper, Thomas, and David James McCord. *The Statutes at Large of South Carolina, Edited, Under Authority of the Legislature*. Columbia: A. S. Johnston, 1837–41.

Dawson, J. L., and H. W. DeSaussure. *Census of the City of Charleston, South Carolina, for the Year 1848*. Charleston: J. B. Nixon, Printer, 1849.

DeBow, J. D. B. *The Industrial Resources, Statistics, &c. of the United States and More Particularly of the Southern and Western States*. New York: D. Appleton, 1854.

———. *Statistical View of the United States*. Washington: A. O. P. Nicholson, 1854.

Digest of the Ordinances of the City Council of Charleston from the Year 1783 to July 1818. Charleston: Archibald E. Miller, 1818.

Dilworth, Thomas. *The Schoolmaster's Assistant*. New York: J. F. Sibell, 1825.

"Domestic Occurrences." *American Monthly Magazine and Critical Review* 3 (October 1818): 469.

Edwards, Alexander, comp. *Ordinances of the City Council of Charleston, in the State of South Carolina, Passed Since the Incorporation of the City, Collected and Revised pursuant to a Resolution of the Council*. Charleston: W. P. Young, 1802.

Forbes, John, Alexander Tweedie, John Conolly, and Robley Dunglison. *Cyclopaedia of Practical Medicine*. Philadelphia: Blanchard and Lea, 1859.

"Frederick Kohne, His Munificent Legacies." *Christian Journal and Literary Register* 13 (July 1829): 224.

Garlington, J. C. *Men of the Time: Sketches of Living Notables; A Biographical Encyclopedia of Contemporaneous South Carolina Leaders*. Spartanburg: Garlington Publishing, 1902.

Gibbes, William Hasell. "William Hasell Gibbes' Story of His Life." Edited by Arney R. Childs. *South Carolina Historical and Genealogical Magazine* 50 (1949): 59–67.

Hagy, James W., ed. *Charleston, South Carolina, City Directories . . .* Baltimore: Genealogical Publishing, various years.

King, William L. *The Newspaper Press of Charleston, S.C.* Charleston: Edward Perry, 1872.

Logan, Dr. [Thomas M.] "Belladonna in Scarlatina." *Western Journal of Medicine and Surgery*, September 1844, 261.

Logan, George. "A Brief Account of the Scarlatina, as It Prevailed in the Orphan House, Charleston, South Carolina." *American Journal of the Medical Sciences*, May 1839, 71.

Metropolitan Catholic Almanac and Laity's Directory for the United States, 1859. Baltimore: John Murphy and Co., 1858.

Mills, Robert. *Statistics of South Carolina*. Charleston: Hurlbut and Lloyd, 1826.

Morse, Jedidiah. *Geography Made Easy*. 19th ed. Boston: Thomas and Andrews, 1818.

Murray, Lindley. *Introduction to the English Reader*. New York: Collins, 1831.

A Naval Encyclopedia: A Dictionary of Nautical Words and Phrases. Philadelphia: L. R. Hamersley and Co., 1881.

"The Orphan House at Charleston." *Spirit of the Times: A Chronicle of the Turf, Agriculture, Field Sports . . .*, November 3, 1860, 465.

"Qualifications of a Guardian of Children." *American Annals of Education* 5 (December 1835): 544.

Ramsay, David. *The History of South-Carolina from its First Settlement in 1670, to the Year 1808*. Charleston: David Longworth, 1809.

Reeve, Tapping. *Law of Baron and Femme, of Parent and Child, Guardian and Ward, Master and Servant . . .* 3rd ed. 1862. Reprint, New York: Source Book Press, 1970.

"Register of the Independent Congregational (Circular) Church of Charleston S.C. 1784–1815 (Continued)." *South Carolina Historical and Genealogical Magazine* 33 (1932): 306–16.

"Review of Bernard M. Byrne, an Essay to Prove the Contagious Character of the Malignant Cholera." *Baltimore Medical and Surgical Journal and Review* 1 (1833): 429–34.

Revised Ordinances of the City of Charleston, South Carolina. Charleston: Walker, Evans, and Cogswell, 1903.

Rules and Regulations for the Government of the Orphan-House at Charleston, South-Carolina. Charleston: W. P. Young, 1806.

Simpson, William. *Practical Justice of the Peace and Parish-Officer of His Majesty's Province of South-Carolina*. Charlestown [Charleston]: Robert Wells, 1761.

South Carolina Digest, 1783–1886, Covering All the Decisions Reported in the 84 Volumes of Law and Equity Reports and South Carolina Reports, Vols. 1–25. St. Paul: West Publishing, 1922.

Stevens, Daniel. "Autobiography of Daniel Stevens, 1746–1835." *South Carolina Historical Magazine* 58 (1957): 1–18.

Tower, David B. *Tower's Second Reader: Introduction to the Gradual Reader*. Boston: Crosby and Nichols, 1863.

US Department of Commerce and Labor, Bureau of the Census. *Heads of Families at the First Census of the United States Taken in 1790: South Carolina*. Washington, DC: GPO, 1908.

Wilson, James Grant, and John Fiske. *Appleton's Cyclopedia of American Biography*. New York: D. Appleton and Company, 1888.

Yearbook, 1910, City of Charleston, So. Ca. Charleston: Daggett Printing, 1910.

IV. SECONDARY LITERATURE

Adams, Donald R., Jr. "American Neutrality and Prosperity, 1793–1808: A Reconsideration," *Journal of Economic History* 40 (1980): 713–37.

———. "Prices and Wages in Maryland, 1750–1850." *Journal of Economic History* 46 (1986): 625–45.

Bardaglio, Peter. *Reconstructing the Household: Families, Sex, and the Law in the Nineteenth Century South*. Chapel Hill: University of North Carolina Press, 1995.

Beadie, Nancy. *Education and the Creation of Human Capital in the Early American Republic.* New York: Cambridge University Press, 2010.

Bellows, Barbara L. *Benevolence among Slaveholders: Assisting the Poor in Charleston, 1670–1860.* Baton Rouge: Louisiana State University Press, 1993.

———. "'My Children, Gentlemen, Are My Own': Poor Women, the Urban Elite, and the Bonds of Obligation in Antebellum Charleston." In *The Web of Southern Social Relations: Women, Family, and Education,* edited by Walter J. Fraser, Frank Saunders, and Jon Wakelyn, 52–71. Athens: University of Georgia Press, 1985.

Billington, Ray Allen. *The Protestant Crusade, 1800–1860.* Chicago: Quadrangle Books, 1962.

Bolton, Charles C. *Poor Whites in the Antebellum South: Tenants and Laborers in Central North Carolina and Northeast Mississippi.* Durham: Duke University Press, 1994.

Bourque, Monique. "Bound Out from the Almshouse: Community Networks in Chester County, Pennsylvania, 1800–1860." In *Children Bound to Labor: The Pauper Apprentice System in Early America,* edited by Ruth Wallis Herndon and John E. Murray, 71–84. Ithaca, NY: Cornell University Press, 2009.

Boylan, Anne. *Sunday School: The Formation of an American Institution, 1790–1880.* New Haven, CT: Yale University Press, 1990.

Bullock, Steven C. *Revolutionary Brotherhood: Freemasonry and the Transformation of the American Social Order, 1730–1840.* Chapel Hill: University of North Carolina Press, 1996.

Burton, E. Milby. *Charleston Furniture, 1700–1825.* Columbia: University of South Carolina Press, 1953.

Brückner, Martin. "Lessons in Geography: Maps, Spellers, and Other Grammars of Nationalism in the Early Republic." *American Quarterly* 51 (1999): 311–43.

Cashin, Edward J. *Beloved Bethesda: A History of George Whitefield's Home for Boys.* Macon, GA: Mercer University Press, 2001.

Cecil-Fronsman, Bill. *Common Whites: Class and Culture in Antebellum North Carolina.* Lexington: University Press of Kentucky, 1992.

Censer, Jane Turner. *North Carolina Planters and Their Children, 1800–1860.* Baton Rouge: Louisiana State University Press, 1984.

Chaplin, Joyce E. *An Anxious Pursuit: Agricultural Innovation and Modernity in the Lower South, 1730–1815.* Chapel Hill: University of North Carolina Press, 1993.

Clement, Priscilla Ferguson. "Children and Charity: Orphanages in New Orleans, 1817–1914," *Louisiana History* 27 (1986): 337–51.

Cmiel, Kenneth. *A Home of Another Kind: One Chicago Orphanage and the Tangle of Child Welfare.* Chicago: University of Chicago Press, 1995.

Coclanis, Peter A. *The Shadow of a Dream: Economic Life and Death in the South Carolina Low Country, 1670–1920.* New York: Oxford University Press, 1989.

Cook, Harvey Toliver. *Life and Legacy of David Rogerson Williams.* New York: Country Life Press, 1916.

Cooper, Donald B., and Kenneth F. Kiple. "Yellow Fever." In *Cambridge World History of Human Disease,* 1100–1107. New York: Cambridge University Press, 1993.

Copeland, J. Isaac. "A Note on South Carolina Teachers, 1811–1860." *Peabody Journal of Education* 44 (1966): 13–16.

Craig, Lee A. *To Sow One Acre More: Childbearing and Farm Productivity in the Antebellum North*. Baltimore: Johns Hopkins University Press, 1993.

Crosby, Alfred W. "Smallpox." In *Cambridge World History of Human Disease*, 1008–13. New York: Cambridge University Press, 1993.

Davis, Richard B., and Milledge B. Seigler. "Peter Freneau, Carolina Republican." *Journal of Southern History* 13 (1947): 395–405.

Degler, Carl. *At Odds: Women and the Family in America from the Revolution to the Present*. New York: Oxford University Press, 1980.

Delfino, Susanna, and Michele Gillespie, eds. *Neither Lady Nor Slave: Working Women of the Old South*. Chapel Hill: University of North Carolina Press, 2002.

Dolan, Jay P. *In Search of an American Catholicism: A History of Religion and Culture in Tension*. New York: Oxford University Press, 2003.

Edgar, Walter B. *South Carolina: A History*. Columbia: University of South Carolina Press, 1998.

Elbaum, Bernard. "Why Apprenticeship Persisted in Britain But Not in the United States." *Journal of Economic History* 49 (1989): 337–49.

Elson, Ruth Miller. *Guardians of Tradition: American Schoolbooks in the Nineteenth Century*. Lincoln: University of Nebraska Press, 1964.

Ezell, John S. "A Southern Education for Southrons." *Journal of Southern History* 17 (1951): 303–27.

Fabian, Ann. *The Unvarnished Truth: Personal Narratives in Nineteenth-Century America*. Berkeley and Los Angeles: University of California Press, 2000.

Fick, Carolyn E. *The Making of Haiti: The Saint Domingue Revolution from Below*. Knoxville: University of Tennessee Press, 1990.

Folks, Homer. *The Care of Destitute, Neglected, and Delinquent Children*. Albany: J. B. Lyon for Charities Review, 1900.

Forret, Jeff. *Race Relations at the Margins: Slaves and Poor Whites in the Antebellum Countryside*. Baton Rouge: Louisiana State University Press, 2006.

Franklin, John Hope, and Loren Schweninger. *Runaway Slaves: Rebels on the Plantation*. New York: Oxford University Press, 1999.

Fraser, Walter J., Jr. *Charleston! Charleston! The History of a Southern City*. Columbia: University of South Carolina Press, 1989.

———. "The City Elite, 'Disorder,' and the Poor Children of Pre-Revolutionary Charleston." *South Carolina Historical Magazine* 84 (1983): 167–79.

Fredrickson, George M. *The Black Image in the White Mind: The Debate on Afro-American Character and Destiny, 1817–1914*. New York: Harper and Row, 1971.

Freehling, William W. *Prelude to the Civil War: The Nullification Controversy in South Carolina, 1816–1836*. New York: Harper and Row, 1968.

Fries, Charles C. "The Rules of Common School Grammars." *Proceedings of the Modern Language Association* 42 (1927): 221–37.

Gilmore, William J. *Reading Becomes a Necessity of Life: Material and Cultural Life in Rural New England, 1780–1835*. Knoxville: University of Tennessee Press, 1993.

Glover, Lorri. *All Our Relations: Blood Ties and Emotional Bonds among the Early South Carolina Gentry*. Baltimore: Johns Hopkins University Press, 2000.

Glynn, Ian, and Jenifer Glynn. *The Life and Death of Smallpox*. New York: Cambridge University Press, 2004.

Graff, Harvey. *Conflicting Paths: Growing Up in America*. Cambridge: Harvard University Press, 1995.

———. *The Legacies of Literacy: Continuities and Contradictions in Western Culture and Society*. Bloomington: Indiana University Press, 1987.

Greven, Philip J. *The Protestant Temperament: Patterns of Child-Rearing, Religious Experience, and the Self in Early America*. Chicago: University of Chicago Press, 1977.

Grigg, Susan. "Toward a Theory of Remarriage: A Case Study of Newburyport at the Beginning of the Nineteenth Century." *Journal of Interdisciplinary History* 8 (1977): 183–220.

Griffin, Richard W. "An Origin of the New South: The South Carolina Homespun Company, 1808–1815." *Business History Review* 35 (1961): 402–14.

Grossberg, Michael. *Governing the Hearth: Law and the Family in Nineteenth-Century America*. Chapel Hill: University of North Carolina Press, 1985.

Grubb, Farley. "Creating the U.S. Dollar Currency Union, 1748–1811: A Quest for Monetary Stability or a Usurpation of State Sovereignty for Personal Gain?" *American Economic Review* 93 (2003): 1778–98.

———. "Growth of Literacy in Colonial America: Longitudinal Patterns, Economic Models, and the Direction of Future Research." *Social Science History* 16 (1990): 451–82.

Hacsi, Timothy A. *Second Home: Orphan Asylums and Poor Families in America*. Cambridge, MA: Harvard University Press, 1997.

Hagy, James William. *This Happy Land: The Jews of Colonial and Antebellum Charleston*. Tuscaloosa: University of Alabama Press, 1993.

Hamilton, Gillian. "The Decline of Apprenticeship in North America: Evidence from Montreal." *Journal of Economic History* 60 (2000): 627–64.

———. "Enforcement in Apprenticeship Contracts: Were Runaways a Serious Problem? Evidence from Montreal." *Journal of Economic History* 55 (1995): 551–74.

———. "The Stateless and the Orphaned among Montreal's Apprentices, 1791–1842." In *Children Bound to Labor: The Pauper Apprentice System in Early America*, edited by Ruth Wallis Herndon and John E. Murray, 166–82. Ithaca: Cornell University Press, 2009.

Hardy, Anne. "Whooping Cough." In *Cambridge World History of Human Disease*, edited by Kenneth Kiple, 1094–96. New York: Cambridge University Press, 1993.

Harris, Robert L., Jr. "Charleston's Free Afro-American Elite: The Brown Fellowship Society and the Humane Brotherhood." *South Carolina Historical Magazine* 82 (1981): 289–310.

Herndon, Ruth Wallis. "The Domestic Cost of Seafaring: Town Leaders and Seamen's Families in Rhode Island, 1750–1800." In *Iron Men, Wooden Women: Gender and Seafaring in the Atlantic World, 1700–1920*, edited by Margaret S. Creighton and Lisa Norling, 55–69. Baltimore: Johns Hopkins University Press, 1996.

———. "Literacy among New England's Transient Poor, 1750–1800." *Journal of Social History* 29 (1996): 963–65.

———. *Unwelcome Americans: Living on the Margin in Early New England*. Philadelphia: University of Pennsylvania Press, 2001.

Herndon, Ruth Wallis, and John E. Murray, eds. *Children Bound to Labor: The Pauper Apprentice System in Early America.* Ithaca: Cornell University Press, 2009.

Hinks, Peter P., *To Awaken My Afflicted Brethren: David Walker and the Problem of Antebellum Slave Resistance.* University Park: Penn State University Press, 1996.

Hollis, Daniel Walker. "Robert W. Barnwell." *South Carolina Historical Magazine* 56 (1955): 131–37.

Humphreys, Margaret. *Yellow Fever and the South.* New Brunswick: Rutgers University Press, 1992.

Humphries, Jane. *Childhood and Child Labour in the British Industrial Revolution.* New York: Cambridge University Press, 2010.

Hunt, Alfred N. *Haiti's Influence on Antebellum America: Slumbering Volcano in the Caribbean.* Baton Rouge: Louisiana State University Press, 2006.

Jabour, Anya. *Marriage in the Early Republic: Elizabeth and William Wirt and the Companionate Ideal.* Baltimore: Johns Hopkins University Press, 1998.

Jackson, Melvin H. *Privateers in Charleston, 1793–1796.* Washington, DC: Smithsonian Institution Press, 1969.

Jacoby, Daniel. "The Transformation of Industrial Apprenticeship in the United States." *Journal of Economic History* 51 (1991): 887–910.

Jernegan, Marcus W. *Laboring and Dependent Classes in Colonial America, 1607–1783.* New York: Frederick Ungar, (1931) 1960.

Jones, Newton B. "The Charleston Orphan House, 1860–1876." *South Carolina Historical Magazine* 62 (1961): 203–14.

Jordan, Laylon Wayne. "Education for Community: C. G. Memminger and the Origination of Common Schools in Antebellum Charleston." *South Carolina Historical Magazine* 83 (1982): 99–115.

Journal of Interdisciplinary History. "The Relationship of Nutrition, Disease, and Social Conditions: A Graphical Presentation," *Journal of Interdisciplinary History* 14 (1983): 503–6.

Kaestle, Carl F. *The Evolution of an Urban School System: New York City, 1750–1850.* Cambridge, MA: Harvard University Press, 1973.

———, ed. *Joseph Lancaster and the Monitorial School Movement: A Documentary History.* New York: Teachers College Press, 1973.

Karasch, Mary C. "Ophthalmia: Conjunctivitis and Trachoma." In *Cambridge World History of Human Disease,* edited by Kenneth Kiple, 897–906. New York: Cambridge University Press, 1993.

Kawashima, Yasuhide. "Adoption in Early America." *Journal of Family Law* 20 (1981–82): 677–96.

Keith-Lucas, Alan. *A Legacy of Caring: The Charleston Orphan House, 1790–1990.* Charleston: Charleston Orphan House, Inc., 1991.

Kierner, Cynthia. *Beyond the Household: Women's Place in the Early South, 1700–1835.* Ithaca: Cornell University Press, 1998.

Kim-Farley, Robert J. "Measles." In *The Cambridge World History of Human Disease,* edited by Kenneth Kiple, 871–75. New York: Cambridge University Press, 1993.

King, Susan L. "Dr. George Logan: Physician to the Orphan House, 1810–1854." *Journal of the South Carolina Medical Association* 92 (January 1996): 19–25.

Klebaner, Benjamin J. "Public Poor Relief in Charleston, 1800–1860." *South Carolina Historical Magazine* 55 (1954): 210–20.

Knight, Edgar W. *Public Education in the South.* Boston: Ginn and Company, 1922.

Koger, Larry. *Black Slaveowners: Free Black Slave Masters in South Carolina, 1790–1860.* Columbia: University of South Carolina Press, 1985.

Lachance, Paul. "Literacy and Provisions for Education in Indentures from New Orleans, 1809–1843." In *Bound to Labor: Varieties of Apprenticeship in Early America,* edited by Ruth Wallis Herndon and John E. Murray, 119–32. Ithaca: Cornell University Press, 2009.

Lander, Ernest M., Jr., "Charleston: Manufacturing Center of the Old South." *Journal of Southern History* 26 (1960): 330–51.

———. "The Iron Industry in Ante-Bellum South Carolina," *Journal of Southern History* 20 (1954): 337-355.

———. "The South Carolina Textile Industry Before 1845." In *Proceedings of the South Carolina Historical Association, 1951,* 19–28. Columbia: South Carolina Historical Association, 1952.

Lebsock, Suzanne. *The Free Women of Petersburg: Status and Culture in a Southern Town, 1784–1860.* New York: W. W. Norton, 1984.

Lesesne, J. Mauldin. *The Bank of the State of South Carolina: A General and Political History.* Columbia: University of South Carolina Press, 1970.

Levy, Barry. "Girls and Boys: Poor Children and the Labor Market in Colonial Massachusetts." *Pennsylvania History* 64 (1997): 287–307.

———. *Town Born: The Political Economy of New England from Its Founding to the Revolution.* Philadelphia: University of Pennsylvania Press, 2009.

Lockley, Timothy J. *Lines in the Sand: Race and Class in Lowcountry Georgia, 1750–1860.* Athens: University of Georgia Press, 2001.

———. "Public Poor Relief in Buncombe County, North Carolina, 1792–1860." *North Carolina Historical Review* 80 (2003): 28–51.

———. *Welfare and Charity in the Antebellum South.* Gainesville: University Press of Florida, 2007.

Lockridge, Kenneth A. *Literacy in Colonial New England: An Enquiry into the Social Context of Literacy in the Early Modern West.* New York: W. W. Norton, 1974.

Mahon, John K. *The History of the Second Seminole War, 1835–1842.* Gainesville: University Press of Florida, 1969.

Malthus, Thomas R. *An Essay on the Principle of Population.* New York: Oxford World's Classics, 2008.

Main, Gloria L. "An Inquiry into When and Why Women Learned to Write in Colonial New England." *Journal of Social History* 24 (1991): 579–89.

Main, Jackson Turner. *The Social Structure of Revolutionary America.* Princeton, NJ: Princeton University Press, 1965.

Margo, Robert A. *Wages and Labor Markets in the United States, 1820–1860.* Chicago: University of Chicago Press, 2000.

Martin, Thomas P. "The Advent of William Gregg and the Graniteville Company." *Journal of Southern History* 11 (1945): 389–423.

McCandless, Peter. *Moonlight, Magnolias, and Madness: Insanity in South Carolina from the Colonial Period to the Progressive Era*. Chapel Hill: University of North Carolina Press, 1996.

McCurry, Stephanie. *Masters of Small Worlds: Yeoman Households, Gender Relations, and the Political Culture of the Antebellum South Carolina Low Country*. New York: Oxford University Press, 1995.

McCusker, John. *How Much Is That in Real Money? A Historical Commodity Price Index for Use as a Deflator of Money Values in the Economy of the United States*. Worcester, MA: American Antiquarian Society, 1992.

McInnis, Maurie D. *The Politics of Taste in Antebellum Charleston*. Chapel Hill: University of North Carolina Press, 2005.

McMillen, Sally. *Motherhood in the Old South*. Baton Rouge: Louisiana State University Press, 1990.

Melosh, Barbara. *Strangers and Kin: The American Way of Adoption*. Cambridge, MA: Harvard University Press, 2002.

Meriwether, Colyer. *History of Higher Education in South Carolina*. Bureau of Education Circular of Information 3. Washington, DC: GPO, 1889.

Mintz, Steven. *Huck's Raft: A History of American Childhood*. Cambridge, MA: Harvard University Press, 2006.

Mitch, David F. *The Rise of Popular Literacy in Victorian England: The Influence of Private Choice and Public Policy*. Philadelphia: University of Pennsylvania Press, 1992.

Montgomery, Florence M. *Textiles in America, 1650–1870*. New York: W. W. Norton, 2007.

Morgan, Philip D. *Slave Counterpoint: Black Culture in the Eighteenth-Century Chesapeake and Lowcountry*. Chapel Hill: University of North Carolina Press, 1998.

Morris, Richard B. *Government and Labor in Early America*. New York: Columbia University Press, 1947.

———. "White Bondage in Ante-Bellum South Carolina." *South Carolina Historical and Genealogical Magazine* 49 (1948): 191–207.

Motes, Margaret Peckham, comp. *Free Blacks and Mulattos in South Carolina: 1850 Census*. Baltimore: Clearfield, 2000.

Murray, Gail S. "Charity within the Bounds of Race and Class: Female Benevolence in the Old South." *South Carolina Historical Magazine* 96 (1995): 54–70.

Murray, John E. "Bound by Charity: The Abandoned Children of Late Eighteenth Century Charleston." In *Down and Out in Early America*, edited by Billy G. Smith, 213–32. State College: Penn State University Press, 2004.

———. "Family, Literacy, and Skill-Training in the Antebellum South: Historical-Longitudinal Evidence from Charleston." *Journal of Economic History* 64 (2004): 773–99.

———. "Fates of Orphans: Poor Children in Antebellum Charleston." *Journal of Interdisciplinary History* 33 (2003): 519–45.

———. "Generation(s) of Human Capital: Literacy in American Families 1830–1875." *Journal of Interdisciplinary History* 27 (1997): 413–36.

———. "Literacy Acquisition in an Orphanage: A Historical-Longitudinal Case Study." *American Journal of Education* 110 (2004): 172–95.

————. "Mothers and Children In and Out of the Charleston Orphan House." In *Children Bound to Labor: The Pauper Apprentice System in Early America*, edited by Ruth Wallis Herndon and John E. Murray, 102–18. Ithaca: Cornell University Press, 2009.

————. "The White Plague in Utopia: Tuberculosis in Nineteenth Century Shaker Communes." *Bulletin of the History of Medicine* 68 (1994): 278–306.

Murray, John E., and Ruth Wallis Herndon. "Markets for Children in Early America: A Political Economy of Pauper Apprenticeship." *Journal of Economic History* 62 (2002): 356–82.

Myers, Amrita Chakrabarti. *Forging Freedom: Black Women and the Pursuit of Liberty in Antebellum Charleston*. Chapel Hill: University of North Carolina Press, 2011.

Oast, Jennifer. "'The Worst Kind of Slavery': Slave-Owning Presbyterian Churches in Prince Edward County, Virginia." *Journal of Southern History* 56 (2010): 867–900.

Olwell, Robert. *Masters, Slaves, and Subjects: The Culture of Power in the South Carolina Low Country, 1740–1790*. Ithaca: Cornell University Press, 1998.

Owsley, Frank Lawrence. *Plain Folk of the Old South*. Baton Rouge: Louisiana State University Press, 1949.

Pease, Jane H., and William H. Pease. *Ladies, Women, and Wenches: Choice and Constraint in Antebellum Charleston and Boston*. Chapel Hill: University of North Carolina Press, 1990.

Pease, William H., and Jane H. Pease. *The Web of Progress: Private Values and Public Styles in Boston and Charleston, 1828–1843*. New York: Oxford University Press, 1985.

Perlmann, Joel, and Dennis Shirley. "When Did New England Women Acquire Literacy?" *William and Mary Quarterly* 48 (1991): 50–67.

Polster, Gary Edward. *Inside Looking Out: The Cleveland Jewish Orphan Asylum, 1868–1924*. Kent, OH: Kent State University Press, 1990.

Porter, Susan L. "A Good Home: Indenture and Adoption in Nineteenth Century Orphanages." In *Adoption in America: Historical Perspectives*, edited by E. Wayne Carp, 27–50. Ann Arbor: University of Michigan Press, 2002.

Poston, Jonathan H. *The Buildings of Charleston: A Guide to the City's Architecture*. Columbia: University of South Carolina Press, 1997.

Presser, Stephen B. "The Historical Background of the American Law of Adoption." *Journal of Family Law* 11 (1971): 443–516.

Pyburn, Nita Katharine. "The Public School System of Charleston Before 1860." *South Carolina Historical Magazine* 61 (1960): 86–98.

Rauschenberg, Bradford L. "Evidence for the Apprenticeship System in Charleston, South Carolina." *Journal of Early Southern Decorative Arts* 29 (2003): 1–67.

————. "A School of Charleston, South Carolina, Brass Andirons, 1780–1815." *Journal of Early Southern Decorative Arts* 5 (1979): 26–75.

Ravenel, Beatrice St. Julien. *Architects of Charleston*. Reprint of the 1964 revised edition of the 1945 study. Columbia: University of South Carolina Press, 1992.

Reinier, Jacqueline. "Rearing the Republican Child: Attitudes and Practices in Post-Revolutionary Philadelphia." *William and Mary Quarterly*, series 3, vol. 39, no. 1 (1982): 150–63.

Ripley, Warren, ed. *Siege Train: The Journal of a Confederate Artilleryman in the Defense of Charleston*. Columbia: University of South Carolina Press, 1986.

Rockman, Seth. *Scraping By: Wage Labor, Slavery, and Survival in Early Baltimore.* Baltimore: Johns Hopkins University Press, 2009.

Rogers, George C., Jr. *Charleston in the Age of the Pinckneys.* Columbia: University of South Carolina Press, 1980.

Rogers, James A. *Richard Furman: Life and Legacy.* Macon, GA: Mercer University Press, 2001.

Roosevelt, Theodore. *The Naval War of 1812.* New York: Modern Library, 1999.

Rorabaugh, W. J. *The Alcoholic Republic: An American Tradition.* New York: Oxford University Press, 1979.

———. *The Craft Apprentice from Franklin to the Machine Age in America.* New York: Oxford University Press, 1986.

Roselle, Daniel. *Samuel Griswold Goodrich, Creator of Peter Parley: A Study of His Life and Work.* Albany: State University of New York Press, 1968.

Rosenberg, Charles. *The Cholera Years: The United States in 1832, 1849, and 1866.* Chicago: University of Chicago Press, 1987.

Rothbard, Murray. *The Panic of 1819.* New York: Columbia University Press, 1962.

Rothman, David J. *The Discovery of the Asylum: Social Order and Disorder in the New Republic.* Boston: Little, Brown and Company, 1971.

Rowland, Lawrence S., Alexander Moore, and George C. Rogers. *The History of Beaufort County, South Carolina,* vol. 1. Columbia: University of South Carolina Press, 1996.

Rusnock, Andrea. "Catching Cowpox: The Early Spread of Smallpox Vaccination, 1798–1810." *Bulletin of the History of Medicine* 83 (2009): 17–36.

Salmon, David, ed. *The Practical Parts of Lancaster's "Improvements" and Bell's "Experiment."* Cambridge: Cambridge University Press, 1932.

Saunders, R. Frank, and George A. Rogers. "Bishop John England of Charleston: Catholic Spokesman and Southern Intellectual, 1820–1842." *Journal of the Early Republic* 13 (1993): 301–22.

Severens, Kenneth. *Charleston: Antebellum Architecture and Civic Destiny.* Knoxville: University of Tennessee Press, 1988.

Smith, Billy G. *The "Lower Sort": Philadelphia's Laboring People, 1750–1800.* Ithaca: Cornell University Press, 1990.

Smith, Daniel Blake. "Autonomy and Affection: Parents and Children in Eighteenth Century Chesapeake Families." *Journal of Psychohistory* 6 (1977–78): 32–51.

Smith, Daniel Scott, and Michael S. Hindus. "Premarital Pregnancy in America 1640–1971: An Overview and Interpretation." *Journal of Interdisciplinary History* 5 (1975): 537–70.

Snell, K. D. M. "Belonging and Community: Understandings of 'Home' and 'Friends' among the English Poor, 1750–1850." *Economic History Review* 65 (2012): 1–25.

Soltow, Lee, and Edward Stevens. *The Rise of Literacy and the Common School in the United States: A Socioeconomic Analysis to 1870.* Chicago: University of Chicago Press, 1980.

Stampp, Kenneth. *The Peculiar Institution: Slavery in the Ante-Bellum South.* New York: Vintage Books, 1956.

Stavisky, Leonard Price. "Industrialism in Ante Bellum Charleston." *Journal of Negro History* 36 (1951): 302–22.

Steckel, Richard H. "A Dreadful Childhood: The Excess Mortality of American Slaves." *Social Science History* 10 (1986): 427–46.

Steffen, Charles G. "In Search of the Good Overseer: The Failure of the Agricultural Reform Movement in Lowcountry South Carolina, 1821–1834." *Journal of Southern History* 63 (1997): 753–802.

Stephens, Lester D. *Science, Race, and Religion in the American South: John Bachman and the Charleston Circle of Naturalists, 1815–1895.* Chapel Hill: University of North Carolina Press, 2000.

Stevens, Edward W., Jr. *Literacy, Law, and Social Order.* DeKalb: Northern Illinois University Press, 1988.

Stowe, Steven M. *Doctoring the South: Southern Physicians and Everyday Medicine in the Mid-Nineteenth Century.* Chapel Hill: University of North Carolina Press, 2004.

Sundue, Sharon Braslaw. *Industrious in Their Stations: Young People at Work in Urban America, 1720–1810.* Charlottesville: University of Virginia Press, 2009.

Terris, Milton. "An Early System of Compulsory Health Insurance in the United States, 1798–1884." *Bulletin of the History of Medicine* 15 (1944): 433–44.

Tolley, Kim, and Nancy Beadie. "Socio-economic Incentives to Teach in New York and North Carolina: Toward a More Complex Model of Teacher Labor Markets, 1800–1850." *History of Education Quarterly* 46 (2006): 36–72.

Towner, Lawrence William. "The Indentures of Boston's Poor Apprentices, 1734–1805." In *Past Imperfect: Essays on History, Libraries, and the Humanities*, edited by Robert W. Karrow Jr., and Alfred F. Young, 36–55. Chicago: University of Chicago Press, 1993.

Vinovskis, Maris A. "Early Childhood Education: Then and Now." *Daedalus* 122 (1993): 151–76.

Wall, Helena M. "Notes on Life Since *A Little Commonwealth*: Family and Gender History since 1970." *William and Mary Quarterly*, series 3, vol. 57, no. 4 (2000): 809–25.

Wallace, David Duncan. *South Carolina: A Short History.* Chapel Hill: University of North Carolina Press, 1951.

Walsh, Lorena S. "Child Custody in the Early Colonial Chesapeake: A Case Study." Unpublished essay, 1981.

Walsh, Richard. *Charleston's Sons of Liberty: A Study of the Artisans, 1763–1789.* Columbia: University of South Carolina Press, 1959.

Ward, Barbara McLean. "Boston Goldsmiths, 1690–1730." In *The Craftsman in Early America*, edited by Ian M. G. Quimby, 126–57. New York: W. W. Norton, 1984.

Waring, Joseph I. "Charleston Medicine, 1800–1860." *Journal of the History of Medicine and Allied Sciences* 31 (1976): 320–42.

———. *A History of Medicine in South Carolina, 1670–1825.* Columbia: South Carolina Medical Association, 1964.

———. *A History of Medicine in South Carolina, 1825–1900.* Columbia: South Carolina Medical Association, 1967.

Warner, John Harley. "The Idea of Southern Medical Distinctiveness: Medical Knowledge and Practice in the Old South." In *Science and Medicine in the Old South*, edited by Ronald L. Numbers and Todd L. Savitt, 179–205. Baton Rouge: Louisiana State University Press, 1989.

———. *The Therapeutic Perspective: Medical Practice, Knowledge, and Identity in America, 1820–1885*. Cambridge, MA: Harvard University Press, 1986.

Wates, Wylma Anne, ed. "From the Archives: Charleston Orphans 1790–1795." *South Carolina Historical Magazine* 78 (1977): 321–39.

Weir, Robert M. *Colonial South Carolina: A History*. Columbia: University of South Carolina Press, 1997. First published 1983 by KTO Press.

———. "'The Harmony We Were Famous For': An Interpretation of Pre-Revolutionary South Carolina Politics." *William and Mary Quarterly*, series 3, vol. 26, no. 4 (1969): 473–501.

Wikramanayake, Marina. *A World in Shadow: The Free Black in Antebellum South Carolina*. Columbia: University of South Carolina Press, 1973.

Williams, Jack Kenny. *Vogues in Villainy, Crime, and Retribution in Ante-Bellum South Carolina*. Columbia: University of South Carolina Press, 1959.

Wood, Peter. *Black Majority: Negroes in Colonial South Carolina from 1670 through the Stono Rebellion*. New York: W. W. Norton, 1975.

Woodman, Harold D. *King Cotton and His Retainers: Financing and Marketing the Cotton Crop of the South, 1800–1925*. Columbia: University of South Carolina Press, 1990. First published 1968 by University of Kentucky Press.

Wright, Gavin. *The Political Economy of the Cotton South: Households, Markets, and Wealth in the Nineteenth Century*. New York: W.W. Norton, 1978.

Wyatt-Brown, Bertram. *Southern Honor: Ethics and Behavior in the Old South*. New York: Oxford University Press, 1982.

Zainaldin, Jamil. "The Emergence of a Modern Family Law: Child Custody, Adoption, and the Courts, 1796–1851." *Northwestern University Law Review* 72 (1979): 1038–89.

Zelizer, Viviana A. *Pricing the Priceless Child: The Changing Social Value of Children*. Princeton, NJ: Princeton University Press, 1994.

Zey, Nancy. "Children of the Public: Poor and Orphaned Minors in the Southwest Borderlands." In *Children and Youth in a New Nation*, edited by James Marten, 173–89. New York: New York University Press, 2009.

———. "'Every Thing but a Parent's Love': Family Life in Orphan Asylums of the Lower Mississippi Valley." In *Family Values in the Old South*, edited by Craig Thompson Friend and Anya Jabour, 19–41. Gainesville: University Press of Florida, 2009.

Zipf, Karin L. *Labor of Innocents: Forced Apprenticeship in North Carolina, 1795–1919*. Baton Rouge: Louisiana State University Press, 2005.

Zmora, Nurith. *Orphanages Reconsidered: Child Care Institutions in Progressive Era Baltimore*. Philadelphia: Temple University Press, 1994.

INDEX OF NAMES

SUBJECT INDEX

Abbeville District, SC, 171
adoption, 8, 70, 131–36, 216n30, 231nn19–20
agriculture, 51, 149, 153, 157–58
Alabama, 141, 143, 147
alcohol, alcoholism, 25, 27, 65, 72, 76–79, 85,
   136, 144, 177, 189, 212n34
American Tract Society, 37–39
Anderson District, SC, 173
Anglican church, clergy. *See* Episcopal
   church, clergy
Anniversary Day (October 18), 2, 41, 92, 98,
   130, 135, 197–98, 243n8
Anson Street, 30
apothecaries, 1, 11, 116, 147, 153, 163, 172

bakers, 107–8, 164–65, 171, 177, 191, 239n49
Baltimore, 15, 36, 194, 220n89, 226n58
Bank of the State of South Carolina, 24, 67
baptism, 38, 58, 68, 176–77
Baptist church, clergy, 35–36, 72, 192
Barnwell, SC, 157–58, 182–83
baths, 22, 44, 123
Beaufain Street, 139
Beaufort, SC, 107, 234n56
belladonna, 124–25
Bell County, GA, 26
bequests to Orphan House, 21–22, 116,
   226n57
Berkeley District, SC, 130
Bethesda, 14, 206nn5–6, 231n19
Bible, 39
blacksmith, 149, 237n26
blindness, 37, 110, 120–22, 156–57, 199
bookbinders, 159, 166

breadwinner frailty, 80–81
brick masons, 74, 167, 188
brothers: adoptive, 135; of children, 1–2, 29,
   75, 78, 83, 99, 137, 162–63, 168, 178–79,
   191; of masters, 75, 165; of parents, 37,
   72, 136, 142

cabinet makers, 72, 148, 161
Camden, SC, 156
Cannon and Bennett, 18
carpenters, 148, 152, 161, 166, 169
Catholic church, clergy, 18, 36–37, 78, 143,
   203, 210n81
chair making, 155, 161, 173, 194
charity sermons, 17–20
Charleston Neck, 1, 16–17, 66, 126, 172
Charleston schools, 87–105 passim
Cheraw Union Factory, 158, 168
Chester, SC, 95, 177
child boarding, 68–69, 85, 163, 187, 216n23
City Gazette, 19, 130, 157, 163
City Guard, 52, 79
City Jail, 17, 27, 190–91
College of Charleston, 17, 22, 47, 98–99, 191
Confederacy: army, soldiers, 31, 202; govern-
   ment, 134–35
Congregational church, clergy, 36, 232n22
corporal punishment, 5, 51–53, 94, 99, 165,
   168
coverture, 140

Darlington District, SC, 158, 170
death: children, 38, 57–58, 113–15, 117–19,
   125–26, 229n52, 229n58; masters, 68, 70,